D0205407

*Psychotherapy Through
Clinical Role Playing*

Psychotherapy Through Clinical Role Playing

By

David A. Kipper

BRUNNER/MAZEL *Publishers* • New York

Acknowledgment of permission to quote from two sources is given below:

1. From Zerka T. Moreno, for the case of the mirror technique, originally published in *Group Psychotherapy*, 1967, *20*, 25-31.

2. From Beacon House, Inc., the Horsham Foundation, for the quotes from Moreno, J. L. (1964), *Psychodrama Vol. 1* (3rd ed.), Beacon, N.Y.: Beacon House.

Library of Congress Cataloging-in-Publication Data

Kipper, David A., 1939-
    Psychotherapy through clinical role playing.

    Bibliography: p. 367
    Includes index.
    1. Role playing—Therapeutic use. 2. Psychotherapy.
I. Title. [DNLM: 1. Psychodrama. WM 430.5.P8 K57p]
RC489.P7K55 1986   616.89'1523   86-14744
ISBN 0-87630-433-1

Copyright © 1986 by David A. Kipper

Published by
BRUNNER/MAZEL, INC.
19 Union Square
New York, New York 10003

MANUFACTURED IN THE UNITED STATES OF AMERICA

To Barbara, Talia, and Tamar
and
to the memory of my father

Contents

Preface

The idea of writing a book on the clinical application of role playing occurred to me a few years ago. I became aware of the need to consolidate the knowledge and techniques associated with this form of therapeutic intervention into a meaningful system, free of its "ideological" polemics. There is, of course, nothing uncommon about having conflicting intellectual views, nor do I find theoretical disputes disheartening. Quite the contrary, theoretical controversies serve an important function. They are stimulating, challenging, thought provoking, and ultimately result in the enhancement of our understanding. But when the main preoccupation of such disputes focuses on establishing intellectual authority, they tend to lose some of their effectiveness and cause stagnation rather than progress. I felt that in some respect this was the fate of role playing. Claims for superiority superseded efforts to provide intellectual frames of reference through which the role playing phenomenon may be examined. Consequently, many arguments centered on issues that may be likened to that of whether the cup is half full or half empty.

I found that the challenge of creating a consensual model for clinical role playing seemed even more urgent as I continued to train an increasing number of professionals in the field of mental health. These were not necessarily prospective psychodramatists. Many of them adhered to other therapeutic approaches, such as behavior therapy, client-centered therapy, Adlerian individual therapy, Sullivanian therapy, or general psychodynamic eclecticism. The interest they had in common was not a search for a new theoretical approach, but rather a quest for professional betterment. They came for training to learn something that they hoped to incorporate into their existing theoretical and philosophical outlooks, not to replace them with a new one. "Can we apply the psychodramatic method, an improved behavior rehearsal, and action techniques or exercises," they asked me, "without subscribing to the theories that gave rise to these interventions?" I knew that in principle the answer to their question was affirmative. But I had to substantiate my conviction by providing an appropriate conceptual frame of reference. It was then that I arrived at the notion of behavior simulation, a general model for the use of the method of simulation in the behavioral sciences. I have also chosen the expression "clinical role playing," a term that encompasses psychodramatic procedures and techniques, behavior rehearsal interventions, and other action-oriented methods, to denote that all these are interventions subsumed under the model of behavior simulation.

I started with the assumption that for all those who see the potential therapeutic advantage of role playing, a model based on the concept of simulation would be a neutral point of departure. To begin with, it does not conflict with their current theoretical preferences. But perhaps more important, it actually leaves room for various interpretations and different utilizations of the procedures that fall under the clinical application of the model. For psychodramatists, this model offers a new outlook on the method they already use. For others, it provides a way of using the psychodramatic and other related methods without a demand, explicit or implicit, for significant theoretical compromises.

My own introduction to clinical role playing was through psychodrama. I was trained for many months by its founder, the late Dr. Jacob L. Moreno, and his wife, Zerka T. Moreno. It was then that I discovered the immense therapeutic potential of role playing. But my training in clinical psychology and the fact that I became an academician prompted me to adopt a broader perspective. Although this has not altered my assessment of the value of role playing, it underscored the problematic issues that needed to be addressed. For one, I could not resign myself to the notion that Moreno's psychodrama is a perfect system that need not be improved upon. I did not share the intellectual contentment evinced by some of my psychodrama colleagues. Also, their historical lack of serious interest in scientific validation of psychodramatic claims concerned me. Such a stance, I feared, would inhibit further progress and refinements of the existing knowledge.

Another concern I had was about the traditional way role playing *techniques* have been discussed in the literature. I was struck by the encyclopedic fashion in which the material was presented. This fashion has been characterized by presenting lists of rules and techniques without analytical explorations of their underlying dimensions. Naturally, this could easily create an erroneous impression that role playing interventions lack a coherent and systematic conceptual structure. Techniques, one might be led to believe, are a "mixed bag of tricks" which have nothing in common and are not related to any fundamental paradigms. But there is no reason for convincing anyone to form such an impression. I have always thought that clinical role playing techniques, or for that matter any other kinds of action-oriented techniques, stem from logical systems that account for their functions and constructions.

One of the major tasks I undertook in writing this book was to demonstrate that quality of role playing. The analytical mode was a dominant posture adopted in the discussions about role playing techniques. The extent to which this has succeeded in dispelling the notion that techniques are merely an assortment of useful "gimmicks" and, instead, advancing the idea that they stem from sound conceptual frames of reference is for others to decide.

So, is this a book about psychodrama? Although the foregoing comments already alluded to this issue, perhaps a direct response is needed. Of course, it depends on understanding the meaning of the question. If it asks whether or not the book deals with Moreno's classic psychodrama, the answer is somewhat problematic. Yes, it is based on the method of psychodrama. Yes, it includes the psychodramatic procedures and techniques because these represent the most extensive use of role playing in therapy. In fact, one can hardly conceive of the use of role playing in clinical practice without reference to psychodrama. Yet, the formulations of some of the models are not Moreno's, though I believe they expand and complement his views. If, on the other hand, the question means does this book intend to provide a broader foundation for what was invented by Moreno, the answer is yes, it does. The best answer for this question, however, may be in the eye of the beholder, that is, the reader. Psychodramatists will undoubtedly answer it one way, and non-psychodramatists, another way.

It is true that the focus of this book is on the application of clinical role playing in therapy. It is primarily written for those who are involved in providing a variety of psychological treatments: group psychotherapy, marital therapy, family therapy, as well as individual therapy. At the same time, however, parts of it concern the application of role playing *in general* and address the entire field of behavior simulation. Therefore, some of the discussions will benefit those who apply role playing in "nonclinical" settings, as well. These include trainers, instructors, and group facilitators involved in conducting self-growth groups, task-oriented groups, management development workshops, training in leadership, interpersonal communication, performance appraisals, problem-solving procedures, public presentation skills, and so forth. These professionals tend to use role playing extensively, usually using single, brief vignettes. Unfortunately, however, judging from what appears to be the prevalent practice, there is reason to suspect that often they are not completely aware of the complexity of the method and its maximal potential. Conventional wisdom would concur with the observation that it is more difficult to conduct an effective role playing intervention through a single, brief episode than through an entire clinical role playing session. Skillfully rendered, the former involves a concentrated effort that requires considerable expertise. There is an element of deception in the belief that just because sometimes role playing "works," even if set in a casual manner, structuring every single scene is a simple operation. The mere act of setting a role playing situation in motion does not guarantee that much will be accomplished. The brevity of the episode tends to affect its psychological quality. Often, it leads to superficiality. For these professionals the message of this book is: There is more to the method of behavior simulation and its application through role playing than meets the eye.

The attention paid to role playing in the teaching of psychotherapy in graduate programs is another issue that I have often wondered about. I must admit that not having comprehensive information about the extent that role playing and/or psychodrama are taught as courses in graduate programs, my thoughts tend to be based on a general impression rather than on data. But I will find it hardly surprising if such a survey, once conducted, reveals that most curricula do not include separate courses devoted to these subjects. This does not mean that the subject of role playing is completely ignored. On the contrary, most students are aware of the existence of role playing through reading about it, having seen it practiced by others, or through allusions made to it by their teachers.

What, then, are the possible reason(s) that role playing has been treated in academic curricula in a cursory manner, even if introduced as a subsection in courses on psychotherapeutic approaches? It is conceivable that this may be related to the historical controversy surrounding psychodrama, to the emergence of a view that role playing is a simple mode of intervention that does not require extended discussions, or perhaps to the teacher's own familiarity (or lack of it) and his or her level of proficiency in this form of therapy. But it could also be related to the traditional tendency of members of the academic world to assume the role of the "impartial observer." The paucity of broad conceptual frames of reference for the application of clinical role playing in therapy makes it difficult to present it in an academic fashion. My own experience led me to believe that, indeed, this reason alone was a considerable impediment. So, in writing this book, I was particularly aware of the need to take the first steps towards a greater systematization and to broaden the scope of role playing and its utilization as a therapeutic modality.

The main thrust of this book is to present clinical role playing as a *primary form* of psychotherapeutic intervention. The idea is to demonstrate how it can be utilized as the fundamental therapeutic approach throughout an entire *course of treatment*, or, at least, throughout an entire treatment *session*. The former is a view held by proponents of psychodrama. The latter, on the other hand, is an approach that could be adopted by therapists of other theoretical persuasions. I anticipate that this second group of potential users will be the main beneficiaries of this book. Having said this, I should emphasize that the therapeutic application of clinical role playing demonstrated in the book does not exclude the introduction of this method in a limited capacity, that is, as *one portion* of a treatment *session*.

The book begins with a brief survey of the emergence of role playing as a form of therapy. This survey, presented in the first chapter, provides a historical background in an attempt to demonstrate the way role playing has earned a prominent place in the behavioral sciences. It is a general outline depicting a trend rather than a comprehensive description of all past and present applications of role playing for therapeutic purposes. This is followed by a discussion of various paradigms of behavior simulation and its fundamental principles. The model itself is presented in Chapter 2, and the principles concerning its clinical application are described in the third chapter.

Chapters 4 and 5 address procedural issues on the structure of the clinical role playing session: its stages, their purpose, the different kinds of scenes and the way they relate to each other, as well as the flow of the various parts of the session and its content, and the management of involvement. Understandably, the *structure* is that of the psychodramatic session because it is the most comprehensive, refined, and clinically sensitive procedure for constructing and administering clinical role playing.

The next topic focuses on clinical role playing techniques, which are addressed in Chapters 6 through 9. The first two of these four chapters present those techniques described as the basic ones. They form two subgroups, a specific and a general one. In addition to descriptions of these techniques and the indications, as well as the contraindications, for their use, each subgroup is presented in relation to a paradigm that

explains its underlying dimensions. Chapters 8 and 9 address the broad
category of situational techniques. The discussion begins with a process-
based paradigm for sorting situational techniques. The paradigm also
provides a psychological explanation regarding the construction of situational techniques for those interested in creative innovations. It consists of four basic prototypes, which are described along with selected
examples.

Chapters 10 and 11 present case illustrations. These include descriptions of full clinical role playing sessions as applied in the contexts of
group psychotherapy, family therapy, and individual treatment. The last
chapter of the book examines some broad issues concerning the present
state of the art, as well as some thoughts regarding possible future developments of clinical role playing.

About style and language: In writing the book I have tried to adhere
to the "he or she" style when speaking in general terms about therapist
or client. At times, however, I resorted to the use of the masculine
pronoun for the purpose of avoiding cumbersome sentences. It ought
to be emphasized that in these instances such language must not be
considered as a deliberate bias. The reader will also note that the words
"therapist" and "director" were used interchangeably. The same holds
true for the use of the words "client," "patient," and "protagonist."

The book also contains case illustrations and excerpts from sessions.
In all these examples the names of the clients/protagonists and the names
of specific places were my own invention and bear no resemblance to
the original. Specific descriptions of situations and many of the dialogues
were deliberately altered, rewritten, and edited in order to protect the
identity of the actual sessions.

There are many individuals who deserve my gratitude for their contributions to the shaping of my ideas. First, I would like to thank my
students and research assistants who inspired me through our joint discussions in various seminars and research projects. They have examined
my ideas, offered constructive criticism, improved them, and studied
them empirically. The idea of writing the book would probably have
remained an "unborn" project if not for the continuous urging and
assistance of Toni Mendez. I also would like to express my deep appre-
ciation to Philip M. Nowlen, Executive Director of the Office of Continuing Education at the University of Chicago, for his help and for
providing me the opportunity to complete the book. Of my colleagues
at the University of Chicago, I am especially grateful to John L. Dreibelbis
for his critical observations, fruitful suggestions, and interest in the development of my views, and to Paul N. Pohlman who was always ready

to offer his expertise and experience, to challenge my ideas, and to help me formulate them clearly. Elane Baum was very helpful in typing the manuscript. Last, but not least, my gratitude goes to my wife, Barbara, for her constant encouragement and for the many hours spent on editing and reviewing the manuscript.

David A. Kipper
Chicago

Psychotherapy Through
Clinical Role Playing

CHAPTER 1

The Emergence of Role Playing as a Form of Psychotherapy

Human beings are born actors. Their ability to act is not only part and parcel of the process of living but also a manifestation of the effort to master the world that surrounds them. All intelligent creatures display their feelings and skills by acting them out. Human beings, however, can plan such behavior in advance and produce it voluntarily. It is precisely this portrayal of concrete behaviors that is subsumed under the concept of role playing. Role playing, therefore, refers to behavior expressed as the result of a conscious decision on the part of the player or at the request of others. To the objective observer this volitional characteristic of role playing behavior endows it with both a dramatic flavor and a sense of artificiality. To the involved participant, on the other hand, it constitutes a genuine mode of expression.

Colorful illustrations of role playing behavior are cited in sociological analyses of rituals in various societies, where it has been practiced in order to mark special events having either a personal meaning to one individual or a cultural significance shared by an entire collective. They commemorated current or historical events whether secular or religious, realistic or fantasized. Perhaps the most interesting examples have been provided by anthropologists who studied primitive societies. A careful examination of these descriptions reveals that role playing behavior was associated with rituals that served very important functions. Some of these are illustrated below.

Role playing has been associated with people's attempts to confront the unknown, that is, to address their need to control, or a least to have some degree of participation in, the forces that influence the fate of their existence. In particular, this was evident with regard to unknowns identified as the intangible powers that control man and nature. Thus,

3

many rituals involved role playing enactments of religious themes, such as pacifying the punishing god or gods and pleasing the good ones, or other themes, such as catering to the forces that affect the provision of food, the creation of climates, and the prospect of war and peace.

Another function served with the aid of role playing behavior, still in connection with addressing the unknown, is the commemoration of special events in the individual's life cycle. Here, too, role playing was used as a vehicle through which people expressed their hopes for the future as each one of them entered a new phase in his or her life cycle. Thus, a host of rituals involving role playing enactments were created to mark unusual events such as birth, marriage, death, and a variety of other initiation ceremonies.

Role playing behavior was also displayed in connection with rituals devised for the purpose of affirming one's relatedness to a shared value system and to a common heritage. It was not only the need for reasserting one's belonging to a large group, to a society, that provided the impetus for such rituals, but also the need to see oneself in a historical perspective as an agent of sociocultural tradition who carries the past into the present and the present into the future. Rituals concerning the affirmation of one's self-identity were evident on both societal and personal levels. The former involved the reenactment of legendary events in the history of the particular society. The latter involved enactments of family traditions maintained throughout several generations.

Role playing behavior was also evident in rituals associated with the practice of healing. For instance, primitive medicine men employed role playing for a variety of purposes. These included efforts to increase their patients' readiness to receive treatment, helping patients cope with painful treatments, or using role playing as a form of a psychological treatment to create a state of extreme suggestibility.

Finally, role playing was used as a mode of communication in interpersonal interactions. Here we no longer speak of role playing in the context of institutionalized rituals but rather as an individualized form of expression. People often resort to concrete reenactments of stories and anecdotes, of ideas or of skills, in lieu of verbal descriptions, presumably because they believe that the demonstrative quality conveys the intended message more clearly. Such a preference has been observed not only in cultures where verbal language is insufficiently developed, but also in modern societies that use highly sophisticated and abstract languages. Whether one deals with a primitive or sophisticated language, one phenomenon seems to be universally true: concrete portrayals serve as a backup contingency to be used in the event that explanations in the abstract fail to accomplish their desired purpose.

It should be emphasized that the presentation of the preceding analysis of rituals and their accompanying role playing behaviors does not exclude the likelihood that such behaviors have been used in additional ways. Nonetheless, limiting ourselves to the examination of the above-mentioned five functions, an interesting trend sems to unfold. Role playing has been associated with the alleviation of feelings of helplessness and uncertainty; with reducing the discomfort caused by fears; with instilling hope; with forming a coherent sense of self-identity; with healing; and with efforts to enhance understanding among people. There is little doubt, therefore, that the immense gratification derived from role playing behavior, as observed among primitive people, stems from its ability to satisfy basic psychological needs and from the inherent therapeutic qualities that it possesses.

In light of this conclusion, it is quite amazing that there are those who try to equate role playing behavior with an inferior level of development or with immaturity. Proponents of such a view maintain that the capacity for self-expression through abstract conceptualization is valued more in modern societies than that which is manifested through concrete portrayals. The problem with this view is that it is superficial and oversimplistic. Not only does it completely ignore the multifarious quality of human behavior, but it also fails to enhance our understanding of it. Clearly the value of role playing depends on the context in which it is expressed. In many instances, the psychological benefits accrued through role playing are quite considerable, if not irreplaceable.

Does this mean that role playing behavior continues to serve the same psychological functions it did in the past? Although, in general, the answer to this question is affirmative, it needs to be qualified. We must recognize that over the years some of the old characteristics of role playing behavior have undergone some changes. For one, the external manifestations of such behavior nowadays differ from those evinced by primitive people partly because contemporary codes of conduct advocate a greater degree of restraint and self-control. Also, with the passage of time many of the old background beliefs have changed, resulting in a change of format of many rituals, including their importance. But the most pronounced change can be seen in a shift where expressions of role playing became associated more with *personal behavior* rather than with institutionalized rituals. Thus, modern men and women no longer resort to role playing behavior in their attempts to control the forces of nature (although some remnants of this continue to exist as evidenced by the fact that pilots, astronauts, firefighters, etc., are still trained by means of role playing and simulated experiences). And there is an increased tendency for modern men and women to rely on logic and the principles of science rather than on role playing behavior in dealing with the unknown.

The belief that communication through role playing is associated with immaturity is also based, in part, on the observation that it tends to be more prevalent among children and less educated adults. On the whole, this observation is accurate. Indeed, there is an inverse relationship between the acquisition of a highly sophisticated language and the prominence of role playing behavior. The frequency of role playing in one's daily activities decreases as one moves from childhood to adulthood. But what does this mean?

It is important to distinguish between displays of role playing behavior as attempts to compensate for a restricted ability to communicate, and those that concern psychological functions other than interpersonal communication. It is true that with regard to communication, an increased verbal proficiency reduces the need to *depend* on role playing as a prime mode of self-expression. As a result the communicator is free to choose between abstract and concrete modes of relatedness. But a reduced dependency does not imply a complete freedom to choose between these two alternatives. In a curious way there is no escaping some "dependency" on role playing behavior. Seen from a developmental perspective, role playing constitutes a primal (perhaps a primordial) form of self-expression. After all, it is the earliest language a person learns in babyhood, and it first precedes and then accompanies the acquisition of verbal language. It was observed a long time ago that under certain conditions people prefer to revert to earlier modes of behavior. This tendency is particularly noticeable under conditions involving emotional duress and a high degree of arousal. Therefore, it is hardly surprising that role playing exists wherever people exist. It is also not surprising that role playing became a form of behavior that subsequently was utilized to increase the effectiveness of modern psychotherapy.

THE EMERGENCE OF ROLE AND ROLE PLAYING IN MODERN TIMES

The task of establishing the time when the term "role playing" was used first in reference to modern psychotherapy is not an easy one. One way of determining the origin of contemporary role playing is to consult the relevant historical documents. But these are scant and not entirely reliable. Two facts, however, may aid us in this effort. One is the fact that role playing is based on the concept of role, and evolved from the first attempts to formulate a role theory. And second is the fact that the introduction of the concept of role playing in modern behavioral and social sciences is traditionally attributed to the work of J. L. Moreno.

In a chapter entitled "The Nature and History of Role Theory," Biddle and Thomas (1966) traced the history of the development of role theory. They listed the names of about two dozen writers whose work appeared during the period 1890 to 1930. These were called the *precursors* of role theory, because their contribution was mainly to the role perspective prior to the emergence of a "discriminable role language and of specialized inquiry into problems of role" (p. 4). The beginning of modern role theory is attributed to the works of George Herbert Mead (1934), Jacob Levy Moreno (1934), and Ralph Linton (1936) some 50 years ago. Mead employed the concept of role taking, along with such related ideas as the generalized other, the self, the I and me, and audience in examining the problems of interaction, the self, and socialization. Moreno discussed the term "role" and pointed out that the genesis of roles goes through two stages: role perception and role enactment. With regard to the latter he introduced the concept of role playing. Linton proposed a distinction between two concepts: status (a socially assigned position) and role. This distinction implied that (a) positions and attending roles are elements of societies, and (b) the behavior of an individual can be construed as role performance, that role is the link between individual behavior and social structure. In the following decades, these ideas were further developed and investigated by other scientists, mostly sociologists and social psychologists.

Historically, however, the notion of role did not evolve from sociology nor from psychology. Its origin is quite different. The following excerpt from Moreno (1960) describes the development of the concept of role throughout the ages.

"Role," originally a French word which penetrated into English, is derived from the Latin *rotula* (the little wheel, or round log, the diminutive of rota-wheel). In antiquity it was used, originally, only to designate a round (wooden) roll on which sheets of parchments were fastened so as to smoothly roll ("wheel") them around it since otherwise the sheets would break or crumble. From this came the word for an assemblage of such leaves into a scroll or book-like composite. This was used, subsequently, to mean any official volume of papers pertaining to law courts, as in France, or to government, as for instance in England: rolls of Parliament—the minutes or proceedings. Whereas in Greece and also in ancient Rome the parts in the theater were written on the above mentioned "rolls" and read by the prompters to the actors (who tried to mem-

orize their parts), the fixation of the word appears to have been
lost in more illiterate periods of the early and middle centuries of
the Dark Ages, for their public presentation of church plays by
laymen. Only towards the sixteenth and seventeenth centuries, with
the emergence of the modern stage, the parts of the theatrical
characters are read from "roles," paper fascicles. Whence each
scenic "part" becomes a role. (p. 80)

Thus the word "role" was a part of English and various European
languages for many years. When, then, did it start to be used in the
behavioral and social sciences as a technical concept? The first sign of
this is believed to have been evident in the early 1920s. Two sources—one
by Simmel (1920), published in Germany, and one by Park and Burgess
(1921), published in the United States—refer to role in a manner reminiscent of its modern connotations. But it was not until the decade of
the 1930s in America that the term was employed technically in writing
on role problems.

It was not until after World War II, however, that extensive use
of role-related terms appeared in the title of empirical studies.
Evidence for this may be found by examining the major index
catagories of *Psychological Abstracts*. Although this journal first appeared in 1927, it was not until 1944 that "role playing" appeared
as a major index category; "role" itself did not appear as such
category until 1945. (Biddle & Thomas, 1966, p. 7)

The notion of role playing as a therapeutic mode of intervention is
also an invention of the twentieth century. Like role, it probably emerged
as a technical concept about 50 years ago. There is some evidence, however, that the idea of acting out roles has been entertained before. One
of the earliest accounts pertaining to the use of role playing in psychotherapy is cited in Zilboorg and Henry (1941). These authors mentioned that in the early 1800s Reil recognized the therapeutic significance
of having mental patients "act out" their interpersonal difficulties (see
Goldfried & Davison, 1976). Moreno (1964a) described the use of spontaneous role playing with children in the gardens of Vienna at the turn
of the century. Nonetheless, such ideas and initial experimentations with
enactment procedures were not translated into a clearly defined psychotherapeutic format until the decade of the 1930s. One of the few
examples of the use of role playing prior to World War II that was not
directly connected with the development of psychodrama is described
by Shaw, Corsini, Blake, and Mouton (1980) as follows:

In 1933 the German Army, limited to 100,000 men by the terms of the Versailles Treaty, began to develop a corps of officers. For the selection of military personnel, Simoneit . . . , a German psychologist, devised a number of action procedures very similar to current role playing by which officers could estimate the qualities of army recruits. (p. 7)

The greatest penetration of role playing procedures into applied psychology began in the early 1940s. It has been reported, for instance, that after the fall of Dunkirk, the British Army incorporated procedures that might be considered as role playing applications in its officer-selection program. Role playing procedures were also used by the U.S. Office of Strategic Services Assessment Staff in the selection of people for secret wartime work. But it was not until after World War II that role playing became widely known as a genuine form of psychological intervention. At that time the early formulation of psychodramatic principles and techniques was disseminated. Furthermore, it was also the period during which the early experimentations with role playing techniques, both in psychotherapy and in industrial training, took place.

As of the mid-1950s, the application of role playing in the United States proceeded in two directions. One was in the area of psychotherapy, which also includes the self-growth groups. Here one finds the use of role playing in treatment modalities that Nichols and Efran (1985) referred to as "modern cathartic therapies." These include, of course, the classic example of role-playing-based therapy (i.e., Moreno's method of sociometry and psychodrama) and the establishment of the psychodramatic movement. They also include the development of gestalt therapy and subsequently the emergence of the many varieties of sensitivity training (e.g., Perls, 1969; Schutz, 1967; Siroka, Siroka, & Schloss, 1971) and of the encounter groups (Goldberg, 1970). Other therapeutic methods that may be classified in this category are: Synanon (see Yablonsky, 1976), primal therapy (Janov, 1970), reality therapy (Glasser, 1965), and, to some extent, transactional analysis (Berne, 1961), to mention a few.

The inclusion of role playing in psychotherapy was also evident in behaviorally oriented treatments, namely those approaches that disclaimed the importance of catharsis in therapy. Here one finds Kelly's fixed-role therapy (Kelly, 1955) and behavior rehearsal (Wolpe, 1958, 1969). In fact, psychodrama may be positioned between the modern cathartic therapies and the behavior therapies, because although it emphasized the importance of catharsis, it also stressed the need for retraining. The same position seems to characterize a number of contemporary family therapy approaches.

A second area in which role playing became a prominent mode of intervention was training in group dynamics. This area became differentiated from the one mentioned above because its declared aim was self-improvement and self-development rather than psychotherapy. It was primarily designed to train people in various skills related to issues such as leadership, the management of small and large groups, dealing with conflicts in groups, cooperation, the formation of accurate perceptions of one's own self and of others, to mention a few. These skills were taught with an extensive use of role playing techniques or exercises by nonclinicians, and for their educational value. Typically, the learning gleaned from such training experiences was meant to improve the behavior of leaders in the military, in business, in educational institutions, in youth organizations, in community centers, in religious organizations, and so forth. The two classic examples of developments in this direction were the establishment of the T-group workshops, and the creation of assessment centers for evaluating vocational and leadership potentials.

Today, the application of role playing is widespread, indeed. It may be found in almost every kind of professional service that falls within the boundaries of the work of psychologists. Yet there is no doubt that the area where it is used to its utmost capability, and where it has the greatest contribution, is psychotherapy.

ROLE PLAYING AS A THERAPEUTIC MODALITY: THREE APPROACHES

There are three therapeutic approaches that have contributed to the emergence of role playing as a recognized form of psychotherapy. These are, first and foremost, psychodrama, which was originated and developed by J. L. Moreno. The remaining two are fixed-role therapy, developed by George A. Kelly, and behavior rehearsal, traditionally associated with Joseph Wolpe and Arnold Lazarus. Before we proceed to present each of these approaches it should be emphasized that the descriptions will be kept brief and condensed. Since the prime consideration of the present chapter is the historical development of role playing, extensive discussions of the three approaches will lead us astray from its main focus. A more detailed exposition of each approach may be found in the references cited throughout the text.

Psychodrama

Moreno gave the date of April 1, 1921, as the beginning of psychodrama, although it took several years before it was formulated as a therapeutic method. Therefore, of the three approaches to be described in this section, psychodrama is not only the method that makes the most extensive use of role playing, but it is also the oldest approach.

Moreno disseminated his ideas regarding group psychotherapy and psychodrama in many articles and books. The main body of his theoretical contributions, however, appears in a book entitled *Psychodrama, Vol. I* (J. L. Moreno, 1964a), which was first published in 1946. Fascinated by the significance of the creative act, Moreno became interested in the idea of the Godhead, but in the sense of God the supreme creator. He believed that people's ability to create is a fundamental quality, and it is this godlike quality within people that produces and makes them responsible for their own creativity. In other words, people share a co-creative power with the Godhead. In search for the determinants that facilitate the creative act, Moreno arrived at the concepts of "spontaneity" and the "moment." These concepts were used to formulate his theory of spontaneity-creativity, the foundation of the psychodramatic method (see also Moreno, 1964b).

Spontaneity. Spontaneity is a fundamental concept in Moreno's theory. But its meaning in the context of psychodrama is not synonymous with that associated with the colloquial usage of the word. In ordinary language, spontaneity implies an instinctive act of the body or of the mind which is not due to consciousness—an uninhibited act produced without external incitement. This definition suggests that spontaneity is characterized by a lack of control. This is not so, according to Moreno's notion. In its psychodramatic sense, spontaneity is capable of moving in prescribed directions. Having such a quality, one must conclude that spontaneity contains an element of control. Although the complexity of spontaneity as a theoretical concept has been discussed elsewhere (e.g., Kipper, 1967), nonetheless, it might be fitting to summarize here some of its discernible characteristics.

First, spontaneity manifests itself in the form of *energy*. Since it is not a concrete substance, it also cannot be seen by the naked eye unless expressed through a carrier. Second, and most important, it is an energy that cannot be stored or accumulated. It is consumed instantly, on the spur of the moment, in an all-or-none fashion. Thus, spontaneity emerges to be spent and must be spent to make place for new emergencies. This *unconservable* aspect of spontaneity is a crucial element in Moreno's existential philosophy. The focus on the immediate present, on the moment, stems from the belief that the here and now is the most important, and psychologically the most meaningful, time unit. A third feature of spontaneity is that it can be *trained* by means of numerous psychodramatic techniques. To Moreno, there is a positive correlation between spontaneity and mental health. In principle, the more spontaneous a person, the healthier—psychologically—he or she is. Conversely, the less "directed spontaneity" expressed, the sicker —emotionally—is the person. Using this terminology, the essence of psychotherapy may be described as "spontaneity training."

How then, we may wonder, do people become endowed with spontaneity in the first place? At the moment, the answer to this question is far from being clear. Moreno proposed that spontaneity exists *sui generis*, and that it is neither strictly a hereditary factor nor an environmental factor but an independent area influenced yet not determined by these two. Simply put, spontaneity is a human quality whose exact origin is not known.

Interestingly, spontaneity was also characterized as an *observable phenomenon*. At first glance, this fourth characteristic of spontaneity appears to be irreconcilable with an earlier one, which classified it as a form of energy. Can energy be directly observed? A closer examination, however, shows that these two attributes are not necessarily in conflict. A phenomenon may be observed even if it is not strictly a concrete event. There is an entirely different category of experiences that may be defined as intangible concreteness, that is, intangible yet real. Love and hate are other good examples of intangible concreteness, that is, a phenomenon that becomes noticeable through the mediation of other expressions of concrete behavior.

Although Moreno considered spontaneity as a general factor, he also suggested that it might be characterized by four independent forms of expression. The first is the *dramatic form*. Here spontaneity gives newness and vivacity to feelings, actions, and verbal utterances, which are *repetitions* of what the individual has experienced a thousand times before. The second is the form of *creative spontaneity*. This kind of spontaneity creates *new* organisms, *new* forms of art, and *new* patterns of environment. The third form is *original spontaneity*. This form does not contain any contributions significant enough to be regarded as creativity. Instead, it is a unique *expansion* or *variation* of that which already exists.

Finally, the fourth form is the *adequacy of the response*. Spontaneous responses must be *well-timed*, and neither too much nor too little in *intensity*.

In fact, the appropriateness of a response and its novelty became the two key components of the formal definition of spontaneity. Accordingly, spontaneity is an adequate response to a new situation or a new response to an old situation.

The creative act. The idea behind this concept is that a distinction has to be made between the creative act proper and some of its final products. Creative acts represent the vehicle through which spontaneity expresses itself in the process of living. One of the salient characteristics of the creative act, therefore, is its relation to *spontaneity,* to the continuous expenditure of energy, and to its observable quality. Another aspect of the creative act is that it contains an element of surprise. It is *unexpected* because the creative act tends to surface suddenly and unpredictably. In addition, it also possesses a quality that has been described as *unreality.* This aspect stems from the observation that the inspirations that produce the creative act are not bound by realistic considerations or constraints, and that it emerges in order to change the reality within which it rises. This notion was echoed by Moreno, who wrote, "Something prior to and beyond the given reality is operating in a creative act" (J. L. Moreno, 1964a, p. 35).

Cultural conserves. Cultural conserves are the products of the creative act. Specifically, they consist of all those cultural products retained in lasting forms. Examples of these are books, paintings, musical compositions, or even well-established behavioral patterns. Thus, any outcome of a creative act that can be packaged so that it is accessible to people other than the original creator to be used repeatedly is considered a cultural conserve. If one were to devise a scale for rating the intrinsic value of creative activity, spontaneous creativity will establish itself in the highest, most valued end, whereas cultural conserves, which represent the containment of spontaneity, will be rated somewhere on the lower end. It should be emphasized that this scale pertains to creativity in its pure, idealistic form. In practicality, many cultural conserves (e.g., certain philosophical, literary, and artistic products) have attained such a degree of perfection that they are highly revered.

Because cultural conserves have been largely responsible for the continuous development of the civilized world, they need to be constantly revitalized and re-created in order to replace the old, outworn ones. It might be concluded that the advantages of cultural conserves are (a) the fact that they can be relied upon for guidance and direction in coping with uncertainty or with threatening situations, and (b) the fact that they constitute a vehicle of perpetuity by facilitating the continuity of our cultural heritage.

The warming up. An additional concept relevant to the present discussion is the warming-up process. Moreno did not provide an elaborated theory of motivation. He simply made a general observation that people possess a drive, which he described as "act hunger," that is, an innate desire to act. This desire is nourished by a continuous force labeled as the warming up, a process that prepares people and makes them ready to embark upon spontaneous-creative behavior.

To summarize: Moreno's theory is based on four concepts: spontaneity, creativity, cultural conserves, and the warming up. The way these form the theory may be described as follows:

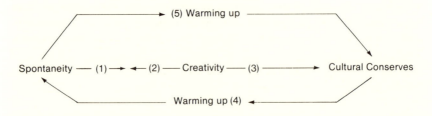

The arrows and their corresponding numbers refer to the relationships among the concepts. Looking at the middle line, left to right, the arrow marked (1) indicates that spontaneity arouses creativity. The arrow marked (2) indicates that creativity is receptive to spontaneity, that the two enjoy a reciprocal relation. The arrow marked (3) indicates that the interaction between spontaneity and creativity results in cultural conserves. Cultural conserves tend to accumulate indefinitely and remain in "storage." Some of them may subsequently be replaced by others and some revitalized or used again and again. This is facilitated by the warming-up process. Looking at the bottom line, the arrow marked (4) indicates that cultural conserves activate the warming up which, in turn, activates spontaneity. Once reactivated, spontaneity may operate in two directions: (a) begin a new cycle leading to the creation of a new set of cultural conserves. This is depicted by the sequence of arrows (1), (2), and (3) in the middle line; or (b) reapply the already existing cultural conserves. This operation is also activated through the warming up and is portrayed, in the top line, by the arrow marked (5).

According to the psychodramatic view, the purpose of the therapy is expressed in terms of enhancing the client's spontaneity as it is expressed through the creative act. Because the latter is displayed in the here and now, on the spot, it is obvious why it focuses on people's actual behavior. The creative act must be dealt with at the moment of its emergence. By its very nature, it inevitably involves the display of concrete behavior.

But why does this have to be conducted in the context of scenes depicting real or perceived life situations? The answer to this question lies in Moreno's notion concerning the relation of the creative act to its *locus nascendi*. The expression means the place of birth, the context of origin. The idea is that the true meaning of things unfolds only when they appear in their original context: "Every thing, form or idea has a place, a locus, which is the most adequate and appropriate for it, in which it has the most ideal, the most perfect expression of its meaning" (J. L. Moreno, 1964a, pp. 25-26). With the removal of a creative expression from the environment it originally sprang from to a new place or media, one "thing" changes into another "thing." "Thus," wrote Moreno, "the 'David' of Michelangelo in its locus nascendi is the true 'David' of Michelangelo. Placed in a museum it is no longer truly itself; it is lending itself to the composition of another 'thing,' the museum" (1964a, p. 25). Similarly, in therapy, talking about behavior in the abstract or even acting out of locus implies a certain loss of the true meaning of what is being dealt with. Ideally, the creative act needs to be observed in its *locus nascendi*, in vivo. Barring that possibility, an approximate simulation of that locus, in the therapist's office, is the next best approach.

Moreno thought of behavior in terms of roles. Roles, he maintained, do not emerge from the self but rather the self emerges from roles. He classified roles into three categories: (a) psychosomatic roles, as the sleeper, the eater, the walker, etc.; (b) psychodramatic roles, as *a* mother, *a* teacher, *a* daughter, etc.; and (c) social roles, as *the* mother, *the* teacher, *the* daughter, etc. The acting of behavior in its original context became role playing.

To conclude this brief discussion we need to add a few words regarding the curative process as seen from the psychodramatic point of view. The healing process is said to be attained through *catharsis* and through *training*. The spontaneity-creativity theory places a great emphasis on catharsis. Catharsis generally refers to the relief of tension. This phenomenon is better described in its modern definition: ". . . catharsis is to be understood as a label for completing (some or all of) a previously restrained or interrupted sequence of self-expression. . . . that which would have occurred as a natural reaction to some experience had that expression not been thwarted" (Nichols & Efran, 1985, p. 55). Moreno identified two kinds of therapeutic catharsis. These, he claimed, are important kinds and they can only be attained through psychodrama and role playing. The first is *action catharsis*, that which occurs by becoming the producer-actor, that is, an active participant in the portrayed drama. The second is *catharsis of integration*, which is predicated on identifying with the positions and problems of others. The concept of catharsis of integration is quite intriguing because of the suggestion that it cannot be attained by merely expressing one's own self. By definition it is a dyadic process which could, of course, involve more people. It requires that the roles and positions of at least two people—the client and a significant other—be taken into account.

The second curative element emphasized in psychodrama is role training. This "healing" process varies, in some respects, from that ordinarily subsumed under the conventional notion of training in the context of psychotherapy. In psychodramatic nomenclature training refers to two goals. One is spontaneity training, and the other, expanding one's existing role repertoire (sometimes also unlearning certain roles) through role playing. It is the latter goal that resembles the process currently known as skill training.

Fixed-Role Therapy

The second approach to be described in the present chapter is fixed-role therapy. This form of role playing was devised by George A. Kelly and described in his book, *The Psychology of Personal Constructs* (1955). It represents a clinical application of his theory of personality. Although in creating his therapeutic method Kelly was inspired by the writings of Korzybky and Moreno, fixed-role therapy itself is much simpler than psychodrama.

Interestingly, many of Kelly's ideas remind us of those that have been expounded, years later, in modern behavior modification. In that respect, fixed-role therapy may be viewed as the precursor of behavior rehearsal. Looking at fixed-role therapy from a historical perspective, it appears that it contributed to the emergence of role playing as a therapeutic modality in several ways. First, it demonstrated that the use of role playing in therapy may be rationalized on the basis of utilitarian considerations as seen by means of direct observations of real-life behavior. Second, it introduced the notion that role playing is therapeutically meritorious, even when initiated and controlled by the therapist rather than predicated on the client's spontaneity. Third, it highlighted the advantages of the "as if" aspect of role playing. It demonstrated the therapeutic power of behaving under an assumed identity rather than being one's own true self. Finally, it was instrumental in promoting role playing as a form of psychotherapy. Since Kelly was not associated with the psychodramatic movement, his interest in role playing gave it a wider exposure among those who were not particularly attracted to Moreno's ideas. In practice, however, fixed-role therapy did not develop into a major form of therapy. In fact, even during the mid- and late-1950s, when fixed-role therapy became publicly known, it did not enjoy a widespread popularity.

Like Moreno, Kelly's ideas about psychotherapy were developed as a reaction to psychoanalysis. He was not impressed with the utilitarian value of psychoanalysis, which, according to him, "had never quite seemed to be the answer to psychological problems obviously arising in a social, economic, or educational setting" (Kelly, 1955, p. 361). His starting point was quite different. The observations that led to the formulation of fixed-role therapy may be summarized as follows:

- *Dramatic experiences have lasting effects.* Kelly observed that actors are influenced by practicing theatrical roles that involve new behavior. Sometimes such practice changes their own behavior, often resulting in long-lasting effects. In that respect, learning new mannerisms late in life does not become more of an artificiality than learning them relatively early.
- *Dramatic roles may become avenues for self-expression.* It appears that certain people are able to express themselves in certain parts of a play with a spontaneity and vehemence that could not be explained simply on the basis of their understanding of the playwright's intent. It is as if they have discovered a verbal vehicle ordinarily not available to them for expressing ideas. This new rehearsed behavior seems to result in a general increase in fluency, both verbal and behavioral.
- *Progress may be achieved through explorations of enactment techniques.* Sometimes a therapeutic progress is attained—a deadlock is broken—by experimenting with enactment techniques. The use of "as if" situations is a good example of this principle.
- *The importance of establishing a social function.* Behavior becomes more meaningful and, therefore, a lasting one when it is perceived as serving a useful function: ". . . there does appear to be a stabilizing effect that accrues from seeing oneself in a functional relationship to one's surroundings, whether those surroundings be things or people" (Kelly, 1955, p. 365).
- *Labeling facilitates corresponding behavior.* There is a tendency for people to adjust their behavior according to the ways they think of, name, or label their predicament. Sometimes people develop real symptoms because they have read about them or have managed to ascribe a label to them. The same phenomenon is observed with regard to changing one's own name (or renaming a given characteristic). Changing one's own name is not only a way of escaping the

social expectations in which one has become enmeshed, but also a way of stabilizing the change one has set for oneself.

- *People seek to change their roles.* People are constantly seeking new ways for readjustment. In that process they tend to seize upon "artificial" roles and assume new labels for them. The search for new roles has important implications for devising therapeutic strategies to help people change.

On the basis of these observations and his general theory of personal constructs, Kelly developed his fixed-role therapy. It is considered a role playing approach because the client is given a role, or a set of roles, according to which he or she must behave (role play) in real life for a specified period. There are three major steps in fixed-role therapy.

1. Writing the fixed-role sketch. Composing the fixed-role sketch is an essential component of the therapeutic endeavor. It is also the most difficult and complex part of it. The client is diagnosed and then asked to prepare a self-characterization of himself or herself. This is done with cards, bearing various descriptions of skills and attributes, which the client sorts along the Q-sort technique, or with the aid of other instruments (e.g., the Rotter Incomplete Sentence Blank). Having such a description, a panel of therapists prepare the fixed-role sketch. It is a detailed, written personality profile which describes the behavior of a person whose characteristics are *sharply in contrast*, but in the therapeutically desired direction, to those that characterize the client. Most important, however, that sketch is written and presented as if it characterizes a *different* (i.e., an imaginary) *person with a new name*, whose identity the client is asked to assume for the duration of the treatment. This "as if" component is crucial to the therapeutic procedure. Kelly emphasizes the importance of having a panel of therapists involved in writing the sketch because the task is too difficult for one person. The following excerpts are taken from a fixed-role sketch prepared for a client named Ronald Barrett. The sketch describes the personality of an imaginary person named Kenneth Norton, and includes a new set of behaviors to be adopted by the client under this new identity. The example is borrowed from Kelly's book (1955).

Kenneth Norton is the kind of a man who, after a few minutes of conversation, somehow makes you feel that he must have known you intimately for a long time. This comes about not by any particular questions that he asks, but by the understanding way in which he listens. It is as if he had a knack of seeing the world through your eyes. The things which you have come to see as being important, he, too, soon seems to sense as similarly important. Thus he catches not only your words, but the punctuations of feeling with which they are formed and the little accents of meaning with which they are chosen. . . . Girls he finds attractive for many reasons, not the least of which is the exciting opportunity they provide for his understanding the feminine point of view. Unlike some men, he does not "throw the ladies a line" but, so skillful a listener, soon he has them throwing him one—and he is thoroughly enjoying it. With his own parents and in his own home he is somewhat more expressive of his own ideas and feelings. Thus his parents are given an opportunity to share and supplement his new enthusiasms and accomplishments. (pp. 374–375)

The remaining two steps are conducted concurrently.

2. *Interviewing and preparing the rehearsal sequence.* Once the client has understood and accepted the sketch, he or she visits the therapist every other day for a period of two weeks. In these visits the two discuss the client's role behavior (see the next step). They also discuss, and sometimes role play in the office, real-life situations as a preemptive measure (i.e., anticipating possible difficulties) or in order to demonstrate the appropriate role play behavior. The interviews cover the enactment of the role(s) in five areas: work, casual relationships with companions of the same sex, relationships involving the spouse or members of the opposite sex, parents, and general life orientation.

3. *Enacting the sketch in real life.* During the period of the treatment, usually two weeks, the client behaves according to the sketch and as if he or she were someone else. This must be carried out regardless of the obvious difficulties involved in operating publicly under an assumed identity. In principle, therefore, the therapeutic practice takes place *outside* the therapist's office, in vivo. Throughout that time, the client is under close supervision, as described in step 2, above.

Behavior Rehearsal

Behavior rehearsal is the last of the three approaches to be described in connection with our historical survey. This form of therapeutic intervention has been, initially, associated with Wolpe and Lazarus and was described in their writings (e.g., Wolpe, 1958, 1969; Wolpe & Lazarus, 1966; Lazarus, 1966). Essentially, behavior rehearsal represents the use of role playing in behavior therapy and behavior modification through the application of learning principles for treatment purposes. The formulation of behavior rehearsal was the latest significant push in the emergence of role playing as a therapeutic modality. Due to the widespread popularity of modern behavior therapy, its use of role playing became widely popular as well. It should be pointed out, however, that within the framework of behavior therapy, role playing (or behavior rehearsal) was considered as *one* of its many *techniques*. It was not regarded as *a separate mode of therapy*, the way it was conceived by both Moreno and Kelly.

Before this technique became known as behavioral rehearsal, it was referred to by other names. During the late 1950s and the early 1960s it was called behaviorodrama, behavioristic psychodrama, or simply role playing. These terms apparently caused some discomfort as they suggested an association with Moreno's method. Given the difference between the theories underlying behavior therapy and psychodrama, a new name, one that conveyed a greater affinity to the principles of behaviorism, had to be found. Some (e.g., Kanfer & Phillips, 1969) proposed the term "replication therapy," but nowadays the application of role playing in behavior therapy is commonly known as behavior rehearsal.

In the beginning, Wolpe considered the technique as one that is based on patient-mediated cues in the context of his theory of reciprocal inhibition. His understanding of the use of behavior rehearsal is described in the following excerpt:

> The therapist takes the role of a person towards whom the patient has a neurotic anxiety reaction and instructs him to express his ordinarily inhibited feelings toward that person. Particular attention is given to the emotion infused into the words. The voice must be firm, and suitably modulated. The patient is made to repeat each statement again and again, being constantly corrected until the utterance is in every way satisfactory. The aim of the rehearsal is, of course, to make it possible for him to express himself with his real "adversary" so that the anxiety the latter evokes may be reciprocally inhibited, and the motor assertive habit established. (Wolpe, 1969, p. 68)

Subsequently, however, behavior rehearsal was seen in a wider perspective. This broader view is described, for example, by Kanfer and Phillips (1969) as follows:

> . . . this technique attempts to simulate or replicate significant parts of the patient's extratherapy environment for observation and manipulation in the therapist's presence. It provides the patient with an opportunity to evaluate his problematic behaviors and to try out new responses without fear of traumatic consequences. Contrived role playing by the therapist and others and the use of verbal instructions and other props foster the replication. In its broadest form. . . [it]. . . may involve construction of an entire therapeutic community, modeled not after a particular patient's particular environment but after the general social setting of the community. (p. 458)

In their systematic description of behavior rehearsal, Goldfried and Davison (1976) rely on the concept of role in order to explain the theoretical basis for the use of this technique. They refer to role theory, as expounded by Sarbin and Allen (1968), where role is generally understood as those socially defined behaviors associated with given positions (e.g., husband, wife, son, daughter). Problems tend to arise when there is a discrepancy between role behaviors available to a person and the expectations held by others in the immediate environment. Such discordance may be attributed to a change in role status, a shift in role definitions due to cultural changes or to an inappropriate social learning history.

The main characteristics of the procedure by which an actor learns his or her theatrical role were described by Sarbin and Allen (1968) as follows. The actor receives information which he must learn in the form of a script, and he must practice in order to perfect his part. Another feature of the dramaturgical model of role learning is the presence of a coach. The coach, using Sarbin and Allen's own words, "can guide and advise the novice, . . . detects mistakes, . . . suggests regime of training, and in a variety of other ways aids the actor in mastering his role" (p. 548). The function of the coach is "to provide social reinforcement to the learner. Praise and criticism provide incentives for the learner, and at the same time furnish feedback which can be used to improve performance" (p. 548). The coach offers an evaluation and critique of the performance, and may serve "as a model," that is, "enacts the role for the novice, explicitly instructing him to imitate" (p. 548). According to Goldfried and Davison (1976) the similarity between this description and behavior rehearsal procedures is striking. In fact, by replacing the words "client" for "actor" and "therapist" for "coach" we have an excellent overview of the way in which behavior rehearsal is used in clinical practice.

Briefly, the behavior rehearsal treatment is said to be divided into four general stages.

1. Preparing the client. The client has to recognize the need for learning a new behavior pattern, accept that behavior rehearsal is an appropriate way to develop this new social role, and overcome an initial uneasiness regarding the idea of role playing in the therapist's office.

2. Selecting the target situation. The client is asked to describe the specific situation in which the behavioral deficits manifest themselves. The therapist draws a hierarchy of items comprising components of the new learning goal. These are ranked by the client according to the complexity of the behavioral skills required. Sometimes, in order to arrive at a beneficial treatment, a significant other in the client's life (e.g., a spouse, a relative, a friend) may be consulted to offer his or her perspective regarding the focus of the hierarchy.

3. The behavior rehearsal procedure. Behavior rehearsal may be construed as a gradual shaping process not only because of the use of a hierarchy, but also because complex social interactions entail a number of skills. During the enactment of each item in the hierarchy, attention is paid verbal behavior (e. g., the tone of voice, the pace of speech), as well as nonverbal behavior (e. g., gestures, eye contact, general posture). The role playing proper uses modeling and direct coaching techniques, and sometimes also role reversals.

4. Practicing the new roles in real-life situations. The client has to understand that transferring the learning attained in the therapist's office into real-life situations is part and parcel of the therapeutic procedure. The in-vivo application must be accompanied by written self-observations, which are then discussed in subsequent sessions. There are various techniques for the use of these home assignments.

Behavior rehearsal is employed in learning specific as well as more general social skills. It is used in cognitive therapy for changing dysfunctional thinking and for attitude change. Many self-control procedures are taught via behavior rehearsal. It is used in assertive training and for preparing individuals for certain novel situations where it may be impossible or inadvisable to acquire "on-the-job" experience.

THE NEED FOR A GENERAL ROLE PLAYING MODEL

The preceding survey has illustrated how, and perhaps also why, role playing developed to become a modern therapeutic procedure. Given its current status it appears that, as far as conceptual models are concerned, those who apply role playing in clinical practice are faced with two alternatives. One is to think of the application of role playing in the context of a theoretical orientation. In that regard, the choice is between one of the two presently most dominant orientations. Therapists can adhere to either the model that constitutes the basis of psychodrama, or that which is associated with behavior therapy. The other alternative is to use role playing purely on the basis of its utilitarian value.

Narrowing the choice to these two alternatives raises several issues that highlight the void created by the absence of a generally accepted role playing model. Let us begin with the first alternative. It is widely acknowledged that the principles underlying psychodrama and behavior rehearsal are, to say the least, very different. The question is, are the differences irreconcilable? Goldfried and Davison (1976) echoed the conventional view that certain points of similarity between these two approaches notwithstanding, the disparity is still too great. The psychodramatic model stems from the notion that therapeutic outcomes are attained by uncovering the individual's blocked affect and through tracing current problems back to their historical origin. The behavior rehearsal model, however, is based on the notion that psychotherapy must focus on helping the individual learn new ways of responding to specific situations.

To be more specific, the disparity between these two approaches may become clearer in the light of our previous discussion of Moreno's theory. A point was made there that, according to Moreno, the two most important curative processes in psychotherapy are catharsis and training. In emphasizing the importance of catharsis, psychodrama has put itself in a sharp conflict with behavior therapy, which refutes the therapeutic significance attached to catharsis. The similarity, then, appears to be attributed to the mutual agreement with regard to the value of training. But even here, a close examination of the two approaches, beyond the general principle, reveals a considerable difference. Behavior rehearsal is more systematic, controlled, and governed by learning principles. As a result, it constitutes a "micro-approach" to role playing. Psychodrama, on the other hand, is governed by the principles of spontaneity, the facilitation of self-expression through action explorations, and the process of self-discovery. Therefore, it may be described as a "macro-approach" to role playing. No wonder that to psychodramatists, behavior rehearsal represents a reductionistic approach, that is, a limited form of psychodrama. Behavior therapists, on the other hand, consider psychodrama to be an unsystematic and an inexpedient training procedure.

It is fitting here to cite Wachtel's comment on his attempt to bring the psychodynamic and the behavioristic views close together. Ironically, this comment was made in connection with a discussion of the issue of resistance in psychotherapy. In deploring *therapist's resistance* to open themselves to views that differ from their own, he wrote,

> Part of the difficulty in getting therapists to look beyond their own paradigms lies in the strong identifications held by therapists with a particular tradition and its own particular language and philosophy. . . . Add to that the centrality of their own personal therapy in the training of many therapists and you have a formula for almost unshakeable commitment not only to a particular approach but to a particular way of talking about what one does. (Wachtel, 1982, p. xviii)

But having to choose between one of these two different approaches not only makes the first alternative undeservedly restrictive; for many therapists it is also unappealing. After all, a large number, if not the majority, of clinicians subscribe to therapeutic approaches other than psychodrama or behavior therapy. Recognizing the effectiveness of role playing, however, they apply this form of therapy without a model.

This void calls for the formulation of a different kind of a general paradigm for the use of role playing. In contrast with previous attempts, which offered separate theory-bound models, the new proposed venture must be governed by a rule that might be labeled "a conceptual neutrality." This rule rests on two interrelated propositions. One is the recognition that it is possible to formulate a set of principles that do not interfere with existing theoretical views. Second is the acceptance of a legitimate coexistence of several, even opposing, theoretical approaches to psychotherapy. The last proposition highlights the difference between a "conceptual neutrality" and a "synthesis." The former accepts, even welcomes, the existence of intellectual conflicts. The latter, on the other hand, represents an integrative effort and intentionally strives to eliminate areas of theoretical frictions and to reconcile between opposing views. Using a literary analogy, a model based on "conceptual neutrality" serves as the *text* for which various theoretical approaches provide the *commentaries.* The next two chapters will describe an attempt to provide such a model for the application of role playing.

CHAPTER 2

A General Model for the Method of Behavior Simulation

As the need for creating a consensual model for the simulation of human experiences becomes apparent, the absence of an accepted vocabulary poses a serious problem. The issue at hand is not simply that of semantics but rather a reflection of a disserving plurality and a lack of coherence. A symptomatic manifestation of the existing confusion can be observed in the way that the words "role playing" appear in the literature. There appears to be no one accepted format. Sometimes they are written as one word: roleplaying. Sometimes they appear as two separate words with one or with two capital letters, (e.g., Role playing or Role Playing). Occasionally, they are written as two hyphenated words, again either with one or with two capital letters, and still in some instances they are referred to as "role play."

On the other hand, the existing confusion is hardly surprising. Perhaps it should be expected of an area that evolved without a central model to develop separate, even parallel, sets of concepts. The proliferation of concepts and the different meanings ascribed to similar concepts is probably a direct result of the fact that role playing terminology was born within the frames of reference of different psychotherapeutic and educational theories or approaches. Since each created a role playing vocabulary congruent with its basic principles, and at the same time strived to maintain its unique character, the prevailing unhealthy plurality is not entirely unjustified.

Of the variety of concepts and terms that are in current use, the most fundamental ones are *simulation* and *role playing*. Is there a difference between these two? The answer to this question, in my opinion, is affirmative but may require further clarification.

The concept of simulation generally refers to techniques of eliciting behavior through the manipulation of the *external* environment. Horn and Cleaves (1980) provided a definition that probably reflects the commonly held view of this concept. According to these authors, simulation is the setting of situations so "that their elements comprise a more or less accurate representation or model of some external reality with which the players interact in much the same way they would with the actual reality" (p. 7). But contrary to their original intent, definitions of this sort produced unexpected results. Instead of eliciting a shared, unanimous understanding, they have led to the formulation of several interpretations of what constitutes a simulated experience.

For instance, one interpretation, admittedly an extremely narrow view, maintained that the concept of simulation is confined to the instances where the actual reality, or at least one aspect of it, is *exactly* replicated in laboratory conditions. Furthermore, according to this view, the simulated environment is restricted to the replication of the *inanimate* background of the situation where the player's action is to take place. In other words, the definition of the external environment excludes the presence of *live* people as part of the simulated *context*. Simulations of this kind typically involve mechanical and electronic devices in the form of computers (Lehman, 1977), flight simulators (e.g., Stave, 1977), a simulated version of a supertanker (Wagenaar, 1975), simulations involving videotape technology (e.g., Berger, 1978), car simulators, or wind tunnels for testing the aerodynamic properties of motor vehicles and airplanes, to mention a few.

At the other extreme, one can find a very liberal interpretation of the concept of simulation. According to this view the essence of simulation is the replication of people's *interactions with their external environments*. Whether or not the environments themselves are concretely replicated is of little significance. In fact, situations where the environment is only visualized in the player's imagination, or exists in the form of a hypothetical model, are also regarded as *bona fide* simulations. Forrester's Urban Dynamic model (1973) is a typical example of this. The model dispenses with the need to replicate a whole city in order to project its future functioning, and instead creates a hypothetical model based on empirical data. Another example is the simulated discussion series shown by Public Broadcasting Service television network where a moderator poses a problem, or a set of problems, to a panel of genuine experts. The moderator describes the issue and then turns to one of the panelists with the question, "How would you handle this?" or "What do you do?"

Between these two extremes one finds a third, compromising interpretation, which tends to reflect the view held by therapists, counselors, and group facilitators. Like the first narrow view, this one, too, insists that simulation is based on the creation of a concrete context, a reality-like environment. But unlike the restricted interpretation, it only requires minimal evidence for a reasonable approximation, that is, a detectable resemblance to the actual reality. Moreover, it also accepts that the contextual environment may be portrayed by either objects or live persons and, when appropriate, both. This view, therefore, extends the definition of simulated experiences to include mechanical and electronic simulators as well as the simulation of interpersonal relations and live rehearsals, *in situ*, that is, in the original location. It will include what Shaw, Corsini, Blake, and Mouton (1980) referred to as *dry runs* and *dress rehearsals*, as well as the use of *prototypes*. Examples of the former two are rehearsals of ceremonies with the original participants or with stand-ins, weddings and receptions, answering samples of test questions before an examination, preparations for interviews, jury simulations (e.g., Hamilton, 1978), mock trials in law schools, and rehearsing for public presentations. Prototypes, or pilot models, refer to activities for which there is little or no history and thus represent a tentative version of what reality might be. They have the advantage of identifying unforeseen problems at a relatively low cost, monetary and emotional alike.

Although the third view gained a considerable popularity, possibly because of its practical ramifications for social scientists and clinically oriented professionals who are the main users of simulation procedures, nonetheless, there are still many who subscribe to the other two extreme views. It will be, therefore, inaccurate to suggest that their influence is marginal. On the contrary, the current literature on simulation is very much affected by the multitiude of views and definitions to the point that often one gets the impression that one group is not communicating with the others. In this apparent chaotic state of the art one can detect a hidden trend where different terms seem to acquire special connotations. Thus, the word *simulation* tends to denote laboratory situations involving interactions with computers or in connection with the design of hypothetical models. The term *games* (or simulation/games) is used in connection with game theory exercises and mathematical simulations (e.g., Colman, 1982). The word *simulator* is reserved for situations involving the use of mechanical-electronic training devices, while *role playing* seems to signify the application of simulation in treatment and education. It should be borne in mind that this trend has evolved informally. It has not been accepted as an official classification.

Turning now to the concept of role playing, we again encounter the problem of a multitude of connotations, meanings, and definitions. Only in this case, the disparity is perhaps not as disturbing as in the concept of simulation. Biddle (1979) refers to role playing in his extensive analysis of role theory as the imitations of behavior and the practicing of roles one sees performed by others. Although this is certainly congruent with the view of role playing in developmental psychology, it is a limited one because of the exclusion of all those enactments that represent spontaneous expressions on the part of the players. Geller (1978) echoed another popular aspect of role playing by describing it as an "as if" behavior. According to this, role playing is actually viewed as an "undisguised deception." It is behavior protrayed as if it were real, although everyone knows that it is not. Again, characterizing role playing solely on the basis of its "as if" quality is somewhat restrictive. It may be an accurate description of the use of role playing in research. Clinical practitioners, for instance, would argue in favor of broadening the definition of role playing. They would maintain that role playing contains both realistic as well as unrealistic components. Furthermore, the unrealistic characteristics are often seen as ingenious circumventing processes for eliciting authentic material. Therefore, since it so often produces genuine self-expression behavior, role playing ought to be regarded as much an "as it is" behavior as an "as if" one.

Another common view of role playing is voiced by Blatner (1973). In describing the concept he wrote:

> . . . most professionals would consider role-playing to be more superficial and problem-oriented. Expression of deep feelings is not usually part of most role-playing operations. Rather, the goal of role-playing tends to be working out alternative and more effective approaches to a general problem. Industry, school, and professional training contexts are more likely to utilize this modality in meeting tasks such as developing interviewing skills, dealing with difficult children, handling customer relations, etc. (p. 10)

The distinction between role playing as a task-oriented, problem-solving behavior and psychodrama or psychodramatic role playing as psychotherapeutically oriented enactments is common among psychodramatists. A similar perception of role playing is also prevalent among group facilitators who see their activities more in the areas of enhancing self-awareness, practicing social and communication skills, and demonstrating the effects of group processes. By the way, it was because of this quite popular nontherapeutic connotation of the concept of role playing that I decided to preface it with the word *clinical* and to refer to it throughout the book as clinical role playing.

The above brief analysis shows that role playing has been described in different ways. The better known ones are acting-out behavior (Starr, 1977), an imitative behavior (Biddle, 1979), an "as if" behavior (Geller, 1978), and a superficial, problem-solving behavior (Blatner, 1973). Perhaps a composite of all these characteristics, lumped together, constitutes a fair definition of role playing.

Given the variety of connotations ascribed to each of the concepts, simulation and role playing, it seemed easier to look at the characteristics these two have in common. Indeed, the two concepts share several important features. For example, both are imitations or replications of real-life occurrences. Both are conducted in controlled laboratory conditions. Both are seen as meaningful learning experiences. And both tend to protect the learner from painful consequences due to their experimental, playlike nature. The result of this similarity was that each concept became associated with a different group of professionals. Simulation was chosen by those engaged in decision-making processes and game theories who based the simulated experiences on mathematical models and computerized technology. Role playing, on the other hand, was adopted by clinicians, counselors, and educators who applied it as a therapeutic and quasi-therapeutic modality. This trend is quite pervasive, and given its long history it is likely to continue to exist.

Turning back to the earlier question regarding the difference between the concept of simulation and that of role playing, I believe that the two *are* different, the similarities notwithstanding. Of the two concepts, simulation is the more general one, implying that a particular intervention is designed as a replication of real-life events in a laboratory condition. Role playing, on the other hand, is a more specific concept. It refers to the implementation aspect of the intervention as expressed in the behavior of the persons involved in the simulated experience. Following this distinction let us begin the discussion with the general concept, and, in order to avoid confusion with its old connotations, a new concept (i.e., *behavior simulation*) is proposed.

BEHAVIOR SIMULATION AND ITS PARADIGM

Behavior simulation was suggested originally as an umbrella concept (Kipper, 1981, 1982) to encompass all versions and forms of simulated interventions used in connection with the treatment of people. The word *treatment* is applied here advisedly and refers to the inducement of learning experiences and psychological changes in general, rather than in its traditional clinical sense. Thus, first of all, *behavior simulation* represents a generic title. Understandably, some clinicians and trainers may find the inclusion of the word "simulation" less palatable because in their minds the old association of this word with nonclinical practice is still alive. Yet the new concept is made of two words, *behavior* and *simulation*. The former denotes that it is concerned with the playing of roles, while the latter implies that the context is set in a laboratory condition. There are two elements associated with the playing of roles. One is the manifestation of the actual activity; the behavior itself, and the second is the portrayal of the situational environment; the various representations of the context of the activity.

The special characteristics of behavior simulation are summarized in two models. One is entitled "The behavior simulation paradigm for the B factor" (Figure 2.1) and the other "A diagram of environmental constellations" (Figure 2.3). These are based on a systematic analysis of the concepts involved in designing and structuring life experiences.

The principles that led to the formulation of the two models are as follows:

1. The models are restricted to the method of simulation. They do *not* pretend to describe behavior in general.
2. The paradigm and the diagram are based on independent concepts and rationale not directly derived from a particular theory or theories of personality and psychotherapeutic approaches. Behavior simulation is seen as an independent field of knowledge in the social sciences; it is a method more than a theory. Its conceptual independence puts it in a neutral position that ought to facilitate its use in a variety of therapeutic approaches.
3. Both the paradigm and the diagram are expected to be sufficiently comprehensive to include all forms of simulated interventions save those that are essentially nonpsychological (e.g., economic models, architectural prototypes, and the like). Therefore, they need to be pertinent to simulation procedures aimed at achieving *complete replications* of the external reality (as, for example, in Stave, 1977, or Wagenaar, 1975), and those aimed at creating only *partial replications* of either internal or external reality (e.g., Colman, 1982; Horn & Cleaves, 1980; Kenderdine & Keyes, 1974).
4. Comprehensiveness also pertains to the scope of the paradigm and the diagram, namely, that they must be applicable in every facet of human functioning. The relevance of behavior simulation is not confined to the clinical practice. It ought to have a broader application: education, rehabilitation, vocational counseling, business, management, and so forth.

To sum up: In principle there are three key elements in every simulated experience. One is the content of the issue to be explored, an element that is not unique to this method. The remaining two are the *behavior* element, that is, the actual responses of the participants in the simulated experience, henceforth referred to as the *B factor*, and the situational backgrounds, the *environmental* element, henceforth referred to as the *E factor*.

CHARACTERISTICS OF THE BEHAVIOR B FACTOR

An observation of the participants' behavior in simulated experiences, either in the role of the star player (the protagonist) or as helpers (the auxiliaries), reveals interesting characteristics. Sometimes the emitted behavior represents a natural and genuine performance, an authentic expression of the player's unique personality. On the other hand, sometimes the exhibited behavior may be of a different sort, which is essentially an imitation of responses more typical of someone else.

This observation suggests that the behavior displayed by the participants in simulated experiences follows two kinds of models. A *model* is defined as a set of response patterns that is presumed to determine not only the overt form that characterizes the expressed behavior but also its quality, that is, the kinds of psychological processes that are being activated. A model can be internal or *endogenous*, one that emanates from within the person and is an integral part of his or her personality. It may include response patterns that originally belonged to someone else but as time went by have been internalized and become integrated into the player's own self. The model can also be external or *exogenous*, one that is typical of an outside source (person) and is temporarily borrowed by the player in order to deal with a given situation or task more effectively. The division of the model according to its two loci explains the perceptions of J. L. Moreno and of Biddle with regard to role playing. Moreno (1964a) emphasized the spontaneity aspect referring to the activation of *endogenous models*. Biddle (1979) emphasized the imitative aspect of role playing thus referring to the importance of *exogenous models*. In other words, behavior displayed in the course of a simulated episode, the so-called B factor, needs to be separated into *spontaneous* behavior and *mimetic* behavior.

Spontaneous behavior refers to the expression of endogenous models. It is behavior customarily described as a display of authentic proclivities: feelings, perceptions, attitudes, beliefs, and skills. In its classical form it is manifested as an immediate, direct, and straightforward response to a given situation and may constitute an ad lib reaction as well as a rep-

etition of past modes of responding. It has high idiosyncratic qualities
and tends to be noticeable best in novel and unexpected situations.

Mimetic behavior concerns the expression of exogenous models. In
principle, it refers to the imitation of an external model, the reproduction
of an already existing response pattern located outside the self. The
dictionary describes the term *mimetic* as "apt to" or "the resemblance to
other forms." It is derived from the Greek word mimos, meaning akin
to, and is used in connection with mimicry and imitation. But in the
present context, mimetic behavior has a broader connotation. Although
it does not exclude superficial, simple, and straightforward imitations,
it primarily refers to imitations blended with personal interpretations.
This view suggests that mimetic behavior involves a wider range of abilities, such as the ability to (a) imitate external examples, (b) assume the
appropriate psychological postures associated with the imitations, (c)
introduce elements of improvisations and elaborations into the emulated
models, and (d) translate abstract codes of behavior into concrete forms.
It is, therefore, a complex and creative behavior that requires a conscious
intervention of cognitive processes.

Given this nature of mimetic behavior it seems appropriate to divide
it further into two separate subcategories: mimetic-replication and mimetic-pretend.

Mimetic-replication behavior is characterized by accurate imitations of
an exogenous model that is *personally known* to the player, one that the
respondent is very familiar with. The model, therefore, is specific and
concrete and must be replicated as accurately as possible. The model
literally must be visible to the player, that is, displayed in front of the
respondent's eyes. Typically, mimetic-replication requires having clear
ideas (or instructions) of what is to be imitated prior to the actual act of
replication.

Mimetic-pretend behavior is characterized by the imitations of certain
kinds of exogenous models. These are models with which the player has
no personal familiarity. They may be composites of traits and qualities of
a vaguely known individual person, or those that exist only as an ideal
(e. g., the perfect lover, the ideal mother). They may be codes of behavior
shared by members of a given culture or subculture (e.g., altruistic behavior, politeness). They may also represent ideas and goals one may
aspire to have for which there are only unspecified models to follow. In
order to qualify as mimetic-pretend, the behavior must be carried out
under an assumed identity and where the original *model is absent* from the
simulation session. If the model represents an individual person, it *must
not be personally known* to him or her.

The following brief summation of the difference between the *mimetic-replication* and the *mimetic-pretend* behavior may highlight their special characteristics.

- In mimetic-replication, the original model participates in the simulated episode. In mimetic-pretend, it is represented in absentia.
- In mimetic-replication, the model, or specific aspects of it, must be accurately replicated. In mimetic-pretend only its general characteristics need to be portrayed.
- In mimetic-replication, the model is clearly defined, hardly allowing any personal input. But in mimetic-pretend it is loosely defined and structured; thus it is susceptible to personal improvisations. In fact, it tends to encourage the introjection of personal contents.

Occasionally one may encounter instances where the differentiation between behavior that is essentially *spontaneous* and that which is essentially *mimetic* is not entirely clear. A seemingly spontaneous behavior may in fact represent an imitation of an exogenous model the player has in mind and does not have the opportunity to say so, or does not know that he or she is supposed to make this distinction. The question is where does one draw the line between a "pure" spontaneous and a mimetic behavior? The answer to this question is not simple. There exists a natural relationship between behavior that we regard as idiosyncratic (spontaneous) and the fact that it tends to be shaped and formed through imitations of external models through the processes of socialization, social affiliation, and learning by means of direct and vicarious modeling (e.g., Bandura, 1977). The prominence of this process may vary in different periods of life. Nonetheless, it is an ongoing process that sometimes introduces further complications. One can, of course, turn to the protagonists themselves to provide the information whether or not their behavior followed a clear exogenous model. But such self-reports are not always very reliable.

The alternative recourse is to rely on external criteria to determine which is spontaneous and which is mimetic behavior. The same criteria should also differentiate between the two mimetic subcategories: the mimetic-replication and the mimetic-pretend. The reliance on external criteria has some clear advantages. Its disadvantage, on the other hand, is that it disallows any input from the players and therefore runs the risk of being inaccurate. Bearing this imperfection in mind, we have nonetheless decided to rely on the external determinants as our main criteria.

What, then, are the aspects that define the three main subcategories or behavior patterns of the B factor, that is, the spontaneous, the mimetic-replication, and the mimetic-pretend? Let us consider two such aspects: the *source* of the behavior and its *scope*. The *source* is concerned with the locus of the model, that is, its internal (endogenous) versus its external (exogenous) origins. These two already have been discussed earlier. The *scope* of the behavior refers to the degree of constraints imposed on the portrayed role itself. There are varying degrees of restrictions that can be imposed. These may range from minimal restrictions (e. g., an instruction such as "I would like you [the protagonist] to behave as naturally as you can") to maximal restrictions (e. g., instructions such as "I would like you [the protagonist or the auxiliary] to show us how angry you were" or "Be as uncooperative as you can").

Figure 2.1 shows how both the source of the behavior and its scope can define the spontaneous, the mimetic-replication, and the mimetic-pretend patterns as well as other combination patterns.

The top two lines in Figure 2.1 describe the characteristics of the model in terms of the *source* of the behavior. Thus, in any given behavior simulation episode the model after which the emitted behavior molds itself can be either *present* or *absent* from the actual session. Considering the former situation, that is, the model is *present* in the session, its pres-

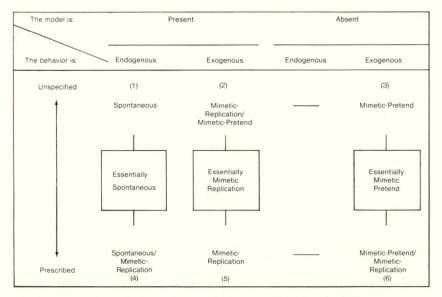

Figure 2.1. The behavior simulation paradigm for the B factor

ence may be expressed in two ways. One, the locus of the model is internal or *endogenous*, that is, it resides within the actor and constitutes a pattern of responses well integrated in his or her own self. The other way is that the locus of the model is external or *exogenous*, that is, it represents a pattern of responses typical of someone else, which is temporarily borrowed by the actor. But when the model is physically *absent* from the session proper, by definition it must be an exogenous one. Otherwise, how can we have an endogenous model (one that resides within the actor's own self) which at the same time is absent from the session? This is the reason why in Figure 2.1 the column under the category, "the model is absent and endogenous," is empty.

The left column in Figure 2.1 shows the characteristics of the *scope* of the model. The scope, it might be recalled, refers to the degree of constraints imposed on the enacted role(s). The expression "degree of constraints" concerns the specificity by which the roles a protagonist is asked to portray are defined. This may range from an essentially unrestricted or *unspecified* role (e. g., "Just act naturally, the way you want") to specific or *prescribed* roles (e.g., "In the next situation I would like you to behave as obstinately as you can"). Given that the specificity of the role is always a matter of degree, the *unspecified* and the *prescribed* categories appear as the extreme ends of a continuum, shown in Figure 2.1 as a two-way arrow. It should be remembered, however, that all roles portrayed in the course of behavior simulation episodes are somewhat defined by virtue of the fact that they are concrete and aim at particular objectives. Therefore, the *unspecified* category does not suggest a complete lack of constraints but rather a relatively low degree of specificity.

Considering all the characteristics ascribed to both the *source* of the model and its *scope*, we have a total of six conditions, henceforth referred to as the *B factor patterns*. These are represented in the paradigm as six cells numbered from (1) through (6).

THE B FACTOR PATTERNS

The B factor patterns shown in Figure 2.1 are arranged in three main columns, each representing one of the spontaneous, the mimetic-replication, and the mimetic-pretend behaviors. The paradigm also shows that each column includes two patterns: a "pure" type and a mixed or combined type. The "pure" ones, looking from left to right, are the patterns marked as (1), (5), and (3). The combined patterns are those marked as (4), (2), and (6). Let us examine each of the patterns more closely.

The column under the heading "the model is *present* and *endogenous*" is characterized as "essentially spontaneous" (see the inside box) primarily due to the fact that the source of the model is endogenous, that is, resides within the player's self. It includes two patterns marked as (1) and (4), which represent the two extreme ends of the spontaneous behavior.

In the pattern marked as (1), the player portrays himself or herself under *unspecified* role behavior. Given the relative lack of specificity, the player finds himself or herself in a simulated environment where a wide range of response options are available. The choice of action is in the hand of the player and, at least a priori, there is a low degree of predictability as to what will be the final selection. The definition of *spontaneous behavior* involves two components. One is that the behavior follows an internal or an internalized model, and the other is that the behavior is emitted in a low predictability constellation. It was J. L. Moreno (1964a) who pointed out that there is an inverse relationship between predictability and spontaneous behavior. Moreno explained that spontaneity is possible only in a universe that is open, where some degree of novelty is continuously possible—a universe not determined by absolute laws. By defining the role behavior as unspecified (e.g., "Just act as natural as you can") one induces a fair degree of unpredictability. In clinical practice, for example, a protagonist will be asked to follow an *endogenous (present)/unspecified* model for general diagnostic purposes in order to evaluate the progress made in the course of the treatment and to reinforce integrative processes.

The pattern marked as (4) also refers to behavior that follows an internal model. But unlike the preceding pattern, the role behavior is *prescribed,* meaning confined to certain kinds of responses. The restrictions imposed on the role behavior introduce a measure of predictability and, therefore, make this condition a less "pure" form of spontaneous behavior. The B factor pattern expected here will be a combination of the *spontaneous* and the *mimetic-replication* behavior, but the *spontaneous* component will be the dominant of the two. This pattern is likely to become evident when a protagonist is instructed, for example, to act "the same way you did when you spoke with your father two weeks ago," or when the role behavior is narrowly defined, for example, to "act as hostile as you can," "be courageous," or "act as compassionate as you can." The reason why this pattern contains a spontaneous quality is quite clear. At first glance, however, one may fail to see the reason for the inclusion of the mimetic-replication component in this pattern because mimetic-replication is said to be associated with an *exogenous* model and not with an endogenous one. On technical grounds, this argument makes great sense. Certainly there seems to be a logical inconsistency here. But from a phenomenological-experiential point of view there seems to be little difference if a person tries to replicate a clearly defined external model or a clearly defined model that is vivid in one's own memory but happened to be an internal one. The act of replication may be the same. There might be only a difference in the player's familiarity with it. Thus, while we agree that this combined pattern is *essentially spontaneous*, it also contains some—perhaps very few—elements of mimetic-replication behavior. These elements may play a greater role when a protagonist is asked to repeat exactly his or her past behavior, as illustrated in the first of the above instructional examples. They may play a weaker role when the instructions are simply to be "hostile," "courageous," "compassionate," and so forth.

The next column to be described appears under the heading "the model is *present* and *exogenous.*" It is characterized as "essentially mimetic-replication" (see inside box) primarily due to the fact that the model is external, that is, derived from an outside source and has not yet become integrated in the player's own self. The stipulation that the model must be *present* may require some further clarification. In the two spontaneous patterns discussed above, there was also a requirement for the actual presence of the model. There, however, the case is simple. Since the model is in fact the protagonist himself or herself, by definition it must be physically present in the session. But when the model is external, its presence may be evident in *two* ways. One is presence in the literal sense, that is, actually being in the session either in person or through recording devices such as audiotapes and videotapes. The other is presence in the sense that it is vividly clear in the player's imagination and memory. This second definition of the notion of "presence" implies that the model is both absent as well as present—absent because it is not available *in person* and present because it exists in the protagonist's mind. According to our paradigm the absence of an external model from the treatment session leads to *mimetic-pretend* behavior, not mimetic-replication. Therefore, in mimetic-replication behavior the requirement of the model to be present means *literally present.*

In the pattern marked as (2), the player emulates another person who is present in the session under *unspecified* role behavior. The relative lack of specificity offers the player a great latitude with regard to which responses to imitate and in what degree of accuracy. The pattern is likely to become evident when a protagonist is instructed, for example, "I would like you to behave exactly as John" (and John *is present in the session)*. Since there is no further hint about what parts of John's behavior are expected to be imitated, the protagonist may try for brief moments to *be* John. When that occurs the protagonist operates under an assumed identity, or partially under an assumed identity. At this point elements of *mimetic-pretend* are being introjected into the intended mimetic-replication behavior. This is the reason why this pattern is characterized as a combination of *mimetic-replication* and *mimetic-pretend* behaviors. *Mimetic-replication*, however, will be the dominant of these two.

It is not difficult to think of instances, especially in the context of group therapy, where this particular pattern is sought. A classic example of it is the clinical role playing intervention known as the Mirror Technique. The technique is essentially a live playback of the behavior the protagonist evinced during the session or a portion of it. Thus, the therapist may ask a helper (an auxiliary) to come forward and behave the way the protagonist did without referring to a particular response, while the protagonist observes the demonstration. The technique is often particularly useful in a family therapy situation. There, one family member is asked to play back to another member the way the latter comes across. Note that our examples concern action feedback where the respondent is *not* given instructions to repeat *a specific* behavior. When this happens we are faced with strictly *mimetic-replication* behavior, a pattern that will be described next.

The pattern marked as (5) is a classic case of *mimetic-replication*. It is characterized by a model that is present and external and with role behavior that is prescribed, that is, *exogenous (present)/prescribed*. Both the external source of the model and especially the specificity of the role behavior make it easy to emulate the desired behavior, thus creating the ideal condition for the occurrence of the *mimetic-replication* pattern. The protagonist is simply asked to repeat and imitate a certain behavior evinced by another individual, or several individuals, who also participate in the session. It is a straightforward modeling situation where the sole emphasis is on copying the performance of someone else. There is no need here to assume the identity of the model, to empathize with him or her, or to understand the underlying motives that have led the model to display the target behavior.

In all four patterns discussed so far (1, 4, 2, and 5), the source of the model, whether endogenous or exogenous, was present in the actual session. What happens when the model is not available and needs to be represented in absentia? What kind of B factor pattern(s) can we expect to see under this condition? The last column (at the right end of the paradigm) addresses this situation. The column appears under the heading "the model is absent and exogenous," which leads to the emergence of an "essentially mimetic-pretend pattern (see inside box). As was already alluded to, the *mimetic-pretend* quality stems from the fact that the model is represented in absentia. As with the other two columns, this one also contains two patterns: one that constitutes a "pure" form of *mimetic-pretend*, and one that is a combination of *mimetic-pretend* and *mimetic-replication*. In the pattern marked as (3), the player portrays a model which is *absent* from the actual session. This portrayal is very general since it takes place with role behavior that is unspecified. The constellation of an *exogenous (absent)/unspecified* model forms an ideal condition for the emergence of a *mimetic-pretend* pattern.

The majority of roles portrayed by auxiliaries in clinical role playing are mimetic-pretend ones. In group therapy this is the case when an auxiliary is asked to portray the mother, the father, the boss, and so forth of the protagonist—people the auxiliary has never met and has some, but very little, information about. The auxiliary has to assume the identity of the other person and with the scant information at his or her disposal tries to represent that person as best he or she can. Protagonists, too, may often be asked to resort to mimetic-pretend behavior. That kind of behavior will undoubtedly become evident when a protagonist is asked to play God, a good fairy, the ideal parent (but not their own or other specific parents they know) or a judge, for example.

The *mimetic-pretend* pattern, especially when it occurs under *unspecified* role behavior, is an interesting simulation phenomenon. Since the role itself is loosely defined and the available data about the original model are limited, players may find themselves somewhat ill-equipped or insufficiently informed to be able to proceed with the tasks assigned to them. They may try to get more information about the role they are expected to play but often it, too, is limited. In order to fill the gap of ignorance and still portray the assigned role, they tend to introject their *own* personality into the role. Sometimes, such self-introjections indeed distort the role to the extent that it no longer resembles the original model. But often these "personal fillers" do not discolor or significantly alter the portrayal of the original model. The dynamics of the mimetic-pretend behavior suggest that the absence of an exogenous model is supplemented by fragments of an endogenous model. In that sense, the classic mimetic-pretend behavior is blended with elements of spontaneous behavior that represent the personal introjections.

The personal introjections into roles portrayed as *mimetic-pretend* create an interesting dynamic. In a sense, they are merely by-products of this behavior simulation pattern. Indeed, from a strictly technical point of view, it is justified to consider them as contaminating material because of their irrelevance to the role(s) and their lack of contribution to the accurate representation of the absent model. But clinically they have some redeeming features. Under the mimetic-pretend pattern the player is cast into a role officially proclaimed as impersonal. Thus, acting under an assumed identity the player is led to believe that whatever happens in the role does not reflect on his or her own personality but rather is ascribed to the persona of the absent model. As this sense of anonymity becomes more pronounced it tends to act as an extra protection and as a shield to the inner self. Inevitably, it results in a decrease of self-guardedness and an increase of perceived freedom. The player begins to feel less accountable for his or her actions, at least in the sense that they will not incur unpleasant consequences. The newly acquired freedom is likely to increase either spontaneous expressions or objective perspectives, or both. The possible effect of the laxity with regard to the use of internal controls and to the enhancement of disinhibition processes is twofold. First, it may facilitate a greater involvement and agility in the task proper. Second, it may spill over and similarly affect the ease in disclosing personal material that is introjected in the formal role(s). It has been repeatedly observed that protagonists find it easier to do or say things ordinarily they would not dare to say or do when put under mimetic-pretend situations.

In the pattern marked as (6) the player also represents an external model who is absent from the session, but this time the role behavior is more specific and *prescribed*. The greater specificity of the role introduces an element of mimetic-replication; hence we predict that the behavior evinced here will be a combination of *mimetic-pretend* and *mimetic-replication*. The *mimetic-pretend* pattern, however, will be the dominant of the two. Examples of this are roles that either the protagonist or the auxiliaries are somewhat familiar with but are not associated with persons they know well. These could be roles such as playing a dishonest person, a policeman, or an impatient boss, all roles which have cultural definitions or formal job descriptions. Many of the role-training exercises are designed so that the protagonist (and the other party involved in the simulation) receives a sheet of paper with some description of a model who is not present in the session. Then he or she is asked to assume the identity of that model and behave according to the instructions, which are quite selective.

The two mimetic-pretend patterns are quite common in clinical role playing. In many respects they epitomize the "as if" quality that has been traditionally ascribed to role playing. Their therapeutic use is widely recognized, though unfortunately it has not been researched sufficiently.

Finally, I should comment on the difference between pattern (2) and pattern (6) in the paradigm. Pattern (2) is described as a combination of *mimetic-replication* and *mimetic-pretend* where the *replication* element is the dominant one. It is true that in this pattern the player may be lured into assuming an identity that is not his or her own. But because of the personal and thorough familiarity with the model, the displayed behavior will be essentially mimetic-replication. The pretend aspect of it is more incidental, perhaps cosmetic. Pattern (6), on the other hand, represents a combination of *mimetic-pretend* and *mimetic-replication* where the *pretend* element is more dominant. In this case the model is not personally known to the player but some selective and specific characteristics of it are available either because the role itself is normatively familiar or because they have been provided deliberately. The limited information demands substantial improvisation and creative imagination which heighten the pretend component of the portrayal.

In conclusion, the B factor of behavior simulation essentially contains three patterns: spontaneous, mimetic-replication, and mimetic-pretend. Each of these may become evident either in a "pure" form or in a combined one. In general, as the role behavior (i.e., the scope of the model) becomes narrow and prescribed, it tends to include more imitative and copying behavior (mimetic-replication).

THE FAMILIARITY WITH THE MODEL

In the preceding section, the discussion focused on the relationships of the three patterns to both the source and the scope of the model. In that discussion the issue of the familiarity with the model was mentioned in a cursory manner. Let us now examine it in detail.

To be sure, the degree of the specificity of the role behavior is not always synonymous with the degree of the familiarity with the model. Both the unspecified and the prescribed instructions may have different meanings to the players depending on whether or not they are personally familiar with the original model. Even the portrayal of a prescribed role, which by definition familiarizes the players with the required behavior, tends to be affected by the presence or absence of previous familiarity with the original model. It must be emphasized, however, that this holds true only in circumstances where the imitated model is external (exogenous). As mentioned earlier, an internal model (endogenous) is always known to the player irrespective of the degree of the specificity of the instructions because it is part and parcel of his or her role repertoire.

Figure 2.2 shows the relationships between the specificity of the behavior (the roles) and the familiarity with the model, as well as their effects on the three B factor patterns.

Figure 2.2 is comprised of two axes, a vertical and a horizontal one. The ordinate represents the specificity of the role behavior and is entitled "The Behavior." It is divided into the unspecified and the prescribed categories with a two-way arrow between them to signify that specificity is a matter of degree. The abcissa, labeled "The Model," is also divided, dichotomously, into two fundamental conditions referring to situations when the player is familiar or unfamiliar with the original model. Here, too, the existence of various intensities of familiarity is acknowledged, although these may have a narrower range than degrees of specificity. Taken together the two axes form four conditions shown in Figure 2.2 as cells separated by the broken lines.

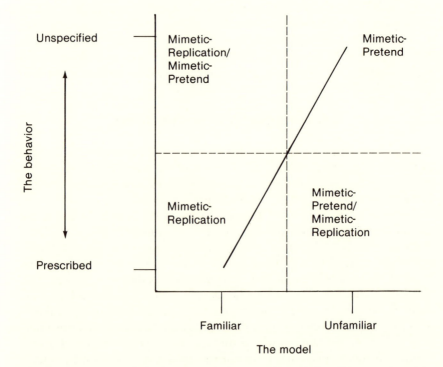

Figure 2.2. The relationship between the specificity of the behavior and the familiarity with an exogenous model

The lower left cell refers to a simple situation where the instructions given to the players are specific and prescribed and the model they portray is known to them. This is probably the easiest of all role playing tasks. Since the players have the maximal information about the role they are asked to assume, their behavior is expected to be essentially mimetic-replication: an accurate imitation of the external model. This is a typical case where a protagonist is requested to portray a specific behavior of his or her own mother, father, brother, sister, friend, employer, and so forth. For an auxiliary, this situation involves playing specific facets of the protagonist's own behavior or those of a group member.

The upper right cell, on the other hand, represents a situation of great uncertainty. The role behavior is unspecified and therefore leaves a void that needs to be filled by intuitive improvisations. Furthermore, the model itself is of little help as the players are not familiar with it and have no additional clues to rely on. This uncertainty is expected to promote mimetic-pretend behavior. This condition is typical of instructions given to a protagonist to assume the role of God, Satan, an angel, or any character he or she is not personally acquainted with. For an auxiliary, this situation may involve playing the protagonist's mother, father, friend, and so forth, assuming that the auxiliary has never met any of these people before.

The diagonal line in Figure 2.2 represents the amount of specific information role players have before and during their simulated portrayals. The bottom of the line (the lower left cell) refers to a situation where maximal information is provided, and its top (the upper right cell) to a situation with minimal information. Between these extremes there are two additional conditions, where one aspect of the information is plentiful and one is meager. These are represented in the two remaining cells.

The lower right cell is one example of the uneven amount of information. The instructions given to the players are specific and prescribed but that is *all* that they get. Since they are not personally familiar with the model, they cannot use additional clues to help them in their portrayal of the role. As most instructions given to players are never complete, the subsequent behavior will be based on a mixture of *accurate* and *self-invented* information. This is expected to be reflected in a combination of mimetic-pretend and mimetic-replication behavior. The predominance of the former or the latter mimetic kind depends on the amount of information given. Experience has shown, however, that under regular circumstances there is a slight dominance of the mimetic-pretend behavior. This behavior is most likely to become evident in those role playing situations commonly known as role training exercises. One of the salient characteristics of these exercises is that the protagonist, and often the other party as well, is asked to portray a role of an imaginary person. The role is specified either orally or through a handout describing the case, the issues, and some elements of the personality (and the behavior) of the involved parties. Such training interventions are typically used for skill development purposes. In clinical settings they are indicated for inhibited protagonists who find it easier to practice under an assumed, even if vague, identity.

The second condition of uneven amount of information is depicted by the upper left cell in figure 2.2. Here the instructions that players receive with regard to the roles to be enacted are unspecified and quite general. But the relative paucity of information imparted through the instructions is well compensated by the familiarity with the original model. This acquaintance is a source of abundant information the players do not get directly from the therapist/instructor. Therefore, it is only natural that they will resort to this source of data for guidance while paying some (moderate) attention to the broad instructions. This condition is expected to elicit a combination of mimetic-replication and mimetic-pretend behavior. The prediction for the presence of some, admittedly few, manifestations of mimetic-pretend behavior is based on the tendency of the unspecified instructions to leave the players somewhat misguided. They must experiment a bit before focusing on the responses relevant to the role played situation. And while engaging in this process they have to rely in their own resourcefulness and intuition.

To sum up: Familiarity with the external model and the specificity of the instructions regarding the role behavior complement, and sometimes also balance, each other. Their various combinations affect the elicitation of the mimetic-replication and the mimetic-pretend behaviors.

The Significance of the B Factor

The importance of the proposed B factor paradigm—its three major patterns and their characteristics—may be self-evident. Nonetheless, let us summarize some of its potential contributions to the future development of behavior simulation.

To begin with, there is little doubt with regard to the advantage of having a general frame of reference that provides a systematic exposition of the key concepts. Like any systematization endeavor in other fields of knowledge, it facilitates a greater coherence and also introduces a sense of order. It is the first step in the effort to gain a better understanding of the simulation/role playing phenomenon.

Additionally, the paradigm is likely to have a unifying effect by offering a broad base foundation as an alternative to the existing, different descriptions of the simulated or the role playing behavior. Using the paradigm, we are now equipped with a set of concepts that affords us comparisons with various interventions and their subsequent outcomes using the same criteria. So far there has been no way one could compare different simulation interventions. The fact that interventions differed in their contents, implementing procedures, and objectives made comparative evaluations almost impossible. The formulation of the three major B factor patterns and their combinations rectifies this situation as it points to some common denominators of several clusters of simulated behavior.

Another advantage is that the attempt to distinguish among several patterns of simulated behavior introduces a useful measure of refinement. Until now, the behavior exhibited by protagonists in simulated experiences was looked upon as a complex performance of *one* kind. This has been the overriding tradition, and this was the way it has been typically described. Adaline Starr's (1977) description of role playing is a good example of this approach. Role playing, according to her, is "the process of assuming the role or character of another person, an animal, an inanimate object, or oneself at another time and acting accordingly" (p. 30). It is referred to as a single process presumably of one kind. The discovery of several underlying patterns and processes of such behavior offers opportunities for a more discriminative research. It is quite possible that the traditional undifferentiated conceptualization of simulated behavior might have hindered a thorough understanding of this phenomenon.

From the very beginning my approach was a different one. Starting from the simple assumption that each set of simulated episodes, instructions, and techniques creates a different constellation, I proceeded to theorize that each group of such constellations puts the protagonists in a distinct phenomenological (psychological) state. I also assumed that each state is likely to activate different psychological processes, hence it ought to result in differential outcomes. In consideration of the three "pure" patterns, the following hypotheses were formulated: The spontaneous behavior was believed to be associated with the elicitation of *integrative* processes; the mimetic-pretend behavior was thought to be associated with the elicitation of *disinhibition* processes and with *cognitive* functioning; and the mimetic-replication behavior was hypothesized to activate processes responsible for learning through *modeling*.

Assuming that the basic premise is correct and that behavior evinced in simulated condition needs to be separated into subcategories or patterns, how can one be assured that the proposed classification is a viable one? Does the theoretical division into the various patterns fit the actual construction of role playing situations as reported in literature?

Let us examine a few examples of role playing studies. But first, a note of caution. The task of sorting the existing studies into the new classification of the behavior patterns may be hampered by several facts. Many of the reported role playing studies do not contain detailed descriptions of the procedures used and the specific instructions given to the subjects. In such cases one can only guess what pattern(s) of simulated behavior were elicited through the experimental manipulation. Also, the extent of role playing used in the different studies varies. Some required minimal enactment which can barely qualify as simulated experiences of the kinds we are concerned with. It should also be pointed out that in some instances multiple interventions were used, that is, role playing and others combined.

Nevertheless, it appears that sorting of studies that used role playing interventions into one (or more) of the B factor patterns is not difficult. For example, eliciting the mimetic-replication behavior in role playing studies is perhaps the most common practice, possibly because the imitation of a defined model can be better controlled experimentally. Customarily, such role playing episodes involve the imitation of live models, videotaped models, or models described either orally or in a written form (e.g., Goldstein & Goedhart, 1973; Gutride, Goldstein, & Hunter, 1973; Newton, 1974; Zimbardo, 1965). The mimetic-pretend behavior (combined with others) was sought in a number of studies. For example, Janis and Mann (1965) asked their smoking subjects to become a patient who receives the news that he or she contracted lung cancer. Others (Johnson, 1967, 1971a, 1971b; Johnson & Dustin, 1970) used the role reversal technique in their studies where the subjects had to become their opponents. Eliciting spontaneous behavior in role playing research is also evident and may take the form of asking subjects to express their rage (Bohart, 1977) or in studies using psychodramatic episodes (e. g., Fleming, 1974; Schonke, 1978; Yablonsky, 1955). It appears, therefore, that the division of the B factor into separate patterns is not merely a theoretical proposition; it corresponds to what occurs in the practical reality.

There are a few studies that provide data in support of the basic assumption that different behavior simulation patterns yield differential outcomes. For example, in some studies the effects of mimetic-pretend behavior were compared to those of the mimetic-replication. One study (Kipper & Har-Even, 1980, reported in Kipper, 1982) investigated the effect of mimetic-pretend simulated behavior, mimetic-replication simulated behavior, and no-simulation control condition on changing the attitude of Israeli students who were unfavorably disposed towards granting new immigrants considerable tax privileges. The results showed significant changes towards the favorable position among subjects in the mimetic-pretend and the control condition but not for the subjects in the mimetic-replication condition.

In another study (Kipper, Har-Even, Rotenberg, & Dagan, 1982) it was found that students who engaged in mimetic-pretend behavior were significantly more involved in their simulated tasks than those engaged in mimetic-replication behavior. In a study of training in empathy (Kipper & Ben-Ely, 1979) subjects who were trained in the Double technique (a mimetic-pretend pattern) significantly improved their empathic performance compared to subjects who were trained in the Rogerian reflecting technique (a mimetic-replication pattern), those trained through lectures (no-simulation condition), and a no-treatment group. One study (Kipper & Har-Even, 1984) compared the effect of mimetic-pretend and spontaneous patterns on the readiness to inflict pain. Since mimetic-pretend is thought to activate disinhibition processes, it was hypothesized that subjects operating under an assumed identity would be less inhibited in delivering (fake) electric shocks as punishment for poor performance than subjects operating under spontaneous simulated behavior. The results confirmed the hypothesis. These initial research data seem encouraging enough to tentatively conclude that our approach indeed opens new avenues for a better understanding of the different effects of the various patterns.

CHARACTERISTICS OF THE ENVIRONMENTAL E FACTOR

In the beginning of the present discussion of the behavior simulation concept, two fundamental factors responsible for the unique features of the simulated experience were identified. The first, expounded in the preceding sections, was the B factor, which addressed the behavioral characteristics associated with the portrayal of roles. We turn now to the second factor, which concerns the environmental characteristics of the simulation: the situational backgrounds created in an artificial "mini-universe." This factor, henceforth referred to as the E factor, pertains to the ecological dimension of role playing (e.g., Barker, 1968; Bellack, Hersen, & Lamparski, 1979; Bellack, Hersen, & Turner, 1978; Wessberg, Mariotto, Conger, Farrell, & Conger, 1979). Thus the letter E may stand for both environment and ecology. Put simply, the E factor deals with the resemblance of the simulated constellation to real life.

It has been argued that an important criterion for the validity of behavior simulation is an affirmative answer to the question, Is there a close resemblance between what occurs in role playing situations and its manifestations in the real world? The assumption is that the closer the resemblance, the more authentic is the behavior displayed in the artificial condition. On its face value, the rationale for this reasoning appears quite plain. If behavior simulation models itself after life, and if it presumes to constitute a medium for training in life skills (e.g., Gazda & Powell, 1981), then the behavior elicited under such circumstances should have the same properties as that displayed outside the treatment sessions.

The available experimental evidence yields conflicting results. For instance, Higgins, Frisch, and Smith (1983) pointed out that assessments of interpersonal behavior commonly use role playing procedures, despite little evidence that they are externally valid and that studies of the extent to which role play behavior predicts in-vivo behavior contain methodological problems. And they further stated, citing two other studies (Curran, 1979; Kazdin, 1979), that "little correspondence has been observed between behaviors in the two types of assessments" (p. 158). Their own study (1981) showed that participants in role playing situations displayed more assertiveness than in realistic situations. Furthermore, they reported that experimental artifacts played an important role in the outcomes, that is, that subjects who knew in advance that the issue was their assertive behavior displayed even more assertiveness in the role playing situations. Other studies (e.g., Gorecki, Dickson, Anderson, & Jones, 1981; Higgins, Alonso, & Pendleton, 1979) also found that under role playing conditions subjects tended to evince more assertive behavior compared to assertiveness displayed in in-vivo situations.

On the other hand, Kreitler and Eblinger (1968) conducted psychodramas with hospitalized psychiatric patients. The patients' behavior was monitored and rated by observers both during the psychodramas and outside the treatment sessions. The researchers reported a high degree of concordance between the two ratings. Wessberg and his co-researchers (1979) compared the heterosocial interactions of male students in role playing simulation conditions and outside the laboratory while they were waiting to take part in the experiment. Their conclusion was that for specific purposes role playing may provide a reasonable approximation to more naturalistic settings for the assessment of heterosexual anxiety and skills. Thus, for distinguishing high and low frequency daters on the basis of anxiety and skills in heterosocial situations,

> role plays of those situations provide similar data to waiting-period interactions involving heterosocial contact. However, if investigators are examining absolute levels of heterosocial skill, the high-demand role plays elicit a much higher level of exhibited skill than do the less constrained, more naturalistic waiting period, although the relative patterning of individual subject's behavior remain fairly similar across the two situations. (Wessberg et al., 1979, p. 534)

The reasons that account for the failure of some studies to demonstrate a correspondence between simulated and natural behaviors are not entirely clear. One possibility is that choices of the assessment criteria and procedures described in several studies might have affected the outcomes. It was noticed, for instance, that sometimes the design of the simulated environments included elements ordinarily not present in the natural situations. These were tests administered during the role playing episodes and the employment of other experimental apparatus for measuring physiological reactions—the introduction of buzzers, tape recorders, etc. It is conceivable that the inclusion of such artifacts could have made the simulated experience unique and atypical. Furthermore, some experimental situations included instructions that unintentionally prompted elements of mimetic-pretend or mimetic-replication behavior, whereas in real life the authentic behavior would have been essentially spontaneous. In such instances, that difference may well have accounted for the new behavior evinced in the simulation because mimetic-pretend behavior, for example, tends to reduce natural inhibitions. Whether for this or another reason, the participants in the role playing simulations in the studies by Higgins et al. and by Wessberg et al., cited above, displayed a greater proficiency compared to their conduct in naturalistic situations. Evidently, behavior simulation situations tend to exaggerate the behavior under observation and somewhat distort its natural proportions. It might be wise, therefore, to redefine resemblance and stipulate it in terms of *pattern* and *kind* rather than as an exact replication of the behavioral *manifestations* and their *magnitude*.

Still, we ought to be concerned about the ways one can prevent excessive distortions under simulated experiences. It stands to reason that in order to increase the probability of a greater resemblance between simulated *behavior* and its natural counterpart, the simulated *situations themselves* must resemble the real-life ones. This topic will be discussed next.

A Typology of Simulated Environments

In principle, the simulated environment contains two components. One is the *physical elements* of the setting, henceforth referred to as the physical context, and the other is the persons who portray various *roles* that are part of the situation, that is, the auxiliaries. The physical context includes all the inanimate objects that characterize the original situation, (e. g., furniture, lighting, and equipment). The auxiliaries include the people, *other than the protagonist,* who characterize the original situation.

The resemblance of both components may be divided into three categories, as follows: no resemblance (none), a fair degree of resemblance (approximation), and a complete resemblance (exact) as illustrated in Figure 2.3.

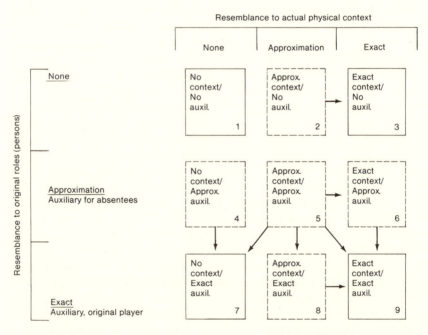

Figure 2.3. A diagram of environmental constellations

The diagram of environmental constellations contains nine types of simulated environments. These are formed by the combinations of the three categories of resemblance to the actual physical context (shown in the upper horizontal axis), and the three categories of resemblance to the original roles as represented by the auxiliaries (shown in the left vertical axis). Each constellation is portrayed by a box drawn with either solid or broken lines.

Of the nine constellations, the four that are illustrated as boxes with the solid outlines serve as prototypes (numbers 1, 9, 3, and 7). These are model environments for Theoretical simulation, Total simulation, Simulator, and Discussion.

Theoretical simulation (box 1): This kind of an environment is usually typical of the "pure" or the mathematical, game theory simulations. The resemblance to any actual physical context is irrelevant and, therefore, does not exist. Often it does not require the presence of human auxiliaries as in the case of interacting with a computer. If a human auxiliary is involved, his or her roles bear no resemblance to any particular person. The function is to play a decision-making role in the abstract, as in the case of the Prisoner's Dilemma game by Albert W. Tucker (see Colman, 1982) and similar games. Simulations of this sort are used primarily in research on decision making and in teaching. They have little relevance, if any at all, in the therapeutic application of behavior simulation.

Total simulation (box 9): Diagonally across from the environment for the Theoretical simulation, at the bottom right corner of the diagram, we have the so-called in-vivo simulation. This is the closest resemblance to a real-life situation one can get in simulated experiences. The physical context is an exact replication of the original, and the auxiliaries (and the roles they portray) are the same persons (and behaviors) involved in the real-life situations. Because of its high degree of resemblance to reality, this environment cannot be *created* under simulated conditions very often. There are many technical obstacles that make the artificial construction of such situations rare. Total simulation environments are typically evident in in-vivo treatments, that is, those conducted in the protagonist's natural habitat with the participation of other, original family members. Total simulation environments are also readily available in group and family therapy situations when a conflict arises *in situ*.

Suppose there is a conflict among several group or family members during the session itself. The therapist, then, may re-create the situation in order to look at the roots of the conflict. Since the players will be the original ones and the physical surrounding is the treatment room, the environment is that of the Total simulation kind.

Simulator (box 3): This environment refers to instances where the physical setting is an exact replica of the real-life one, except it does not require the involvement of a human auxiliary. Typically, these constellations contain specially designed environments (with specific equipment) to simulate highly complicated settings such as a pilot's cockpit, a driving vehicle, or control rooms. Protagonists are put in these simulators *alone* and are requested to respond to preprogrammed problem situations. These are controlled from the outside either by a computer or by an instructor. Simulators are expensive to build and, therefore, are reserved for the technical training of people engaged in high-risk occupations or in ergonomics research. They are not used in the psychotherapeutic application of behavior simulations.

Discussion (box 7): The fourth prototypical environment is the exact opposite of the preceding constellation. Here the physical context bears no resemblance to the original one, but the roles played by the auxiliaries are identical to those that occur in real life, that is, the auxiliaries are the original persons. Protagonists interact with significant persons in their life in the treatment room with a complete *disregard* of the nature of the original physical context. If the interaction is a demonstration of an encounter that occurred *in the past,* then the enactment (conversation) falls within the definition of a simulated event. It will also be considered a simulated event when the interaction is of the "what if" *hypothetical* type. Examples of these are an encounter of a daughter with her mother (who is present in the session) without actually re-creating the original scene, or an encounter of a son with his original father when the former says, "Suppose I would come and tell you that I have decided to join the Marine Corps. Let's see what will happen." On the other hand, if the encounter between a protagonist and an original auxiliary is other than a replication of the past or of a hypothetical situation, then it is not classified as a simulation at all. It is simply a conversation, an authentic discussion.

Interestingly, the four environmental prototypes described above have *limited practical* value. They are difficult to design. Except for the Theoretical simulations, which have no resemblance to both the physical context and the original roles, the remaining three contain overbearing constraints. Each of them requires that at least one of the two components—the physical context or the roles portrayed by the auxiliaries—will be an *exact replication* of the original environment. In the reality of training and therapy, that degree of exactness is frequently unobtainable. Instead, the only available alternative is to approximate the real environment.

Of the nine constellations shown in figure 2.3, five are illustrated as boxes with broken outlines (numbers 2, 4, 5, 6, and 8). The broken lines signify that the constellations include at least one element of approximation that makes them easier to construct in laboratory conditions. Still, only three of these five (boxes 2, 4, and 5) represent complete approximations. Two are in-vivo simulations (boxes 6 and 8) and, by definition, must contain a measure of exact resemblance to the authentic situations. Their advantage is that they are easily attained, good, and practical substitutions of the Total simulation prototype.

(a) *In-vivo Individual Simulation* (box 6): This environment requires that the physical context will be an exact replication of the original one, but the roles portrayed by the auxiliaries may only approximate the real-life ones. In fact, the auxiliaries are confederates who have *not* been involved parties in the original scene(s). The simulation still must occur in the protagonist's natural habitat.

(b) *In-vivo Group or Family Simulation:* Box 8 pertains to this constellation where the physical context can be approximated in the laboratory. But the roles of the auxiliaries must be identical to the origin, namely, performed by those who were the original parties to the conflict or the problem raised by the protagonist. Because this environment concerns issues involving several *original persons*, it must be in a group or family therapy situation and possess some in-vivo characteristics.

The next two environmental constellations represent an *approximation of the Simulator* prototype (box 2), and an *approximation of the Discussion* prototype (box 4).

(c) *An Approximate Simulator* (box 2): This environment does not require an exact replication of the original situation. In fact, of its two components (the resemblance to the physical context and to the original roles), only the physical context is of importance, but merely as an approximation. The introduction of a measure of inexactness changes the entire function of the Simulator. It no longer serves as a medium for training highly technical skills and instead acquires important placebo qualities. Its main contribution now is to increase the protagonist's involvement in the scene. The absence of resemblance to the original roles means that no auxiliaries are involved and that the protagonist enacts the scene alone. An example of this environment is a simulated episode

where the protagonist is asked to use chairs and tables to represent
his or her office, and then to sit at the desk and soliloquize.

(d) *An Approximate Discussion* (box 4): This environment represents
the opposite of the previous one (box 2). Again, it requires no
exact replications of the original, and only one component of the
environment is of importance. But this time it is the approximation to the original roles, that is, the use of auxiliaries to represent the *original persons in absentia*. The physical context is
ignored completely. In fact, of all the nine environmental constellations, the Approximate Discussions is the least expedient.
Unfortunately, experience has shown that many role playing episodes are designed that way.

The box that appears in the middle of the diagram (number 5) represents a *Total Approximation* environment. *It is the most common environmental design seen in the clinical application of behavior simulation interventions.*
The psychodramatic approach, for example, dictates that every scene
must begin with the description (approximation) of the space where the
action takes place and the persons and their roles in the situation. Since
it is so often hard to make exact replications of either the physical context
or the original roles, the Total Approximation simulation is the best
available solution.

(e) *Total Approximation* (box 5): In this constellation the designer of
the situation addresses both components of the E factor: the physical context and the roles. These, however, are represented as
approximations of the original. The arrows that point from this
box toward four other boxes signify that it is the best available
substitute in instances where the environments marked as numbers 6, 7, 8, and 9 cannot be implemented because no measure
of exactness can be attained.

The typology of simulated environments provides us with a set of
principles for comparing different simulated experiences. At this point
there is no sufficient research evidence to advise us regarding the effects
of different simulated environments on the final outcomes. Other than
a general suggestion that some role playing outcomes may be situational-
specific, the literature in this area has not been very helpful. Perhaps it
is partly the result of the fact that until now there were no serious
attempts to offer any typology for simulated environments.

Finally, the concept of *approximation* was used in this chapter as if it is as clear and definite as the concepts of *no resemblance* and of *exact resemblance*. This, of course, is inaccurate. There are many shades of approximations. Furthermore, there are some who maintain that it is enough to establish a resemblance to the original which is only in the eyes of the beholder, that is, the protagonist, and that there is no need for it to be evident to the impartial observer. Thus, as long as the *protagonist feels* that the simulated episode is similar to the original, the main function of the E factor has been achieved. We have used the concept of *approximation* as a degree of resemblance to the original that contains sufficient ingredients to capture the unique characteristics of the authentic situation. At the present state of the art, this seems to be a comfortable definition.

CHAPTER 3

Therapeutic Principles of Behavior Simulation

It is perhaps paradoxical that in order to treat those who seek psychological help to cope effectively in the *real world*, conventional psychotherapy confined itself to the secluded environment of the therapist's office. Since the ultimate goal of the psychotherapeutic endeavor is to make clients better functioning individuals, one would assume that it would adopt a model that incorporates, as closely as possible, the learning conditions that make people well-adjusted human beings in their natural settings. These conditions are marked by continuous interactions with external environments, as is evident in the process of socialization and in the ensuing adult social learning processes. That logic is apparent in the philosophy espoused by the early behavior therapists. Their premise was that the same learning principles that produce adaptive behavior are also responsible for the development of maladaptive and pathological behavior; hence, both natural growth and "artificial" remedial processes are, in essence, quite similar.

Yet traditional, especially psychoanalytic, therapy followed a different model. It was based on the notion that the problems that prompt clients to seek treatment can be addressed independently of the reality contexts where these problems manifest themselves. And if references to these contexts are called for in the course of the treatment, they are made only in the abstract. This approach was based on the theory that psychological difficulties stem from the interplay of forces that reside *within* the individual and are caused by intrapsychic processes, conscious as well as unconscious. The prediction was that interventions pertaining to these forces and processes will eventually result in a change of behavior. That change will generalize from the therapist's office to real-life situations. Therefore, concrete representations of the environmental contexts in the treatment session are unnecessary or may even be looked upon as distractions.

It appears that the validity of this prediction was not left unchallenged. For instance, in her comments on some inadequacies in psychoanalytic theory, Durkin (1981) addressed the issue of therapeutic effectiveness, a discussion that is relevant to the paradoxical phenomenon described above.

> Psychoanalytic theory has been one of the great leaps forward in the history of modern thought, yet it has rarely been free from criticism. Much of the criticism has been the result of misunderstanding on the part of the critics and of the misuses on the part of clinicians. But other criticisms were quite warranted and must be examined because the results of analytic treatment have not been as far-reaching as had been anticipated. It has been assumed that explicit behavior change would naturally follow from genuine insight . . . In the long run, however, it became apparent that while analyzed patients excel in self-understanding, the ability to change their behavior too often lagged behind. (p. 175)

Durkin's own specific suggestion for improving the effectiveness of the analytic treatment was, of course, in accordance with the principles of the psychoanalytic model. The analysis ought not to be restricted to content interpretations, but a shift is required towards process interpretations. Thus, these therapeutic advantages and shortcomings notwithstanding, the paradox itself remained unaltered.

J. L. Moreno, the founder of psychodrama, was greatly perturbed by the dissimilarity between the context within which psychodynamic therapy had been traditionally rendered and real-life situations. He sought to bridge the two and minimize the disparity. The approach he advocated may be illustrated by a story told about a meeting he had with Freud in 1912, in Vienna. Moreno, then a student, attended one of Freud's lectures where a telepathic dream was analyzed. At the end of the lecture, Freud asked Moreno what he was doing. The reply was, "Well, Dr. Freud, I start where you leave off. You meet people in the artificial setting of your office. I meet them on the street and in their home, in their natural surroundings. You analyze their dreams. I try to give them the courage to dream again . . . (J. L. Moreno, 1964a, pp. 5-6).

WHY SIMULATION?

The notion that the inclusion of concrete representations of real-life situations in psychotherapy is both feasible and meritorious was introduced early in the twentieth century. But it has begun to gain more popularity only in the last two or three decades. Slowly, psychotherapists seriously entertained the possibility that such an inclusion is not only advantageous but often constitutes an important ingredient of the treatment process, as is evident, for example, in the treatment of agoraphobia (e.g., Mathew, Gelder, & Johnston, 1981). In principle, combining therapy with real-life situations may be achieved in two ways. These, using the analogy of Mohammed and the mountain, are to bring Mohammed (i.e., the treatment hitherto rendered in the therapist's office) to the mountain (i.e., situations in the outside world) or to bring the mountain (i.e., real-life situations) to Mohammed (i.e., the treatment in the office). The former is known as in-vivo therapy, and the latter as behavior simulation or clinical role playing.

The in-vivo approach may take many forms. Some are known as milieu therapy, community therapy, and rehabilitation. Others are referred to as live-exposures, treatments in situ, or simply in-vivo treatments. These therapies were based on a variety of orientations including eclectic, psychodynamic, even psychoanalytic models (e. g., Bettelheim, 1967). But it was the behavior modification movement and its developments in the last two decades that made considerable use of the in-vivo approach. These developments led to the conclusion, for example, that the most effective desensitization procedures in the treatment of classical phobias and hypersensitivities to fear of criticism, rejection, and disapproval appear to include exposures to real-life situations (e. g., Bandura, 1977; Emmelkamp, 1982). Gradual exposure to anxiety-provoking objects, people, situations, and events were regarded as critical ingredients in the effective treatment of phobias (Marks, 1978). The technique of flooding used in the treatment of obsessive-compulsive disorders is another example of the incorporation of real-life conditions in therapy. Token economies programs for psychotic inpatients, autistic children, and delinquent youths were conducted in natural surroundings, such as hospital wards, cafeterias, recreational rooms, classrooms, homes, and correctional and rehabilitation settings (e. g., Hersen & Bellack, 1978; Kazdin, 1977). Similarly, in-vivo home assignments were said to be crucial in the cognitive treatment of anxiety (Beck, Emery, & Greenberg, 1985). These are only a few examples of a vast literature summarized in a recent review by Lazarus and Fay (1984), which affirmed the importance of in-vivo exposures in the treatment of various psychological problems.

Indeed, in describing the principles of psychodrama, J. L. Moreno (1964a) referred to the ways in which patients can be provided with new opportunities for "psychodynamic and sociocultural reintegration . . . in lieu or in extension of unsatisfactory natural habitats" (p. xxii). One is in-vivo therapeutic interventions, that is, "existential psychodrama within the framework of community life itself" (p. xxii). A second alternative is an adaptation of the laboratory method—the in-vitro approach—that is, conducting treatments in "the neutral, objective, and flexible therapeutic theater" (p. xxii). In other words, this alternative suggests utilizing behavior simulations of existential realities through role playing *inside* the therapist's office.

In his book, *Role-playing for Supervisors,* Towers (1969) begins the first chapter with the question, "Why role playing?" Obviously, the issue underlying this question is quite fundamental to the present discussion. Put plainly, is it appropriate to justify the use of role playing and behavior simulation simply as a back-up contingency, a second-best strategy in the event that technical or other difficulties prevent the effective use of live, in-vivo exposures? In order to rely on such a justification one must first demonstrate that in-vitro simulations accurately resemble real-life situations and that they contain all essential properties that characterize the actual reality. Furthermore, one also needs to show that the therapeutic outcomes of simulation experiences are the same as those of the in-vivo ones. Unfortunately, the evidence pertinent to such a contention is equivocal. Some supports it and some does not. Even the supportive research at times claims that although role playing may elicit material similar to that obtained in the authentic situations, it tends to be exaggerated. Evidently, given the present knowledge, although role playing tends to resemble (approximate) real life, it is not sufficient to justify its use in therapy solely on the ground that it appears to be technically convenient, an easier-to-manage method of approximating real-life exposures. The answer to the question "Why role playing?" must include other reasons.

One such answer may be found in Biddle's (1979) discussion of role theory. Following an analysis of some of the current uncertainties with regard to role playing, he wrote:

> Nevertheless, there are strong reasons for advocating the use of role playing in therapy. Role playing is a natural phenomenon that is practiced by children in the process of growing, therefore it forms part of the normal repertoire of roles that are performed and enjoyed by everyone. The client who plays roles in therapy may provide insights concerning roles that are played elsewhere by others or by him or herself. The therapist and other clients (if present) can also gain insight or add their interpretations in the role-playing session. Role playing also allows the client to practice alternative roles (rather than simply talk about them). It is also

inherently a "dramatic" technique . . . which implies that the client
may have "peak experiences" when deeply involved in role playing.
These experiences can also lead to insights or to the reliving and
resolving of painful episodes from the client's past. (p. 329)

Towers' own answer to the question he raised may be captured in
three words: effectiveness, flexibility, and practicality. These imply that
role playing is an effective tool for teaching (in his case the teaching of
supervisory techniques), that it provides the player with an opportunity
to deal flexibly with a variety of problems, and that it fosters learning
by doing. Acording to Towers all these are highly commendable attributes. Interestingly, the identical question, "Why role playing?" was also
raised by Shaw, Corsini, Blake, and Mouton (1980) in the second chapter
of their book, *Role Playing: A Practical Manual for Group Facilitators*. The
summary of their answer is well expressed in the following excerpt:

A human being is complex. Most of us think, feel and act at the
same time. We may not have the three in focus; we may think one
thing, say another, and feel a third. The most effective way to reach
a person, to communicate with or teach him, is to deal with the
totality; the thinking, feeling, behaving individual. It is precisely
this that role playing accomplishes. (p. 19)

The usefulness of role playing has been debated among social psychologists. The issue was introduced first by Vinacke (1954) in connection with the ethics of conducting research on human subjects. Social
psychologists traditionally adopted a research strategy known as the
"deception" approach, that is, human subjects were put in experimental
conditions where they did not know the true purpose of the studies they
participated in or they were provided with false "cover stories" about
the purpose of the studies. Although the continuous use of the "deception" was not without logical reasons, there was also a mounting discomfort with the ethics of such a practice. In the search for a better
alternative, the use of role playing was recommended to replace the
"deception" strategy. Under role playing conditions, it was argued, subjects may be informed about the true purpose of any given study but
then are asked to proceed and behave as if they have not heard it (informed consent). This could eliminate the ethical issues raised in connection with the use of "deception." The validity of the new proposition
became, then, an empirical question of whether or not studies conducted
under role playing experimental conditions could produce the same
results as those conducted with naive subjects. As expected it generated

many studies, which, taken together, yielded inconclusive results. Some supported the viability of role playing as an alternative research methodology, and some did not. Still, the literature occasionally presents improved models in favor of the utilization of role playing options.

Important as it is, the issue of whether role playing is or is not a good substitution for traditional research methods is not exactly at the heart of the present discussion. The debate is mentioned, in this context, because even those who were opposed to the new suggestion were not oblivious to other advantages of role playing. For instance, Freedman (1969), who strongly rejected the role playing alternative, saw a redeeming feature in the use of role playing in research: "There is one special and somewhat unusual use of role playing that deserves special consideration. This is the use of role playing as a 'simulation' of the real situation" (p. 112). In that respect, he agreed, role playing studies may be a fruitful technique for gathering other people's intuitions and ideas about human behavior. And studying what affects people's guesses may be one way of getting ideas about what is important. But even according to this minimalistic view, the (debatable) contention that role playing is not a sufficiently reliable indicator of how people actually behave in real life does not negate the application of role playing *in therapy* because a substantial portion of the psychotherapeutic endeavor is focused on the clients' *subjective* perceptions of their own thoughts, feeling, and actions, as well as those of significant others. In order to place these perceptions in proper contexts, approximations of reality-like situations may suffice. For psychotherapy, this is good enough.

Interestingly, from a clinical perspective as evidenced in the practice of psychotherapy, it is also possible to argue that the fact that behavior simulation often *does not* exactly replicate the external reality may be an advantage. It has been repeatedly said that in order to alter the operation of a given system one needs to change at least one of the existing rules that govern the behavior of the system. This is often accomplished by stepping outside the system, evaluating it through conscious criticism, and eliminating—sometimes replacing—one, or one set, of its rules.

The therapeutic milieu was conceived on a similar notion. Clients come to treatment because they cannot function satisfactorily in the natural environments (system) they live in. Evidently, these natural environments by themselves have therapeutic limitations. Thus, in order to help clients investigate other options for coping, they have to be asked to step outside that system, to abandon it temporarily, and enter a different system—the therapeutic environment. The new system includes rules that do not exist in the natural one. These have been described by different words such as unconditional regard, permissiveness, sheltered environment, and nonpunitive atmosphere. As clients and their therapists begin to interact under the new system, other corollary rules gain prominence. Examples of these are "the system is geared to deal with the content of the clients' complaints," or "the system will analyze both the content of the clients' complaints and their behavior *inside* the therapy room," or "the system will regard the clients' contents and behavior in the therapy room as a representative sample (and a symbolic evidence) of behavior evinced outside the system."

Therefore, there is good reason to assume that, being a corrective system, the treatment situation might have lost its unique advantage if it were designed as an exact replication of real-life events. On the other hand, the two systems cannot be completely different. Since clients use the benefit of the therapeutic "system" to get better not in the therapist's office but rather in the natural (environment) system, the ease of moving from one system to the other can be facilitated if the two share common denominators. How can such a similarity be attained? One logical answer to this question is that it can be achieved through the use of behavior simulation.

There is another, intriguing aspect of the therapeutic situation that has not been sufficiently noted. The special environment where psychotherapy is conducted, even in its traditional verbal form, may, in fact, be construed as a simulated endeavor. Clients are placed in an unusual situation (therapy) and are asked to respond to their therapists. Regardless of how active or inactive therapists choose to be, their mere presence and certainly their more active behavior serve as stimuli that elicit responses on the part of the clients. These responses produced in the therapy room are the total reality that therapists deal with. In that respect, the therapeutic situation is akin to any other experimental setting because it is constructed as a self-contained, planned environment controlled by the therapists who design and set its specific rules (e. g., encouraging freedom of expression, instituting an atmosphere of permissiveness). It also resembles other experimental settings in the sense that, occasionally, it includes attempts to model or activate behaviors that eventually will have to be exercised outside the treatment room. In traditional psychotherapy the simulation aspect of the treatment environment ends here. The rest of the treatment is focused on analyzing contents and processes. Evidently, therapists have been content with the limited utilization of simulation in psychotherapy. One wonders why. Since therapeutic settings already have some simulation characteristics, the suggestion to expand these by incorporating the behavior simulation method through the use of clinical role playing seems reasonable. It certainly is consistent with some of the premises that serve as the basis for contemporary practices of conventional treatments.

There are, however, three issues that could be raised against the acceptance of such a suggestion. First, one might argue that by incorporating the clinical role playing application of behavior simulation, the emphasis in psychotherapy will shift away from treatment through theoretical learning, understanding, and insights towards treatment through experiential learning: learning by doing. The response to this contention is that such a shift is already in progress. The use of experiential learning becomes more and more popular as evidenced in marital counseling and family therapy, for example. Some of the reasons for the change were mentioned in the beginning of our discussion: The use of insights and interpretations did not produce the results therapists hoped they would. There are reports concerning skill-training practices that indicate that the use of experiential learning results in improved skills as well as other, more general improvements. As research outcomes concerning nonverbal behavior and the communication of emotions increases (e.g., Buck, 1984), so does our understanding of these areas and our ability to infer practical applications from the findings.

A second, perhaps corollary, argument is that the shift towards a greater emphasis on experiential learning may change the way therapists operate. Instead of viewing their responsibility solely in the area of interpreting the meaning of contents and processes, they will have a considerably greater responsibility for setting concrete situations, that is, creating opportunities for the emergence of relevant, curative processes. Since this does alter the kinds of interventions that the therapist employs, the question is whether or not this shift in the therapist's responsibility is really needed.

The answer to this question is that the occurrence of such a change is believed to represent an enrichment of the therapist's function rather than an attempt to trim and restrict his or her traditional role. We have already seen that there are sufficient indications to suspect that, paradoxical as it may sound, it is the heavy reliance on analysis of contents and processes in the abstract that causes the greatest danger of restrictiveness. It directs the therapist's efforts to *one* avenue at the expense of utilizing others (e.g., concrete experimentations or experiential learning). The suggestion to incorporate a behavior simulation approach with the application of clinical role playing does not imply an abdication of the therapist's traditional role. Rather, it positions it in a different perspective relative to other useful therapeutic interventions. It proposes that a good portion of the therapist's interpretative function may be delegated to the process, that is, attained through the activation of simulation processes. With the application of clinical role playing techniques one can rely more on clients to gain insights through self-realization.

Finally, it could also be argued that it is somewhat inaccurate to suggest that traditional verbal therapies do not offer clients opportunities for remedial experiences. Clients are encouraged to relive old, new, and even hypothetical life situations by using their imagination, which is reminiscent of the "Theoretical simulation" environments described in Chapter 2. Changing traditional practices by incorporating clinical role playing applications may not, after all, represent a significant added value to what is already accomplished in conventional psychotherapy. The claims to the contrary, it might be argued, are more polemic than substantive.

The response to this argument is that, indeed, verbal therapies —especially those that subscribe to what has become known as the "eclectic approach"—contain simulations in the abstract. Clients are encouraged to recount, and therefore also experience, incidents that occurred either in their past or in the here and now.

But there is a difference between these kinds of abstract simulations and the concrete, clinical role playing one. Observers of human behavior are familiar with the discrepancy between the things people say about what they did or intend to do and that which has actually occurred or will actually happen in the future. Intentions and actions do not always go hand in hand, and a gap between performance and design is not an unusual phenomenon. Furthermore, in abstract simulations, clients are in full control of the situation. Since they are the ones who produce the entire scenario, it is likely that they may avoid creating opportunities involving unexpected, embarrassing, difficult-to-handle, or helpless moments. The clients respond, and thus feel the need to become accountable, only to the material *they choose* to raise. In concrete clinical role playing (simulations), part of that control is handed over to the auxiliaries: the therapeutic helpers. These auxiliaries may respond in ways the clients have not anticipated, or even may not like. In that respect the role-played situations contain an important element that the verbal therapeutic situations tend to play down. That element highlights a real-life characteristic, namely, that behavior often occurs under conditions where one's own control over the surrounding environment is incomplete.

Unlike real life, however, where a given decision of action leads to results and consequences that the player must live with for a while, in simulated situations the results and their consequences are easily revocable. If the client (player) does not like them, they may be discarded. This has at least two important advantages. First, given the significant reduction of the fear of adverse consequences clients tend to be more open, more spontaneous and more adventurous. Second, seeing clients actually behave in concrete situations adds credence to the validity of what they say about their behavior.

BEHAVIOR SIMULATION AND CLINICAL ROLE PLAYING

At this point it might be fitting to further clarify the distinction between behavior simulation, a concept that has been used until now, and clinical role playing, a term that I intend to use throughout the book. The notion of *behavior simulation*, presented in the preceding chapter, refers to the recreation of situations that depict people interacting with their environments. As previously indicated, the reasons for resorting to the behavior simulation method and the areas in which it can be applied may vary. These may include, for example, attempts at generating new ideas and new procedures in any conceivable human involvements, initial testing of the appropriateness of such ideas and procedures, rehearsing important activities before they are enacted in live situations, and perfecting existing skills. They may also include presenting concrete examples of models, issues, dilemmas, and processes. In other words, the relevance of the behavior simulation method extends over a broad spectrum of purposes and activities.

Role playing was described as the tangible manifestation through which the behavior component of the method expresses itself. And it may take many forms ranging from simple (minimal) enactments to complex sets of activities. Again, the relevance of role playing is not necessarily limited to a specific content area or purpose.

But the term *clinical role playing* is different. By adding the word *clinical*, I have narrowed the relevance of role playing to a specially designated use, that is, to the application of the model of behavior simulation in clinical practice. Thus, in the general scheme, clinical role playing should be viewed in the proper perspective: as *one subset* of behavior simulation. At the same time, keeping such a perspective also requires us to emphasize that of the several potential application areas of behavior simulation and role playing, the clinical is a very important one. Furthermore, not only is this an important area, but as we shall attempt to demonstrate in the book it is also the most sophisticated use of role playing technology.

Given the unique characteristics of the psychotherapeutic endeavor, special adaptations of the general rules that govern the application of role playing had to be made. These were formulated in a set of principles to be described next. The principles were tailor-made to suit clinical role playing and may not be relevant to other applications of behavior simulation.

THERAPEUTIC PRINCIPLES

In the past, there were at least two attempts to formulate principles for the use of role playing in psychotherapy (Z. T. Moreno, 1959, 1965). Described as psychodramatic rules, these principles were presented with a special reference to the practice of psychodrama as related to the theory espoused by J. L. Moreno. The presentation of the new version of principles is consistent with our effort to provide a broader conceptual basis for the use of role playing interventions in psychotherapy. Therefore, most of the previously stated psychodramatic rules were reformulated and at times even expanded to suit the clinical role playing approach. To those who identify themselves as psychodramatists, these will merely represent a different outlook of the method they already employ. To clinicians and psychotherapists of other persuasions, they are meant to serve as a comfortable set of guidelines for using role playing in much the same extensive and sophisticated way it is used in psychodrama.

Principle 1: Clinical Role Playing Is Based on Concrete Portrayals

The most distinct characteristic of clinical role playing interventions is that the information dealt with during the treatment sessions is presented in concrete forms. This holds true for information coming from the clients as well as from the therapists. Indeed, the first psychodramatic rule (Z. T. Moreno, 1965) stipulates that clients act out their conflicts instead of talking about them. Concretization, therefore, means *enactments*. The therapist will say to the client, "*Show* me what happened," rather than, "*Tell* me what happened."

Although the definition of concretization as enactments is appropriate, it does not include all aspects of concretization evident in clinical role playing. It might be recalled from our earlier discussion that behavior simulation has two factors: one referring to the client's behavior, the other to the environment in which his or her actions take place. The definition is incomplete because it applies only to the client's behavior and to that part of the environment factor represented by the behavior of the auxiliaries (the therapeutic helpers). However, it should be noted that the principle of concretization also refers to the inanimate part of the environment, that is, the situational context, the part that does not involve human beings or cannot be personified. The merit of concretizing the inanimate part of the environment is often undeservedly overlooked in clinical practice as evidenced by the frequent tendency to conduct role playing as if it occurs in a situational vacuum. Perhaps the reason for this is that the relative contribution of such concretizations to the total process is judged (sometimes misjudged) to be miniscule compared to that of concretizing human behavior. Nonetheless, the principle of concretization applies to the entire simulated constellation, even if it can be designed only in the form of approximations.

The advantage of dealing with concrete phenomena is that they tend to enhance the meaningfulness of the data. Not only does this attribute of concretization make intuitive sense, but it is also congruent with the experience of many practitioners, as well as having some indirect support from research. For example, Borgida and Nisbett (1977) argued that information is utilized in proportion to its vividness and that in their study imparting information in a concrete form had advantages over imparting the information in the abstract. Also, Nisbett, Borgida, Crandall, and Reed (1976) suggested that access to scripts is more readily achieved by information that is concrete and vivid than by information that is pallid and remote.

Concretization enhances the meaningfulness of the presented issues because it offers optimal opportunities to express both the spontaneous, involuntary kind of communication and the symbolic, intentional kind (Buck, 1984). In his extensive work on helping human relations, Carkhuff (1969a, 1969b) identified three functions for concretization. These three clearly demonstrate the advantages of the principle of concretization. Thus, for therapists, concretization secures that their responses will not be far removed from the clients' own responses and experiences. For the interactive process, it facilitates the clarification of misunderstandings and increases perceptual accuracies. For clients, concretization becomes helpful when they try to directly address their problems and emotional conflicts.

Principle 2: The Displayed Behavior Must Be Authentic

Like any other form of psychotherapy, clinical role playing must ensure that the behavior and content dealt with in the simulated episodes are authentic. Authenticity is commonly defined as reliability and genuineness, which in the context of role playing has two connotations. One is the absence of a deliberate deception. It must ascertain that the portrayal is not fake in the sense that it fails to represent the true feelings and thinking of the client *at the moment of acting.* Second, it also connotes a maximal resemblance to the original experience. Thus, given that the client acts in good faith, authenticity implies that the re-created portrayal must truly reflect the psychological state that existed when the situation first occurred.

Achieving the former is easier than the latter. There are certain measures that can be taken in order to increase the probability that the simulated behavior will not turn into a fake portrayal. Furthermore, there are observable clues that can verify whether or not this authentic quality of the players' reactions prevails; for example, the presence of involuntary responses associated with emotional arousals, logical consistencies, reaction time, remembering basic information, and the absence of the "falling-out-of-the-role" phenomena, to mention a few. On the other hand, making sure that the simulated portrayals are qualitatively identical to the original behavior is generally extremely difficult. This aspect of authenticity often must remain an assumption verifiable only on the basis that clients say so. Is this unique to clinical role playing? Not at all. The same difficulty exists in every form of psychotherapy.

But is this a real problem? Should therapists question more the validity of their clients' self-reports and check with other reliable (objective) sources whether or not they accurately reflect what actually occurred? Therapists would argue that although occasionally it might be necessary to verify the clients' perceptions, in most instances it is not important. They would claim that proving the existence of perceptual distortions does not make any difference as far as the therapy is concerned, and that checking activity of this kind could only have an adverse impact. It runs the risk of upsetting the essential trusting relationship that ought to exist between therapists and their clients. The claim is further supported by two observations. One is that such verifications are frequently impractical; and the other, that some instances do not lend themselves to any form of objective verification. Examples of these are hypothetical issues such as projections into the future or fantasies. Since these have no past reality, they cannot be evaluated against an unbiased baseline. It is not surprising, therefore, that therapists do not seem perturbed in operating under the assumption that whatever clients bring to the treatment session (verbally or in action) is genuine material.

Some of the measures (subprinciples) that can be adopted to ensure the authentic quality of the clients' portrayals are as follows.

1. Portrayals in the here and now. This principle implies that clients present their difficulties as if they are happening now, in the present. This holds true regardless of when the actual incident(s) occurred or were fantasized—past, present or future (Z. T. Moreno, 1965). The idea of the here and now is rooted in existential philosophy, and it applies to all forms of psychotherapy that subscribe to an existential approach, clinical role playing included. (Elements of the philosophy are discussed elsewhere in the book along with the rationale for its application in psychotherapy.)

2. Maximizing clients' involvement. Authenticity is directly related to the degree of involvement in the enactments. A heightened involvement ensures authenticity, whereas a minimal involvement may not. It is true that although the importance of involvement has long been recognized, regretfully it is frequently taken for granted. Thus, even in contemporary practice of role playing, involvement is often underplayed, if not ignored. There are still practitioners who introduce role playing interventions without due attention to the players' level of involvement. They presumably operate under the assumption that involvement will emerge spontaneously, simply due to the fact that the players are actually *acting out* their conflicts. There is ample evidence to show that this supposition is erroneous. The need for the warm-up stage (see next chapter) is one example of such evidence.

The idea that involvement in role playing might be a crucial variable in the success of role playing simulation has also been emphasized by Greenberg (1967). Sarbin and Allen (1968) spoke of *orgasmic involvement* and provided a continuum ranging from noninvolvement (Level 0) to bewitchment (Level 7). It has been suggested that the third level, engrossed acting, is a minimal (and good) requirement for role playing. The relationship between involvement in role playing and genuine responses (e. g., obedient behavior) was clearly demonstrated by Geller (1978).

There are several interventions and techniques that can be used by therapists to encourage and maximize their clients' involvement in clinical role playing. These will be described in other chapters of this book.

3. Spontaneous portrayals. Spontaneity is understood here in the way it is described in J. L. Moreno's theory (Moreno, 1964a). It has several characteristics and modes of expression, which were discussed in the previous chapter. It might be recalled that spontaneity was said to be in the form of energy that cannot be accumulated, stored, and conserved, but rather released in an "all-or-none" fashion. Spontaneity must emerge to be spent and must be spent to make place for new emergence. This means that spontaneous responses (portrayals) are: (a) genuine, that is, emanating from within the individual (energy that is endowed *sui generis*, as a constitutional factor); and (b) released openly and fully, in an uninhibited fashion (an "all-or-none" expenditure of energy). Given these characteristics, the encouragement of spontaneous responses by definition secures their authentic quality.

It ought to be emphasized that responding spontaneously does not necessarily mean quick or immediate responses. Spontaneity is not synonymous with fast reaction time or the lack of premeditation. On the contrary, since spontaneity requires that responses will be *appropriate* (adequate) to the situation, and at times also novel ones, it must be assumed that these are mediated by cognitive processes such as contemplation, evaluation, selection, and setting priorities. There are several techniques at the therapists' disposal to enhance their clients' spontaneity through training. One of them is *training in improvisation*. The technique uses the element of surprise. Protagonists are confronted with unexpected responses from the auxiliaries or with unexpected situations to which they should respond adequately, openly, and often in innovative ways.

Principle 3: Clinical Role Playing Therapy Uses Selective Magnification

On many occasions where behavior simulation is used, the details of the enacted episodes must accurately resemble the original situations. Such resemblance means: (a) that all the major components of the original situation have to be represented in the simulation; and (b) that the representation of each component or aspect is in the correct proportion, similar to the way it appeared in the original situation. These kinds of simulation do not permit disproportional exaggerations of any facet of the authentic model.

This is not so in clinical role playing. In this case, exaggerations of certain aspects of the portrayals are permissible, even desirable. In fact, experience has shown that although exact replications of the original situations may have advantages, they tend to minimize the *psychotherapeutic* (clinical) quality of the simulation. Selective magnifications, on the other hand, *enhance* it.

The principle of selective magnification is analogous to the technique of "blow-up" in photography. In photography, an entire picture, or typically a part of the picture, is magnified beyond its original dimensions

so that minute details become clearly visible. Similarly, magnifying selective parts of simulated portrayals in clinical role playing facilitates a
better scrutiny of small, yet potentially important, details. Once these
have been exposed, it is easier to proceed with treatment interventions.

The principle of selective magnification is not unique to clinical role
playing. Indeed, it is applied in other forms of psychotherapy as well.
For example, in verbal therapies small indications such as slips of the
tongue, unexpected hesitations in clients' reactions, or small, seemingly
trivial anecdotes told by clients are often regarded as symptoms of an
important issue. Whereas in real life these could pass virtually unnoticed,
in therapy they acquire different dimensions, "bigger than their life
size." In clinical role playing, selective magnifications are primarily
achieved by altering the time dimensions and by externalizing internal
processes dramatically. These two procedures serve as "psychological
magnifying glasses."

1. Altering the time dimensions. In real life things happen very fast. We
respond to a successive bombardment of stimuli rapidly, often under
time pressure and at a pace beyond our control. Under these circumstances there is hardly time to pay attention to the motives that lie behind
our actions, to past influences that might be responsible for our present
tendencies, and to the genuine feelings and thoughts that accompany
and follow our reactions. In that sense there is a limited therapeutic
advantage in simulations where we simply reenact our life events at the
same speed that they actually occurred.

What is needed, instead, is an opportunity to examine selected issues
more closely. To do this, certain elements of the portrayals must be
magnified, and the way this can be done is, first, to slow down the pace,
that is, to "stop the clock," "expand given moments," or rerun the entire
portrayal in a "slow motion" manner. Things that occur in life in a matter
of seconds are portrayed in clinical role playing at length without any
time constraints.

2. Externalizing internal processes dramatically. One of the salient characteristics of psychotherapy is the effort to uncover, understand, and
change internal (psychological) processes. This is definitely true for all
the psychodynamic therapies. It is also true for some major behavior
therapy interventions such as enhancing self-control and modifying dysfunctional thoughts or attributions. In clinical role playing the same
effort manifests itself dramatically, by acting out these internal feelings
and thoughts, by personifying them. Thus, guilt, shame, dilemmas, con-

flicting wishes, aspirations, tensions, and so forth are externalized as protagonists or auxiliaries assume roles that personify each of these psychological phenomena. In such dramatic portrayals the client interacts openly with the auxiliaries (representing the feelings and the thoughts) with the full knowledge that in reality such interactions occur internally. The consequences of these acts are that the internal dynamics acquire different proportions both in terms of their magnitude and their complexity. Therefore, one should be aware of the fact that these psychological phenomena appear in clinical role playing in an exaggerated form largely as a result of magnification. In assessing their "true" or "natural" dimension, they need to be scaled down.

Principle 4: Clinical Role Playing Offers Expanded Learning Experiences

One of the reasons that prompts therapists, counselors, group facilitators, and other experts in the helping professions to use the behavior simulation method (and clinical role playing therapy) is that it offers an unusual learning opportunity. This opportunity may be characterized as a new chance for psychological and sociocultural reintegration. Clinical role playing constitutes a temporary corrective environment, which leads to the emergence of learning opportunities a person failed to seize in real life. In that respect, the relation of clinical role playing to natural learning opportunities as manifested in real life is complicated and perhaps even somewhat strange. On the one hand it must apply the same learning principles that govern all human learning, and on the other hand it has to represent an experience that is "beyond real life," one that differs from the unsatisfactory, natural reality. The features that enable clinical role playing to become an expanded learning experience are as follows:

1. The notion of the sheltered environment. The simulated situation is a manmade environment. It is designed so that players who become part of it will feel more secure and protected than they normally feel in similar natural environments. This is achieved by giving the players complete control over significant aspects of their enactments. They can control *time.* This means that they are at liberty to determine the time factor as they wish. If, for example, a client says, "I would like to do something that may happen in the future," "I would like this to last longer," "Let's do this quickly. In real life it takes so long," or "I want it to be evening now," he or she gets his or her wish complied with. The client can control *space.* So, if a given client wants to set up the situation in a way that is more comfortable, less threatening, and if this may help the client to learn better, he or she is at liberty to do so. The client also can control *actions* and *consequences*. Often people refrain from making decisions or taking certain actions in life because they fear the potential adverse consequences. Avoidance of this sort may deprive them of important learning experiences. In clinical role playing they can be protected from such fears in two ways. One is by setting up the situation in a manner that guarantees the exclusion of adverse consequences. For example, the therapist may say to the client, "I want you to express your disappointment to your father, but this time we will provide you with a truly understanding parent." The second way is to tell the client, "Let's do this anyway. If you find the outcome too painful we can scratch that and do it all over again in a different way until you feel satisfied."

2. *Corrective experiences.* Sometimes clients need to reexperience events so that they can have a new positive outcome associated with the event. But often clients complain that they *missed* an experience they should have had and reality did not provide them with a second chance. Such new opportunities can be created in the therapy session through the application of clinical role playing to fill the experiential void.

3. *The notion of surplus reality.* The term "surplus reality" was coined by J. L. Moreno (e.g., 1965). It is based on the notion that "there are certain invisible dimensions in the reality of living, not fully experienced or expressed . . . and for those who failed to experience them, life is incomplete . . . that is why we have to use surplus operations and surplus instruments to bring them out in our therapeutic settings" (J. L. Moreno, 1966, p. 151). One of the most popular techniques that brings out such hidden dimensions is *role-reversal.* A full description of this technique appears in Chapter 6. Briefly, it requires the client to assume the role of his or her counterpart(s) in the simulated situation. Indeed, one of the psychodramatic rules states that, in the course of their therapy, protagonists (i.e., clients) must assume the role of all other persons with whom they are meaningfully related in order to understand the way(s) these persons relate to both the protagonists themselves and to each other (Z. T. Moreno, 1965).

4. *Adjusting the pace of the learning process to each individual client.* Although one of the aims of clinical role playing is to encourage clients to maximize their expressions, actions, and verbal communications, they are also permitted to be as unspontaneous or inexpressive as they feel

at any given moment. This position is not self-contradictory. It assumes that the ability to express oneself fully is the desired, ultimate goal. But it also suggests that in order to attain it the therapist must operate on the basis of the client's present strengths and weaknesses. The therapist must respect his or her client's fears, inhibitions, and deficiencies rather than exert undue pressures to get rid of them. Progress is predicated on the application of two learning principles, *gradual progression* and *individual adjustment.* Gradual progression implies that learning objectives need to be broken into small, successive steps where each step by itself is easy to master and poses no threatening challenge. Individual adjustment means that in designing the steps one has to take in account the particular idiosyncracies of every given client. Similar learning objectives may be paced and designed differently for different clients.

5. *Expanded learning experience may involve the learning of restraint.* The emphasis on learning maximal expressiveness can be misleading. It holds true only as long as it is rewarding. Reward has two interrelated aspects. One pertains to intrinsic gratifications, that is, personal feelings of relief and happiness. The second aspect pertains to gratifications with regard to the attainment of objectives in which the cooperation of an external recipient is sought. Thus a person may fully express his or her feelings towards a colleague and experience an internal relief (reward) but at the same time this may hurt the colleague and end or damage the relationship. Paradoxical as it may sound, often one has to learn to restrain oneself spontaneously. Some clinical role playing interventions are designed to increase a client's ability to derive internal reward from willingly imposing adequate measures of self-censorship and self-control.

Principle 5: Clinical Role Playing Involves a Succession of Interrelated Simulated Episodes

The basic notion behind this principle is that clinical role playing consists of a number of interrelated simulated episodes, and that maximal therapeutic effectiveness is attained through a progressive move from one scene to another. At first glance, this principle appears to be in conflict with the approach marked by a sporadic use of individual simulated episodes often seen in nonclinical as well as clinical contexts. Does this mean that an occasional introduction of one or two unrelated role playing scenes is therapeutically ineffective? Not at all. Experience has shown that even this, rather minimalistic, use of clinical role playing can enhance the effectiveness of the treatment and has genuine benefits to the overall curative effort.

In its ideal format, clinical role playing serves as the therapist's primary *modus operandi*. Thus, although at any given session some nonactional verbal exchanges (e.g., brief interviewing, occasional side explanations, background clarifications, or integrative discussions) may occur, they should be kept at a minimum. Most of the material dealt with in the course of the therapeutic encounter is portrayed through clinical role playing. In practice, however, this ideal format may be compromised so that the ratio between the time devoted to actional and nonactional intervention is altered more in favor of the latter. The idea that therapeutic effect is related to the portrayal of a sequence of episodes is alluded to in the assertion, "Catharsis begins in the actor as he enacts his own drama, scene after scene, and climaxes the moment when its peripety is reached" (J. L. Moreno, 1964a, p. 16). This process follows the rule of "from the periphery to the center." It starts from a peripheral scene, which leads to a succession of interrelated scenes, until it reaches a certain climax and then comes to a closure.

Therefore, it should be borne in mind that in most instances, the therapeutic quality of this method is achieved through the *movement from one scene to another* and not from an extensive (often tedious) exploration of a single scene. This principle is discussed further in subsequent chapters of the book.

Finally, the presentation of the basic therapeutic principles will not be complete without mentioning three additional principles. These are not unique to clinical role playing; they are relevant to any form of psychotherapy. We will mention them very briefly below:

(a) Maintaining adequate therapeutic relationships with clients. Every therapeutic involvement, clinical role playing included, requires that the therapist and his or her client(s) form a special kind of professional relationship. The particular characteristics of this relationship have been described by many authors and need not be expanded here again. Some of them are common to all forms of psychotherapy, and some are unique to each special method. At this point our interest is in the common characteristics. Examples of these are the need to establish a mutual trust and confidence; the creation of a nonpunitive atmosphere where clients feel safe to express themselves freely; the instillation and maintainence of hope and faith in the treatment mode (e.g., Yalom, 1975); providing clients with the feeling that they are unique and respected persons, that their difficulties are considered genuine, and when other auxiliaries are involved, as in role playing, that this kind of a relationship exists among all the participants in the treatment session(s).

(b) Therapists have the responsibility to comply with the ethical code of their profession. The psychotherapeutic endeavor is a professional undertaking. It is based on an explicit or an implicit (often generally defined) contractual agreement between therapists and their clients. The contract must conform to the norms and shared values that prevail in the sociocultural environment in which the concerned parties live. In addition, it has to conform to the specific code of ethical (professional) conduct for therapists. Again, a full discussion of this code is beyond the scope of the present book. It will be sufficient to mention here only a few illustrative points. Thus, therapists must make it clear that the special relationship that exists between them and their clients is restricted to the therapeutic situation, and that they are prevented from entering other forms of relationships with their clients while serving in their professional capacity. The therapy is conducted under complete confidentiality within the confinements of the law. Therapists must live up to their responsibilities as experts in their profession and to help their clients become well-functioning members of society.

(c) The need for therapists to have confidence in the interventions they employ. Therapists must be proficient and have confidence in the kind of psychotherapeutic interventions they use. This confidence should be based on professionally accepted scientific, empirical, and theoretical criteria. Given the existence of such validity, the method they use must be carried out in a proper and a consistent manner. In clinical role playing, too, the effectiveness of the therapy depends, among other factors, on the therapists' readiness to use it without undue compromises. Halfhearted applications are bound to reduce the potential efficacy of this psychotherapeutic intervention.

CHAPTER 4

The Structure of the Session and Its Stages

Clinical role playing is more than a form of behavioral expression or a form of communication expressed by means of actional language. It is more than the concretization of verbal interactions or phenomenological experiences such as feelings and internal thoughts. And it is also more than a collection of exercises and techniques for the purpose of eliciting information or confronting hitherto avoided encounters. Clinical role playing is a systematic method of psychotherapy—a method that is carried out through a highly organized, well-structured procedure, which requires that the enacted behavior be treated according to the rules of that procedure. Labeling a therapeutic intervention "clinical role playing" is warranted only if it complies with such a requirement.

THE DEFINITION OF THE CLINICAL ROLE PLAYING SESSION

What Constitutes a Clinical Role Playing Session?

Earlier in the book I have tried to clarify a few concepts and terms regarding the general area commonly known as role playing. Indeed, the existence of so many loosely defined terms is quite disturbing and often causes unnecessary confusion. Another example of such concepts is the treatment *session*. Put differently, there seems to be a considerable ambiguity concerning the definition of what constitutes a clinical role playing session. On the surface, the issue may seem to be quite trivial, one that can be resolved easily. A clinical role playing session, it might be contended, is a session that uses the *as if* kind of role playing, the *as it is* kind, or a combination of both. Unfortunately, this is too simple and unsatisfactory an answer. It overlooks the problem that in practice role playing sessions vary so much that it seems as if they do not belong to the same method of psychotherapy. Some people consider a session a clinical role playing when it is entirely based on role playing enactments. Some will label the session a clinical role playing one if only a portion of the time is used for role playing enactments. There are also those who describe their therapeutic intervention as clinical role playing if they introduce one technique of role playing, even for a few moments only.

Of course, it is possible to argue that there is really no urgent need to define the clinical role playing session, and in fact, there is no harm in having several definitions. If the method of role playing can be administered in a variety of ways, perhaps it is appropriate to have several definitions of the clinical role playing session. The point that is ignored here is that the absence of a basic definition, or at least a clear description, will make it impossible, and certainly meaningless, to compare treatments of different clients. Naturally, this will tend to block further advancements regarding the effectiveness of this method of therapy.

The term "session" usually refers to a time unit. Traditionally, a psychotherapeutic or treatment session has been thought of as a meeting that lasts for 50 minutes. Still, in many instances the length of the session may vary from the traditional notion as in the case of some behavior therapy interventions. Sessions may be shorter (e.g., Kelly & Drabman, 1977; Ost, Gotestam, & Melin, 1976) or longer, as, for instance, in the case of group psychotherapy. Furthermore, the length of the session often depends on the presenting problem, its severity, complexity, and the responsiveness of the protagonist. In fact, there is very little about time per se that makes it an important criterion for the definition of therapeutic sessions, in general, or a clinical role playing session, in particular. Indeed, experience has shown that the time needed for conducting a clinical role playing session may vary within some limits. It is extremely difficult to have a meaningful session in a time period of less than 15 to 20 minutes. On the other hand, a session that lasts longer than an hour and a half tends to become unproductive.

Another criterion for defining the clinical role playing session (e.g., Kipper, 1978) concerns the use of the special role playing techniques. It was thought that a session that includes one or more such techniques could be considered a clinical role playing session. Although the use of special techniques may be considered a component of a good criterion, by itself it is unsatisfactory. This is because it does not capture the essence of clinical role playing as a therapeutic modality. One would not consider a session in which the therapist offers a few reflections to be a Rogerian treatment, nor would one consider a session in which dreams are interpreted to be a psychoanalytic treatment. Obviously a psychotherapeutic treatment must be characterized by its *entire procedure*, not merely by the use of one or more of its techniques.

Thus, the clinical role playing session, too, should be defined in terms of the application of its special procedure. And the answer to the question, what constitutes such a session? is *a session that uses the entire clinical role playing procedure*.

THE STRUCTURE OF THE SESSION

The clinical role playing session includes three parts or three basic stages. In principle, this three-stage structure is identical to the one that characterizes the psychodrama session. (e.g., Blatner, 1973; Buchanan, 1984; Moreno, 1964a; Starr, 1977; Yablonsky, 1976).

In classic psychodrama, the session consists of three portions: the warm-up, the action portion and the post-action sharing by the group.

It is appropriate to mention here that Moreno also suggested a fourth stage, the analysis, which was thought to serve as a complementary stage to the third one. The sharing stage was originally designed to facilitate emotional closure—that is, a reduction in the level of emotional arousal—by providing the protagonist with the feeling that he or she is not alone, that his or her psychological difficulties are shared in varying degrees by others. The analysis stage was supposed to serve as the cognitive counterpart to the sharing. Such an analysis would evaluate the appropriateness of the role playing portrayals, discuss their meaning, and suggest conclusions and future directions. Though Moreno spoke about the need for such a fourth stage, he did not describe it in writing. The result was that subsequent publications on psychodrama adhered to the three-stage structure of its session.

But the adherence to the three-stage structure neither overlooked nor eliminated the need to add a cognitive element to the closing sharing stage. On the contrary, several writers tried to combine the third and fourth stages proposed by Moreno into one stage so that the three-stage structure would be retained. Some of these attempts were very clear and some less so. For instance, Yablonsky (1976) retained a three-stage structure but called the third part the post-discussion rather than sharing. His description was as follows:

There are three phases to a psychodrama session as follows: (1) the warm-up, (2) the action, and (3) the post-discussion. The warm-up and the action in a session are vital; however the post-discussion is also highly significant. This is the portion of a session during which the group *shares* empathy and experiences with the protagonist. (p. 13)

At first glance it appears that replacing the name of the third stage with the term "post-discussion" is merely a matter of terminology. Yablonsky's third stage is still characterized by sharing processes. But a closer look suggests some interesting subtlety. The very choice of the term "discussion" is interesting since it has more of a cognitive connotation than the term "sharing."

Hollander (1978) addressed the same issue, but he was quite clear about the need to combine emotional and cognitive procedures into the third stage. Like Yablonsky and Moreno, he, too, retained the three-stage structure of the session, where the first two stages were the warm-up and the action. But his third and final stage was termed "integration." According to Hollander, this stage is comprised of three components as follows: (1) self-disclosure—audience reporting, which is actually identical to the sharing process, (2) dialogue, and (3) summary. The three components have a sociometric significance in that they address every person who is present in the session or, in sociometric conceptualization, every "participation role." The self-disclosure refers to the reactions of the group to the protagonist. The dialogue is the interaction among the group members. And the summary is the director's responses to the group and to the protagonist. But there is also an affective-cognitive dimension to the composition of the integration stage. It was already pointed out that the first self-disclosure, audience reporting, is a sharing process. The summary and dialogue portions, on the other hand,

> build from an affective focus to a cognitive one. As the members endeavor to integrate their feelings, experiences, and thoughts into a congruous whole, they simultaneously insure themselves against the possibility that . . . [no one] . . . will exit from the session . . . in a state of incompleteness, pain, or panic. (Hollander 1978, p. 11)

In order to resolve the unsettled issues regarding the structure of the session, I would like to propose a scheme that will integrate the various points raised above. This scheme is presented in Figure 4.1 and it will serve as our basic model for the session's structure. Future discussions throughout the book will refer to this model whenever relevant.

The abscissa for Figure 4.1 divides the session into three stages: the warm-up stage, the action stage, and the closing stage. The first two stages are identical to the stages proposed by Moreno, Yablonsky, Hollander, and others. I term the third and last stage simply the closing stage, because from a structural point of view this is its purpose: to bring the session into some comfortable closure.

THE WARM-UP STAGE

A clinical role playing session begins with the warm-up stage. Generally, the purpose of this stage is to provide the protagonist with the best opportunities for developing sufficient involvement, willingness, and readiness to proceed to the next action stage. The rationale for the insistence on a mandatory inclusion of such a stage in the session is multifaceted and is described below.

First, clinical role playing, and for that matter any behavior simulation method, models itself after real life. In real life most of our activities are preceded by a warm-up stage. The only exceptions to this are situations in which we are caught unprepared. Then it is incumbent upon us to quickly "reorient" ourselves and warm up simultaneously with the onset of the response.

With the exception of surprises, the warm-up precedes the action and it may be a very brief state of preparation or a prolonged one, an au-

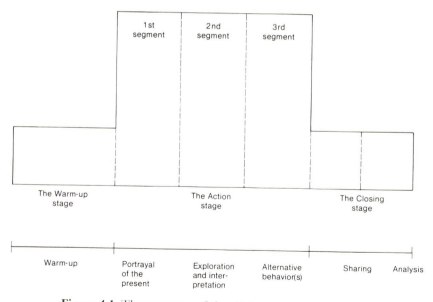

Figure 4.1. The structure of the clinical role playing session: the three stages and their internal division

tomatic or a deliberate one, with or without our awareness. Let us consider a simple, routine activity as an example. People who hold jobs usually go every morning to their office or place of employment. The acts of leaving home on time, commuting to the office, punching the time card, greeting colleagues and entering the office, all constitute the warm-up stage for starting the daily work. Ordinarily, these warming-up activities are executed automatically without the awareness that they are an essential preparatory phase. The exceptions are those days, typically following the weekend or a vacation, when the habitual warm-up activities are insufficient. On such days, people have to add other activities in order to warm up themselves to their work. Thus, people often talk to themselves in an attempt to be convinced that they should go to work, and they may spend time in the office engaging in routine, sometimes unproductive, administrative activities to become gradually involved in their work. In short, their warm-up stage is prolonged and requires a special, deliberate attention. The same holds true for almost every act, no matter how small it is: It must be preceded by some warm-up stage. If clinical role playing models itself after real life, then it should begin with the warm-up.

Second, people are natural role players in the sense that their behavior is expressed in terms of verbalizations accompanied by gestures and activities. They are natural role players also in that they can easily perform roles and behave according to the requirements of a wide range of situations. But that which is easy to do naturally becomes difficult when asked for on command. And role playing is no exception. It might be natural for a given person to become angry, to throw a book or other objects, and to hit the table with his or her fist. The same person will find it difficult and awkward to demonstrate the same behavior upon request. One of the purposes of the warm-up stage is to bring the protagonist to the point of sufficient involvement so that such a request is easy to comply with.

Third, people who seek psychotherapy are looking for help to overcome psychological difficulties, to improve their coping ability, and to be relieved of their mental anguish. In the course of their treatment they must, at some point, confront these difficulties, explore their vulnerable parts, and address themselves to their weaknesses. These are threatening tasks that are always accompanied by anxiety. Studies of personality have shown that such anxiety is handled through defense mechanisms and various forms of resistance which, though natural to the way human beings behave, are not conducive to the therapeutic process, at least not if they persist for a long period of time. The warm-up stage aims at reducing the activities of defense mechanisms and resistances to an acceptable minimum and hence to increase the chances for therapeutic gains during the remainder of the session.

Finally, although the primary purpose of the warm-up stage is to increase the protagonist's involvement in the session, it is also designed to monitor and control the *pace* of the involvement. It is quite clear that there is little merit in asking a protagonist to get into the action stage without ensuring that he or she is ready to become involved in the role playing. Most protagonists will probably resist such a request, and the therapist will find him/herself in a position of "fighting" his or her clients. If they succumb and comply with the therapist's request, chances are that the ensuing role playing will be meaningless, more of an exercise in "going through the motions without emotions." But there is also a need to monitor and sometimes control the pace of the involvement, which is enhanced during this warm-up stage, because overinvolvement—an excessively emotional, hystrionic state—is equally unproductive. Overinvolvement puts the protagonist in a euphoric state, which makes it extremely difficult to concentrate on the treatment issue. The rate at which the involvement is increased is sometimes crucial. An excessive emotional involvement attained rapidly often results in a crisis that prevents orderly progression to the action stage.

The Warm-Up Process

The warm-up is both a psychological and a biochemical process through which one becomes ready and motivated to embark on a given act. It appears that one is born with the ability to warm up, but it needs to be developed through experience. Since the ability to be warmed up to an act is a natural phenomenon, a deficiency in such an ability is considered a pathology, as, for example, in the case of autism and catatonia.

The warm-up process may vary in pace, intensity, and adequacy. The pace refers to the speed with which the process is put into action. In the extremes it varies from fast and quick to a very slow pace. The intensity refers to the forcefulness of the process and it, too, may vary in degrees. Adequacy is related to the fact that every warm-up process has to end with an act. Thus, if it has culminated in an act and the act was perceived as a satisfactory one, we speak of an adequate warm-up. Interestingly, intensity is related to adequacy. Usually, in the extremes, the very low and the very high intensity do not lead to a satisfactory act.

What stimulates the warm-up process and how does it operate? According to Moreno's (1964a) spontaneity theory of child development, the warm-up process is triggered by *starters*. There are two kinds of starters, *physical* and *mental*.

Physical starters typically refer to bodily activities such as rhythmic movements: walking, pacing, ranning, and singing. They are the ones that develop first and that tend to be dominant in the first period of the infant's life, even prior to birth. As the child grows, the mental starters (sometimes also referred to as the interpersonal starters) become more functional and usable.

But physical starters never lose their importance, remaining operative throughout the person's life. With the availablity of mental starters, they tend to acquire a rescue quality. This means that adults resort to them especially in emergencies or when taken by surprise. For instance, a common example of this "rescue" quality of physical starters is the tendency of people to start pacing in their room or office when confronted with an unexpected or difficult question. Some theories will construe the pacing as nervousness or anxiety, with an overtone of an inappropriate response. On the other hand, according to the notion of the warm-up process, such seeming restlessness is perceived as a positive manifestation which may indicate an appropriate behavior. It signifies the process of getting ready to act.

Mental starters refer to activities influenced by (a) *psychological* triggers, such as fantasies, dreams, aspirations, fears, and guilt feelings, or (b) *sociocultural* triggers, including effects of social norms, group pressures, social status, moral obligations, ethical codes, and external incentives. Mental starters begin to develop as soon as the child is able to differentiate between the self and the environment. The environment includes objects as well as people, and this is why mental starters are often referred to as *interpersonal* starters.

All the starters—physical and mental—may be triggered by internal stimulations (self-initiated) or by external stimulations. The former are produced by the protagonist and the latter by the therapist. Both have the same impact on the warm-up process. Furthermore, there is a reciprocal relationship between the starters. Thus, once put into motion, the warm-up becomes a self-propelled process. Physical starters can warm up a person mentally, and mental starters can warm up a person physically.

People tend to develop warm-up habits. Some have their own favorite starters for certain acts, which they will repeat whenever appropriate. For instance, some like to pace in their room before they begin to write, light a cigarette before they begin a speech, or drink beer before they watch a ball game. Encouraging potential protagonists to resort to their favorite starters may help to initiate a warm-up process, but it is not a must. Therapists may use any kind of starters, of their own choosing, perhaps the ones they, themselves, like best. In fact, there are many exercises (e.g., milling around, dancing in circles, moving chairs, and stretching arms and legs) that serve as warm-up starters. And although, at first glance, they seem to be unrelated to the therapeutic endeavor proper, they do serve an important preparatory function as starters of the warm-up process.

Specific Goals of the Warm-Up Stage

The overall purpose of the warm-up stage still leaves us wondering about the *exact* objectives that need to be met during this portion of the session. What, one may ask, does the phrase "increasing the protagonist's readiness to act" actually entail? The short answer is that there are three specific goals: familiarizing the protagonist with role playing as a mode of expression, building an atmosphere of trust, and enhancing the protagonist's spontaneity.

The first of these three goals concerns helping the potential protagonist to accept the idea that the method of portraying his or her presenting problem(s) and the ensuing explorations will be by means of an actional language. People are accustomed to describe their experiences verbally. They do so when they speak to each other under normal circumstances, and in the special therapeutic relationship in the course of their psychotherapy. A full behavioral demonstration of their experiences is uncommon and often regarded as a primitive, unnecessary, or even comical form of expression. These difficulties and prejudices must be overcome during the warm-up stage. Once involved and properly warmed up, role playing seems natural.

The second goal is related to the first one but this time it concerns the need to develop an atmosphere of trust. The issue of trust is important in every therapeutic endeavor; yet, in the context of clinical role playing, it contains an extra dimension. Potential protagonists may not know what to expect in the session or how they appear to the other using actional language. They may feel that their proficiency and "eloquence" in communicating through such a language is deficient. It is, therefore, the trust in themselves, as good communicators, that needs to be built during the warm-up stage. Again, the apparent initial lack of trust in communicative effectiveness is more presumed than real. Once involved, these fears and uncertainties usually disappear completely.

Finally, the third specific goal for the warm-up stage refers to the need to prepare the protagonist to be as spontaneous as he or she can be. Put differently, it ought to increase the protagonist's willingness to take risks. The risks have to do with allowing oneself the freedom to behave in a manner that may differ from that typical of everyday life. In everyday life, behavior is controlled to some extent by conventions. On certain occasions one has to control one's emotions, one has to speak politely to people, or one must accommodate one's behavior in a manner that will not jeopardize vital interests. During the clinical role playing session most of these restrictions do not apply. But it takes a special intervention on the part of the therapist to convince the protagonist that such freedom of expression is legitimate, and that during *the session proper* the otherwise sanctioned expression will not be penalized. The purpose of the warm-up stage is to help the protagonist to be ready to take such risks.

Being spontaneous or having freedom of expression does not necessarily mean that protagonists may portray anything they wish or fantasize without restrictions. On the contrary, one must distinguish between a freedom that pertains to the *content* of the enactment and that of its *form*. Although there are no restrictions regarding the content, the form is subjected to several rules and regulations. For instance, a protagonist who needs to express aggression may do so, but he is prohibited from expressing physical violence that may cause injuries to himself, his co-therapist or helpers, his therapist, or for that matter anyone who is present in the session. The same principle applies to forms of expression that are not permitted on professional-ethical grounds. Such restrictions are described in various ethical guidelines for giving psychological services (e.g., American Psychological Association, 1977).

The Progression of the Warm-Up

The warm-up stage has content, that is, it is comprised of topics that are discussed, situations that are role played, and tasks that need to be performed. In principle, the content that the therapist may choose to introduce is unrestricted, except that it should not be that of the presenting problems. Every other issue is acceptable. That rule is known as the rule for the progression of the warm-up, which proceeds *from the periphery to the center.*

The rule actually means that the therapist should not use potentially threatening content in the warm-up stage. The first target is to get the warm-up process started; the content is less important. Unfortunately, novice therapists who use role playing often ignore that rule. They get "right to the point," presumably to save time, and in that process the protagonist not only fails to warm up him/herself, but also becomes threatened.

To demonstrate how one can follow the *from the periphery to the center* rule, the following case will be described. Note how the therapist uses a side issue to warm up the protagonist and to bring her to the point of (a) readiness to move to the action stage, and (b) connecting the end of the warm-up stage with the main complaint, to be dealt with in the second stage of the session. The last point makes the transition from the warm-up stage to the action stage a very elegant one.

The protagonist was a woman in her late thirties who had been in therapy for some time. The session began with the usual procedure, that is, with the *director* asking a few questions and a brief discussion, which essentially summarized the previous session. Then, the *director* asked the protagonist if she had any particular topic or issue which she wanted to concentrate on. (Note that *director* is used here instead of *therapist*. As we shall see later in the book, director is the clinical role playing term for the person who conducts the session; the therapist. From now on these two words, director and therapist, will be used interchangeably.)

Director: Well, Mary, is there any particular issue or subject that you wish to bring today?

Mary: Hmmm . . . not really, no. I can't think of anything special right now. As a matter of fact I'm tired. I don't know why I feel that way because I had a very good day today. But suddenly I feel very tired and reticent.

At this point the director thought that the issue of the sudden tiredness might provide a clue for the main issue to be dealt with in the session. The sudden tiredness appeared to be some sort of a defense; it looked like an attempt to avoid something. The question was, of course, what that "something" could be. It could have been an important issue that had never been raised so far. It could have been an attempt to prevent the therapist from further probing an issue related to the previous session that had been summarized a few moments ago. It could also have been a sign of a general tendency on the part of the protagonist to avoid a confrontation with a potentially threatening issue. Of course, it could have been a genuine tiredness, but it did not sound that way. Whatever the real reason was for the sudden tiredness, it seemed a worthwhile issue for further exploration. Having decided to focus on the issue of her tiredness, the director should now pick up on another issue, according to the rule of *from the periphery to the center,* and explore tiredness in the action stage.

The director decided to introduce another small role playing vignette to serve as a warm-up. Here is how he proceeded:

Director: I understand. You suddenly feel tired, is that it?

Mary: Yes, that's correct.

Director: Do you often find that you suddenly get tired?

Mary: Sometimes, not really. I don't think so.

Director: Did you have a physical checkup recently? Could it be that you are ill?

Mary: No, I feel fine. As a matter of fact two months ago I went for my physical and the doctor gave me a clean bill of health.

Director: You're not pregnant, are you?

Mary: (Laughs) No, no way.

Director: OK. Let's begin with something else, and we'll see where it will bring us. Is that agreeable with you?

Mary: Fine.

Director: Mary, didn't you tell me in a previous session that you usually take the bus to come to the sessions?

Mary: Yes, I take bus number 46. I took it today, too.

Director: Is that a long bus ride?

Mary: No, it takes about 20 to 23 minutes. I usually leave the office at 3:30 and get here about five minutes before our sessions.

Director: And today you took the bus as usual. Is that right?

Mary: Yes.

Director: Fine. Mary, on your way to the session today in the bus, what did you think? What went on in your mind?

Mary: Oh, all kinds of things. I was just thinking.

Director: Let's reenact today's bus ride here, now, but this time I would like you to express your thoughts openly. OK.?

Mary: It's fine with me. That's easy. But there was nothing special or particularly interesting in my thoughts.

Director: Let's see anyway. Why don't you set the bus scene here in the room. Take a few chairs and arrange them like a bus, will you please? *(Mary gets up and takes three chairs. She puts two next to each other, and places the third chair behind the two).* That's fine. Was there anybody important who sat in any of these chairs, except yourself, of course?

Mary: Not really. They were just people. I didn't even pay attention to them. I suppose you want me to sit in my chair and start talking, right?

Director: Yes, whenever you're ready.

Mary: (sits in one of the chairs and begins) I thought that I really should pay my telephone bill tonight. It was . . .

Director: Hold it Mary. I want you to say it in the present tense as if it is happening right now. This is the bus. The time is what? About 3:30? *(Mary nods yes.)* And you're in the bus. OK.?

Mary: I really should pay my telephone bill tonight. It's long overdue. If I don't they'll disconnect it and then I'll be in trouble. Apropos of telephones, I must call Debbie. She's having trouble with her children. I wonder if I should bring this to the session. Maybe I could give her good advice. Ah, better not to mention it. If I do, he'll make a big fuss about it and start asking me why I talk about my friends. Psychologists know how to make a big issue out of everything. It's really not important. Maybe I'll have time to get an ice cream cone before the session. I'm getting too fat . . .

Director: Mary, let's expand on these thoughts. What we can do is to have a dialogue between the two parts of Mary. It's like having an internal dialogue that we can see and hear in this room. Let's decide that Mary A sits where you're sitting now, and Mary B sits on the chair next to you. When you talk as Mary A, you'll sit on your chair. When you talk as Mary B, you'll move to the one next to you. You can move from one chair to another as you wish. Sometimes I may suggest a change in chairs. OK.?

Mary: OK.

Director: Go ahead.

Mary A: Where was I? Yes, I remember. I'm too fat. I can't get into some of my clothes anymore. I shouldn't have an ice cream cone. Oh well, I'll start dieting tomorrow.

Mary B: I've heard that before.

Mary A: Now, what's that supposed to mean?

Mary B: Just what I said. You always let yourself loose with food and then start a diet. Then you can't discipline yourself and after four days or so it's "eating like a pig" again. Why don't you get hold of yourself? Get organized, get some discipline, plan ahead.

Mary A: Wait a minute. Don't get excited. I'm OK. So I forgot to pay my telephone bill, so what? *(A pause. Mary stays in the Mary A seat and does not move.)*

Director: Change seats. Let's hear Mary B's response to that.

Mary B: The bill? It's more than *a* bill. You'd better say "the bills." Do you want me to remind you how well organized and disciplined you are? Very well. Let's start with balancing your checking account. When did you do that last? And what about the letter you promised

Joe to write? And how about running out of the exact change every time you take the bus? Why don't you buy some tokens? And . . . *(Mary jumps into the Mary A chair.)*

Mary A: Oh, leave me alone. I'm tired.

Director: Thank you. Will you please get out of the bus and forget Mary A and Mary B. Now, you're again one Mary. Now, about being tired, didn't I hear that expression before, in the beginning of our session?

Mary: (visibly upset) I guess so.

Director: Why don't we look further into that. I see that you're a little upset, so maybe it's important. We'll explore that slowly. Is that all right with you?

Mary: I guess so.

Director: OK. The easiest way to begin is like this. Can you think of a situation, past or present, when you remember being very enthusiastic about something and that enthusiasm disappeared quickly? suddenly you became bored and tired?

Mary: (After a moment or so of thinking) Well, there was that thing with the concert.

In terms of the structure of the session, the point at which the director terminated the bus scene and asked Mary to step out of the bus marked the end of the warm-up stage. At that point the protagonist seemed to be sufficiently involved in the role playing "language," emotionally involved in the content of the scene, ready to pursue the clue (i.e., the tiredness) picked by the director, and motivated to continue with the session. The last two interactions between the director and Mary marked the transition from the warm-up stage to the action stage. The latter began with the enactment of the situation concerning the concert, which will not be described here.

To sum up, it should be noted that the director complied with the rule of *from the periphery to the center* by using a strategy that may be characterized as temporal antecedents. According to this, the warm-up consists of the situation(s) that preceded in time the situation that represents the main complaint. This *temporal antecedents* strategy is frequently used and it has many advantages. It refers to a situation known to the protagonist; hence it is unlikely to make him or her uncomfortable. The outcomes of that situation are also known, a fact that adds to the protagonist's feelings of comfort. And finally, it seems neutral enough. The use of the Mary A and B intervention was, in fact, a form of a physical starter, as the protagonist had to actually move from one chair to another. The reason why the externalization of the internal debate was kept brief was a practical one. Moving from one chair to another several times is a physically tiring task. At this early stage of the session it is important to keep the protagonist alert and fit rather than bringing him or her to the point of exhaustion.

Undirected and Directed Warm-Ups

The kinds of warm-up interventionns that a therapist may employ may also depend on whether or not the potential protagonist appears to be ready to act from the very beginning of the session.

1. The undirected warm-up. An undirected warm-up may be *focused and specific.* In this case the protagonist enters the session ready to deal with a specific issue. That state of readiness is easy to identify because usually the protagonist will say something like: "I thought about my difficulties with my father, our inability to understand each other, and I would like to work on that problem today" or "I had a terrible argument with my wife and I would like to show you what happened and work on that." In such situations there is really no need to go through an elaborated warm-up stage. But this does not mean that the therapist should start the action stage immediately. A brief warm-up might be still in order. Often, such protagonists are overexcited and may benefit from a slight "cooling off" period. The simplest way to achieve this is for the therapist to sit with the protagonist and ask him to describe verbally the circumstances that brought about the problem or brought him or her to decide to work on that problem. That discussion is very brief and must not exceed a few minutes. Then the protagonist can be permitted to begin the action stage.

An undirected warm-up may also be *general and diffuse.* In this case the protagonist enters the session already prepared to participate in role playing enactment. No specific issue is mentioned. In fact the typical expression of such readiness is: "I feel like doing something really good today, but I do not have a particular problem to work on. I'll do whatever you suggest" or "If you want me to, I am ready to role play today."

The focused and specific kind of undirected warm-up already suggests the clue(s) for the first scene or scenes. But in the second kind of undirected warm-up—the general and diffuse—only a general state of readiness to participate in a clinical role playing enactment is expressed. Specific clues about how to begin the action stage are yet to be identified. Therefore, it is incumbent upon the therapist to look for such clues. The procedures for achieving this goal are similar to those used in the direct warm-up to be discussed in the following section.

2. The direct warm-up. This situation is the most typical and it refers to those instances when the protagonist enters the session still not ready to role play. Here the task of the therapist is to use the warm-up stage for all the purposes it is designated to accomplish.

There are numerous ways to conduct the warm-up stage, and many of these have already been mentioned. Briefly, one can conduct the warm-up stage purely on the verbal level, which may include interviewing, discussions, pep talks, and persuasion. One can also use the non-verbal approach, by asking the protagonist to perform one or two short nonverbal exercises. And, naturally, the warm-up stage may be conducted as a brief role playing vignette. This form not only combines the verbal and the nonverbal approaches, but it also introduces an example of the actional language mode.

The Warm-Up of the Director

The person who directs the clinical role playing session has to be ready for his or her involvement, too. Like any other human being, the director's own state of readiness to assume the role of the therapist may vacillate from one case to another, from one hour to another, and from one session to another. It is not uncommon for a given director to be caught in a state of insufficient warm-up to conduct a clinical role playing session. Experienced directors are quite familiar with this situation, and as a rule they warm up themselves simultaneously with the warm-up of their protagonist or potential protagonists. They will attempt to activate self-starters by becoming physically active—pacing a little, moving chairs, etc.—or by using mental starters such as talking to the group or to the individual client.

In addition, the warmed-up director becomes a model for the potential protagonist. Observations of clinical role playing sessions, especially those conducted as group therapy, show that warm-up can be "contagious"; it enhances the warm-up of other participants. Often, the mere presence of an already warmed-up individual is sufficient to positively affect the warm-up of others. Such a "covert warm-up leader" can be anyone who is present in the session, including the therapist.

THE ACTION STAGE

Clinical role playing is not an artistic experience in the theatrical sense, and the "acting" part of the role playing has no dramaturgical value. Instead, clinical role playing can be thought of as a vehicle that facilitates behavioral and social changes or as a form of psychotherapy; it is a medium that enables a person to experience a fuller and wider life pattern. It is true that role playing in real life has some theatrical aspects. "Performances" in everyday life contain elements of *as if* behavior, and so do the performances of the actor in the theater. But this similarity does not make the two types of performances identical. On the contrary, they are very different modes of behavior, which differ in form, purpose, quality, and substance.

Acting as a profession is a make-believe performance which assumes a split between the actor's private life and the corresponding roles played on the theater stage. Furthermore, the playing of such roles is based on scripts written by others. It is also guided by *artistic* considerations rather than *authentic* ones. The legitimacy of acting as a profession stems from its entertainment value.

Role playing in everyday life is authentic, original, and serves functions other than mere contentment and satisfaction. It is an effort to further one's accomplishments, a form of communication by compliance with shared socioclutural norms, and a way of protection from self-exposure, where such exposure threatens to disturb a comfortable internal equilibrium. Role playing in the "action stage" models itself after acting in real life and adds to it a therapeutic value. This value becomes the main thrust of the action stage.

One of the most important characteristics of the action stage is that it has an internal structure. This structure is expressed in terms of segments and scenes.

The Internal Structure: The Segments

Figure 4.2 shows the internal structure of the action stage. According to this illustration the action stage is comprised of three segments where each is designed to fulfill a certain function or functions as described at the bottom of the rectangles representing the segments. Each segment includes two types of scenes which are represented by small and slightly larger boxes. These are the key scenes and the connecting ones, which will be described in full in the next section. In the segments of Figure 4.2 there are small circles marked by the word "clue." These are various signs and indications that direct the therapist in deciding how to proceed from one segment to another and what scenes to construct. We will discuss the issue of clues and the selection of clues in the next chapter.

The discussion of the internal structure of the action stage begins with the three segments. The function of the first segment is the portrayal of the present, that is, a role playing description of the problem to be explored during the session. Here the protagonist is asked to show his or her presenting problem and its scope. Typically, this is done through a role playing enactment of a scene, a situation where that problem appears to manifest itself most vividly. In that portrayal it is customary to request that both the difficulties and their consequences will be shown. The protagonist is allowed to demonstrate this with complete freedom in an entirely subjective manner, no matter how distorted this may appear to the observer. This is the best way to understand and evaluate the problem, its characteristics, and magnitude. It is also the best way

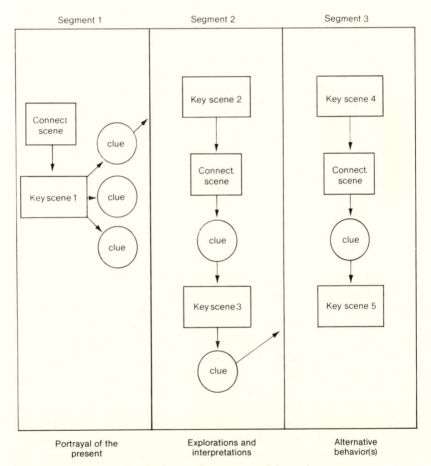

Figure 4.2. The internal structure of the action stage

to provide the therapist with an opportunity to pick up important clues regarding the possible maintaining variables or causes that are related to the presenting problem. The selection of clues is the central task of the therapist in the first segment. Such clues ought to direct him or her how to proceed with the session, what areas need explorations in the second segment, and what scenes ought to be constructed.

The function of the second segment, which is described as explorations and interpretations, is actually twofold. It has a diagnostic part and a corrective one. The diagnostic part refers to role playing explorations of factors associated with the presenting problem. By factors associated with the presenting problem we mean issues such as early traumatic experiences that establish a certain mode of responding in a given set of circumstances or a lack of adequate skills in handling certain tasks.

The corrective part of the second segment of the action stage refers to the elimination of debilitating anxieties. Actually, it is a disinhibitory function. Therapists who adhere to theories that advocate catharsis will attempt to provide the protagonist with the opportunity to achieve catharsis here. Those therapists who subscribe to other theoretical models may offer the protagonist an opportunity to overcome such anxieties through a gradual encounter with the anxiety-evoking stimuli. Whatever the therapeutic approach, the common goal of the disinhibitory procedure is to bring the protagonist to a state where he or she is amenable to explore new modes of responding.

The learning of such alternative behavior is done in the third segment of the action stage. Its function is described as "alternative behavior," that is, experimentation with various ways of overcoming or solving the presenting problem. In this segment the therapist trains and guides the protagonist in new modes of responding to the old, troubling situation. It is absolutely mandatory that the process of such experimentations will include not only scenes where the new behavior is practiced but also the consequences of the behavior. The best criteria for assessing the appropriateness of the practiced solutions are (a) whether or not the protagonists themselves feel comfortable with the consequences, and (b) whether or not they significantly reduce the chances for the recurrence of the original presenting problem. One of the greatest advantages of clinical role playing and other simulation procedures over many other forms of psychotherapy is that the former offer protagonists a unique opportunity to explore unknown consequences in a nonthreatening environment. Protagonists are protected in the sense that they know that this is only a test situation—a trial, an exploration in which there is a substantial amount of control over the external environment. Therefore, they do not have to pay an emotionally painful price should a wrong solution be chosen. They can simply discard it and try a different solution.

The effectiveness of the treatment—the successful attainment of the goals described through the function of each of the three segments—is predicated on the therapist's skill to construct the scenes. The selection of scenes that address critical incidents that highlight the most important issues relevant to the treated problem, is vital to the success of the treatment. This is a special skill based on the sensitivity of the therapist, the wisdom and the knowledge of how to construct scenes and relate them to each other in a meaningful way.

Scenes and the Setting of Scenes

In the final analysis, the action stage manifests itself through the enactment of role playing scenes. Scene refers to a well-defined situation portrayed by means of role playing. Every conceivable situation can become a scene. It can be a situation that occurs in the present, one that took place in the past (whether the recent past or the remote past), a situation that may occur in the future, or even a fantasized situation. In fact, it is difficult to think of a situation that could not be portrayed in clinical role playing. Every scene, whether realistic or fantasized, common or bizarre, is always portrayed as a real situation, as if it actually happened.

There are two categories of scenes: *key scenes* and *connecting scenes*. The division into these two categories is according to the function of the scenes rather than their content.

Key scenes. This category of scenes is very difficult to define because it includes the vast majority of the scenes portrayed through role playing. Since scenes vary in their content, their length, the number of people who are involved in them, and the different techniques that they use, a simple definition of what constitutes a key scene is an impossibility. Generally speaking, a key scene portrays an independent situation. It is independent in the sense that it may be construed as one complete unit. The easiest way to describe a key scene is by process of elimination, that is, a key scene is every role playing situation that does not fall under the category of connecting scenes. Admittedly, this description is far from being satisfactory but it has practical implications for the therapist who is about to construct an action stage.

Connecting scenes. This category includes special kinds of scenes. They are very brief and serve as introductions or summaries to key scenes. Typically, the connecting scene is a very simple one. Most connecting scenes use the following procedure. The protagonist is asked to walk in the treatment room in a fairly wide circle and to soliloquize openly, that is, to describe his or her feelings and thoughts at the present moment. The connecting scenes are also aided by two techniques: the Soliloquy and the Double (see Chapter 6).

When a connecting scene is introduced to *preamble* a key scene, its purpose is twofold. One is to provide the therapist with an opportunity to identify significant clues that can be useful in subsequent scenes. And the second is to assess the protagonist's expectations prior to the start of the key scene. For instance, a protagonist brought a problem concerning his feelings of inadequacy in starting conversations with members of the opposite sex. It was decided that the first key scene would be a portrayal of an evening in a singles' bar (to which the protagonist went every Friday night). The therapist, however, wanted to begin with a connecting scene, which he designed as follows:

Director: On your way to the bar do you think about what may happen there?

Protagonist: Yes, I'm trying to figure out what to do and contemplate various options.

Director: Let's start with a small scene. It's now Friday evening, and you're on your way to the bar. Is that correct? OK then, let's say that this room is the street leading to the bar. I'd like you to walk in the room and let me hear your feelings and thoughts. I know that ordinarily those feelings and thoughts are kept inside. But, here, let's have them in the open.

This connecting scene is kept very brief. Once the therapist is satisfied that he or she has sufficient information, he or she may terminate the scene and begin with the key scene. This is simply done by saying, "Thank you. Now I want you to enter the bar and show me what usually happens."

When a connecting scene is introduced *following* a key scene its purpose is to help the therapist to assess the impact of the previous scene and what was learned from it. At the same time it helps the protagonist to evaluate, and perhaps integrate, the experiences he or she has had thus far in the session. The following illustrates a typical way of introducing a connecting scene which represents the aftermath of a key scene.

Director: So now you left the bar. Are you alone?
Protagonist: (sadly) Yes.
Director: What time is it?
Protagonist: You mean right now?
Director: Well, in the scene, what time is it?
Protagonist: Before midnight. I'm going back home.
Director: And on your way home do you think about what happened tonight?
Protagonist: (sadly) Yes, very much so.
Director: OK. Let's hear these feelings and thoughts. You're going back home. Walk around this room and tell me what goes inside your head, what're you feeling and thinking as you walk home.

Again, like all connecting scenes, this one should be very brief. In general, the end of such a connecting scene may be the end of the session, the end of one portion of the session, or a bridge to the next key scene. In the latter instance, the connecting scene actually serves a dual purpose. It explores the aftermath of the previous key scene and at the same time becomes an introductory connecting scene for the next key scene.

Connecting scenes ought to be employed sparingly. There is no need to precede and supplement every key scene with a connecting one. In fact, it is recommended *not* to do so. Otherwise the action stage will be too long, cumbersome, and tiring. Therapists should exercise their best judgment as to when to introduce a connecting scene and when it is not needed.

Setting the scenes. Once the protagonist is ready to move to the action proper, it is up to the therapist to set the scene, that is, to construct the situation that is to be role played. Ordinarily, this task is performed as a joint venture, in collaboration with the protagonist. The procedure for setting the scene may take a few minutes and may resemble a short interview. The procedure involves four steps: (a) designating the *action space* (only in the first scene); (b) describing the *situation;* (c) determining its *time;* and (d) identifying the most *important people* involved in the situation.

The *action space* is that part of the treatment room where the actual role playing takes place. This space ought to be delineated either by physical signs (e.g., a circle marked with chalk, the edges of a carpet, chairs) or by visualizing imaginary boundaries. Although the marking of physical boundaries is preferred, the use of imaginary boundaries may suffice. The rationale underlying this procedure has to do with the need to differentiate between the simulated world and the real world. Clinical role playing is based on the notion of the psychological simulator. It creates a special reality. This reality is characterized by minimal constraints. Here the protagonist is the master of the environment: he controls it; he can shape and change it as he wishes. In real life, however, such a degree of control is not available. Delineating the boundaries of the *action space* symbolizes the difference between the role playing reality and what prevails outside.

The *situation* must be described as meticulously as is needed. Such a description addresses first the physical characteristics of the situation. Though at times this may seem an unnecessary distraction, in fact it is very important to both the therapist and the protagonist. To the therapist it offers an opportunity to see the physical characteristics of the protagonist's world and may help the therapist to detect clues that otherwise might be difficult to identify. To the protagonist it offers an additional opportunity to increase the involvement in the enactment. Visualizing the original situation, even if only in the imagination, puts the protagonist back in the original scene. The description must also address the *time* when it took place. All role playing enactments are portrayed in the present, as if they occur now for the first time. Therefore, establishing the time when the original situation occurred helps to set it in the present.

Finally, the therapist needs to know who was involved in the situations besides the protagonist. There is no need to represent everybody who was there. Only the most *important people* must be brought into the action.

Scenes must have a clear beginning and a clear end. A scene begins when the therapist invites the protagonist to enter the action space and show what has happened. The instruction here is very simple. For instance, "I would like you to enter the action space and start the scene. Go ahead." When a scene comes to an end, the therapist asks the protagonist to stop. Many therapists who use clinical role playing pay little attention to the need for providing clear clues for when to begin a scene and when it is over. The unfortunate result is that the action stage turns out to be one long and arduous role playing session as scenes blend with each other. This inevitably makes it very hard for the protagonist to reconstruct the session and to evaluate what has happened.

The following is an example of an individual session with an actual case treated with clinical role playing. For the purpose of the present discussion we will illustrate the setting of scene one (in the first segment of the action stage).

The protagonist, a male in his mid-thirties, was an executive manager in a large corporation. His complaint, in this session, was that he tended to talk too much, to say openly everything that came to his mind, and to get into trouble because of it. He said that as much as he wanted to, he could not control the need to be overly talkative. The therapist decided to begin with that issue and see where it would lead him.

Director: Can you recall a typical situation, perhaps from the recent past, which illustrated the problem you have just described to me?

John: (thinks for a while) Sure. There was a cocktail party given by the company that I'm working for. We had a two-day seminar for all the managers and the executives and at the end of the first day we had a cocktail party. So, here I was standing at the bar talking to Jim, our vice-president. Actually he started. He came to me and asked me how things were in my department. So, I told him that . . .

Director: Hold it, John. Don't tell me right now what you said. I would like to see that in action. But before we get to that, I would like to know a little more about the situation. Where was the bar?

John: Do you want the address? *(laughs)*

Director: Not really. Suppose that the action space here is the place where the cocktail party took place. Now, where's the entrance?

John: Say here *(Points two yards to the left. Both the director and John move to the entrance.)*

Director: OK. I want you to give me the "grand tour." You enter the room and I'll follow you. Now, which side is the bar?

John: If this is the entrance, the bar was to the left. You know, they'd tables moved together, covered with white tablecloths and drinks.

Director: What's here on the wall behind the bar?

John: Well, behind the tables there were two bartenders and on the wall . . . yes, there was a huge curtain.

Director: What color, do you remember?

John: Terrible one. Some kind of a yellow which I hate. And by the way every room has the same type of curtain, even my office. Terrible. *(a clue?)* . . . Now, on the wall opposite the bar they had tables with some food.

Director: What kind of food?

John: Good food. Oh, shrimps, and small sandwiches, and so on.

Director: And on the wall behind these tables?

John: A painting, some sort of scenery, a river. I like fishing, you know.

Director: OK. Why don't you take a few chairs and put some to represent the bar and some to represent the tables with the food.

John: (arranges the chairs)

Director: And what's on the third wall, the one opposite the entrance?
John: I don't remember.
Director: Look at this wall, look at it. Is there anything on the wall?
John: No, I do not . . . wait a minute. *(laughs)* There's a picture of our complex of buildings. Ha! *(a clue?)*
Director: Anything else important here?
John: I can't think of anything else.
Director: Can you remember the day and the time of the cocktail party?
John: It was . . .
Director: Say, *it is.*
John: OK. It's Wednesday, 5:30 in the afternoon. We don't have cocktails early in the morning. *(smiles)*
Director: Who's here? Who are the most important people for the scene?
John: There are about 50 people, but only Jim, the vice-president, is really important.
Director: OK. And you stand next to the bar. Do you have a drink?
John: Yes, vodka on the rocks.
Director: In a minute we'll begin the role playing scene. I'm going to be Jim. As long as I play Jim I'm not the therapist. If you want to talk to me as the therapist, you and I have to step aside from the action space. Is there anything you want to ask me before we start? *(John nods to signify no.)* OK. Let's begin. Step into the action space and start.

THE CLOSING STAGE

The closing stage is the third and final portion of the session. Its general purpose is conveyed by its name, that is, to bring the entire session into some form of closure both structurally and psychotherapeutically.

Therapeutic Aspects of the Closing Stage

From a treatment point of view, the closing stage is expected to accomplish several goals. These may be described as deroling, emotional stability, comfort, optimism, understanding, and future plans.

1. Deroling. Deroling is an expression that refers to the act of getting the protagonist out of the role or roles that he or she portrayed during the action stage. Recently, there has been an increasing awareness on the part of many therapists regarding the importance of deroling. The transition from the end of the action stage to the beginning of the closing stage is not always smooth. This is especially true when the protagonist was extremely involved in the role playing enactments—when the action portrayals elicited intense emotional reactions on the part of the protagonist. It is during the closing stage that any residual feelings of this sort need to be dealt with. Deroling often takes the form of brief discussions, sharing, debriefing, and follow-up procedures (e.g., telephone conversations), which extend beyond the formal closing stage.

The need for deliberate interventions aimed at deroling the protagonist was always recognized when dealing with psychotic clients, that is, protagonists who find it difficult to draw clear boundaries between reality and fantasy. It was assumed that with mild neurotics the process of deroling occurs automatically. Experience has shown that such an assumption must not be made.

2. Emotional stability. Restoring the protagonist's emotional stability may be seen as part of the deroling process. During the first and particularly the second stage of the session, the protagonist is encouraged to expose himself or herself and to confront painful conflicts. Inevitably, this process contributes to an increasing sense of vulnerability on the part of the protagonist. To compensate for that the rules that govern the action stage provide ample protection in the form of substantial controls over the actions. In that way the emotional vulnerability becomes tolerable and somewhat safe. In the closing stage, however, the rules are changed and the control is drastically reduced. Now that such a state of vulnerability is less tolerable and certainly no longer safe, the protagonist must be protected in a different way. Ideally, the therapist must see that his or her protagonist leaves the session in a *better* emotional state than when the session began. In instances where this goal is unattainable, it is incumbent upon the therapist to ensure that the protagonist's emotional state has not deteriorated compared to that which was evident prior to the onset of the session.

3. Comfort. Comfort is a subjective feeling and depends on the individual's ability to alleviate his or her own anxiety, to reduce stress, and to tolerate uncertainties. The kind of comfort that the closing stage is concerned with refers to the perception that the problems and difficulties one may have are somewhat shared by others as well. During the first two stages of the session the protagonist struggles with his or her difficulties, a process that involves a considerable personal anguish. While immersed in his or her portrayals, the protagonist cannot appropriately assess the seriousness of the problem(s). As the session comes to a close that ability must be regained, and personal difficulties have to be evaluated in their correct perspective. Often, the ability to objectively evaluate one's own situation in itself enhances the feeling of comfort. At the very least, the therapist ought to help the protagonist see that his or her difficulties are not exceedingly unusual, and that others may have similar or even more disturbing problems.

4. Optimism. Ending the session on a hopeful note is another therapeutic goal of the closing stage. Such a sense of optimism can be attained by helping the protagonist see that he or she is in a better position to cope with the presenting problems, or at least that the prospect for being in such a position is good. Of course, efforts to provide an optimistic outlook must be true and genuine. The discussion during the closing stage must emphasize the positive aspects of the portrayals, the healthy parts of the protagonist, and the skills (or potential skills) that he or she may have.

There are several strategies that therapists may use for the purpose of instilling the feeling of hope in their clients. They may use encouragement, they may ask group members, in a group therapy situation, to join them in this endeavor, and they may also design a brief role playing episode to convey the message through action.

5. Understanding. Enhancing the clients' understanding of themselves, of their behavior, and of its impact on others is a therapeutic goal shared by most, if not all, treatment modalities. Typically, it is attained through interpretations provided by the therapist. Why is it, then, that the process of interpreting the protagonist's behavior is considered a task to be accomplished in the closing stage? Would it not be more appropriate to ascribe it to the action stage where it can serve as an integral component of the protagonist's enactments?

In clinical role playing a distinction is made between two forms of interpretations: *action* and *verbal*. Ordinarily, action interpretations are offered during the action stage, whereas the more traditional verbal interpretations may be provided, if needed, in the closing stage. Sometimes, however, exceptions have to be made and action interpretations need to be introduced in the closing stage as well.

The notion of action interpretations may require further explanation. Unlike verbal interpretations, which represent a component of conventional approaches to psychotherapy, action interpretations are unique to clinical role playing and psychodrama. The use of action interpre-

tations is consistent with the fundamental premise of behavior simula-
tion-based therapies, namely, that therapy is rendered through actional
language. Thus, whenever a therapist wishes to introduce a point of
interpretation, it, too, should take the form of a role playing enactment.
There are two ways in which this may be accomplished: 1) to add a role
playing enactment or technique to an already existing scene; and 2) to
design a special situation, a critical incident, that will highlight and bring
into the open the intended message. To the impartial observer, action
interpretations may appear as an indirect way of making the protagonist
aware of the meaning of his or her behavior. Nonetheless, experience
has shown that this can be a powerful form of interpretation. Furthermore, the elegance of this method of interpretation tends to reduce the
protagonist's resistance to accept the therapist's point.

It is not surprising, therefore, that in clinical role playing and psychodrama the recommended strategy is that, in principle, action interpretations should precede verbal interpretations.

The following excerpt illustrates the use of action interpretations. This
role playing vignette is taken from a group therapy session. The protagonist, Bill, was a white male in his late forties. He made a point to
repeatedly present himself as an "extremely liberal person" and regarded
his conduct and life-philosophy as fitting this image of himself. Early in
the action stage it became apparent that he was in the process of divorcing
his wife. He also had a girl friend, a black woman, whom he loved and
planned to marry as soon as the divorce was finalized. As the first two
scenes unfolded, his proclamation of "extreme liberalism" came under
suspicion. He also resisted the therapist's attempts to make him reexamine his liberal convictions. The turning point occurred as a result of
the following dialogue:

Director: Does your wife know that you are dating another woman?
Bill: I'm not sure. I think she does.
Director: Why aren't you sure?
Bill: Well, I didn't tell her. You see, our decision to get a divorce was
    not based on the fact that I love another woman. We realized long
    ago that there is no reason for us to stay together, before I met my
    girl friend.
Director: What's your girl friend's name?
Bill: I prefer not to say.
Director: How about her first name?
Bill: As I said, I prefer not to say.
Director: Can you give her a fictitious name? It's easier for us to talk
    about someone when we know his or her name . . . any name.

Bill: OK. Let's call her Jane.

Director: (smiling) This is not her real name by any chance, is it?

Bill: (smiling) No, I made it up.

(The therapist wanted to reflect to the protagonist that his lack of openness indicates unnecessary self-guardedness. But he already knew that any direct suggestion to that effect will be denied by the protagonist. Instead, the director decided to make this point through action interpretation. He decided to design a hypothetical scene, a scene that may occur in the future.)

Director: Bill, five years from now, where are you?

Bill: Oh, I'm still in my home happily married to Jane.

Director: And your ex-wife, where is she?

Bill: She's living in the same town.

Director: I would like to set a situation that you and Jane are shopping in the supermarket and suddenly you meet your ex-wife. Please choose one group member to be Jane and one to be your ex-wife.

(Bill and Jane start walking in the supermarket and suddenly the ex-wife appears.)

(Ex-wife): (surprised) Bill. How are you? You look good.

Bill: (visibly uncomfortable) Fine, fine, and how are you?

(Ex-wife): OK. *(A long pause, then she looks at Jane. Silence.)*

Bill: Oh, this is Jane.

(Ex-wife): Hello, Jane.

Bill: Jane's . . . my wife. *(Suddenly, Bill sits down and starts crying.)*

Director: What are you crying about, Bill?

Bill: You see, when I introduced Jane I felt uncomfortable, but worse, for a moment I wished she was white. *(still crying)* I'm not ashamed. I love Jane, but as a liberal person I shouldn't have felt that way. *(turns to Jane)* I do love you very much.

(Jane): I know you do. And I love you too. I know that it isn't me whom you're uncomfortable with. What is it, then?

Bill: I suppose I'm still uncomfortable with the value system I grew up with.

(Jane): With the value system?

Bill: Well, with my parents who taught me that value system.

Director: When you say "parents," do mean both of them?

Bill: Yes, but actually I thought of my mother.

Designing techniques and scenes that can serve as action interpretation interventions is a very difficult task. In the example above, the intervention succeeded and the message was understood. Therefore, there was no need to reinterpret the situation in the ensuing closing stage. But sometimes therapists do not try to introduce action interpretations at all. Even if they do, their efforts may turn out to be ineffective either because of a faulty design or because the protagonist misses (or rejects) the intended message. In such circumstances there is a need to offer verbal interpretations. The recommended place for these is during the closing stage.

6. *Future plans.* Many sessions require that the protagonist implement the new learning in the outside world, especially when alternative modes of responding were practiced. Plans and strategies for such implementations can be discussed in the closing stage. These may include "home assignments" and discussions on future clinical role playing sessions and issues that they should focus on.

The closing stage usually closes the *session* and not necessarily the *issue* or the problem dealt with during the action stage. The closing stage, therefore, often serves as a *temporary closure,* the ending of one unit of the entire treatment process. Sometimes the same problem needs to be explored in several ways in several sessions. On other occasions, one session addresses only certain aspects of the problem and requires several sessions to be fully explored. A temporary closure implies that the issue will be reopened or further explored in the future, and in these cases future planning is indicated.

It is probably impractical to attend to all these six goals in one closing stage, which is supposed to last for about 20 percent of the session's time. Obviously, therapists must set priorities for each session, and depending on the circumstances, focus on those therapeutic goals that require their attention. The decision about which of the goals is to be addressed in the closing stage of a particular session is related to the nature of the presenting problem, the protagonist's behavior during the action stage, and the phase of the treatment. Having said this, it should be noted that some goals may be attended to simultaneously. Deroling is an issue that stands on its own. But the sharing process tends to address the protagonist's emotional stability and the issues of comfort and optimism together. The process of analysis typically includes the issues of both enhancing the protagonist's understanding and future planning.

The Third Segment of the Action Stage and Closure

The discussion of the three stages of the clinical role playing session addressed each stage as if it were an independent unit. But at the same time one should not forget that the three stages are intrinsically related to each other and together they form one whole structure. The significance of this point is that it is quite usual for two adjacent stages to overlap. For instance, the first stage, the warm-up, was said to prepare the protagonist to become involved in the role playing session. Increasing the protagonist's involvement is the central task of this stage, but this does not mean that a portion of this task cannot continue into the next stage. The action stage itself continues to deepen the protagonist's involvement, though at that point this becomes a secondary task.

The overlap between two adjacent stages is particularly relevant to the present discussion on the closing stage. Here we have a clearer illustration of how the central function of one stage is partially taken care of in another. Very often the closing of the session begins in the third segment of the action stage.

The general rule is that the closing stage does not include action, that is, closure here is not achieved by role playing enactments. The closing stage uses verbal techniques such as sharing, discussion, or analysis, or it may use nonverbal techniques such as the shaking of hands or a pat on the back to convey the message of sharing. At times, however, it is necessary to close the session through actual role playing enactments. For example, many issues explored in the action stage end with role playing scenes that indicate possible solution(s), alternative modes of responding, or the practice of new skills. Typically, these are introduced in the third segment of the action stage. These scenes are, of course, part and parcel of the treatment procedure, a phase in the therapy itself. But, in addition, they represent a closure, a way of bringing the entire issue to some sort of resolution. Therefore, such scenes actually serve as a part of the closure process, and it would be correct to say that the closing stage has, in fact, begun in the third segment of the action stage.

There are also sessions where the third segment of the action stage does not include solutions. Many times it is too early to suggest solutions, and further exploratory sessions are needed. Yet in order to close the session, a closure in terms of role playing enactments is often needed. Even if this is only a temporary closure, an attempt should be made to facilitate the transition from behavior under the rules of the psychological simulator to behavior that conforms to the environment outside the clinical role playing session. In this case, too, the third segment of the action stage serves as the beginning of the closing stage—a closure through action.

Like the construction of any scene, the ways to close the session through role playing enactments are indefinite and are left to the creative imagination of every therapist. But there is also a standard strategy for closing the action part that is commonly used and that can be introduced routinely. The idea is to construct a scene where the protagonist talks to someone or to a group of people about his or her experience in the session. This conversation may center on the conclusion that the protagonist drew from the session or what he would recommend to others who may have similar problems. The following illustrations will show the implementation of this principle in two separate cases.

The first example is the case of a protagonist who had a session on a problem that he described as his fear of being aggressive. In the exploration process, it became clear that this fear became prominent 16 years previously, when he was in the armed forces. During his military service he was involved in combat situations where he had killed numerous people on several occasions. But the most traumatizing experience was the first person he had to kill. The action stage itself included several scenes: a reenactment of the disturbing episode and scenes that focused on the protagonist's present reaction to the memory of the episode. During the role playing enactments the protagonist became very emotional. He cried out of fear and sorrow, mourned his victim, and felt guilty. The closing stage began with a scene that was triggered by a clue, as given in the following first line.

Protagonist: (at the end of the scene) You know that I'll never tell anyone outside therapy about this. Not even my family.
Director: And what would you do if they ask?
Protagonist: Who, my children?
Director: Whoever. Your children, your wife . . .
Protagonist: My wife knows she shouldn't ask. If my son, say, asks me, I won't tell him.
Director: I don't understand what you mean.
Protagonist: I'll lie if necessary.
Director: Why?
Protagonist: (a pause, then says in a quiet trembling voice) I don't want him to think that his father was a killer, though I know it was during a war. This is not my image of an ideal father.
Director: Is there an additional reason for not telling the truth as it was?
Protagonist: I guess I'm also afraid that he'll hate me.
Director: I'll tell you something. In real life you may choose not to tell. But here in the session you may. Why not try this, as an imaginary situation. See what it does to you.
Protagonist: OK, but only here.

Director: Very well, if that's what you want that's fine with me. Let's set a future projection scene. Your son is 20 years old. The two of you are talking on the porch. How do you think the subject will come out?

Protagonist: I don't know. Maybe he'll ask me.

Director: Ask what?

Protagonist: Well, you know, if I ever killed anyone during military service.

The scene was then enacted with the protagonist talking to his adult son. The point about whether or not he would eventually talk with his son was not an important objective of that scene. Rather the therapist wanted to bring the protagonist to relate to his disturbing experiences in a more rational, intellectual manner. Following the strong emotional outlet, a cognitive perspective could help the protagonist to "cover the wound" without avoiding the issues. This was the rationale for suggesting the scene, and it was the therapist's way of starting the closing stage.

The second example is that of a protagonist, a female in her early fifties, whose problem was that she could assert herself only by acting helpless and weak. One of the areas where she encountered difficulties was with her own family, specifically in her relationship with her son and daughter. At the end of the action stage, the therapist suggested the following scene:

Director: I have an idea for the last scene for today's session. Let us see if you think you can and want to do it. Now that you have explored one aspect of your behavior and how it is related to your relationship with your children, we can do a future projection scene. You are invited to a P.T.A. meeting to talk about some ways in which parents may get into trouble with their children and what they can do about it. The reason why you were invited as the guest speaker is that you have a personal experience which is worthwhile sharing with others. Would you like to try it? Your speech does not have to be long, say only a few minutes.

(The protagonist agrees.) OK. Here we are in the meeting. There are two dozen people in the room. *(The therapist puts two chairs to represent the audience and one chair in the front for the speaker.)* I will be the moderator and will introduce you.

The scene was set. The protagonist sat on the speaker's chair and the therapist introduced her to the imaginary audience. The protagonist gave a brief speech explaining her experience, what was found to be the problem, and so forth.

These kinds of closing scenes not only allow the protagonist to integrate his or her experiences in a more rational way, but they also help the therapist to see what was learned and if that corresponds to what the therapist wanted the protagonist to learn. With that information, the main closing stage could begin and generate meaningful discussion.

One final issue regarding the closing stage needs to be addressed. Sometimes, a seemingly well-conducted closing stage fails to accomplish its intended goal(s). I call this phenomenon *a premature closure*. A premature closure is usually evident in the behavior of a protagonist who responds to the sharing process in an inadequate manner. Behavior of this kind may be classified into two groups of responses. One group conveys a general posture of detachment. The protagonist appears preoccupied with himself or herself, inattentive to the statements of sharing, and tense. The protagonist feels restless, agitated, frustrated, emotionally aroused, and finds it difficult to concentrate on the discussion that constitutes the closing stage. The second group of responses reflects a general posture of negation and resistance. The protagonist appears impatient, argumentative, and combative. He or she will deny the relevance of the statements of sharing to his or her situation, will find such statements unhelpful, and will fight for more "air time" to dominate the discussion by talking about his or her problem(s).

The message conveyed through such responses is that, from the *protagonist's* point of view, the closing stage has been introduced prematurely and that the third segment of the *action stage*, which is supposed to result in a comfortable resolution, even a temporary one, has missed its target. Frustration on the part of the protagonist typically indicates that he or she feels displeased, dissatisfied, and perhaps short-changed. The expression of restlessness and anxiety indicates that the protagonist still feels helpless and lacks adequate control.

Therapists tend to respond to the manifestation of a premature closure with an extended discussion of possible resolutions. They try to complete the third segment of the action stage, after the fact, using verbal explanations and interpretations. The best approach, however, is to return at this point to the action stage: to design an additional role playing scene that will finish the action stage properly. It appears that the most satisfactory way to complete an action stage is to use the same actional language that characterized its first two segments.

CHAPTER 5

Planning the Scenario

In the preceding chapter the clinical role playing session has been presented in terms of its internal structure. The discussion focused on each of the three main components of the session: the warm-up stage, the action stage, and the closing stage. But the fact that each stage was discussed separately, was described as having some unique characteristics, and was said to serve a special function does not exclude an interdependency among stages. Indeed, each stage is regarded as one phase in the entire structure. The three stages are interrelated and together they form a complete structural whole.

The last point alludes to another facet of the clinical role playing session that deserves further elaboration. There are issues that transcend the specific characteristics of each individual stage and address the session as one entity—a complete unit. The term "scenario" denotes this facet and includes issues concerning the management of the entire session: its content, as well as the people who play important roles in it. Specifically, the present chapter will discuss the planning of the scenario, including strategies for managing the content of the role playing enactments and for planning the scenes, the length of the stages and the scenes, and the function of the clinical role playing team.

CLUES AND THEIR SELECTION

Determining the content of a scene depends on the kinds of clues that the therapist identifies in the process of observing the protagonist's role playing. A clue is an indication—a hint of the existence—of an actual or a potential area of difficulty related to the main complaints. There are several kinds of clues that therapists use in the course of every psychotherapeutic process, clinical role playing treatments included. Generally, the two main kinds are verbal and nonverbal clues. In clinical role playing, because the protagonist's difficulties are expressed through action, the nonverbal behavior becomes a richer source for generating clues than in traditional verbal forms of psychotherapy. Furthermore, an incongruence between the verbal and the nonverbal behavior itself often constitutes an important clue.

Kinds of Clues

Generally, clues may be divided into three kinds: verbal, nonverbal, and an incongruence between the verbal and the nonverbal behavior.

Verbal clues are expressed in a variety of ways. They may be explicit verbal statements given by the protagonist. For example, "I always feel anxious in the presence of someone in authority." Some verbal clues are subtle, that is, they are not offered directly by the protagonist but rather stem from the therapist's inferences from the presented descriptions. These may be expressed in the form of irrational beliefs, inconsistency in reporting a series of incidents, or in the symbolic meaning of the words chosen to describe a given fact, thoughts, or feelings. An example of the use of verbal clues can be seen in the case of John, the manager who role played a meeting with the vice-president of his company described in the preceding chapter (see p. 100). The reader may recall that the protagonist mentioned his dislike of the color of the curtains in the cocktail room and added that his office had the same kind of curtain. Later he failed to remember a picture that hung on one of the walls which was a view of his office building. These clues might indicate the presence of conflicting feelings regarding the place where the protagonist works. The therapist could have pursued this further to find out what was the meaning, if any, of these clues. Another form of verbal clue is a slip of the tongue. For example, a female protagonist was in the middle of a scene regarding her relationships to her father and mother. She maintained that she felt close to both of them. But at a certain point she responded to the question, "So, you feel close to your mother?" as follows:

Protagonist: Oh yes, I loathe my mother.
Director: Did I hear you saying loathe or love?
Protagonist: (begins to sob) I didn't think that I'd ever be able to bring myself to say that I have difficulties with mother.

Director: Well, now that you did, don't you think that it might be important to examine your feelings towards your mother in greater detail?

Nonverbal clues are sometimes harder to detect. They require good observation skills. Often even very experienced therapists miss them, especially if they happened to look in the wrong direction. The following is an example of a nonverbal clue based on an actual case. The protagonist was a university professor, a man in his early fifties. His presenting problem was that he contemplated changing his place of work; he had several offers from other universities but could not make up his mind. The first key scene took place in his office. At the end of the scene, where his inability to decide became clear, the therapist asked him whether he would seek advice from anyone. The protagonist replied that ordinarily he would discuss this with his wife, and in fact he did so. The therapist suggested that the next scene would be at home. The protagonist left the office and moved to the next scene. He got to his home, opened the door, and said "Hi" to his wife (portrayed by a female co-therapist). The greeting was brief and lacked warmth.

Director: Is that how you greet your wife when you come home?
Protagonist: Yes.
Director: Only "Hi"? No more words? No hug or a kiss?
Protagonist: Well, you caught me, didn't you?
Director: Tell me more, please.
Protagonist: Actually, we don't get along very well. As a matter of fact, we are in the process of divorce.
Director: Does this have anything to do with your inability to change your place of work and which offer to take?
Protagonist: Yes. I have a girl friend and she lives in another city. But she said that after the divorce comes through she'll join me wherever I decide to work, even at the university where I work now.
Director: Shall we explore that part of the issue in a separate scene?
Protagonist: (after a pause) I think we should.

The most intriguing clues are those based on a *disparity* between the protagonist's verbal and nonverbal behavior. Again, this kind of clue is often hard to detect. Furthermore, in terms of frequency it is less common than the other kinds of clues. Here is an example of a clue based on the incongruency between the verbal and nonverbal behavior of the protagonist. The protagonist was a female, a chief social worker with 25 years of experience. Her husband took a job in another city, and she, too, had to change her place of work. She had applied for the position of chief social worker in a large psychiatric institution. Prior to the scene she said that she was very confident that she would get the position (she did) and that she was not anxious at all. The scene was in the room of the superintendent at her final interview. Indeed, as the scene of the interview progressed her answers conveyed confidence, but her non-verbal behavior was awkward. She kept pushing her skirt in an attempt to continuously cover her knees. This behavior repeated itself so often that she looked terribly uncomfortable. At one point the therapist decided to use the Mirror technique (see Chapter 6). He asked the protagonist to step outside the action space and to watch an auxiliary portraying her behavior. After a few minutes the therapist joined the protagonist outside the action space and the following interaction took place:

Director: Did you notice anything in particular about the behavior of Linda mirrored by the auxiliary?

Linda: She kept pushing her skirt all the time.

Director: Why did she do this? Was she nervous about the interview?

Linda: It had nothing to do with the interview. You see *(now she changes from referring to herself in the third person, as the observer, to the first person),* one of my legs is thinner than the other. I was always self-conscious about it.

Director: Does it bother you?

Linda: You know, here I am almost a grandmother and I worry about this like a teenager. But it does disturb me. It always makes me feel insecure when I talk to people I don't know.

Director: We can end the interviewing scene here and explore these feelings in another scene. Shall we do that?

Linda: I should have mentioned this problem when we began instead of bringing the issue of that silly interview.

Selecting the Clues

The method the therapist uses for selecting the clues eventually leads to the formation of the clinical role playing scenario. The operation of this process requires further discussion of the meaning of clues, their relation to the setting of the scenes, and the effect of using different strategies for selecting clues on the shaping of the content of the session.

One way of understanding the meaning of clues is to regard them as signs for the beginning of creative acts. Characteristically, there is no distinction between conscious and unconscious in the creating mind. The unconscious is the reservoir that feeds the act of creation and is continuously filled and emptied by the creator. The creative act is spontaneous, unexpected, and strives to produce mimetic behavioral effects. The following excerpt captures the essence of the creative act, which is also true for the understanding of the meaning of clues.

> In the spontaneous-creative enactment emotions, thoughts, processes, sentences, pauses, gestures, movements, etc., seem first to break formlessly and in anarchistic fashion into an ordered environment and settled consciousness. But in the course of their development it becomes clear that they belong together like the tones of a melody; that they are in relation similar to the cells of a new organism. The disorder is only an outer appearance; inwardly there is a consistent driving force, a plastic ability, the urge to assume a definite form. . . . (Moreno,1964a, p. 36)

Clues, too, manifest themselves as hints, shapeless concepts, and fragments of ideas. As the beginning of a creative act they seem first to break formlessly but then they require a platform, a medium where they can be expressed in an orderly fashion. That medium can be provided by the therapist in the form of a scene, a situation where the act may be consumed for the purpose of fulfilling the need.

The shaping of the content of the scenario is, therefore, a joint effort. It is a creative act shared by both the protagonist and the therapist. The protagonist produces the clues and the therapist helps to set the scenes, that is, arranges situational circumstances and provides the necessary conditions, which facilitate enactments that bring the protagonist to attain psychotherapeutic gains. It is obvious that the role of the therapist—his or her contribution to the development of the scenario—can be quite substantial.

This role of the therapist is not always as simple as it may appear at first glance. It puts him or her in a very delicate position because he or she must maintain an appropriate balance between his or her input and that of the protagonist. It requires a constant awareness and an active attention to ensure that the therapist's understanding of the presented clues is correct and in harmony with the protagonist's intentions and needs. The setting of scenes ought to be congruent with the direction that the protagonist wishes to pursue. This point becomes further complicated because clues may come from the protagonist as well as from the therapist. The therapist can become a partner to the creative act by intuition, that is, he or she intuitively identifies a clue that the protagonist does not offer directly. Examples of such clues are those that are *inferred* from the behavior of the protagonist. The potential difficulty in these situations is that here the therapist, in addition to his or her role as facilitator, acts also as an initiator in that he or she not only sets the scene, but also provides the clues.

The danger is, of course, that the therapist may err in his or her intuition and judgment. Even if the therapist is right, his or her timing might be inappropriate. Even if the timing is right, he or she might be too forceful. Therefore, a sensitive strategy for selecting the clues is needed in order to maintain an appropriate balance between forcing a scene on the protagonist and moving along with his or her needs and state of readiness.

In the extremes there are two strategies: *self-initiated* and *externally initiated*. The *self-initiated* strategy or approach maintains that the freedom for determining the content of the scenario lies entirely in the hands of the protagonist. The scenes are built around clues provided only by the protagonist or by the protagonist together with auxiliaries. The function of the auxiliaries will be described later in this chapter. The assumption is that there is a relationship between the protagonist's state of readiness and the offering of relevant clues. Therefore, a lack of a clue may signify that the protagonist is not yet ready to confront the issue. When a therapist has a hypothesis concerning the presenting complaints but no clues are offered by the protagonist, he or she should wait and refrain from setting scenes concerning that hypothesis until a relevant clue comes along. The selection of the clues is limited to those produced by the protagonist, directly or indirectly, openly or covertly.

The *externally-initiated* strategy or approach differs from the former one. Thus, clues may come from either the protagonist or the therapist. In fact, there is a greater emphasis on clues that emanate from the therapist. The assumption here is that while the protagonist provides the basic data related to his or her difficulties, it is the therapist who can make the interpretations and the judgments and who can formulate what accounts for their emergence. Scenes may be constructed on the basis of clues provided by the protagonist. But most of the important scenes are based on clues offered on the initiative of the therapist.

The *externally-initiated* strategy is mostly favored in role playing enactments used for teaching, demonstrations, and training purposes. Many of the group, as well as individual, role playing exercises that appear in the literature on group training stem from this approach. The scenes (i.e., the role playing situations) are set in advance, based on predetermined clues (see, e.g., some of the exercises described in Morris & Cinnamon, 1974, 1975). In clinical role playing (i.e., when role playing is used as a method of psychotherapy) the *self-initiated* strategy is often favored. In the context of psychotherapy there is a danger involved in selecting clues based on the *externally-initiated* strategy. This strategy may invite, or often even evoke, resistance on the part of the protagonist. It tends to encourage therapists to exercise undue pressure on their protagonists. And perhaps the most common pitfall associated with this strategy is that therapists may become preoccupied with their own clues at the expense of missing clues provided by the protagonist.

But there are also advantages to the *externally-initiated* strategy, even in the context of clinical role playing. The best recommendation for a method for selecting the clues is, therefore, a combination of both strategies with a somewhat greater emphasis on the *self-initiated* one.

THE FLOW OF THE SCENARIO

The scenario consists of a number of role playing situations—key and connecting scenes—which ideally should flow in a certain pattern. The term "flow" refers to the way these scenes move from one episode to another, to the rhythm in which they reach the climax of the session and its ending. The management of the flow is often a difficult task. First, it largely depends on the protagonist's involvement and cooperation. Second, it depends on the topic, the issue presented for the role playing enactment. Third, it is not unusual for therapists to have no preconception of what is involved in the presenting problem until its various aspects unfold during the action stage. This excludes preplanning, and the flow has to be handled on the spot, step by step, like an impromptu production. Notwithstanding these complications, there are some guiding principles that can help attain a smooth and elegant flow. These will be discussed in the next sections.

Gradual Progression

The content of the scenario progresses from the superficial manifestations of the problem to the core. It begins with the overt manifestations and reaches the basic, underlying components of the problem, those that contribute to its emergence and maintain the disturbing behavior. The direction of this progression follows the principle of *from the periphery to the center*, which was already described in the preceding chapter in connection with the discussion on the development of the warm-up process.

Another characteristic of the progression of the scenario is that the content (i.e., the scenes) moves in a *gradual* manner, step by step. The enactment begins with a scene in the first segment of the action stage and gradually reaches its peak in the last scene of the second segment of this stage. Sometimes the pace of this gradual development is slower and the peak is reached in the third segment of the action stage.

To illustrate the principle of the gradual progression of the content, let us consider a hypothetical case. Suppose a therapist conducts a clinical role playing session that include two key scenes in each of the three segments of the action stage—six scenes altogether. For the purpose of our illustration we shall disregard the connecting scenes. The ideal line of progression should look like the illustration shown in Figure 5.1, Part B, as represented by the shading and the curved line. Each step in the shading represents a key scene, and one can clearly see the gradual progression in the action stage from the first segment to the peak at the second segment followed by a gradual decline in the third segment. The ascending curve represents the emotional intensity of the role-played content, its importance, and its relevance to the core of the difficulty. The closer it comes to the peak, the more emotionally intense and more relevent is the scene.

Determining the Focus of the Scenario

The protagonist who presents a problem or a conflict for the clinical role playing session does not make a judgment whether the complaint encompasses the entire scope of the problem, parts of it, or even if the presentation is merely the façade for another, more important problem. The presenting problem is a statement of anguish, not necessarily a psychological diagnosis of what discomforts him or her. It is the task of the therapist to make such evaluations and diagnoses based on his or her professional knowledge and skill.

In order to plan the flow of the scenario, the therapist must make a decision prior to the enactment proper. As the therapist hears the presenting complaint, he or she must *decide where to begin*. Basically the therapist is confronted with two options or clinical strategies. One, he or she may regard the presenting complaint as an accurate statement of the *real issue*. Second, he or she may regard it as the outward manifestation of *something else*, a more important issue. The criteria for adopting the first or the second strategy are complex and often vary depending on (a) the nature of the problem or the stated difficulty, and (b) the therapist's own conceptualization of the relationships between overt manifestations and core factor—symptoms and their causes. Our concern, here, is merely with procedural aspects, that is, how each of the two strategies determines the planning of the scenario.

Figure 5.1 illustrates that point. The figure is divided into two parts: A and B, one above the other. Each part illustrates one of the two strategies mentioned above.

Part A of Figure 5.1 illustrates the first strategy where the therapist considers the presenting complaint as the *real issue* and therefore decides that it will be the high point, the focus of the session. The circle around the second segment of the action stage represents this decision. It implies that the exploration and interpretation part of the action stage will address the presenting complaint as stated by the protagonist. Having decided on this strategy, the therapist is faced now with the task of finding a way to begin the session with scenes that *preamble* the central

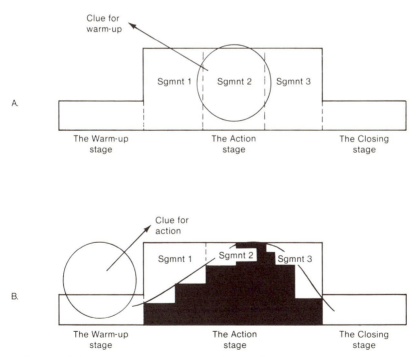

Figure 5.1. Illustration of two approaches for determining the issues to be dealt with in the action stage.

scene. He or she must find clues for scenes that will gradually lead to the enactment of the presenting complaint now slotted to be portrayed in the second segment of the action stage. That task is represented by the arrow that points from the circle to the left of the diagram, to the beginning of the session. Pursuing this task may take different forms and we will mention only two very common ones.

One is the use of the *temporal regression* principle described in the case of Mary and her tiredness (see pp. 88-90). In that example the therapist decided to go back in time and explore the situation(s) preceding that in which the main complaint expressed itself. Such scenes serve as the role playing antecedents of the main scene.

Therapists may also use the principle of *moving the context of the presenting complaint.* "Moving the context" implies the transfer of the presenting difficulties to another time dimension, another situation with other people. This is a somewhat sophisticated operation and it works in the following way: The therapist begins the action stage by asking the protagonist to role play and demonstrate a current situation where the presenting difficulties manifest themselves. But in the mind of the therapist this enactment is regarded as a preamble, not the focal scene. Following this, the therapist asks the protagonist to think of another typical situation in a more distant past, in a different place, involving the same or preferably other people, where he or she encountered *similar difficulties.* Now the second segment of the action stage focuses on the same presenting complaint but in the context of past analogue(s).

Part B of Figure 5.1 illustrates the second strategy where the therapist considers the presenting complaint as the outward manifestation of *something else,* a more important issue. The presenting complaint is merely a symptom of a more substantive disturbance, which may still await uncovering but ought to be dealt with in the second segment of the action stage. This more substantive disturbance is the focus of this session. Here the therapist's decision is illustrated in Figure 5.1, Part B, and represented in the circle. The arrow that points to the right of the diagram signifies that the real issue, the focus of the session, will come later, pending the solicitation of pertinent clues.

The most common way in which the second strategy is implemented involves the process of *action associations.* This process is similar to the technique of verbal associations used in traditional forms of psychoanalysis, except that action association is based on the protagonist's total behavior: experiential—cognitive, emotional, and actional—similarities between one set of behavior and another set. The way the action associations process works is as follows: The therapist begins the action stage with a scene that portrays a situation where the present difficulties manifest themselves. During this enactment a new clue ought to be identified. This clue serves as the basis for another scene during which, again, a new clue is sought. The idea is that through the process of action associations the protagonist will lead the scenario to the central core of his or her difficulties. At each point in that process the therapist must asssess any additional clue in terms of whether or not it helps to reach the desired peak. Ideally, two or three scenes built on the basis of the action associations' process ought to bring the scenario to its high point.

Sometimes, however, one encounters a situation where the protagonist does not provide meaningful clues as readily and as quickly as one would wish. Consequently the use of the action associations' process as an attempt to find a central scene that captures the focus of the presenting complaint seems chaotic. One scene follows another in a manner that appears to lead nowhere. Once the development of the scenario begins to take this shape, the therapist will be wise to end the process and resort to other means if possible. Alternatively, the therapist may opt to change the emphasis of the session and to look for a new focus for the scenario. This new focus may address a less important aspect of the presenting complaint than the original focus. But having *a* focus is better than an aimless search to *the* focus. Sometimes in the course of using action associations there is a point where the scene is virtually over but there is no clue to suggest how to proceed. Here, therapists often fall into common traps. Either they tend to continue the scene endlessly hoping that with more action something will come up, or they construct a new scene "out of the clear blue sky," often forcing an issue where it is not indicated.

In the event that the session comes to a dead end it is advisable to terminate the scene altogether. At this point the therapist may proceed with a connecting scene, the kind used after a key scene (see p. 97). Alternatively he may simply ask the protagonist, "What shall we do next?" or "Where do we go from here?" He may also ask the protagonist, "What does this scene remind you of?" or "Do you recall a situation where you felt somewhat similar to the way you felt in the last scene?" In a group therapy situation the therapist may turn to the group members and solicit their ideas. The basic principle underlying these kinds of solutions is that therapists must take actions that increase the chances of picking up new clues. And if *they* cannot find such clues, *others* might.

THE LENGTH OF THE STAGES AND THE SCENES

In the beginning of the discussion of the clinical role playing session it was already pointed out that the length of the session may vary. A clinical role playing session may be brief, as short as half an hour or as long as 90 minutes depending on the circumstances. Therefore, a discussion on the length of each of the three stages will be more meaningful if expressed in terms of the percentages of the session's time rather than in absolute time units.

Figure 5.2 illustrates the division of the session in terms of its duration. The horizontal line under the diagram displays the time dimension and the numbers represent the points where each stage ends and the next one begins. Underneath the time dimension continuum the ideal duration of each stage is presented in terms of percentages of the session's time. Thus 15% of the time is allocated to the warm-up stage, the action stage gets about 65% of the time, and the closing stage is recommended to last for the remaining 20% of the session's time.

This division of the session's time ought to be regarded as a recommendation, not as a rigid rule. There are many circumstances that require departures from this time plan. Some of these will be discussed in the next section.

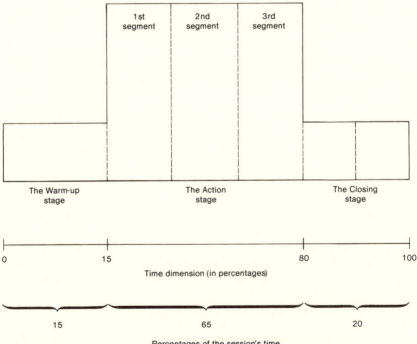

Figure 5.2. The length of the stages

Changing the Length of the Stages

There are times when the therapist may decide or even may be advised to alter the recommended length of one or more stages of the session. The circumstances that call for such changes vary but generally fall into two groups: changes predicated on protagonist-related factors, and on therapist-related factors.

The most important *protagonist-related* factors are the degree of readiness or warm-up and the familiarity with the role playing language. Protagonists who are quick to warm up or who come to the session already warmed up may require a shorter time for the warm-up stage. But those who are slow to warm up made need an extended warm-up stage, one that lasts longer than 15% of the time. Naturally, the length of the warm-up stage determines the length of the action stage. A brief warm-up stage allows a longer period for the second stage, whereas an extended warm-up will curtail the action stage. In either case, the length of the closing stage should not be altered. The other factor is the protagonist's familiarity with the role playing "language." Protagonists who are familiar with that mode of expression may require a shorter action stage. Familiarity enhances the process and more can be accomplished in less time. A lack of familiarity may slow the process and hence may require a longer action stage.

Therapist-related factors refer to the purpose of the session as determined by the therapist. Obviously these factors cannot be divorced from those discussed above. Thus, a therapist may decide to devoted most of the session to warming-up the protagonist. This is a typical situation, especially in the beginning of the treatment. In that case the action stage will be quite brief, or even becomes part of the warm-up where the entire session is construed as a warming-up session. Or a therapist may decide that he does not want his protagonist to role play every aspect of the problem during the session. Instead, he may ask the protagonist to focus on two scenes only. The rest of the related aspects he may choose to discuss verbally. In that case the action stage may last less than the recommended 65% of the session, and the closing stage becomes longer.

Notwithstanding the reasons for changing the length of the stages, it is strongly recommended that the 15:65:20% ratio should not be upset to any great degree, except when an unusual situation demands it.

The Length of the Action Stage with Complex Problems

When the presenting problem seems very complex, there are more related issues that need exploration. If each of these issues must be portrayed in a separate scene, the action stage becomes very long. Such an action stage may result in several adverse effects. It may leave no time for the closing stage. It may cause an early fatigue on the part of the protagonist, and it may also cause him or her to lose the focus of the session.

When a therapist realizes the complexity of a given presenting problem, his or her best strategy is to deal with it in *several sessions*. Each session may address one part of, or one set of aspects related to, the problem. In this way the action stage of every session will not exceed the recommended duration, and the entire session can be treated as a complete interim whole. Protagonists usually prefer that approach and acquiesce to it readily provided it is clearly explained to them by their therapists.

Omitting Any Stage

In principle a clinical role playing session should include the three stages. None should be omitted. The fact that some therapists tend, sometimes, to omit the warm-up stage or the closing stage can only be deplored. But experience has shown that when one works with the *same protagonist* over a long period of time, the warm-up and the closing stages become shorter and shorter. The more experienced the protagonist in the role playing procedure, the greater the emphasis on the action stage.

A related issue is that of omitting not an entire stage but a portion of a stage. In the action stage this may be expressed by focusing on diagnostic issues and excluding corrective ones or vice versa. In the closing stage it may be expressed in introducing the sharing part only, or omitting the sharing and instead focusing on the analysis. There is no question that such omissions are allowed, but only when the therapist has good reasons to support the decision to omit one part or another. In the process of contemplating an omission the therapist ought to weigh both the advantages and the disadvantages of such a decision. The omission of the sharing part may affect the protagonist in one way, and excluding the analysis part may affect him or her in another. Unfortunately, there are no hard rules to facilitate such decisions. The therapist has only his or her best professional judgment and sensitivity to rely on.

The Length of Scenes

Perhaps the most important aspect concerning the length of scenes is that, on the whole, they are short episodes. Generally, there is no observed direct relationship between the effectiveness of a scene and its duration except in the extremes, where an adverse relationship is usually noted.

Establishing clear rules regarding the recommended length of clinical role playing scenes is obviously a difficult, if not an impossible, task. For instance, the length of scenes might depend on the duration of the entire session and in particular that of the action stage. The length also depends on the content of the scene: whether it lends itself to complex and involved interactions or not, and whether it represents the focus of the scenario or a step leading into it. The length of a scene may vary depending on its kind. A connecting scene is brief, while a key scene is usually noticeably longer. Recognizing these considerations and limitations, the therapist can use one guiding rule with some degree of certainty: Experience has shown that the 15-minute mark ought to serve as a warning signal. A scene lasting for that length of time without a sign of near termination is too long. Typically, the scenario should not exceed five key scenes and two or three connecting scenes.

In the process of building the scenario, on the way to reaching the focus of the session, *an important clue* given in the course of a scene *justifies the termination of this scene*, even abruptly. The clue is used now for constructing a new scene. Once the session has reached its focus, longer scenes might be appropriate, but again within reasonable time limits.

THE CLINICAL ROLE PLAYING TEAM

In the preceding chapters there have been several allusions to the fact that a classic clinical role playing session involves more than two persons: a therapist and his or her client. The example of Bill, his ex-wife, and Jane (see Chapter 4) clearly indicates that other people may join the enactment by portraying significant persons in the protagonist's life. Where do these helpers come from? Traditionally, clinical role playing is applied in a group setting, that is, group therapy, a couple's therapy, or a family therapy. The availability of group members who may also serve as helper, the therapist, and a single protagonist who emerges from the group led to the creation of the concept the clinical role playing *team*.

Most writings on the clinical role playing team describe it in terms of the role or roles of each member of the team (e.g., Blatner, 1973; Moreno, 1964a; Starr, 1977; Yablonsky, 1976). This is based on the assumption that each team member had a number of functions to perform and that these functions are unique to his or her role. But experience has shown that sometimes the same person may serve in several functions, one at a time. In fact, the number of people that comprises the clinical role playing team may vary. In the extreme—admittedly a rather unusual situation—the "team" is comprised of one individual. This is the case of an autodrama where the protagonist serves also as his or her own therapist as well as in the role of the auxiliary. In individual role playing treatment, both the therapist and the protagonist may temporarily assume the function of the auxiliaries. Therefore, I prefer to discuss the clinical role-playing team not in terms of the *people* who comprise the team but rather in terms of the therapeutic *tasks and functions* that are being served. The clinical role playing team consists of people who must fulfill at least three functions: the function of the *director* (the therapist), the function of the *auxiliaries* (the co-therapists), and the function of the *protagonist* (the client, the patient). Where three or more people are present in the treatment situation, a fourth function is added: that of the *group member(s)*. Each of these four functions will be described in detail in the remaining sections of this chapter.

The Function of the Director (the Therapist)

The "director" is the clinical role playing or psychodramatic term for the "therapist." The main function of the director is to conduct the treatment session: to assume the responsibility for its psychotherapeutic aspects and for the proper use of the clinical role playing method.

The preceding definition of the function(s) of the director is too general to convey the complexity of the task. According to Moreno (1964a) the director's functions are: a producer, a chief therapist, and a social analyst.

> As a producer he is an engineer of coordination and production . . . he tries to find his audience and characters first, drawing from them the material for a plot. With their assistance he turns out a production which meets the personal and collective needs of the characters as well as the audience at hand. As a therapeutic agent, the last responsibility for the therapeutic value of the total production rests upon his shoulders. It is a function of over-all guidance whose manipulations are often carefully disguised. His task is to make the subjects act, to act on that spontaneous level which benefits their total equilibrium, to prompt . . . and to stir up the audience to a cathartic experience. As a social analyst

he uses the auxiliary egos as extensions of himself to draw information from the subjects . . . to test them, and to carry influence
to them. (p. 252)

The role of the director and his or her function(s) was also described
as follows:

The director is the prime coordinator and the *catalyst* of a session.
With the group input he determines who will be the protagonist
and orchestrates the flow of the session.

The director must constantly diagnose the situation . . . and
create new situations by means of which self-defeating patterns
have maximal opportunity for being resolved. It is essential that
the director have the ability to think on his feet and observe the
nonverbal as well as the verbal communication cues in the protagonist and the group . . . in such a manner that insight and learning
is achieved. (Yablonsky, 1976. p.111)

A survey of the literature shows that the function of the director is
described in many different ways. A compiled list of these includes terms
such as a catalyst, a coordinator (Yablonsky, 1976), a producer, a therapist, a social analyst, a social investigator (Moreno, 1964a), an enabler
(Fink, 1968), to mention only a few. The existence of such a list does
not necessarily indicate a disagreement regarding the function of the
director. In fact, some of the terms are somewhat synonymous. More
likely the list reflects the realization that this fuction is multifaceted and
complex. The role of the director involves several functions, responsibilities, and tasks. Although each of these can be described independently
they are interrelated and together comprise what is commonly known
as "the function of the director." The following list (Table 5.1) summarizes the many facets of the role of the director.

The functions, responsibilities, and tasks of the director summarized
in the list require some further clarification, which is offered in the
following.

1. Therapist. The clinical role playing director is first a psychotherapist.
This function stems from appropriate professional training and skills
which qualify him or her to treat psychological conflicts and behavioral
disorders. As a theraupeutic agent it is the director's responsibility to
render a professional psychotherapeutic service. In the context of clinical
role playing the following tasks are needed:

TABLE 5.1
The Role of the Director: A Summary List

Function	Main Responsibility	Central Tasks
1. Therapist	Securing the psychotherapeutic value of the session	a. Observation b. Assessment c. Planning
2. Producer	The introduction, construction, and maintenance of the method of clinical role playing	a. Warming-up b. Identifying clues c. Selecting scenes d. Closing
3. Catalyst	Facilitating the therapeutic value of the session through the medium of clinical role playing	a. Constructing scenes b. Using auxiliaries c. Using special techniques d. Participation e. Modeling and coaching

(a) *Observation.* As a therapist the director is not physically involved in the action, that is, he places himself outside the action space. He works " . . . with the minimum expenditure of emotional energy . . . keeping himself at a distance, objective and uninvolved"(Moreno,1964a, p. 257). Unlike other forms of therapy he need not carry the responsibility of actually running the session. The stimuli for the interactions are provided by others, auxiliaries if available, and by the very nature of the scene itself. In that way he has the time and the freedom to observe the enactments.

(b) *Assessment.* Using this time and freedom the director assesses and evaluates continuously the presented material. This constant assessment allows him to introduce different interventions, shift the focus of the action, and entertain the possibility of changing scenes.

(c) *Planning.* The director is under a continuous obligation to make decisions. In the context of clinical role playing this is an especially taxing duty, since he must make not only therapeutic decisions, but also role playing decisions. There are literally dozens of such decisions that are being made in every session.

2. Producer. This function of the director is unique to the method of clinical role playing. Production involves the responsibility of introducing the method of clinical role playing, that is, getting the protagonist to work on the presenting complaints through role playing enactments. This function also involves the responsibility of moving the protagonist through the three stages of the session.

(a) *Warming-up.* This task concerns the preparation of the protagonist to protray his or her difficultios by means of role playing. In group treatment it requires the creation of an atmosphere conducive to the emergence of a potential protagonist.

(b) *Identifying clues.* The director actively seeks clues for the scenes. This may be achieved by means of questioning and interviewing the protagonist, by observing the behavior during the actual enactments, and by consulting the auxiliaries—the co-therapists or members of the group—if available.

(c) *Selecting scenes.* The director establishes, preferably in concert with the protagonist, the content of each scene. In determining the content, only minimal coercion on the part of the director is allowed. This is because clinical role playing is conducted on the premise that protagonists act out the truth as they perceive it in a completely subjective manner and regardless of how distorted this appears to the observer (Z.T. Moreno, 1965). Gradually, with the successful progress of the therapy the subjective truth ought to become compatible with adequate coping. Selecting the scenes also involves decisions concerning their length: when a scene should be prolonged, shortened, or completely terminated.

(d) *Closing.* The director decides on the form by which the session is to be closed, taking into consideration the nature of the portrayed enactment, the individual needs of the protagonist, the reactions of the group members, and their needs.

3. *Catalyst.* This function combines the functions of the therapist and the producer. Here the director serves as the brain and the designer behind the production. In a nutshell, the function of the catalyst is to accelerate the therapeutic process by providing the protagonist with the best opportunities for achieving optimal relief and new learning. The function of the director as a catalyst is the culmination of his expertise as a therapist.

(a) *Constructing the scenes.* A good scene is that which addresses a critical incident and provides a combination of circumstances that can best help the protagonist. Scenes should be constructed in such a way to facilitate the elicitation of the psychological processes and the behavioral skills most relevant to the issue under treatment. They should stimulate the protagonist to react and interact in the desired direction. For example, if the issue is the expression of anger, the scene must offer the best context for expressing anger. If the issue is that the protagonist is unaware of his or her self-defeating behavior, the scene ought to provide the best context for confronting the protagonist with the existence of such behavior on his or her part. The construction of good scenes is one area where the functuon of the director as a catalyst can be expressed best.

(b) *Using auxiliaries.* Auxiliaries are helpers—co-therapists in roles other than that of the protagonist, which are introduced in the action (the function of the auxiliaries will be discussed in the next section). Auxiliaries direct the action to meaningful avenues and to central issues. They also serve as training agents. Therefore, they are one of the most important therapeutic tools available to the director.

(c) *Using special techniques.* The effectiveness of clinical role playing is directly related to the use of its special techniques (see also the next chapter).

(d) *Participation.* The director's participation in the clinical role playing treatment is a very delicate issue and to some extent is influenced by personal style. The rule, however, is that on the one hand he should stay as the catalyst behind the scene, yet on the other, he also must form, at least in certain crucial moments, a cooperative relationship with protagonist acting as a partner. Partnership might be established in two ways: direct and indirect. Direct partnership is expressed through actual involvement, that is, when the director assumes the role of an auxiliary. The indirect partnership involves imparting feelings of care, empathy, understanding, and support which manifest themselves through the act of directing the session and verbal communications on the part of the director. Acting in a direct partnership manner has serious disadvantages. First, it leaves the session without a director, at least for a few moments. Second, since the director cannot be an observer and a full participant simultaneously, there is the danger that neither role will be performed properly. Finally, it may have an undesirable impact on other group members or the auxiliaries. They may feel untrustworthy or failing to serve as competent helpers. Notwithstanding these disadvantages, direct participation on the part of the director may be indicated in crucial moments. In clinical role playing used in individual therapy it is unavoidable.

(e) Modeling and coaching. Therapeutic progress can be attained through the use of modeling procedures: direct-contact or vicarious modeling (Bandura, 1977). Directors should shy away from offering personal modeling except when it is the best alternative. Other alternatives are the use of auxiliaries or instructing the protagonist to behave differently along prescribed guildelines.

Finally, in a clinical role playing session there *can be only one* director. That person may be assisted by other participants in several ways. But the final responsibility rests on his or her shoulders. Where a professional co-therapist is available, both the director and the co-therapist must agree to coordinate their functions in a manner that leaves the ultimate decisions and responsibilities to the director. Furthermore, the director is advised not to leave the session leaderless—a practice that is unfortunately common—by assuming other roles. The exceptions to this rule are (a) in individual treatment where in the absence of auxiliaries the director has no alternative but to assume the role of a helper from time to time, and (b) in instances where the contribution of an auxiliary is limited to a very brief input. Here the director may step into the role of the auxiliary but only for a very short period of time.

The Function of the Auxiliaries

The auxiliaries are individuals who participate in the clinical role playing session as helpers—co-therapists. In the psychodramatic nomenclature these are referred to as the auxiliary-egos, a term coined by Moreno (1964a). I prefer to call them simply the *auxiliaries,* though their function is identical to that ascribed to the auxiliary-egos. The auxiliaries can portray aspects of the protagonist when required but typically they portray other persons, concepts, and objects not actually represented in the treatment situation, but having a direct relevance to it. They are instrumental in the construction of the action through the ". . .representation of absentees, individuals, delusions, hallucinations, symbols, ideas, animals, and objects. They make the protagonist's world real, concrete, and tangible" (Z.T. Moreno, 1966, p. 152).

The representations made by the auxiliaries need not be exact replications of the objective reality. Approximations of that reality are usually sufficient, provided that they are close enough to *make the protagonist believe and feel as if he or she confronts the real things.* The assumed role must be protrayed in a manner that is authentic enough to make the protagonist *imagine* that the situation is real. Furthermore, the auxiliaries' portrayals are often exaggerated and amplified beyond their real proportions. This process of exaggeration is one of the unique characteristics of this method and makes it a powerful therapeutic tool.

The role of the auxiliaries is summarized in Table 5.2 which is divided into three categories: function, responsibility, and tasks.

The auxiliaries, when asked to participate in a clinical role playing session, serve in a dual capacity. They function as extensions of the protagonist and at the same time as extensions of the director. These functions are performed simultaneously. For the purpose of the present discussion each will be described seperately.

1. An extension of the protagonist. Protagonists are often overwhelmed by the scenes in which they find themselves. At such times, they need help to promote self-disclosure and self-expression. They also need external stimulations to get going, in order to confront a difficult situation and to mobilize their yet undeveloped coping mechanisms. It is the function of the auxiliaries as the extension of the protagonist to provide such help.

(a) *Facilitating expressions.* The auxiliary establishes close and empathic relationships with the protagonist. He facilitates the protagonist to reach a fuller self-disclosure, a cathartic experience; to ventilate fears and anxieties; and to openly discuss wishes, hopes, and disturbing memories.

TABLE 5.2
The Role of the Auxiliaries: A Summary List

Function	Main Responsibility	Central Tasks	
1. Extension of the protagonist	Helping the protagonist in self-expression, confrontations, and coping	a.	Facilitating expressions
		b.	Focusing the action
		c.	Support
2. Extension of the director	Assisting the director in his diagnosis, guidance, and implementing corrective procedures	a.	Providing information and clues
		b.	Developing the interactions
		c.	Rehearsing the protagonist

(b) *Focusing the action.* Through the process of achieving a fuller self-disclosure, the auxiliary helps the protagonist to articulate his or her thoughts and actions. The purpose of this is to focus the attention on what is experienced as the most important issue of the presenting complaints.

(c) *Support.* In the course of the enactment the protagonist often feels alone in his or her difficulties, bewildered and paralyzed by the conflicts that he or she experiences, and weak or inept in the attempt to cope with the problems. In these very common instances it is the task of the auxiliary to come forth and to give support and encouragement. These may be expressed in the form of offering empathy, opening new possibilities for evaluating the issue at hand, and reinforcing the healthy and strong aspects of the protagonist's behavior.

2. *An extention of the director.* Auxiliaries are also co-therapists. They serve as therapeutic agents used by the director in order to implement the treatment. Therefore, the auxiliaries must be in concert with and attuned to the thinking of the director, supply him with maximal information and clues, and execute his instructions. They are expected to accomplish these tasks to the best of their ability whether or not they fully understand or even accept the director's approach. If they strongly disgree and hence find it difficult to execute the directives, they should step down and be replaced by other auxiliaries. The main tasks of the auxiliaries here are as follows:

(a) *Providing information and clues.* Often the information provided by the protagonist spontaneously is not sufficient to shed light on the presenting complaints or to suggest a direction which the role playing can go. Auxiliaries can assist the director and elicit more information through their interactions with the protagonist. Similarly, often protagonists do not offer *meaningful* clues. The auxiliary who has established some degree of empathic relationship with the protagonist is in an ideal position to help. He can identify key words that may serve as clues, he can offer them directly, and he can solicit clues from the protagonist through through intensive probing and self-search.

(b) *Developing the interactions.* The auxiliaries who portray roles of others have the responsibility to maintain the flow and the development of the scene because a protagonist who role plays by himself or herself may quickly reach an impasse. The following excerpt illustrates this and the task of the auxiliary.

Director: Here, David, is an empty chair. You said a few moments ago that you would like to meet your sister, Jane, who lives in another country, right? *(David agrees.)* OK, I'd like you to imagine that Jane is sitting in the empty chair. Tell her whatever you wanted to tell her.

David: Hi! Actually I wanted to see you *(He talks to the empty chair.)* and tell you that I am angry with you. No! To be honest, I hate you. Now that I look back on what happened between the two of us I realize that you really hurt me. I just wanted to tell you that.

Director: Anything more you want to say? Maybe you want to explain yourself?

David: No, that's it. Believe me it's quite enough.

Director: Why don't you select someone who may help you, say someone who will be Jane. Let that person sit in the chair as Jane. OK? Who looks a little bit like Jane? *(David selects an auxiliary.)*

Jane (Auxiliary): What the hell do you mean, David?

David: I've said enough.

Jane (Auxiliary): No you haven't. You throw this to me like that? I think I deserve an explanation. You know it hurts me, too, to hear you saying such things about me.

David: All right, I'll tell you. During all these years that we were together you . . . (etc.).

(c) *Rehearsing the protagonist.* When the director wishes to offer the protagonist an opportunity to practice a new way of responding, he uses auxiliaries as helpers. The auxiliaries portray roles that encourage the protagonist to practice, which can help him or her to gain some success. Their performance should gradually resemble what one might be expected to encounter in the real world. Such rehearsals can be made as easy or as difficult as the director deems advisable.

Auxiliaries may be professional people, that is, individuals who are trained as therapists, nurses, social workers, group facilitators, and so forth. They may also be individuals who have experience in clinical role playing. Such auxiliaries are usually preferred in clinical role playing sessions conducted with hospitalized clientele—protagonists with severe disturbances. In other instances, including a hospital situation, where clinical role playing is conducted in group therapy sessions, other members of the group serve as auxiliaries. In individual therapy sessions, the role of the auxiliaries has to be portrayed by the therapist himself and sometimes by the protagonist.

The number of auxiliaries that can be introduced in the course of clinical role playing session or in one scene may vary from one to many more. It depends on the nature of the particular scene and the availability of the auxiliaries. One may use a few auxiliaries simultaneously, though usually no more than four or five.

The Function of the Protagonist (the Client)

The protagonist (protos-first, agony-pain) is the client, the patient, and the subject of the treatment. His or her function in the clinical role playing session is similar to that of the client in any other form of psychotherapy.

Clinical role playing is a place where protagonists can dream and fantasize and then live it in actuality to see the possible consequences of their fantasy. They can venture new and alternative modes of behavior, uninhibited and unintimidated by the effect of the possible consequences. Clinical role playing is not merely a method of replicating past and present experience. Most important, it is a method that offers *more* than life itself. Protagonists are encouraged to behave in any way they have always wanted but were unable, afraid, or uninspired to do so.

In a clinical role playing session there is usually *one person* who is the protagonist. Even if the session involves two people (e.g., a husband and a wife, a mother and her child, two group members), the director must decide in advance who is the protagonist and who is the auxiliary. Thus in one session the husband may be the designated protagonist and the wife the auxiliary, and in the next session the wife becomes the protagonist and the husband the auxiliary. Experience has shown that it is virtually impossible to have two or more protagonists simultaneously.

The Function of the Group Members

Clinical role playing, in its psychodramatic version, was originally created as a form of group psychotherapy (Moreno, 1964a; Moreno & Kipper, 1968). And although clinical role playing can be applied in individual and marital therapy, its maximal potential is expressed in group therapy situations.

In clinical role playing, members of the group are also members of the therapeutic team because they serve the following three functions:

They are potential protagonists, they participate as auxiliaries, and they provide support.

(a) *Potential protagonists.* The director in a group therapy situation regards each member as a potential protagonist. Often several members offer themselves as protagonists. In such instances it is usually the task of the group to select one protagonist. The selection process may be intense and emotionally loaded where the needs of each candidate are seriously considered and compared with those of the other candidates.

(b) *Serving as auxiliaries.* Most of the auxilitaries, if not all of them, emerge from among the group members. This is also true where a trained co-therapist is available, because often scenes require several auxiliaries. Furthermore, it is not uncommon to have protagonists who have already established, prior to their session, special relationships with certain group members(s). In the event that these relationships seem beneficial for the purpose of the session, the director is advised to take advantage of them and use the particular member(s) as an auxiliary.

The availability of group members increases the number of models that can be used in the treatment. For example, a protagonist may role play his or her reactions in a given situation. The director then asks several members, one at a time, to show how they behave in the same situation. This provides a range of alternatives for the protagonist to choose from and try for himself.

(c) *Support.* At the end of the action stage, group members are asked to share their experiences with the protagonist. This is one way in which members lend their support to the protagonist (and to each other). In fact, they communicate that the protagonist is not alone in his or her problem because others have experienced it too. They also convey that the protagonist's difficulties ought not be regarded as catastrophes either because others may have experienced them in greater severity or overcome them.

The present chapter completes the discussion of the clinical role playing session, its stages, and the planning of the scenario: content, duration, and the therapeutic team. The next chapter will describe the basic clinical role playing techniques.

CHAPTER 6

Basic Techniques:
The Specific Subgroup

Role playing techniques are hard to define. There are many different kinds of techniques. Some are aided by props such as toys (e.g., the Matrioshka Doll technique, Robbins, 1973); others use paper-and-pencil exercises as the basis for the technique proper (see examples in Pfeiffer & Jones, 1973-1979). Some are based on a prepared script to be role played (e.g., Shaw, Corsini, Blake, & Mouton, 1980, pp. 126-127); others are entirely spontaneous (e.g., Corsini, 1966; Z.T. Moreno, 1965; Starr, 1977; Weiner & Sacks, 1969). Many techniques are essentially verbal (e.g., Elms, 1969; Maier, Solem & Maier, 1975) but some are nonverbal (e.g., Morris & Cinnamon, 1975).

As a general rule, role playing techniques have a skeletal structure that under normal circumstances ought not to altered. Characteristically the techniques are externally induced, that is, introduced into the protagonist's enactment by the therapist. They take the form of new role behavior—new in the sense that they are not part and parcel of the natural flow of the protagonist's role playing portrayals. The declared purposes of role playing techniques are to further the exploration of an issue, to activate a particular psychological process, and to facilitate a painful confrontation. An additional aspect of role playing techniques is that the vast majority of them require the participation of at least one auxiliary. Very few are designed to involve the protagonist alone.

ROLE PLAYING TECHNIQUES: TYPES AND GENERAL CHARACTERISTICS

Types

The number of role playing techniques that were invented in the last two decades alone is enormous. If one were to compile even those tech-

137

niques that have been written up, the list would undoubtedly consist of several hundred items. Obviously such a task is beyond the scope of this book. But the availability of so many different role playing techniques creates a dire need to sort them into a workable classification system. The purpose of such an endeavor is far from being an academic exercise; rather, it is (a) to bring some order into a vast amount of bits and pieces of information scattered in many volumes; (b) to increase our understanding of the usefulness of these techniques by providing a general overview; and (c) to facilitate the storing of this information in our memory.

Role playing techniques can be classified in various ways. Each has certain advantages but at the same time is likely to be short of being fully comprehensive. For instance, it is possible to classify them according to the kind of expressive language they predominantly use: verbal, nonverbal, actional, or paper-and-pencil types. It is also possible to categorize them in terms of how well defined and organized they are, that is, into structured versus unstructured types. Techniques can be sorted into separate categories according to the number of people that they address, namely, into individual, dyadic, triadic, and group techniques. They can be also divided on the basis of content, that is, techniques dealing with leadership issues, with aggression, with assertive behavior, with communication styles, and so forth. They can be categorized, for example, according to their therapeutic goals, such as facilitating catharsis, or enhancing self-disclosure, desensitization, or skill training.

The point is that although all these and other classification systems have merits, we regard them as subcategories of a more fundamental line of division between two distinctly different types of role playing techniques. These are the *basic* techniques and the *situational* techniques. The criterion that we suggest for differentiating between these two types concerns *the degree to which a technique is directly related to the specific content of the issue portrayed in the enactment.*

The *basic* techniques have a broader base of application; in a way they seem to have a universal psychological value. They are not related to a specific content of the presenting problem. In principle they can be introduced to any psychological or behavioral problem and conflict *regardless* of its content. There are very few basic techniques and all of them are essentially psychodramatic ones (Z.T. Moreno, 1959, 1965) derived from J.L. Moreno's theory (Moreno, 1934, 1964a). However, they can just as well be formulated in terms of other psychotherapeutic approaches, such as, behavior theory (Sturm, 1965, 1970, 1971).

The *situational* techniques, on the other hand, represent behavior simulation interventions that have a more restricted psychological basis. Their pertinence to the specific content of the portrayed problem is strong; hence their usefulness might be best served with one set of issues but not with another. Being content-bound techniques, their range of application is somewhat limited.

The situational techniques will be discussed separately in Chapters 8 and 9. The present chapter focuses only on the basic techniques. But first let us briefly describe some of the general (i.e., common) characteristics shared by *all* the techniques, basic and situational alike.

General Characteristics

At this juncture two questions may be raised. First, what is the central function of role playing techniques? There are several ways to respond to this question. Let us focus on the one aspect that is probably the most interesting for the practicing therapist—the pragmatic point of view. Role playing techniques serve as therapeutic tools. They are means available to the therapist to utilize his or her professional skills effectively. The contribution of the techniques to the treatment process is analogous to that of the computer to the process of solving a complex mathematical problem, the scalpel to surgical treatment, or the drilling hand-piece to the dental treatment. Techniques that do not increase the treatment efficacy, generate a greater refinement, or simply save time have little value.

The second question is, what are the most important prerequisites of role playing techniques? Considering both the basic and the situational techniques, it is possible to identify five such requirements.

1. Every role playing technique must have a *psychological rationale*, an underlying reason why it was created and what purpose it hopes to achieve. The rationale is closely related to another quality common to all role playing techniques (to be discussed later), namely, the ability to elicit and activate certain psychological processes. For example, if the rationale for a given technique concerns improving one's care and understanding of a fellow human being, the technique should be designed to activate and promote empathy.
2. Role playing techniques ought to be designed in a relatively *simple way*, easy to grasp and easy to perform.
3. Somewhat related to the previous point is the issue of duration. Role playing techniques should be *brief*. Obviously the time needed

to perform a given technique is a function of its complexity as well as the number of participants it involves. It cannot be divorced from the time required for the psychological process it purports to activate to fully develop. But in principle it ought to be as brief as possible.

4. A role playing technique must be *well designed* and structured. It should follow a clearly defined procedure and have clearly stated rules.

5. It is necessary that role playing techniques offer protagonists *guidance and support*. The process of psychological exploration and the search for relief, better self-understanding, and more effective coping skills tends to open new possibilities for protagonists. In the face of these, protagonists often become overwhelmed, confused, or even frightened—overwhelmed by the new discoveries, confused by the number of new options opened to them, and frightened becaused they are confronted with action directions whose consequences are somewhat unknown. It is the function of the techniques to help them choose a direction to go, and to guide them in the process of learning in a relatively pain-free experimentation. The last point brings us to the supportive aspect of role playing techniques. It requires that techniques will not be intimidating. On the contrary, they should have built-in reinforcing qualities that can encourage protagonists to continue in their pursuits.

THE NINE SPECIFIC TECHNIQUES

There are *nine specific* (basic) *techniques* in our listing. These are: Self-presentation, Role-playing, Dialogue, Soliloquy, Double and Multiple Doubles, Aside, Role-reversal, Empty-chair, and Mirror. Each technique will be discussed separately in the following sections.

Self-presentation Technique

Self-presentation represents one of the simplest forms of role playing techniques. In essence it comprises a series of brief role playing enactments where the protagonist portrays himself or herself and any other significant person in his or her life. In these enactments the protagonist is the sole participant and the presentation is done in complete subjectiveness. J.L. Moreno described this technique as follows:

The simplest psychodramatic technique is to let the patient start with himself; i.e., to live through, in the psychiatrist's presence, situations which are part of his daily life, and especially to live through crucial conflicts in which he is involved. He must also enact and represent as concretely and thoroughly as possible every person near him, near his problems, his father, his mother, his wife, or any other person in his social "atom" [a social nucleus towards whom he is emotionally attached]. The patient does not present "roles". . . . It is not *the* father, *the* mother, *the* wife or *the* employer; it is *his* father, *his* mother, *his* wife, *his* employer. (Moreno, 1964a, p. 184)

The two basic premises underlying this technique are subjectiveness and exclusiveness: subjectiveness, in that the portrayals rest entirely on the protagonist's idiosyncracy, his personal perceptions and judgments; exclusiveness, in that the protagonist is the sole source for these perceptions and experiences. The protagonist has total control with regard to what impressions will be portrayed, their extensiveness, and the aspects that will be emphasized.

Strictly speaking, the technique of Self-presentation is used every time protagonists act as themselves or take the role of a specific other. In that respect it amounts to the elementary ingredient in any clinical role playing portrayal: the action representation of people via role playing. In the technical sense, however, the classic manifestation of this technique is primarily evident in two forms. One is when protagonists are asked to provide a brief overview of themselves, as well as of significant others, in successive episodes as if it were a parade of people and personalities. The other form is also known as a *monodrama*. Here the protagonist enacts a series of complete situations all by himself or herself. All the roles and personalities are portrayed solely by the protagonist. As suggested by the prefix mon or mono (from the Greek word *monos-alone, single)*, this form of role playing production is done without the participation of any auxiliary. Sometimes the technique of Self-presentation may be conducted as an interviewing situation (e.g., Kipper, 1977). This is especially useful when the protagonist portrays the part of the technique that involves enacting the role of another person. The protagonist is interviewed in that role responding in the same way as the original person would. The following interactions illustrate this variation of the Self-presentation technique.

Director: (to the protagonist) I'd like to meet your wife and get a feeling as to how she sees you. Since your wife is not present here, why don't you assume her role. After all between the two of us you know her best. *(The protagonist assumes the role of his wife.)*
Protagonist: (as the wife) Hello . . .

Director: Hello, my name is Dr. David, I don't think we've met before but I'm your husband's therapist. I really wanted to meet with you for a few moments and talk with you. Do you mind? What's your name?

Protagonist: (as the wife) Oh! I'll be happy to talk with you. I'm Tracy. Nice to meet you.

Director: Your husband told me that you're an emotional type, that you get excited easily. Is that true? Could you perhaps tell me a little more about that?

Protagonist: (as Tracy) That's what *he* thinks. Me excited! I'll tell you what's his problem. He simply doesn't know the difference between excitement and concern, that's what it is. He. . . , *(etc.)*.

Rationale. The Self-presentation technique is based on three interrelated reasons. The first concerns the specific use of this technique in the form of portraying significant others in sucessive episodes enacted either spontaneously or through the interviewing situation variation. Why would one have to do this through role playing? Is it not simpler to describe these other persons verbally? The reason for resorting to the Self-presentation role playing technique is not because it is superior to the strictly verbal descriptions. The point is one of neither simplicity nor superiority but of consistency. One of the purposes of the Self-presentation technique is gathering information about the protagonist's behavior, as well as that of the people with whom he or she interacts or is affected by. That information will be processed through role playing treatment. If the therapeutic process is to be conducted by means of role playing enactments, then for reasons of consistency the same means should be used in the information-gathering phase.

The second reason for the use of the Self-presentation technique concerns the psychological state that characterizes clients in the beginning of their therapy or often in the beginning of many individual sessions. Clinical experience has shown that at the onset of treatment sessions clients often go through an "initiation anxiety." This anxiety tends to manifest itself in the form of feelings of apprehension, trepidation, uncertainty, and helplessness. They have a need to remain protected in the face of requests for emotional exposures or confrontations with painful experiences. That need may be satisfied by encouraging self-disclosure while being in control of the extent of the exposure. This is precisely what is being offered through the Self-presentation technique: self-disclosure regulated and controlled by the protagonist. And although the need for control might be pronounced in the beginning of sessions, it might persist or even be further heightened at any point throughout the role playing production. In cases where protagonists are suspicious and threatened by the participation of auxiliaries over whom they have limited control, Self-presentation in the form of a monodrama might be the best first approach.

The third reason concerns the warm-up quality of the Self-presentation technique. Being a simple and a relatively nonthreatening role playing task, this technique tends to reinforce the protagonist's readiness to become further involved in the clinical role playing treatment. The reader may be reminded here of a point made earlier in the book regarding the need to maintain and promote the warm-up process throughout the entire action stage. With the use of Self-presentation, that facet of the treatment is also being nurtured.

Instructions. Obviously there are several ways for introducing the Self-presentation technique to the protagonist. There is no particular reason to adhere to one form of instruction provided that the main task is clearly explained. Basically there are two kinds of instructions: one concerning the presentation of oneself and the other concerning the presentation of another person. Here are two examples:

> "I would like to see you, now, behaving in a way that is typically you, exactly as you do in real life. You may do this while you sit, stand up, or move around the action space."

> "I would like to meet your mother (father, sister, wife, boss, etc.). Since she (he) is not present here, you take her (his) role. Please portray her (him) the best you can. Try to feel like she (he) does and think like her (him). Let us see what kind of a person she (he) is."

Indications. The following list briefly describes those typical instances where the technique seems to be particularly useful. It should be emphasized, however, that therapists have the freedom of introducing this technique any time they deem it necessary, provided they have considered the contraindications and found them nonapplicable.

1. At the beginning of sessions or as an introduction to a particular scene. It also may be incorporated into, and serve as a part of, an intake: a general interview that ordinarily precedes the onset of

the treatment. This might be especially indicated in the case of group therapy for the purpose of familiarizing group members with the protagonist and his or her personal social network.

2. With protagonists who are inhibited and guarded, where a slow pace or gradual self-disclosure is sought.

3. With overwarmed-up protagonists. While it provides them with an opportunity to express themselves, it also requires that they focus on the task given to them and hence exercise some control.

4. With protagonists who are suspicious of others and cannot accept or trust any auxiliary. For instance, with protagonists with paranoid tendencies—psychotics or otherwise—monodrama might be the best way to begin the treatment.

5. When protagonists find it difficult to work with auxiliaries in general, or a particular one, because they are perfectionists, they do not like the auxiliary personally, they find the auxiliary unsuitable for a given role, or the auxiliary failed to play the role to their satisfaction.

Contraindications. The term *contraindication* refers to the instances where a given technique, in the present context the Self-presentation, should *not* be introduced into the protagonist's role playing enactment. One must bear in mind, however, that in most cases the contraindications for role playing techniques do not carry the same warning value as those for the use of medications, for example. They do *not* imply that if ignored, a serious iatrogenic effect (i.e., a deterioration in the patient's condition as the result of the treatment) will occur. But the contraindications suggest that under certain conditions a given technique may not be effective, may not serve the therapeutic goal, or may confuse the protagonists and sometimes elicit noncooperation or a sudden resistance to comply with the instructions (see also Moreno, 1973). The contraindications for the Self-presentation techniques are as follows:

1. When protagonists are not sufficiently warmed up and they find it hard to enact all the roles alone. What they need is a constant stimulation from auxiliaries who will keep them involved and responsive.

2. When protagonists find it emotionally difficult, either personally threatening or culturally unacceptable, to portray the role of a given person. I recall a case of a protagonist from one of the Latin American countries who refused to portray the role of his mother. He would enact any other person except his mother or his grand-

mothers. "Don't make me do this," he said. "In our family one does not challenge the role of the lady of the household."

Role-playing Technique

Before we proceed to describe this technique, a point of clarification must be made concerning the use of the term *role playing*. I use the expression Role-playing (capitalized and hyphenated) to denote a special behavior simulation intervention, a basic technique. This should not be confused with "role playing" (separate words), a term commonly used to describe general behavior expressed through action language which is often contrasted with other forms of expression (e.g., the verbal or the nonverbal languages).

Rationale. Role-playing is unquestionably the most important ingredient, the backbone, of clinical role playing. Without it the method loses its unique character and perhaps its value. Role-playing, simply described, is *the act of assuming the role of someone else*. At first glance this description looks quite clear and straightforward. A closer examination, however, suggests further elucidation, especially with regard to two points. One concerns the definition of the phrase "the role of someone else." Customarily such a role is thought of as the portrayal of *a person*, whether living or dead, real or fantasized. But since clinical role playing deals with the protagonist's subjective perceptions of his or her relationships with the *entire* surrounding world, there is no reason for limiting the portrayed roles to human beings. The world that affects us consists of different kinds of elements, many of which play important roles in our lives. Therefore, the role of that "someone else" could be the role of a part of the body (e.g., the heart), the role of an animal (e.g., a beloved pet), the role of an inanimate object (e.g., a souvenir), and even the role of a notion or a concept, such as time, confinement, or death. The second point requiring further clarification is that the technique of Role-playing refers to the act of assuming the role of *someone else*. In terms of techniques this should be distinguished from the act of portraying *one's own role* or any aspect or variation of it. The latter portrayal would be a part of the Self-presentation technique. We will return to this point later.

In the early 1930's two terms appeared in the psychological and sociological literature concerning man's ability to assume the role of the other. One was "role taking ," a term coined by G.H. Mead (1934), which referred to a sequential, self-correcting process through which the individual can experience another's subjective state (Scheff, 1967). But role taking has been interpreted in various ways and, with the absence of sufficient empirical evidence, has lost some of its importance. Recently, it was thought to be the ability of a person to hold "veridical expectations in which he or she (correctly) maps the expectations of a sentient other" (Biddle, 1979, p. 189). It appears, therefore, that role taking focuses particularly on the *veridicality* of *thoughts*.

In the same year, J.L. Moreno (1934) suggested the term "role playing," which referred to a person's ability to (correctly) imitate another's role. Moreno observed that role playing appeared spontaneously in the behavior of children and, therefore, he considered it to be a fundamental force of self-development, a basic strategy for learning. Unlike role taking, role playing concerns the *imitation* of *behavior,* both of oneself and others. The existence of two techniques—Self-presentation and Role-playing—provides a further refinement in the role playing concept. The former focuses on the "imitation" of one's own behavior (i.e., spontaneous behavior), and the latter on the imitation of the other's behavior (mimetic-pretend/mimetic-replicaiton).

As a rule, the technique of Role-playing concerns the performance of the auxiliaries. Typically, it is they who portray roles of the others with whom the protagonist interacts, and they are the ones who represent animals, objects, or concepts that affect the protagonists's behavior. The only instances where auxiliaries do not portray roles of others are those that require the Dialogue technique (see the next basic technique).

Since protagonists generally portray *themselves,* the technique of Role-playing usually does not apply to them. There are, however, three exceptions to this rule when this technique may be used by the protagonists. The first exception is when the Self-presentation technique is used and the scene is conducted as a monodrama. There, protagonists enact roles *alone,* including those of persons with whom they are emotionally involved. The second is when the Role-reversal technique is used. We will explain more about this technique later. For the moment it will be sufficient to say that in this technique the protagonist briefly exchanges his or her role with that portrayed by the auxiliary, e.g., the mother. The protagonist becomes the mother and the auxiliary assumes the role of the protagonist. The third exception is when, in a training situation, the protagonist is asked to assume a new role, one that is not typically his or hers, or is not a part of his or her existing repertoire of roles. A classic example of this is when a protagonist is asked to role play a case that has not been taken from his or her own environment.

Instructions. The instruction for using the technique of Role-playing could be as simple as "I would like you to be the mother (the father, the boss, etc.)." It can also be more detailed, as follows:

"I would like you to be the mother (the father, the boss, etc.). Try to protray her (him) as accurately as you can. Talk like her (him), use her (his) gestures, and try to feel the way you think she (he) does."

Indications.

1. When for maintaining the action and the flow of the plot the protagonist needs an auxiliary who will portray the role of someone else.
2. When a protagonist needs training in a role or skill he or she does not have. The training is designed along a modeling procedure (mimetic-pretend/mimetic-replication combination) where the protagonist assumes the role of someone else (expert model) and stays in that role.
3. When the enactment is performed for demonstration purposes, as an educational technique. Here both the protagonist and the auxiliary play roles of other people usually as described in an already made text.

Contraindications.

1. When a protagonist rejects the idea of working with an auxiliary because of either the nature of his or her psychological disturbance (e.g., paranoia) or personal reasons.
2. When a protagonist is not ready to become very involved in the role playing enactment and defers the idea of working with an auxiliary for a later time. Protagonists feel that the introduction of an auxiliary intensifies their involvement and are ready to accept such help only when appropriately warmed up.

Dialogue

The *Dialogue* technique is a role playing enactment of relationships among the *original* participants. The auxiliaries are the same people with whom the protagonist interacts in real life. In fact, this technique is sometimes regarded as a special case of the Self-presentation technique or a variation of it. The roles the auxiliaries portray in the Dialogue technique are not those of someone else but their own. Everybody plays himself or herself, the protagonist as well as the auxiliaries. This technique is seen as most applicable in conflict situations between, say, a husband and his wife, a parent and his or her child, various members of an entire family or a part of it, and between two friends, *provided* all are present in the role playing scene(s). As in any clinical role playing enactment, here, too, there can be only one protagonist at any given time. For each session, or alternatively for every scene, the therapist must decide, in advance, who will be the protagonist. The remaining involved participants serve as auxiliaries regardless of the magnitude of their own contribution to the emergence of the presented complaint.

Rationale. This concerns the veridicality of the data: behavior, as well as information, provided through the enactments proper, and its resemblance to the real life situation(s). In a typical clinical role playing session the only authentic source available is the protagonist. The contribution of all the other participants, especially the auxiliaries, is merely an approximation of the real behavior of the original people with whom the protagonist is emotionally and functionally involved. By necessity this contribution depends on information given by the protagonist and is used at the risk of being very subjective. When the actual people involved happen to be in the therapist's office during the session they can serve as additional sources of information. They can simply play themselves. In this way all the portrayed roles become genuine and none needs to be an approximation any longer. The Dialogue technique, therefore, depicts the most authentic protrayals a therapist can hope for in the context of a clinical role playing session.

Instructions.

"I would like you to be yourselves. Try to behave as naturally as you can. Please, do not feel like an actor on a stage. This is not a show. Just behave exactly as you did when the real situation took place, or as you would if this were the real thing."

Indications.

1. When a scene is set for diagnostic purpose, in an attempt to identify the source(s) of the protagonist's difficulties. The Dialogue tech-

nique offers an opportunity to replicate exactly the relationships of the protagonist and his or her real partner(s).

2. When a scene is designed for a training or retraining purpose, to teach, show and rehearse the protagonist in new skills, new approaches, or new behavior. The Dialogue technique provides an opportunity to practice the new behavior in a context which is almost identical to a real life situation yet under due guidance and in a protective simulated condition. This is perhaps the closest one can get to real life experimentation.

Contraindications. The contraindications for this technique are the same as those listed for the technique of Role-playing. In addition, once the Dialogue technique *has been* introduced, it should be stopped under the following circumstances:

1. When the person who serves as the auxiliary is involved in the scene to such an extent that instead of helping the protagonist he or she competes for the protagonist's position. In this case the therapist is advised to release this auxiliary and substitute him or her with another one, a less involved party. The Dialogue technique is, thus, replaced by the techique of Role-playing where the new auxiliary assumes the role of the original partner, who in turn now becomes an observer.
2. When the protagonist and the original partner (serving as an auxiliary) interact continously in a manner that perpetuates or even reinforces their existing pathological relationships. Again, the therapist might want to substitute the Dialogue technique with the technique of Role-playing or any other technique that will set the scene on a more therapeutically productive course.

Soliloquy

In the *Soliloquy* technique protagonists are requested to recite their feelings and thoughts as if they were having an open (yet intimate) consultation with themselves. The Soliloquy may appear as narrative comments (feelings and thoughts) on their role playing enactments in the middle of the scene, before it begins, or upon its completion.

Rationale. An examination of previous writings on this technique reveals two issues in need of further clarification. One concerns the number of soliloquy types, and the other concerns timing, that is, at what points in the enactment might this technique be introduced? Regarding the issue of types, Moreno (1964a) distinguished between two kinds of soliloquy. The first, according to him, represents an *enlargement of the self*, an act of complete exposure. It allows hitherto secret mental processes to "flow to the person to whom they should have been communicated originally" (p.207). This kind corresponds to my understanding of the Soliloquy technique, and it is in this sense that I refer to it throughout this book. The second kind of soliloquy in Moreno's classification concerns that which constitutes a *resistance to a full development of the role*. This kind manifests itself where the official, portrayed act and the soliloquy that accompanied it are on different, even conflicting, levels. While Moreno considered this to be a variant of the Soliloquy technique, I have classified it in a separate category: the *Aside* technique (described later in this chapter).

According to Starr (1977) "the soliloquy is used whenever it is important for the audience to hear what the patient is thinking" (p.14). This is, of course, a rather general statement. But originally, this technique was invented (Moreno, 1964a) in order "to duplicate hidden feelings and thoughts which he [the protagonist] *actually* had in a situation with a partner in life or which he has *now*, in the moment of performance"(p. 190). Accordingly, the soliloquy has been described as "a monologue of the protagonist *in situ*" (Z.T. Moreno, 1965), or as the recitation of thoughts "in the middle of a scene" (Yablonsky, 1976). In terms of timing this means that the Soliloquy may be introduced on two occasions: (a) in order to supplement the action portrayed during a regular, key scene, and (b) to form a specialized, that is, connecting, scene. (The latter was described in Chapter 4.)

How does this technique work? Upon receiving the instruction to soliloquize, the protagonist moves away from the center of the action space where the scene was enacted to the periphery. There he or she begins to walk around the action space at a slow pace in fairly wide circles, always moving forward. While walking, the protagonist expresses openly his or her feelings and thoughts *at this moment*. Usually, a soliloquy lasts for a brief period and may vary from a few seconds to about five minutes, depending on how candid the protagonist is and the issues concerned. The reason why the Soliloquy is performed while the protagonist walks rather than in a stationary position is because bodily movements act as physical warm-up starters and tend to promote involvement. But should the protagonist insist on soliloquizing in a sitting position, that wish ought to be honored. The reason for suggesting a circular, forward walk rather than walking back and forth across the action space is that the latter tends to cause restlessness, repetitious behavior, and is physically taxing.

Often, *the Soliloquy is combined with the Double technique.* Experience has shown that protagonists may need external stimulations to help them in their soliloquies. An auxiliary serving as a double (i.e., in the role of the "soliloquizing protagonist") may be introduced to maintain the flow of the soliloquy.

Instructions.

"I would like you now to soliloquize. Go to the edge of the action space and begin to walk slowly around it. As you walk, let us hear what you are feeling and thinking *right now* about the meeting, confrontation, your actions, or about anything else." (In a soliloquy that preambles a key scene one should say ' . . . about the meeting, confrontation, etc., you are to have; your expectations, mood, anxieties, etc.') While you are soliloquizing keep on walking around the action space."

For protagonists already familiar with this technique the therapist may simply say "Let's have a soliloquy now."

Indications.

1. When the therapist suspects that the protagonist is withholding information, or that there are important unexpressed feelings and thoughts which ought to be brought into the open.
2. When the protagonist is about to be involved in a very important scene, and it would help both the therapist and the protagonist to face the protagonist's expectations, anticipatory anxieties, etc.
3. At the end of a scene when the therapist sees that the protagonist is left with residual feelings in need of expression.
4. When the therapist is looking for clues to begin the next scene.

Contraindications.

1. When the communication seems to be open and clear, and the protagonist expresses himself or herself in what appears to be an uninhibited fashion.
2. When the enactment flows smoothly and the pauses created by the soliloquy may interfere with the protagonist's involvement.

The Double

Of all the basic techniques described in this chapter, two techniques—the *Double* and the *Role-reversal* (to be discussed later)—stand out as perhaps the most ingenious and therapeutically powerful clinical role playing interventions.

The *Double* technique, often referred to as the *alter-ego* technique, was originally designed as a psychodramatic intervention and was invented a few decades ago (e.g., Toeman, 1948). Since then, presumably because of its reported effectiveness, it became an important component in many forms of psychotherapy that are aided by behavior simulation procedures (see, e.g., in behavior modification, Sturm, 1971; in the Adlerian approach, Starr, 1977; in group psychotherapy, Goldstein, 1971; and in some other therapies, Yablonsky, 1976). In principle, the idea of using the double as a therapeutic agent is quite simple. An auxiliary is assigned to portray a specialized role, one that duplicates that of the protagonist. The auxiliary plays this role simultaneously with the original protagonist and attempts to become his or her "psychological twin," to serve as the protagonist's inner voice and conscience, to reflect his or her feelings, to uncover concealed thoughts and concerns, and to assist the protagonist in expressing these fully and openly. In practice, however, the role of the double is rather complex and ought to be analyzed step by step.

Let us begin with the issue of the double's physical position, that is, his or her place in the action space in relation to the protagonist. Is there a preferred place for the double? Some writers advise the double to stay right behind the protagonist. Others may take a compromised stance. For example, according to Blatner, "The best physical position for the double is to place himself behind, slightly to the side of , and facing the protagonist at about 30 degrees angle" (1973, p. 31). I join those who recommend that the double position himself or herself *close to the protagonist at his or her side* (perferably the side that is not close to the audience). The reason for this recommendation is that the double cannot have a complete view of the protagonist from behind, or even from a slightly backward position.

In order to function successfully the double needs to establish a feeling of oneness—as close a psychological identity as possible—with the protagonist. This may require a deliberate effort on the part of the double, who must now initiate a process of establishing similarities. Such a process begins with the imitation of the protagonist's physical postures. When the protagonist stands, the double stands, too. If the protagonist sits, scratches his head, plays nervously with his fingers, lowers his shoulders, screams, laughs, whispers, etc., the double repeats these behaviors exactly. The purpose of this imitation is twofold:

(a) To help the doubles in extricating themselves from their own identities and becoming as completely involved as possible in the role of the protagonist. Realistically, however, a complete immersion in that role is hardly possible. It is more a question of the degree of the involvement since one never abandon one's own identity entirely.

(b) To direct the double's attention to physical clues with the hope that these will facilitate the detection of clues concerning the psychological state of the protagonist.

At first, protagonists, especially novice protagonists, react to this mimicry with caution and a sense of discomfort. They find themselves unexpectedly feeling exposed and embarrassed. But soon, if the double does a credible job, these feelings dissipate. Instead, there is a shift in the protagonist's preoccupation from the physical mimicry to other aspects of the double's performance.

Imitations of body postures are only the first step leading toward the development of psychological "oneness." The double must now ascertain that his or her verbal statements are congruent with the protagonist's thoughts, attitudes, preoccupations, and feelings. Intuition and empathic ability might be a great asset here, but there is a simple procedure that can help the double. The double may resort to the safest approach by repeating the protagonist's verbalization, not word by word but primarily that which expresses moods, concerns, or wishes. The protagonist, in turn, is instructed to talk with his or her double "as if it were an internal conversation." During their verbal exchanges the protagonist has to confirm his or her agreement with the double's reflections if they are correct, or refute them if they are wrong. The more affirmative feedbacks the double receives, the sooner an identity will be established.

The double is now in a position to expand and elaborate his or her role. The effort is directed to "become the link through which the patient [protagonist] may try to reach out into the real world" (Z.T. Moreno, 1965, p. 80). The double must read between the protagonist's lines and openly voice that which is not being expressed directly. Sensitivity, empathy, understanding, and perhaps wisdom should be mobilized here in order to fulfill this role effectively. Sometimes the double must take a chance and express a feeling or a thought that he or she *assumes* is being hinted at by the protagonist. The protagonist may either agree or disagree with the double. In the latter instance the double may (a) go along with the protagonist and reverse the previous statement, (b) adhere to his or her statement regardless of the protagonist's protest, or (c) probe a little further into the source of the protagonist's disagreement. The double reaches now a deeper level of similarity with the protagonist.

It is appropraite to point out here that the double need not be of the same sex as the protagonist. A male can double for a female and vice versa.

To summarize, the double's role is comprised of several steps as follows:

1. Imitating the protagonist's physical gestures and mannerisms.
2. Assumming mental (i.e., attitudinal), as well as emotional, similarities with the protagonist by repeating key words.
3. Reading between the protagonist's lines and exposing hidden concerns, thoughts, and feelings.
4. Focusing particularly on fears, inhibitions, and dilemmas the protagonist might have.
5. Taking chances in expressing hypotheses regarding the protagonist's preoccupations.
6. Encouraging the protagonist to express openly these (#4 above) and cope with them directly.

Often doubles fail to function successfully because they tend to assume the position of "a professional, *objective* observer" rather than that of "a *semi-objective,* involved party." Such doubles readily offer their own interpretations of the protagonist's behavior and constantly conduct mini-interviews in their role. They ask a lot of questions. The best doubling is performed through statements, not questions, echoing the protagonist's concerns and not by providing interpretations.

Rationale. The double's role can be conceptualized by numerous theories. These include psychodynamic approaches, as well as learning theories (Strum, 1965, 1970). But since the double's role has originated in psychodramatic thinking, we would like to present this approach especially as interpreted by Z.T. Moreno in her article, "The significance of doubling and role reversal for cosmic man" (1975). Doubling is viewed as a developmental need and a developmental stage. As soon as the young child discovers himself capable of moving independently into space, he needs to be assured that being himself is a positive category;

he requires self-affirmation. That can be transmitted by the parents through affirmative doubling and later through noninjurious role-reversal.

> The parent precedes the child in the world. Regrettably, he cannot pass on his experience of that world to his child. It is the tragedy of the human race that every child and each generation needs to explore life from the very start. Very little experience or wisdom can be passed on. But through doubling first and later role reversal, some of these gaps can be bridged. (Z.T. Moreno, 1975, p. 57)

The notion of doubling as a therapeutice process is theoretically congruent with the Rogerian approach, especially in reference to the importance of the concept of empathy (e.g., Rogers, 1975). The role of the double and its function are in harmony with many of the characteristics ascribed to empathy. In fact, the double technique has been regarded as the actual embodiment, the operational definition, of being empathic. There is some experimental evidence that one can increase one's ability to empathize through this technique, and that doubling is one of the best training methods for improving empathic skills (Kipper & Ben-Ely, 1979). The therapeutic effectiveness of the Double technique in group psychotherapy was also demonstrated experimentally by Goldstein (1967) and, in a more refined version of that study, by Goldstein (1971). Both studies showed the doubling method to be effective in involving severely withdrawn patients in the psychotherapeutic process. These patients were reported to be so withdrawn prior to their participation in the studies that they were not amenable to any form of psychotherapy. The Double technique can be used as a part of a full clinical role playing session or as an independent therapeutic intervention. It may be used in the therapist's room or *in situ* (e.g., Pankratz, 1971).

In terms of clinical or therapeutic responsibility, the auxiliary who assumes the role of the double has two functions to perform. The first is to serve *as an extension of the protagonist* with a duty to assist the therapist in understanding the protagonist. The double must continuously provide the therapist with clues and explanations regarding the protagonist's feelings and thoughts, and ascertain that the therapist is getting these messages. The second function is to serve as *an extension of the therapist*, that is, to act as an intermediary agent through which the therapist can implement desirable changes in the protagonist's behavior. The double, therefore, has a dual function: to be a co-protagonist as well as a co-therapist.

Multiple Doubles Technique

The *Multiple Doubles* technique is an extension of the Double technique. It is subjected to the same principles and regulations that characterize the Double technique with one exception: The role of the double is divided among *several* auxiliaries. Each auxiliary portrays one aspect of the protagonist's behavior, one side of his or her conflict, one personality trait of the protagonist. This technique should be used primarily whenever a protagonist is overwhelmed by the several facets of his or her presenting problem, and is unable to address them as a whole. The Multiple Doubles technique makes it easy to deal with each facet separately. In principle a therapist may introduce as many doubles as he or she wishes. The limits are essentially practical. It is important to remember that one should not have too many people in the action space for a long period. Having several doubles in addition to the protagonist and perhaps one or two auxiliaries makes it extremely difficult to manage the scene. Also, too many doubles tend to overwhelm the protagonist. These auxiliaries inevitably will take over the running of the scene, leaving the protagonist quiet and in an observer's position. Experience has shown that for all practical purposes one ought not involve more than three or four doubles simultaneously.

The last point brings us to the question: Who is entitled to have a double, or for that matter, multiple doubles? Although Blatner (1973, p. 29), for example, wrote that a double may be given to the protagonist as well as to his or her auxiliaries, I share the view of those who recommend that the double or the multiple doubles can be assigned only for doubling *original players*. The reason for this recommendation is that effective doubling must portray the protagonist authentically. This is achieved best when the double has opportunities to check his or her portrayal with the original: the protagonist. There seems to be little advantage in providing an auxiliary who represents an absentee with a double since that auxiliary is not the original person with whom the protagonist interacts in real life anyway. If the auxiliary happens to represent the assigned role unsatisfactorily he or she should be replaced by another auxiliary rather than be given a double. Morever, assigning a double or multiple doubles to all the key participants in the enactment will unnecessarily crowd the action space. Therefore, the rule to follow is that *only players who portray themselves may be given a double or multiple doubles*. This means that only protagonists may have doubles. The only exception is in the case of the Dialogue technique where all the participants—the protagonist and the auxiliary —role play their own selves. There the auxiliary may also be asssigned a double whenever indicated.

Instructions. In introducing the Double technique or the Multiple Doubles technique the therapist must instruct the protagonist and the auxiliary designated to be a double separately.

To the protagonist: "Like all of us you must sometimes have conflicting thoughts or experience conflicting feelings. You probably find yourself at times holding an internal debate. I would like to give you a double. This person will try to become you and will represent an inner aspect of your personality. Your double will try to help you by clarifying your thoughts and feelings. You may talk with your double as if you are having an internal debate. If the double is right tell him (her) so. If the double is wrong, and says things that do not reflect your thinking and feeling, please correct him (her)."

To the double: "As a double you become part of the protagonist. Try to imitate his (her) behavior, and empathize with him (her). You are an extension of the protagonist, the part of him (her) that is not vocal. Talk in the first person, and try to bring out that which is concealed and unexpressed. Check with your protagonist, periodically, that you are on the same track of thoughts. Remember, you talk *only with your protagonist.*"

For experienced protagonists and auxiliaries the therapist may simply say: "I would like to give you (the protagonist) a double. Is it OK with you? Whom do you want to be your double?" It is important to check with protagonists whether or not they want to have a double. Sometimes they do not. In addition, whenever possible it is preferable that the protagonists pick out their double. Chances are that they will choose those with whom they have already established close relationships. If the therapist wants to have a particular person as the double he or she should assign the role to that person *without* offering the choice of selection to the protagonist.

Indications (for Double and Multiple Doubles technique).

1. When the protagonist is in a conflict of experiencing undue stress.
2. When the protagonist feels alone, sad, depressed, or hurt.

3. When the protagonist seems inhibited or intimidated by the encounter he or she experiences with the other auxiliary.
4. When the level of interaction between the protagonist and the other auxiliary is superficial and needs to be either deepened or directed to the core issue(s).
5. When the therapist is looking for clue(s) for how to proceed to the next scene.

Contraindications (for Double and Multiple Doubles technique).

1. When the protagonist needs to meet challenges alone.
2. When the protagonist is very open and the role playing enactment flows smoothly (although the introduction of a double here is not really disruptive).
3. Use with caution when dealing with schizophrenic patients.
4. Use with caution when dealing with persons having paranoid tendencies.

The Aside

The *Aside* is a basic role playing technique which somewhat resembles the Soliloquy and the Double techniques described earlier. Its rationale, too, is very similar to that described for the Soliloquy. To some extent it combines several characteristics of both these techniques and in principle shares a similar therapeutic goal, that is, eliciting the protagonist's inner thoughts and feelings and bringing them into the open. Within this general frame of reference, however, the Aside stands out as a separate technique in two respects. First, unlike the Soliloquy or the Double technique, the Aside is introduced into the role playing production *only* when there are clear indications that the protagonist's communication is inaccurate in the sense that it *deliberately* conceals the real truth. The objective of the Aside technique is to address that concealed part of the communication and to make it publicly known. Second, the Aside technique is always used in combination with either the Roleplaying or the Dialogue techniques. It requires a context of an interaction between at least two persons: a protagonist and auxiliary who portrays the role of someone else.

The way the Aside technique operates is as follows: Consider a role playing situation in which the protagonist interacts with an auxiliary who portrays his wife. Let us also assume, for the purpose of our example, that the enactment reflects a replication of the real-life situation where the protagonist chooses to be less than candid with his wife. Here the therapist may decide to introduce the Aside technique. The protagonist does it by turning his head away from the auxiliary with whom he is talking (i.e., representing the wife), covering the side of his mouth that is toward her and then openly saying what he is really feeling, thinking, or planning to do. The Aside is relevant to instances where there is a discrepancy between the things the protagonist says and those that he or she keeps to himself or herself. The Aside is carried out with the understanding that the auxiliary continues to act as if he or she did *not* hear that which was said in the Aside. The following brief excerpt illustrates this technique.

Protagonist: OK Pam, what was it that you wanted to tell me?
Auxiliary (as Pam): Would you please call John and set a date for dinner with Gail and him. You know how much I like Gail and we haven't seen them for a long time.
Protagonist: I don't have their number with me, it's at the office. *(Aside: turns his head away from Pam, covers the side of his mouth and says, "Actually I remember their telephone number but John is such a bore! Maybe if I postpone it until tomorrow she'll forget to ask me again. I'm not going to call them tomorrow, that's for sure.")*
Auxiliary (as Pam): Will you remember to call him tomorrow, then?
Protagonist: I'll do my best.
Auxiliary (as Pam): You like John, don't you? I know you will enjoy an evening with them.
Protagonist: OK *(Aside: "There's no use starting an argument now. She has never understood my feelings towards John.")*

Ordinarily, the Aside is performed by the protagonist, but occasionally the auxiliary may use it, too. One such instance is when the role playing scene involves the protagonist and the original other as the auxiliary, that is, the real wife, real mother, real friend, and so forth. Thus, when using the Dialogue technique, all the participants may also use the Aside.

As mentioned above the Aside technique is used in interpersonal communication situations where the protagonist creates, consciously and deliberately, a discrepancy between his or her explicit message and another unspoken or hidden message. This phenomenon is commonly known as "a communication with a hidden agenda."

Rationale. Since psychotherapy requires that protagonists will be as completely honest as possible, it cannot allow them to behave in a manner that is less than candid. On the other hand, sometimes protagonists may find it difficult to be completely honest with the people near to them. For the moment, they need to adhere to a communication style characterized by "hidden agendas." The Aside technique permits them to retain that style but at the same time exposes the existence of such a hidden agenda. This is believed to be the first step towards altering the communication and making it completely open.

Instructions.

"I would like you to continue the scene the way you normally talk with your wife, mother, father, friend, employer, etc. But whenever there is a difference between what you say to him (her) and what you *really* think or feel, use the Aside technique: Turn your head aside, away from the auxiliary, cover the side of your mouth that is towards him (her) with one hand and tell us what you are really thinking, feeling, or planning to do. Then everyone continues the scene pretending that no one heard your Aside."

Indications.

1. When the therapist sees signs that the protagonist is withholding certain information, or that "something else is going on behind the overt messages."
2. When there are interpersonal problems based on one-sided or even mutual misunderstanding. This is especially true when certain assumptions are being taken for granted without direct checking through open communication.
3. When the therapist is looking for a clue for the next scene.

Contraindications.

1. When the communication seems to be open and clear, and the protagonist expresses himself or herself in what appears to be an uninhibited fashion.
2. When the enactment flows smoothly and the pauses created by the aside technique may interfere with the participants' involvement.

The Role-reversal

The *Role-reversal* technique, or simply *Role-reversal,* is one of the most important and potent therapeutic interventions of all the basic techniques described in this chapter. It is also the most popular role playing technique as evidenced by numerous case illustrations and experimental studies. These pertain to clinical applications (e.g., Alperson, 1976; Blume, 1971), as well as to uses in teaching and education (e.g., Carpenter, 1968), in industrial training (e.g., Kelly, Blake, & Stromberg, 1957; Shaw, Corsini, Blake, & Mouton, 1980; Speroff, 1955), in the training of interpersonal communication (Johnson, 1971b), in developing procedures for the understanding of intergroup processes, in the dynamics of bargaining, and in the study of attitude change (e.g., Johnson, 1967, 1971a; Johnson & Dustin, 1970; Kipper & Har-Even, 1980; Muney & Deutch, 1968), to mention only a few. The technique itself is remarkably simple. Two persons switch their roles for a brief period of time where A becomes B and B becomes A.

As a cognitive process Role-reversal is a very familiar phenomenon. Indeed many of our social interactions involve using mental role reversals. It is through such cognitive exercises that we articulate many of our responses to other people. Often people *think* how they would act if they were someone else and then proceed to fantasize an entire series of events imagining themselves being that other person. Often we are confronted by someone who asks us, "How would you react if you were me?" or "Put yourself in my position. Can you see my point of view?" In clinical role playing such cognitive "exercises" are translated into concrete experiences in the form of *actual* role reversals.

In the Role-reversal technique the two involved parties actually switch their physical positions with each other and assume each other's posture, mannerisms, and mental and psychological states. In the context of psychotherapy, *Role-reversal always involves the protagonist as one of the two role-reversing parties.* The protagonist temporarily becomes the auxiliary, while the auxiliary assumes the role of the protagonist for the duration of that reversal episode. During the enactment of a given scene the protagonist may reverse roles with the auxiliary back and forth several times if necessary, and do this on several occasions. But Role-reversal can be an emotionally demanding task and may lead to mental fatigue if used excessively. Since people often need time to gradually "ease their way" into the role of the other and for reorienting themselves in the newly assumed role, the length of staying in the reversed role is important. Experience has shown that this should not be very brief (unless it is used for the purpose of providing information, see Indications, below) and ordinarily ought to be measured in minutes rather than in seconds. As in the case of other basic techniques, it is not required that the involved parties be of the same sex; males can reverse roles with females.

The notion of role reversal stems from the existential approach in philosophy especially with regard to the concept of "encounter." In 1914 Moreno described the idea of "encounter," i.e., role reversal, in his philosophical poetry as follows:

> A meeting of two: eye to eye, face to face
> And when you are near I will tear your eyes out
>   and place them instead of mine
>   and you will tear my eyes out
>   and will place them instead of yours
>   then I will look at you with your eyes
>   and you will look at me with mine.
>   (Translated by J.L. Moreno, from Moreno, 1914, p. 3)

Expounding on the existential dynamics of Role-reversal, Bratter (1967) explained that the shift in roles, from one's own role to that of the other, creates a dialectic process of thesis and antithesis which produces a synthesis. This ultimately creates not only anxiety but also provides insight. Brind and Brind (1967) write:

> Initially, the protagonist, upon assuming the character of his "opponent," may actually intend to act as the "devil's advocate". . . . Yet the effect of the mere consent to relinquish one's own self, be it ever so deceptively or superficially, the very attempt to desist from the stance of confrontation, the sheer movement to the "other side," is of unfailing value . . . . Properly conducted, the ongoing process naturally compels the psychodramatic protagonist to deepen and to widen his empathic identification with the opponent, just as this same process compels him to see his own self-enactment through the eyes of the adversary or the adversary substitute (auxiliary ego) who now portrays him. (p. 176)

Similar positions were also taken by others (e.g., Speroff, 1955; Sylvester, 1970), including the hypothesis that Role-reversal promotes reconciliation, which is the basis of any mutual understanding (Cohen, 1951). It is also fitting here to mention that both J.L. Moreno (1964a) and later Z.T. Moreno (1975) saw the ability to properly role reverse as a developmental process essential for the social growth of the child. In the course of this growth, children have to learn to overcome three critical stages. They must learn to reverse roles with (a) inferior subhuman beings such as animals, (b) nonhuman objects, and (c) superior and powerful beings like parents, teachers, God, or the devil (Moreno,

1964a; see also Nolte, Smallwood, & Weistart, 1975). Experimental studies with Role-reversal showed that it produces more agreement in individualistic rather than in competitive conditions (Johnson & Dustin, 1970), and that the most important variable in effective Role-reversal is the accuracy of the sender's message coupled with the expression of warmth and acceptance of the sender (Johnson, 1971a).

Instructions.

"Reverse roles! I want you (the protagonist) to sit (stand) here, where the auxiliary was and be the person portrayed by the auxiliary. Behave and talk exactly like him (her). And you (the auxiliary) move here where the protagonist was and try and be him (her) exactly. Now (to the auxiliary who portrays now the protagonist) will you, please, repeat the last sentence that the protagonist has just said?"

For experienced protagonists and auxiliaries it is sufficient to say "Reverse roles."

Indications.

1. When an auxiliary portrays the role of someone well known to the protagonist but requires further information to do a credible job. This information can be provided by the protagonist through an action method, that is, by becoming that person and offering the missing information through modeling and demonstration. Typically these kinds of Role-reversals are very brief.
2. When the therapist needs more information about the protagonist. Many protagonists venture to reveal more about themselves once taken out of their own roles and placed in a role of the auxiliary. Getting out of their roles often reduces their original defensive and guarded postures.
3. When the role played interaction between the protagonist and the auxiliary needs to be further intensified, or when it gets close to a dead-end while the main issue(s) remains largely unexplored.
4. When dealing with a conflict between intimates, a conflict that ought to be resolved through reconciliation and the recognition of everybody's needs.

Contraindications.

1. When the action proceeds smoothly and openly in a meaningful fashion.
2. When the protagonist is too threatened or intimidated by the personality, traits, or behavior portrayed by the auxiliary (e.g., a liar, a sadist, a rapist, a saint, an adversary).
3. When, according to Starr (1977), the therapist deals with psychotic patients.

> Some patients can enact a person in authority but not one who accepts authority. Many psychotic patients are unwilling to play the role of the other and either respond with terror, taking the role as real, or make no effort to influence or change the course of events.(p. 44)

4. Too many Role-reversals may cause fatigue both physically and psychologically.

The following illustrates the use of Role-reversal. This is a part of a session with Susan, the protagonist, who was 18 years old and who complained of having endless arguments and quarrels with her mother. When asked for a typical example of such arguments she responded, "Well, take her attitude towards the boys I date." The scene involved Susan and her mother as played by an auxiliary, and it took place in her parents' kitchen after dinner.

Mother (played by the auxiliary): Are you going out tonight?
Susan: Yes.
Mother: With John, again?
Susan: Yes, *again! (makes a mockery of the last word).*
Mother: (disapprovingly) As usual, I don't suppose you're interested in my opinion?
Susan: That's right.
Mother: Frankly, I don't know what you see in him. You deserve better.
Susan: (explodes) I told you that I'm not interested in your opinion. But you gave it anyway. It's *my* life and I'll do with it as I please. I'll date anyone *I* want. Stop interfering. You don't own me, you know! *(gets up from her chair to leave the kitchen in a protest)*
Director: Wait a minute. Maybe that's how you end the conversation usually. But what I want you to do here is to reverse roles with your mother. You take the role of mother and sit here *(points to*

mother's chair) and you *(the auxiliary)* move to the protagonist's chair and be Susan. *(to the auxiliary)* Who are you? What's your name? And who's sitting in front of you?

Auxiliary (as Susan): I'm Susan, and this is my mother. *(points to the protagonist)*

Director: (to the auxiliary) Susan, will you please repeat the last sentence said by the protagonist?

Auxiliary (as Susan): . . . You don't own me, you know!

Mother (now played by the protagonist): But you are *my* daughter.

Auxiliary (as Susan): That doesn't give you the right to run my life.

Mother (Susan): Listen, I'm not running your life. I've experience and I only want the best for you.

Auxiliary (as Susan): Ha!!!

Mother (Susan): We always seem to fight. Always! I'd dreamt that my daughter would be my closest friend.

Auxiliary (as Susan): You're not my friend, you're my mother.

Mother (Susan): That really hurts. *(begins to cry)*

Auxiliary (as Susan): Look, Mom *(holds her hand affectionately)*, I don't want to hurt you, you know that. But I really don't understand you. Are you afraid that something will happen to me or what?

Mother (Susan): Maybe.

Auxiliary (as Susan): What is it?

Mother (Susan): I don't know. Maybe I'm afraid that *my* hopes for you will never come true. Maybe I'm afraid that if I don't protect you something terrible will happen to you. Oh! I'm so confused and scared.

Auxiliary (as Susan): I *am* grown up, mother. I don't need your protection.

Mother (Susan): I don't want to lose you. *(sobs)*

Auxiliary (as Susan): You're not going to lose me, Mom. Don't you feel happy if I'm happy? Isn't that the most important thing?

Mother (Susan): But you don't share your happiness with me, you only fight with me.

Director: Reverse roles again. Everyone resumes her original role. *(to the auxiliary)* Repeat the last sentence said by the protagonist as her own mother.

Mother (played now by the auxiliary): But you don't share your happiness with me.

Susan: (still in tears from her previous role) I guess I don't. God knows why but I feel that mothers are only good for fights and to argue with.

Director: Thank you. Let's stop here. Susan, would you like to explore the answer to your last question in another scene?

Susan: Yes.

The Empty-chair Technique

The *Empty-chair*, sometimes also referred to as the *Auxiliary chair* (e.g., Lippitt, 1958; Z.T. Moreno, 1965), is one of the better known role playing techniques and has been widely employed, especially in psychodrama and gestalt therapy. It is one of the techniques, like Self-presentation, that is performed by the protagonist acting without the help of an auxiliary. To be more precise, in this technique the protagonist interacts with an imaginary counterpart represented by one or more empty chair(s). The *chair*, serving in an auxiliary capacity, represents an absentee. It may represent an inanimate object such as a crib, a crutch, or a home. It may represent a concept, a trait, a skill, or a handicap, (e.g., a place in the sibling hierachy; dominance; a profession or a trade; a fear, an inferiority feeling, or a barrier; a block to be conquered). Most frequently, however, the Empty-chair is introduced to represent a person with whom the protagonist is emotionally involved. That person may be alive or dead, someone else, one's own self or an aspect of the self.

In this technique the protagonist talks with the imagined absentee as represented by the empty chair. In the beginning this takes the form of a monologue but soon it is supplemented by the Role-reversal technique. The protagonist keeps changing roles, as well as seats, with that absentee, alternating between that role and his or her own. This "two-ways monologue" maintains the flow of the interaction. It is also important that subsequently the Empty-chair will be filled with a concrete person, an auxiliary, with whom the protagonist can communicate as if the imagined absentee were really there.

In its simplest form, the Empty-chair technique uses one chair. But it can also be extended to become an elaborated scene using several empty chairs representing a number of roles. For instance, two empty chairs may stand for the nice-guy part of a protagonist and the bad-guy part. A group of empty chairs may represent an entire repertoire of one's role (e.g., the husband, the father, the provider, the boss, the handyman, the tutor, the intellectual companion, the social secretary). The Empty-(auxiliary)-chair has been known to be useful as a warm-up technique (Weiner & Sacks, 1969), as a therapeutic intervention proper (Z.T. Moreno, 1965), and as a didactic technique (Warner, 1970). There have been numerous variations of this technique including its adaptation as a Self-presentation technique (e.g., Kipper, 1977).

Rationale. The use of the Empty-chair concerns those instances in which protagonists are not ready to face painful confrontations with which they should deal therapeutically. Under ordinary circumstances such protagonists will be inclined to avoid and deny these unpleasant experiences altogether. The Empty-chair technique helps them to acknowledge these feelings, and encounter them in a less threatening context. This technique offers a vehicle for using "sheltered" confrontations in which protagonists can exercise full control over the situation. It also provides opportunities for projections and displacements.

Instructions. The therapist introduces this technique by placing an empty chair in the center of the actions space facing the protagonist (or the group members in the case of a group treatment). Then the following instructions might be given:

> "I would like you to focus on this chair. Do not look at me, just concentrate on this empty chair. As you look at the chair, try to seat in it, in your imagination, someone with whom you have 'unfinished business.' Try to visualize that person as vividly and as accurately as you can and hold that image for a few seconds."

The therapist then asks the protagonist, or members of the group, for the identity of their imagined absentees. Often people report that they have seen a parade of persons before they were able to focus on a particular person. Sometimes they report that the chosen absentee kept coming and disappearing. Then the therapist proceeds:

> "Now, I would like you (a protagonist, or one group member at a time) to address the person you have just visualized in the chair, and tell him (her) whatever you would like to tell him (her)."

When the situation is such that the chair or chairs represents an already known absentee(s), the following instructions might be offered:

> "We have here several empty chairs each representing one of the list of absentees you have mentioned (e.g., several members of one's family, a number of traits and skills one has, a list of responsibilities or roles one assumes in a given function). I would like you to tell me which chair represents which absentee. You may also move and arrange each chair so that its distance from you indicates how important it is for you. The closer the distance the greater the importance. Then tell me which chair you want to address first, and you may begin.

Indications.

1. In the beginning of a session as a warm-up technique. In a group therapy situation the Empty-chair can also serve as a method for selecting a protagonist. Using the Empty-chair as a medium for projection, participants may bring out "unfinished business" with significant people in their lives. The therapist may use this material to select a protagonist he or she, as well as the group members, wants to work with.
2. *Any time* the therapist is looking for a significant clue to begin a scene.
3. When dealing with a protagonist who needs to express negative feelings, especially anger in the form of physical violence. This can be done by channeling the aggression towards the empty chair (appropriate measures must be instituted to physically safeguard all participants).
4. When dealing with a protagonist who needs to express an intense positive emotion toward an absentee, but refrains from doing so in order not to embarrass the actual person.
5. When a protagonist has profound feelings of guilt and needs to work them out (Z.T. Moreno, 1965).

Contraindications. There are no particular instances where the Empty-chair technique is contraindicated. The technique is appropriate for a variety of needs and situations and often lends itself to become a basis for a complete session. As long as it is properly handled, it has not been reported to have had adverse impacts.

The Mirror Technique

This technique is a behavior simulation intervention specifically designed to provide the protagonist with live feedback. In principle, it operates and actually serves the same therapeutic functions as videotape replays (Berger, 1978). The main reasons why clinical role playing uses the Mirror techniques rather than videotape technology are that (a) historically it was invented long before such technology was easily available, and (b) since the Mirror technique uses action language, it fits better the role playing approach.

The *Mirror* technique is performed by an auxiliary who assumes the role of the protaganist for a brief period of time while the latter observes that portrayal from a distance, outside the action space. The auxiliary's task is first to replicate the protagonist's behavior but occasionally it could also involve a slight exaggeration of certain aspects of that behavior. In that respect the auxiliary's function is that of a "psychological" mirror. For this the auxiliary must use his or her sensitivity and judgment, often in a prior consultation with the therapist, as to which parts of the protagonist's behavior should be mirrored accurately and which overemphasized. Traditionally, this technique is used within the context of a closed-door therapy session. But it can also be used effectively on the spot, in a hospital ward, for example (Pankratz, 1971).

Rationale. This is based on the role of the self-confrontation concept in psychotherapy. An extensive discussion of this subject is beyond the scope of the present context. The interested reader may be referred to other sources (e.g., two chapters in Berger (1978), one by H.H. Garner, "A review of confrontation in psychotherapy from hypnosis to the problem-solving technique," and one by M.M. Berger, "Confrontation through videotape"). By way of a short summary we might quote the following excerpt:

> Confrontation in treatment is a form of psychotherapeutic intervention. However, whether it serves as more of an interference or intrusion than a constructive intervention will depend upon the scientific and artistic skills of the therapist, his intuitive sense of timing, and the goals for confrontation envisioned by the therapist. (Berger, 1978, p. 19)

The following is an illustration of the Mirror technique. It is a segment of a psychodramatic treatment used with an actual case reported by Hollander (1967). It shows the use of the Mirror technique and how it can eventually lead to the involvement of a reluctant protagonist in a role playing session. We will bring the description of the first scene as reported with minor editorial changes in the explanatory text so that the reader may follow it easily. The protagonist in this case was Mrs. W., a 49-year-old white divorced female who had been diagnosed as suffering from chronic brain syndrome with "regression." She was one of nine children and had been living in isolation from her consanguinal family. Her nuclear family had all but dissolved, with an only son, Richard, living elsewhere. Mrs. W. had been hospitalized several times and her most recent nursing home experience was terminated because of "unmanageable" behavior. She talked about her preoccuation with her son's death (a false belief that he had met a violent death on the "freeway") and her own irrevocable death (which she believed would soon take place). In the following excerpt, the actual Mrs. W. will be referred to as "protagonist," the auxiliary who mirrors her is called "Helene," and the auxiliary who portrays the role of the protagonist's (as well as Helene's) mother will be referred to as "Mrs. Smith." As the scene starts, the protagonist who refuses to participate and who is confined to a wheelchair, watches the action from a distance.

Helene (an auxiliary mirroring Mrs. W.'s screaming behavior): Richard's dead! Richard's dead! No, no, no , no!

Director: Helene, can you tell me how Richard died?

Helene: Richard, Richard. He's dead! The highway killed him. No, no, no, no.

*Protagonist (from her observation place):*No, no, no, no, the *freeway.* Ha, ha, ha, ha. *(laughing hysterically, sliding rigidly from her wheelchair, laughing and screaming, "Richard, Richard, Richard, Richard")*

Helene: The freeway *killed* him. I am going to die.

(The director helps to put the protagonist, now in tears for the first time, back into her wheelchair and stays next to her.)

Director: Who can help her? *(pointing to Helene)*

Protagonist (from her observation place): No one. No one. Oh, oh, no one! *(screaming).*

Helene: I love children! I love children. I want my mommy and daddy!

Director (to Helene): Are they warm and loving parents?

Protagonist (whispering): My mother was.

Director (to the protagonist): What is mother's name?

Protagonist (still in her observation place): Mrs. Smith.

Director (to the protagonist): Where were you born?

Protagonist: In Sand Creek, Colorado.

(The director set the scene at the hospital delivery room in Mrs. W.'s birthplace.)

Director (as the doctor to an auxiliary who portrays the mother, Mrs. Smith): Mrs. Smith, Mrs. Smith.

Mrs. Smith: Yes doctor. Is it over? Oh God, that was terrible. *(begins to scream as the protagonist usually screams)*

Doctor: You have a little girl.

Mrs. Smith: Is she OK? Does she have ten fingers and ten toes?

Doctor: Yes, she's all right. However, she will need corrective therapy on her legs and feet. *(later it was found that this was not true)*

Mrs. Smith: Oh, no! Why me? I don't want it. I don't want the baby!

Protagonist (from her observation place): No! No! No! She loved me! Oh, no.

(At this point it was apparent that the protagonist is very involved and ready to take a part in the scene. She was lifted from her wheelchair and put in Mrs. Smith's [the auxiliary's] lap).

Director (to the protagonist now in *the scene playing herself as the little baby girl):* Mrs. W., Betty *(the auxiliary)* is going to be mommy. You sit on mommy's lap. Mrs. Smith, how is the baby Helene eating? Is she colicky? Does she sleep well or does she cry?

Mrs. Smith: She's a wonderful baby.

Protagonist: (in a weak baby voice) Oh, mommy, mommy!

Mrs. Smith: (beginning to rock the protagonist) Now Helene, it's all right. Mommy's here. I love you.

The initial purpose of the session was to obtain additional information about Mrs. W. and the Mirror technique was an attempt to get her involved. The session continued with two episodes from her own childhood. In these she was a little more cooperative. On the basis of her responses to the entire session it decided that another session ought to be conducted.

Instructions.

(To the protagonist): "Could you please step outside the action space, and stand here, with me. I am going to ask someone to portray you in the scene. Watch that portrayal for a while. You may observe it quietly or make comments to me or to the auxiliaries any time you wish."

(To the mirroring auxiliary): "I would like you to assume the role of the protagonist in this scene. Behave exactly as the protagonist did in terms of mannerisms, gestures, and tone of voice. Go ahead."

Indications.

1. When the protagonist is *reluctant* to follow the therapist's instructions to respond to the auxiliaries, is withdrawn, and is not sufficiently warmed-up (Yablonsky, 1976), or chooses not to become involved in the role playing enactment of a scene.

2. When the protagonist does take part in the scene but evinces a lack of insight into his or her own actions, and into the impact of his

or her own actions, and into the impact of his or her attitude and behavior.

3. When dealing with protagonists who have been unable to interact with others appropriately, with depressed individuals, misbehaving children, or fantasy-ridden persons (Starr, 1977).

Contraindications.

1. When dealing with protagonists who are overly defensive and sensitive, especially those demonstrating low self-esteem.
2. When dealing with protagonists who have suicidal tendencies or paranoid inclinations.

It is quite obvious from the *indications* for the use of the Mirror that this basic specific technique is designated to address resistance on the part of protagonists. But what forms of resistance are likely to disappear through the application of this technique? And is this the only behavior simulation intervention available for the treatment of resistance? The answers to these two questions require further discussion of the manifestations of resistance in clinical role playing.

Resistance is a complex construct. It has a motivational as well as a behavioral dimension. The former concerns the *reasons* that cause protagonists to resist some aspects of the therapeutic endeavor, while the latter refers to the *way(s)* they display their resisting attitude(s). It would be helpful, perhaps, to emphasize from the outset that the conceptualization of resistance in clinical role playing offers no new theoretical insights with regard to these two dimensions. One may subscribe to psychodynamic conceptualizations or alternatively to those espoused by behavior modification and cognitive-behavioral therapy. The ways these two groups of approaches view resistance have been discussed at length in a recent book by Wachtel (1982) and need not be reiterated here. Actually, regardless of one's conceptual preference, any one of these approaches will lend itself to the application of clinical role playing. Therefore, the unique contribution of clinical role playing to the issue of resistance is not in the theoretical domain but rather in the area of application.

Let us elaborate some more on the motivational and the behavioral dimensions. The motivational one is associated with the issue: What is it that resistance resists? Briefly, it seems fair to conclude that, in general, all therapies agree that resistance resists a change. If therapies differ from each other it is in the answer to the question: Why do people resist a change? The emphasis in the cited reasons for resistance varies from those attributed to unconscious, to preconscious, and to conscious processes. Some attribute resistance to suppressed infantile desires and other hidden wishes, to a reluctance to depart from the comfort accrued by "secondary gains," or to pessimism, hopelessness, and hostility. Others ascribe it to an unwillingness to take risks, and expression of the fear of becoming involved with the unknown and acting upon unfamiliar expectations and unverified outcomes.

The behavioral dimension is concerned with the manifestations of resistance. It addresses the various forms that resistance is communicated by the protagonists. These are usually divided into two groups of modes of expression: overt and covert. The overt ones are fairly easy to read and understand, and most therapies will agree on their meaning. Any disagreement among therapies will express itself in reading, understanding the meaning of, and indeed the significance attached to, some of the covert clues. But even here, the extent of the agreement by far exceeds the instances of dissension.

The foregoing discussion offers a general answer to the question, what is it that resistance resists? But the same question may also be treated differently. It can be understood as: What *specific elements* in the treatment can induce resistance on the part of protagonist? Generally, every form of psychotherapy contains four elements that may elicit resistance: the content of issue under treatment, the therapist, the treatment format, and the therapeutic process. Of course, we are familiar with the argument that the separation of these four is superfluous because resistance to each of them merely reflects a different expression of the same basic resistance stance. But experience has shown that this is not necessarily true in every case. The view that resistance always stems from one basic stance tends to obfuscate and generalize intervention strategies rather than refine them. The distinction among these elements has practical advantages because each may be addressed somewhat differently.

Looking at these four elements in the context of clinical role playing it becomes apparent that resistance to the first two, that is, the issue and the therapist, expresses itself in the same manner it is displayed in other forms of therapy.

- *Resisting the issue:* Protagonists may resist a confrontation with the issue both overtly and covertly. Examples of explicit resistance are: denying the existence of the problem, requesting (sometimes demanding) that the subject be dropped or not be raised at all. Examples of implicit resistance are: changing the topic in the middle of the discussion, falling out of the role, mishearing the director or the auxiliaries, commanding the scene by talking incessantly and occupying most of the "air-time," decreasing the involvement in the enactment, silence, or missing appointments.

• *Resisting the therapist:* Protagonists may resist the therapist, that is, reject his or her expertise and leadership, for a variety of reasons. Typically, this eventually results in the termination of the treatment contract. Protagonists leave and seek other alternatives. Explicit resistance in this case is displayed in a request to terminate the therapeutic relationship. Examples of implicit resistance are: continuous arguments with the way the therapist conducts the treatment, criticism of certain traits in his or her personality, or comparing the therapist to other therapists in an uncomplimentary fashion.

But in clinical role playing, resistance to the last two elements, that is, the treatment format and the therapeutic process, manifests itself differently. This is due to the fact that this therapeutic modality is conducted in an unconventional manner; it uses auxiliaries and role playing enactments.

• *Resisting the therapeutic format:* Protagonists may resist working with auxiliaries, in general. Typically, this reflects a preference to participate in an individual rather than a group therapy. But some protagonists may not object to the group format yet they do refuse to be assisted by auxiliaries. This kind of a resistance is rare. It may occur with psychotics, especially with paranoid protagonists. A more common resistance, in this category, is a rejection of a particular auxiliary. The protagonist may prefer to work with some group members but not with others. The explicit manifestations of this are, for instance, changing an auxiliary chosen by the director, or declining an offer by a given person to serve as an auxiliary. Examples of implicit resistance are: correcting the behavior and statement of the auxiliary constantly, voicing frequent requests for Role-reversals, a reduced involvement in the scene when interacting with one auxiliary but not with others, or not allowing sufficient "air-time" for the auxiliary.

Usually, directors allow protagonists to have their choice of auxiliaries. They do not make an issue of such a form of resistance because it tends to subside and disappear with time. If if does not, the resistance may be brought up as a subject for a session, but only in a later phase of the treatment.

• *Resisting the therapeutic process:* The term "therapeutic process" is used in this context in an unorthodox way to convey the specific characteristic of clinical role playing, i.e., the use of actional language. Protagonists may resist requests to describe their conflicts and difficulties in the form of role playing. Often they will say, "I don't want to role play. Let's talk about my problem," or "I don't like role playing," or "Role playing is not useful," or "Role playing is childish," or "I'm not good as an actor. I've never been good in acting." Obviously, most of the expressions of resistance to use the actional language are explicit, simply because protagonists wish to prevent getting involved in role playing. Sometimes, however, they agree to give it a try. Then, if the resistance persists, it may express itself implicitly by frequent falling out of the role, running out of things to say, or behaving in an extremely controlled and guarded manner.

We can turn back now to the questions raised in the beginning of the present discussion. What forms of resistance are likely to disappear through the use of the Mirror technique? It seems that its greatest usefulness is in dealing with resistance to the issue. This holds true when it is expressed overtly, but perhaps more so when it is manifested covertly. Is the Mirror the only behavior simulation intervention available for the treatment of resistance? The answer is no. Other basic specific techniques may be used to handle resistance, as well, but they have not been designated specifically for such a purpose. For example, resisting the assistance of auxiliaries may be handled through the use of the Empty-chair technique. Often, protagonists become tired of talking to an empty chair for a long time, and *ask* for the help of an auxiliary. The Double technique is also very useful in countering resistance. Suppose a protagonist resists a confrontation with a threatening issue. The director may ask one auxiliary to represent the protagonist and to face the "dangerous" encounter, while the protagonist becomes the double (i.e., to double the auxiliary who is playing himself or herself). This allows the protagonist to become involved intermittently, at will. As soon as the double (portrayed by the protagonist) feels comfortable in the scene, he or she may reverse role with the auxiliary, assume the protagonist role, and continue the confrontation under the self-identity. The Role-reversal technique, too, may serve to counter the element of resisting the issue. Often, people reveal information about themselves under an *assumed* identity that they will not reveal while under their *own* identity.

Finally, the Mirror technique tackles resistance in an explicit mode.

Other techniques may do it implicitly. The implicit-explicit dimension of clinical role playing techniques is discussed in detail in Chapter 8.

THE TECHNIQUES' PARADIGM

In the beginning of this chapter, clinical role playing techniques were divided into two major catergories identified as the *basic* and the *situational* groups. The ensuing discussion focused on nine interventions grouped under the heading: the *specific techniques*. What is the reason for singling out these techniques as a separate subgroup? Do these nine specific techniques have a shared characteristic that justifies their inclusion in one distinguishable category? At first glance it seems quite difficult to detect a common feature that unites these techniques. A closer examination, however, uncovers an interesting structural basis underlying these role playing interventions. This structural basis is to be henceforth referred to as "the techniques paradigm." It portrays all the possible combinations of the interactions among the principal participants in a given enactment and the kinds of roles that they assume.

With regard to the principal participants, every clinical role playing scene requires the presence of one protagonist, or at least one auxiliary, but preferably both. Essentially, these two participants can portray three kinds of roles: They can portray *themselves*, they can represent *someone else* who is not personally present in the scene, and they can assume the role of *each other*. Let the code letter P stand for the protagonist, and the code letter A for the auxiliary. The code letter *s* will represent the the portrayal of the self role, that is, playing one's own self. The code letter *o* will represent the portrayal of the role of someone else, usually an absentee. Let the code letter *a* stand for those instances when the protangonist assumes the role of the auxiliary, and the code letter *p* for scenes when the auxiliary assumes the role of the protagonist. The techniques' paradigm lists all the possible combinations of the protagonist playing his or her three roles (i.e., P*s*, P*o*, P*a*), either alone or with an auxiliary playing his or her three roles (i.e., A*s*, A*o*, A*p*). It also includes the three combinations of the auxiliary portraying his or her three roles alone.

Table 6.1 is arranged in three columns which, looking from left to right, are: a list of all the possible combinations presented in code letters, the descriptions of the meaning of each code combination, and a list of the relevant technique(s), that is, the specific techniques(s) that corresponds to each of the 15 combinations.

The left column is divided into four sections. The first 12 combinations

TABLE 6.1

Players and Their Roles Combinations Paradigm with the Corresponding Specific Techniques

Code	Description		Relevant Technique(s)
	Group I: Protagonist plays him/herself		
1. Ps : —	P plays him/herself.	A outside the action.	Soliloquy. Self-presentation. Empty-chair. Aside.*
2. Ps : As	P plays him/herself.	A plays him/herself.	Dialogue.
3. Ps : Ao	P plays him/herself.	A plays someone else.	Self-presentation/Role-playing combination.
4. Ps : Ap	P plays him/herself.	A plays the protagonist.	Double. (Multiple Doubles).**
	Group II: Protagonist plays someone else		
5. Po : —	P plays someone else.	A outside the action.	Role-playing. (solo).
6. Po : As	P plays someone else.	A plays him/herself.	Role-playing/Self-presentation combination.
7. Po : Ao	P plays someone else.	A plays someone else.	Role-playing. (Dyadic).
8. Po : Ap	P plays someone else.	A plays the protagonist.	Role-playing/Role-reversal combination.
	Group III: Protagonist plays the auxiliary		
9. Pa : —	P plays the auxiliary.	A outside the action.	Role-reversal. (Mirror).
10. Pa : As	P plays the auxiliary.	A plays him/herself.	Double (in reverse).
11. Pa : Ao	P plays the auxiliary.	A plays someone else.	Role-reversal/Role-playing combination.
12. Pa : Ap	P plays the auxiliary.	A plays the protagonist.	Role-reversal.
	Group IV: Auxiliary plays solo roles		
13. — : As	A plays him/herself.	P outside the action.	Soliloquy. Self-presentation. Empty-chair. Aside.***
14. — : Ao	A plays someone else.	P outside the action.	Role-playing. (solo).***
15. — : Ap	A plays the protagonist.	P outside the action.	Mirror. Double for absentee P.

P = The protagonist. A = The auxiliary. s = the *role* of oneself. o = The *role* of someone else, usually an absentee.
p = The *role* of the protagonist. a = The *role* of the particular auxiliary.

*The Aside technique is always combined with another technique.
**It becomes Multiple Doubles with two or more auxiliaries.
***This is a possible but rather atypical combination because when the auxiliary is alone and plays s or o, he or she actually becomes the protagonist. In that case it is the same as numbers 1 and 5, respectively.

are arranged according to the roles portrayed by the protagonist. Thus, combinations 1 through 4 are those where the protagonist plays himself or herself either alone or with an auxiliary who portrays each of the three roles. Combinations 5 through 8 are those where the protagonist assumes the role of someone else who is not personally present in the scene, again either alone or with an auxiliary in each of the three roles. In the third section, combinations 9 through 12, the protagonist portrays the role of the participating auxiliary. The fourth section, that is, combinations 13 through 15, is arranged according to the roles of the auxiliary but *only* in those instances when the protagonist does not take part in the enactment. There are clinical role playing situations where the protagonist is temporarily removed from the action space, as in the use of the Mirror technique. These, admittedly, are rather unusual situations because when the protagonist is removed from the action for a longer period of time the auxiliary actually becomes the protagonist.

Turning now to the right column in the paradigm, one can see how the nine specific techniques correspond to the combinations listed in the left column. A glance at Table 6.1 shows that each of these nine specific techniques is represented by at least one of the following combinations: 1, 2, 4, 5, 7, 9, 10, 12, 13, 14, and 15. Table 6.1 also shows that sometimes there are several techniques that correspond to one combination pattern (e.g., 1, 13, and 15).

On the other hand, sometimes the same technique may correspond to more than one combination pattern. For example, the Soliloquy, the Self-presentation, the Empty-chair, and the Aside are a group of specific techniques that corresponds to both combinations 1 and 13. The Role-playing (solo) technique corresponds to both combinations 5 and 14, and the Mirror technique corresponds to combinations 9 and 15. The Double technique, for example, also corresponds to two combinations (4 and 10). Again, in combination 4 the auxiliary doubles the protagonist, whereas in combination 10 the protagonist doubles the auxiliary. Two techniques, the Role-playing and the Role-reversal, can be applied in situations involving a single player (combinations 5 and 14, and 9 respectively) or in situations involving two players (combinations 7 and 12 respectively).

Of all the combinations listed in the left column of the paradigm, four do not correspond to any of the nine specific techniques singly. Instead, they describe a combination of two techniques used simultaneously. There are two combinations of the Self-presentation and the Role-playing techniques (nos. 3 and 6), and two combinations of the Role-playing and the Role-reversal techniques (nos. 8 and 11). The fact that basic role playing techniques may be combined and applied simultaneously is an essential characteristic of this kind of therapeutic intervention. For instance, the Aside is always combined with another technique or the Double is often used in a combination of Self-presentation (the protagonist portraying himself or herself) and Doubling (the auxiliary playing the role of the protagonist).

In conclusion, the features that the nine specific techniques have in common are: (a) they are clinical role playing interventions that can be introduced in the enactment of any psychological or behavioral problem and conflict regardless of its content; and (b) they represent the clinical application of the combinations of the interactions among the principal players in any role playing scene and the roles that they portray.

Table 6.1 describes a simple case involving only one and two players. But what happens to the paradigm when more players participate in the enactment, for example, one protagonist and *two* auxiliaries? The answer is that the basic paradigm remains intact, but the extra auxiliary and his or her roles need to be added to the existing list of combinations. For example, suppose the protagonist is in a family therapy situation and the scene involves both his parents who are present in the session. This is a three-party Dialogue technique (combination 2 in Table 6.1). Every participant plays his or her self role, that is, Ps:A1s (father), A2s (mother). If, however, the real parents are absent from the session and need to be represented by other auxiliaries, the situation becomes a Self-presentation/Role-playing combination (3 in Table 6.1). The protagonist plays himself, and each auxiliary assumes the role of one parent, that is, Ps:A1o (father), A2o (mother). Suppose, the Multiple Doubles technique is used (combination 4 in Table 6.1). The protagonist is assisted by two auxiliaries, each serving as a specialized Double, for example, one representing the protagonist's anger and one his guilt. The combination code here will read Ps:A1p (anger), A2p (guilt).

Often a scene may involve more than one technique, and as the scene unfolds different techniques are introduced. For instance, consider the situation described earlier where the protagonist confronts his parents who are represented by two auxiliaries (not the real parents). This is a two-way Self-presentation/Role-playing combination (3 in Table 6.1) and, therefore, can be described as follows: Ps:A1o (father), A2o (mother). After a few minutes the protagonist is instructed to reverse role with the A1o (father) auxiliary. The protagonist now portrays the role of his own father, whereas the auxiliary assumes the role of the protagonist. This new situation will become a combined Role-playing/Role-reversal techniques (combination 8 in Table 6.1) and, therefore, is described as: Po

(father) : A1*p*, A2*o* (mother). In this manner, it is possible to describe the behavior of the participants in any portion of a given scene provided a basic specific technique is used.

In situations where four or more players are involved, the techniques' paradigm needs to be expanded accordingly, bearing in mind that there is only one protagonist in the scene. The added players are auxiliaries who may portray different kinds of roles.

The division of the participants' roles in three basic types—the *s*, the *o*, and the *a* or *p* roles—reminds us of the spontaneous, mimetic-pretend, and mimetic-replication patterns (see the Behavior Simulation Paradigm in Chapter 2). Indeed, there seems to be a great degree of congruency between the techniques' paradigm and the Behavior Simulation Paradigm. The relation between these two paradigms becomes clearer when one combines them together. Table 6.2 shows the Behavior Simulation Paradigm and the way each of the nine specific techniques fits in it.

The nine specific techniques are arranged in Table 6.2 in three columns. The second from the left pertains to simulation conditions where the *model* is *present* in the session and is the *player himself* or *herself*. Essentially, these conditions fall into the spontaneous category and fit five techniques. The first four can be employed with unspecified instructions (behavior), are more spontaneous, and appear in the spontaneous portion of the column at the top. The Self-presentation is a more prescribed behavior and therefore contains some elements of mimetic-replication. Its place in the Table is at the bottom of the first column. It should be recalled that the Self-presentation technique sometimes involves the protagonist in the role of significant others. That part of Self-presentation actually falls under the Role-playing technique.

The third column from the left refers to simulation conditions where the *model* is *present* in the session and it is *someone else*. Essentially, these conditions fall in the mimetic-replication category and fit three techniques: the Double (and the Multiple Doubles), the Role-reversal, and the Mirror. The Double technique can be an unspecified task (i.e., "be the protagonist") but usually involves some specific instructions about the behavior to be portrayed. Therefore, it appears in Table 6.2 somewhere in the middle of the unspecified-prescribed continuum. The same applies to the Role-reversal technique. The Mirror, on the other hand, is strictly a mimetic-replication situation. Therefore, it appears at the bottom of the column.

Finally, the right column in Table 6.2 pertains to simulation conditions where the *model* is *absent* from the session and is *someone else*. Essentially, these conditions fall in the mimetic-pretend category, and fit the Role-

TABLE 6.2
The Relations of the Specific Techniques and the Behavior Simulation Paradigm

The behavior is:	Present				Absent			
	Endogenous		Exogenous		Endogenous		Exogenous	
	Essentially Spontaneous		Essentially Mimetic-Replication				Essentially Mimetic-Pretend	
	Technique	Code	Technique	Code	Technique	Code	Technique	Code
Unspecified	Soliloquy	1, 13			—	—	Role-playing	5, 7, 14 *3, 6, 8*
	Empty-chair	1, 13	Double	4, 10				
	Aside	1, 13	Role-reversal	9, 12 *8, 11*				
	Dialogue	2						
Prescribed	Self-presentation	1, 13 *3, 6*	Mirror	9, 15	—	—	Role-playing	5, 7, 14 *3, 6, 8*

playing technique. The Role-playing technique is usually a combination of behavior simulation categories. It is always a mimetic-pretend situation. The reason why the Role-playing technique appears twice in the column is so that it can occur under two types of situations: one characterized as mimetic-pretend/spontaneous combination, and the other as mimetic-pretend/mimetic-replication combination. The former refers to the portrayal of a vaguely known model, whereas the latter refers to the portrayal of a model which is *somewhat* familiar to the player.

The numbers that appear inside Table 6.2 refer to the code combinations as listed in the techniques paradigm (Table 6.1). The numbers in italics are those that represent a combination of techniques.

COMBINATIONS OF THE SPECIFIC TECHNIQUES

We now turn to the discussion on the various combinations of role playing techniques: the combinations within the *specific techniques* subgroup. This is an extremely important issue because often the techniques' combination patterns provide clinical role playing with its therapeutic strength.

Let us begin with an illustration of two of the nine specific techniques. Consider the combination of the *Soliloquy* and the *Double*. In this situation the protagonist soliloquizes walking around the periphery of the action stage accompanied by an auxiliary in the role of a double. The double helps the protagonist to be open and spontaneous and adds to the effectiveness of the soliloquy itself. Or consider another example of the combination of *three* specific techniques, say, the *Double, Role-reversal,* and *Role-playing.* The protagonist interacts with an auxiliary portraying his father (the Role-playing technique). Then he is provided with a double, a second auxiliary (Double and Role-playing combination). At this point the protagonist is asked to reverse role with the auxiliary portraying the father to become the father, while the auxiliary temporarily assumes the protagonist's role. During this episode the double continues alongside the auxiliary who now represents the protagonist.

But not every single specific technique may be combined with each of the remaining eight techniques. Some can be grouped together and some cannot. Table 6.3 shows the alternative combination patterns.

Consider the upper portion of Table 6.3, the part that presents the specific techniques under the heading *Specific Techniques.* Taking into account the vertical list on the left and the horizontal list on the upper axis, we now can summarize the various specific techniques' combinations. It should be emphasized, however, that for the sake of providing a complete list some combinations might be repeatedly mentioned.

1. The *Self-presentation* technique is usually performed alone. But when the protagonist's presentation concerns other significant persons in his or her life, it must be combined with:
   (a) *Role-reversal.*
2. The *Role-playing* techniques may be performed alone or combined with the following techniques:
   (a) *Soliloquy.* The auxiliary leaves the center of the action for a brief moment and soliloquizes while the others remain silent (or continue the action very quietly).
   (b) The *Double* or the *Multiple Doubles.*
   (c) The *Aside.*
   (d) *Role-reversal.*

TABLE 6.3
Combinations of the Basic Techniques

Basic techniques	Specific techniques								
	Self-presentation	Role-playing	Dialogue	Soliloquy	Double(s)	Aside	Role-reversal	Empty-chair	Mirror
Specific techniques									
Self-presentation							x		
Role-playing				x	x	x	x		x
Dialogue				x	x	x	x		x
Soliloquy					x				
Double(s)							x	x	
Aside							x	x	
Role-reversal								x	
Empty-chair									
Mirror									
General techniques									
Future-projection	x	x	x	x	x	x	x	x	x
Time-regression	x	x	x	x	x	x	x	x	x
Spontaneity test	x	x	x	x	x	x	x	x	x
Dream technique	x	x	x	x	x	x	x	x	x
Psychodramatic shock	x	x	x	x	x	x	x	x	x
Role playing under hypnosis	x	x	x	x	x	x	x	x	x

(e) The *Mirror* technique. This combination is a matter of necessity because as the protagonist is removed from the action to become the observer, an auxiliary must substitute for him or her to continue the role playing, and hence provide feedback.

3. The *Dialogue* technique may be performed alone or combined with the same techniques and technique combinations listed for the *Role-playing* technique (2[a-e] above).

4. The *Soliloquy* technique can be performed alone or combined with the following techniques;

   (a) *Role-playing*.
   (b) The *Dialogue*, which is the same case as with the *Role-playing* combination.
   (c) The *Double* (but usually not with the *Multiple Doubles*).

   These three combinations are shown in Table 6.3 in the column under *Soliloquy (Role-playing* and *Dialogue)* and horizontally, on the *Soliloquy* line *(Double)*.

5. The *Double* and the *Multiple Doubles* technique may be performed alone or combined with the following techniques:

   (a) *Role-playing*.
   (b) The *Dialogue*.
   (c) The *Soliloquy*. This combination holds true for the *Double* technique only. It is usually not combined with the *Multiple Doubles* technique.
   (d) *Role-reversal*.
   (e) The *Empty-chair*.

   The combinations (a), (b), and (c) are shown in Table 6.3 in the column under the *Double(s)*, whereas combinations (d) and (e) may be seen on the line marked as *Double(s)*.

6. The *Aside* technique may be performed combined with the following techniques:

   (a) *Role-playing*.
   (b) The *Dialogue*.
   (c) *Role-reversal*.
   (d) The *Empty-chair*.

   The combinations (a) and (b) appear in the column under *Aside*, whereas combinations (c) and (d) are shown on the *Aside's* line.

7. The *Role-reversal* technique may be performed alone or combined with the following techniques:

   (a) *Self-presentation*. For explanation see 1 above.
   (b) *Role-playing*.

(c) The *Dialogue*.

(d) The *Double* or the *Multiple Doubles*.

(e) The *Aside*.

(f) The *Empty-chair*.

The combination (a) through (e) are shown in Table 6.3 in the column under *Role-reversal*. Combination (f) appears on the *Role-reversal* line.

8. The *Empty-chair* may be performed alone or combined with the following:

(a) The *Double* or the *Multiple Doubles*.

(b) The *Aside*.

(c) *Role-reversal*.

These three combinations appear in the column under the *Empty-chair* technique (see Table 6.3).

9. The *Mirror* technique, by definition, is always combined with the *Role-playing* technique because as the protagonist is removed from the action to become the observer, an auxiliary must be brought in to serve as the protagonist's substitute and to provide the necessary feedback. Thus, when the *Mirror* involves two original adversaries (a *Dialogue* technique), it inevitably becomes combined with the *Role-playing* technique.

The combination patterns are far more simple than they may appear at first. We can illustrate this by describing a few examples of the meaning of the combinations in terms of the role playing situations that they address.

Let us consider a couple of combinations involving one player (i.e., the protagonist). Combination 1a above states that *Self-presentation* may be combined with *Role-reversal*. The role playing situation is that the protagonist is asked to show what his or her mother, father, wife, etc., looks like. He or she, then, reverses role with each of these persons and portrays them one at a time. Another example is the combination of the *Empty-chair* and the *Role-reversal* (combination 7f above). The protagonist places an imagined person, an absentee, in the empty chair and addresses him or her. Occasionally the therapist instructs the protagonist to switch roles, sit in the empty chair in the role of the absentee, and respond to the statements made by the portagonist.

Some combinations involve two players (i.e., the protagonist and an auxiliary). Combination 2c above refers to *Role-playing* combined with the *Aside*. The situation is that the protagonist interacts with an auxiliary representing another person. During this interaction the protagonist occasionally turns his or her head aside and openly voices his or her true feelings and thoughts. Another example is the *Empty-chair* combined with the *Double* technique (combination 5e above). The role playing situation here is as follows: The protagonist addresses an absentee, represented by the chair, with whom he or she has unfinished business. Then a double is introduced to help the protagonist express his or her feelings as openly as possible towards that absentee.

Finally, let us consider a couple of examples of combinations involving three players (i.e., one protagonist and two auxiliaries). This situation calls for a combination involving three techniques. Table 6.3, however, does not show combinations of triads. These can be formed by joining two pairs, together. For instance, the combination marked as 2d above refers to *Role-playing* combined with *Role-reversal*. The protagonist interacts with two significant persons in his or her life represented by the auxiliaries. Then he or she reverses role, with one of them assuming the role of the person played by the auxiliary while the auxiliary becomes the protagonist's substitute. As the enactment proceeds, the protagonist, now representing someone else (Role-reversal), continues to interact with the two other auxiliaries (Role-playing). Another illustration is a triple combination of the *Empty-chair* and the *Double* (combination 8a above). Picture an empty chair scene with the protagonist "facing" an absentee, represented by the chair. The protagonist is then provided with a double (an *Empty-chair* + *Double* combination). During the scene the protagonist is asked to assume the role of the absentee and sit in the empty chair; (an *Empty-chair*, *Double*, and *Role-reversal* combination).

It is fitting to conclude the discussion of the basic specific techniques with the observation that Table 6.3 contains a portion that depicts the combination patterns for the (basic) *general techniques*. What are these general techniques? What are their relationships to the specific subcategory? The answers to these questions will be provided in the next chapter.

CHAPTER 7

Basic Techniques: The General Subgroup

We now turn to the second subgroup, which has been identified as the general techniques. What is the the difference between the specific and the general techniques? Why are they classified as separate subgroups? The titles *specific* and *general* already suggest the nature of the distinction between these two clusters of techniques. Let us illustrate two issues where the difference between these subgroups is most pronounced.

The first illustration concerns the issue of techniques' combinations. In the last section of the previous chapter the possibility of combining several techniques was described. With regard to the specific techniques subgroup, it was shown that each of its nine techniques may be combined with a number of other techniques. In a complex portrayal, several pairs of specific techniques may be joined together. But some techniques go together and some do not; in any event, none goes with every other specific technique. The general techniques, on the other hand, represent a different situation.

The lower portion of Table 6.3 (see p. 183) lists six general techniques. It shows that each of the six is related to the specific techniques; in fact, it *must be combined with at least one specific technique* in order to become operationally meaningful. The most important point, however, is that unlike the specific techniques, the general ones may be combined with *any of the specific nine.* This does not suggest that a given general technique should use only a single specific technique, one at a time. On the contrary, each of the general techniques could, even should, use any of the combination patterns that apply to the specific techniques.

Second, the distinction between the specific and the general subgroups is also related to the different conceptual premises that led to their formulation. The specific techniques, for example, are based on com-

187

binations of the interaction of the principal participants in role playing enactments and the roles that they portray, as illustrated in Table 6.1 (see p. 177). These techniques represent the concretization of this interactive paradigm. The general techniques are based on an entirely different conceptual frame of reference. In his article "Psychiatry of the Twentieth Century: Function of the Universalia: Time, space, reality, and cosmos" Moreno (1966) made the observation that every psychotherapeutic system could be analyzed in terms of the degree to which it has utilized each of these four universalia. The general techniques subgroup refers to two of the four universalia. Their prime concern is with *time* and *reality*, and the utilization of these two in a concrete form in the therapeutic process.

THE GENERAL TECHNIQUES

The list of the general (basic) techniques, according to my classification, includes six techniques: *Future-projection, Time-regression, Spontaneity test,* the *Dream technique, Psychodramatic shock,* and *Role playing under hypnosis* (or in an *Altered State of Consciousness*). The first three represent different dimensions of the time universal, whereas the last three represent different aspects of the *reality* universal.

Techniques Related to the Time Universal

With regard to time, clinical role playing treatments are guided by the rule that every simulated enactment is portrayed in the *here and now.* The behavior is dealt with in the context of the moment, the warming-up to the moment, and all its immediate personal, social, and cultural implications. But time has *three* dimensions of which the present is only one. People live in time in the past, present, and future. They may suffer from behavioral or psychological disorders related to each of these dimensions.

Indeed, theories of personality development do vary with regard to the assumed relationship between psychopathology and the dimension of time. The deterministic approach emphasizes the importance of the past in determining one's present difficulties. The teleologists speak of the effect of the future in shaping one'e current behavior. This approach will agree with Rollo May who wrote that "personality can be understood only as we see it on a trajectory towards its future" (see Bratter, 1967, p. 91). The existentialists propose a different view. They maintain that the future and the past meet in the present to form the moment of action. Therefore, the present time dimension must be regarded as the moment of action. Therefore, the present time dimension must be regarded as the focal point of attention. From the practical therapeutic aspect, the problem is how to translate the three time dimensions into meaningful operations: "It is not sufficient that they figure as 'abstract' references; they must be made alive within treatment modalities" (J.L. Moreno, 1966, p. 146). Three of the general (basic) techniques appear to address that need. The *Future-projection* technique in concerned with the future dimension. *Time-regression* addresses the past dimension. The *Spontaneity test* technique focuses primarily on the present dimension.

Future-projection

Future-projection is a technique designed to portray anticipated events. It requires the protagonist to act out a meaningful situation in which he or she expects to become involved in the future. In other words, the protagonist role plays a new situation that *has not happened yet* but is likely to occur at a *later* time. For instance, suppose a protagonist is scheduled to have an employment interview, an event that he or she anticipates with anxiety and uncertainty. The Future-projection technique will place that protagonist in the interviewing situation and will provide opportunities to (a) examine the protagonist's intended performance, and (b) rehearse him or her for the eventual interview. Or suppose a protagonist is planning to confront his parents with a difficult issue but postpones the encounter lest it results in a "catastrophe." The Future-projection technique offers such a protagonist the opportunity to role play different scenarios with different outcomes and see which one works best for him or her. The following scenes, taken from a group session, illustrate this point.

Director: Let me see if I understand your situation. You said that you want to move away from your parents' home to Los Angeles. You have a job offer there, right? You've had this plan for sometime but you haven't told your parents about it. Why didn't you?

Protagonist: Because I want them to approve of the move but I'm pretty sure they'll feel hurt and rejected.

Director: You want them to feel happy and glad that you've decided to move away. Is that it?

Protagonist: Well, that's a bit of an exaggeration.

Director: How so?

Protagonist: Let me put it this way: It would be nice if they felt that way but I know it's unrealistic. I only want them to *really* understand that I don't reject them.

Director: Now, between you and me, are you rejecting them?

Protagonist: No! Well, rejection is a strong word. I need freedom and more "breathing space." With them around me I don't feel I have it. Let's say that want to get away from them. Oh . . . , maybe 2% is rejection, no more.

Director: Suppose you tell them of your plan. How do you expect them to react?

Protagonist: My father won't say much. But my mother will feel hurt and she'll make sure that I get that point. She knows how to do this so that I'll feel guilty. Then I become very defensive or nasty.

Director: Can you think of another alternative?

Protagonist: Not right now.

Director: Why don't we try the first possibility, the one that makes you defensive. I realize that this situation hasn't happened yet, but it's happening now, for real, OK? Now, where and when are you telling them of your plan, and who's involved in the situation? Remember, this is for real.

Protagonist: OK. We are in the kitchen, in the evening—my mother, my father, and myself.

(The protagonist describes the kitchen and arranges it with some chairs. He chooses two auxiliaries to play the roles of his mother and his father. They all sit around the kitchen table.)

Director: Who begins the conversation?

Protagonist: I will. I wanted to talk with you about something . . . *(pause)* . . . a very important . . . something. . . . *(turns to the director and says: "I'm stuck")*

Director: Maybe I can give you a double to help you? You already know what a double is; we've used it before. Your double will try to be you, too, as if the two of you are one person having an internal conversation. When your double is right, tell him so. If he's wrong, please correct him. You may consult your double whenever you wish. Who can be your double? (The protagonist chooses an auxiliary to serve as a double.)

Double: *(sits like the protagonist at his side and waits silently for a few seconds)* I'm stuck.

Protagonist: Right.

Double: I don't know how to begin. It's so difficult!

Protagonist: Right.

Double: I'm afraid to begin.

Protagonist: Right.

Double: I wish I didn't have to do this at all.

Protagonist: Right, you can say that again.

Double: Maybe I'll leave it as it is. If it's difficult for me, I'm better off avoiding this unpleasant situation altogether.

Protagonist: I can't do that.

Double: No, I can't do that. I must have the courage to go through with this. Hell, I've been through worse situations.

Protagonist: Right. *(to the parents)* I . . . er . . . I want to. . . . The reason we are all here is because I wanted to tell you something . . . a decision I made.

Double: That's right.

Father: What is it?

Mother: I hope it's something nice.

Protagonist: Well, . . .

Double: She had to say that, ha! Now what do I say?

Protagonist: (to the double) I've started it, I must go on. *(to the parents)* It's nice for me. I've decided it's time for me to be more independent.

Father: Good.

Protagonist: (takes a deep breath) I want to move to L.A. I have a job there, and I'll be OK.

Mother: (after a pause) If you feel that we don't allow you to be independent, well . . . what can I say? If you feel you *have to leave us* and go somewhere else, there's no point in arguing, is there?

Protagonist: (to the double) I feel the guilt mounting.

Double: And how! She did it again!

Protagonist: I'm not *leaving* you . . . I mean I'm not running away from you or anything like that.

Director: You're doing fine. Behave as defensively as you can.

Protagonist: It's not that I don't love you. Of course I do. I'm not saying that you're not good parents. I'm just trying to grow up without your help. Come on, don't look at me that way. I only mean that I need to be alone.

Double: I feel so bad that I can't even make it to sound right.

Protagonist: That's right. And the more I try to explain, the more guilty I feel.

Double: Isn't it supposed to be like this?

Protagonist: No, it should be the other way. The more you talk about it, the easier it should get.

Director: OK. Thank you all. Let's start the whole situation all over again. But this time use the other reaction you mentioned: get nasty, OK?

(The situation is repeated from the beginning to the following point.)

Mother: (after a pause) If you feel that we don't allow you to be independent well . . . what can I say? If you *must leave us* because you feel that way, there's no point in arguing, is there?

Protagonist: That's not what I'm saying. Why don't you understand me?

Double: I feel angry.

Protagonist: Aha. Every time I try to explain myself to you, you turn it upside down. You always understand it the way *you* want to, and not the way I mean. I'm simply saying that I need more freedom. Isn't that clear?

Double: It's very clear to me.

Father: One thing is clear. You've still got to learn how to talk to your mother.

Protagonist: (excited) What's wrong with the way I talk to her? Why is it always *me* who is wrong? Have you ever considered the possibility that *you* might be wrong for a change?

Double: I feel angrier and angrier, and I'm getting nowhere.

Protagonist: (to the double) You see, I told you I should keep my mouth shut.

Double: I can't keep my mouth shut with them, but whenever we talk I get into trouble.

Protagonist: (to the double) So what shall I do?

Director: OK. Thank you all. What do you think? How did you do?

Protagonist: I feel terrible. Can I ever do it right?

Director: We can try other alternatives, if you want to.

Protagonist: Yes, I do.

Director: Let's talk for a couple of minutes about what these might be, and then you'll role play them. OK?

Protagonist: OK.

Another version of the Future-projection that also deals with evaluating the protagonist's ability to cope in the future is the *Exit Test.* This is a prognostic procedure, based on Future-projection role playing, and it is used with hospitalized or institutionalized patients prior to their discharge. In the Exit Test the protagonist role plays a series of situations he or she is likely to encounter in the outside world. These situations always involve minor and common frustrations. The series includes a homecoming situation, meeting the spouse or the parents, seeking employment, dating, socializing, and dreaming. The performance in these situations may serve as an indicator of the protagonist's readiness to face the real world on his or her own.

In general, the Future-projection technique addresses the unknown elements of one's prospective involvements by making these somewhat obscure and uncertain elements alive and concrete. It familiarizes the protagonists with their future aspirations, and with whatever significant relationships they may develop in the future. Psychologically, the technique focuses on the elimination or the substantial reduction of one's debilitating anticipatory anxieties, particularly those that affect one's present attitudes and behavior. This technique has been considered effective as a rehearsal technique (Haskell, 1957; Starr, 1977). Although this is true, its main impact seems to be that of building self-confidence, encouragement, and reinforcement—encouragement in the sense that it supports the protagonist's *belief* in his or her ability to satisfactorily cope in future confrontations; and reinforcement in the sense that it helps the protagonist *develop* the necessary skills for future performances.

In terms of our model for behavior simulations (Chapter 2) the Future-projection technique combines elements of the two mimetic behaviors. By definition, it is primarily an *as if* situation since it includes many unknown and assumed elements. Both the protagonist and the auxiliaries must behave pretending that the projected (or imagined) future situation represents a feasible reality.

The literature concerning the Future-projection technique (e.g., Yablonsky, 1954, 1974, 1976) suggests that its therapeutic effectiveness depends on meeting the following four conditions:

1. The portrayed situation has to be important to the protagonist.
2. The protagonist is actually going to become involved in such a situation.
3. The auxiliaries must be able to project the protagonist into the future situation, to make him or her feel as if it is real.
4. Future-projection should be introduced only following an effective warm-up.

Instruction.

"Let's move the clock forward to . . . (establish the date; the year, and if necessary the month, the season, or the day).
We are now in the year ———. How old are you? What do you do for a living? Where does the meeting, interview, discussion, etc., take place? What time of the day is it? Besides you, who else is involved? Please arrange the action space, and let's begin."

After each question the therapist waits for the protagonist's answer.

It is important to ask these and other questions to help the protagonist "enter the role." If the protagonist is already married one can ask, if he or she has children and what are their names (imaginary), etc.

Indication.

1. To test the protagonist's attitudes, reactions, and skills and their consequences as related to his or her ability to cope in future encounters.
2. Diagnostically, to check whether or not the protagonist's ambitions and aspirations have a realistic basis. To help the protagonist evaluate the validity of his or her future goals.
3. To use it as an Exit Text situation.
4. To alleviate pressures; to address a lack of motivation to pursue goals caused by poor self-confidence.
5. To reduce anxiety that inhibits action for fear of its unknown consequences.
6. To prepare the protagonist to perform more effectively in future situations, that is, to rehearse him or her for prospective eventualities.

Contraindications. Ordinarily, the Future-projective technique should not be introduced in the first scene of the session.

Time-regression

Time-regression is a technique that concerns the past. It requires the protagonist to recreate, through role playing enactment, significant events from his or her past and act them out as if they occur in the present. The rule that every simulated role playing scene is portrayed in the here and now has an important implication as far as Time-regression is concerned. All the participants—the protagonist and the auxiliary(s)—must use the present tense. For example, the protagonist will say: "I *am doing* it because . . ." rather than "I *did* it because. . . ." The use of the past tense tends to put the actor in the role of a spectator, whereas the use of the present tense makes him or her an involved party. Suppose an adult protagonist is concerned with an event that happened years ago in grade school, when she was eight years old. With the Time-regression technique the protagonist assumes the behavior of an eight-year-old girl and portrays the scene as if it is happening now for the first time.

In terms of our model for behavior simulation (Chapter 2) the Time-regression technique emphasizes the spontaneous mimetic-replication behavior. The protagonist *repeats* or *replicates* that which took place before as accurately as possible.

The therapeutic advantage of reliving the past has been discussed by many theoreticians. It has been a central psychotherapeutic issue that has resulted in both agreements and some controversies. In clinical practice, however, most treatment modalities address the issue of the client's past in one way or another. The Time-regression technique is the way clinical role playing deals with it.

The usefulness of the Time-regression technique often depends on the extent to which the protagonist remembers the situation to be recreated. But the technique can be introduced in instances when the recollection is fragmented or minimal. In fact, Time-regression can be used even if the recreated scene is fantasized, imagined, or exists only as a delusion. The key criterion is that the protagonist truly believes that it actually happened and that it is portrayed honestly to the best of his or her recollection.

Most classic clinical role playing sessions involve at least one scene based on this technique. A typical example may be seen in the case of the family therapy presented in Chapter 11, key scene 2 (see p. 323).

Instruction. The way this technique is introduced to the protagonist is similar to that described for the Future-projection technique with one exception. Instead of moving the clock *forward*, here it is moved *backward*.

> "Let's move the clock backwards to the year. . . . (establish the date, and if needed, the season, the month, or the day). It is now 19—. How old are you? Where do you live? Where does the meeting, conversation, incident, etc., take place? What time of the day is it? Besides you, who else is involved? Please arrange the action space and let's begin."

Indications.

1. When the protagonist is troubled by a traumatic, or unpleasant, past experience.
2. Whenever the therapist thinks that the protagonist's present difficulties are related to past experiences.
3. When a therapist believes that a cathartic experience can relieve (or undo) an emotional burden that was created in the past.
4. When a therapist wants to identify the protagonist's response pattern to certain situation(s) over a long period of time.

Contraindications. None. It is important to remember that Time-regression can be effective only if the protagonist has been duly warmed up.

Spontaneity Test

The *Spontaneity test* is a role playing technique that concentrates on the present. Almost half a century ago, J.L. Moreno wrote that the Spontaneity test "is able to uncover feelings in their nascent, initial state. Through it we get a better knowledge of the genuine attitudes an individual may develop in the course of conduct and clinch acts in the moment of their performance" (Moreno, 1934, p.193). Theoretically, spontaneity is regarded as a mental state characterized by the readiness of a person to respond as freely as possible. The acts that follow such a state reflect the experiences of the present, the culmination of one's *total* behavior as evident in the moment of action. In practice, the emergence of present-oriented behavior largely depends on the *novelty* of the situation and on the extent to which the respondent is caught/reacts *off guard* by *surprise*.

The Spontaneity test has also been referred to in the psychological literature by other titles, such as the situation test (Starr, 1977), the impromptu experience, or the improvisation technique. It has been primarily used for diagnostic purposes. Since it was invented many years ago, there have been several versions of it. Among the known ones are the Spontaneity test (improvisation) as a method for personality assessment (Bronfenbrenner & Newcomb, 1948), and as a projective-action-test (Haas & Moreno, 1961). Basically, however, this technique and all its variations are designed to confront the protagonist *unexpectedly* with a new situation. Thus, the role playing episode is structured by the therapist with one or more auxiliaries *without the knowledge of the protagonist.* The auxiliaries receive clear and detailed instructions on how to behave in the situation and often regardless of the protagonist's responses. Then, the protagonist is introduced to the role playing situation and is asked to act as naturally as possible.

I recall an example of the Spontaneity test with a female protagonist, a student in a university. The role playing episode was designed to take place in the office of the chairman of her department. The chairman's role was portrayed by an auxiliary who was instructed to tell her that she could not continue her studies in that department. The protagonist was a very energetic, assertive, combative, and strong-willed person. She was unaware of the nature of the situation until she actually confronted it. While role playing the situation she surprised everyone. Instead of fighting and resisting the decision, she broke into tears, admitted that she did not take her studies seriously and that she was more vulnerable than people imagined, and pleaded for another chance to prove herself. An entirely new facet of her behavior was suddenly uncovered.

The Spontaneity test may consist of one role playing scene, about 10-15 minutes long, or it may include two or three usually shorter scenes. Sometimes it may be designed in the form of brief *series* of episodes, about three minutes each, as a projective-action-test (e.g., Haas & Moreno, 1961). This series may be comprised of a number of standard situations involving common conflicts (e.g., a parent-child conflict, tension with an authority figure, a conflict with a member of the opposite sex). It can also be designed in the form of personal situations involving (a) samples of the protagonist's relationships with family members and other significant persons, (b) the expression of feelings—frustrations as well as happiness, and (c) fantasies. The purpose of this use of the Spontaneity test would be to get a profile of the protagonist's behavior and response repertoire.

Instructions. The Spontaneity test is introduced to the participants in two, separate stages. The first concerns the auxiliaries in the absence of the protagonist. The second stage involves instructions given to the protagonist.

1. During the first stage the therapist designs the scene and instructs the auxiliaries about what attitudes and behavior they should display. The details of these instructions vary, of course, depending on the content of the scene and its particular purpose.
2. In the second stage, the protagonist is brought in and is introduced to the scene. Here, too, the specifics of the instructions vary from one case to another. In principle, the protagonist ought to be briefly warmed up, followed by a short introduction. For example:

   > "You are now in . . . (describe the place where the scene takes place), and the time of the day is . . . (establish the time). In a few seconds I want you to . . . (sit in your car, do your home chores, meet. . . , describe the person portrayed by the auxiliary, etc.). Do you have any questions? Now, let's begin. Please behave as naturally as you can."

Indications.

1. When the therapist wants to assess the protagonist's current skills, relationships to other persons, abilities to cope with stressful situations, and so forth.

2. When the protagonist needs to be trained to trust his or her abilities, to overcome anxieties concerning self-confidence, and to become more spontaneous in his or her responses to other people.

Contraindications. This technique is not recommended with very anxious and inhibited protagonists, at least not in the beginning of their treatment.

Techniques Related to the Reality Universal

Clinical role playing, like many other psychotherapeitic approaches, is concerned with the relationship between two dimensions of the reality universal: the percieved and the objective ones. The former dimension is idiosyncratic by definition and includes personal biases, errors of judgment, misinterpretations, as well as wishful thinking. The later dimension represents an external criterion defined by normative expectations and consequences. These two dimensions are always evaluated one against the other when determining the psychotherapeutic process and its target. A substantial portion of the therapeutic effort is invested in the perceived, or the psychological, dimension of reality, in order to uncover the reasons that led to the formation of the individual's biases and perceptual distortions, and to understand their impact on the decision-making processes or the overt behavior that is accrued as the result of such processes.

The perceived, psychological dimension of reality may be expressed in several forms. One—an adaptive manifestation of a surrealistic expression—is dreams. The *Dream* technique offers a way of dealing with dream contents. Another general technique related to the perceived reality dimension is the *Psychodramatic shock* (Moreno, 1939a,b). This term was introduced to describe an extreme emotional state which may be manifested through fantasies, realistic or surrealistic, or through hallucinations and delusions. The third technique in this group is role playing under *Hypnosis*, which is not necessarily concerned with biases and misinterpretations but rather with psychological contents that reside at a subliminal level.

The Dream Technique

In principle, the clinical role playing approach to the portrayal of dreams follows the basic procedure used for the enactment of any other presenting problem or conflict. Therefore, a session devoted to the treatment of dreams begins with a warm-up stage, continues with an action stage, and ends with a closure stage (see Chapters 4 and 5). This three-stage structure, however, is further divided into six parts, which will be described later in this section.

What, then, are the special characteristics of the Dream technique, and in what ways does it differ from the traditional approach to the treatment of dreams? One important difference is the *manner* in which the dream content is presented and explored. Like any other clinical role playing procedure, the dream content is presented by the dreamer in action rather than through strictly verbal description. The dreamer is asked to reenact the dream as it occurred originally. The task of unraveling the possible meaning of the dream is also achieved through the process of reenactment. The dreamer portrays his or her dream again, this time, however, taking advantage of the various specific (basic) techniques. This provides him or her an opportunity to discover the meaning of the dream through a process of self-realization.

The Dream technique differs from the traditional approach to the treatment of dreams in yet another respect. This concerns the learning task to be attained at the end of the therapy session. One may begin with the assumption that every dream has a message. It could be a statement of a problem, a reflection of the dreamer's attitude towards that problem, a real concern on the part of the dreamer, or a wish he or she may have. But the language of the dream is typically unclear and often bizarre; it is lacking in internal cohesion and may appear illogical. It often reflects a subconscious anxiety or a censored wish which is communicated in a highly personalized and subjective language. According to the traditional, primarily psychoanalytically oriented approach, the sole purpose of the treatment of dreams is to uncover their meaning, to *interpret* the message communicated through the dream. This requires an understanding of the "dream work," that is, the rules through which a would-be coherent message is distorted by the dream process. Since according to this approach the content of the dream is conveyed in symbols, it also requires having a code dictionary through which highly abstract symbols can be translated into a simple and coherent language.

The purpose of the treatment of dreams through clinical role playing is a different one. While the Dream technique does not ignore the need to make some sense out of the dream, its main objective is to *train the dreamer to dream better.* In fact, the clinical role playing approach to the treatment of dreams begins with the premise that dreaming fulfills important psychological needs and serves valuable emotional as well as cognitive functions. Contemporary research on dreams and sleep heavily supports this premise. Thus dream activities ought to be encouraged provided that they serve the dreamer well. The purpose of clinical role playing therapy as far as dreaming is concerned is, therefore, helping and teaching people to dream more effectively and more productively. The Dream technique is actually a dream *training* technique whereby the dreamer is taught to positively change the ending or the nature of his or her disturbing dreams.

The idea of overcoming disturbing dreams by introducing a positive change in their content is hardly a novel one. Garfield (1974), for example, wrote the following recommendation: "Engage in activities relevant to the dream change you wish to produce; expose yourself to the positive thing you wish to dream of; experience the negative things that you dream of in a positive way" (pp. 202-203). Noone (1972) reported of an interesting anthropological observation regarding the handling of dreams in another culture. Children of the Temiar tribe of Malaya, a division of the Senoi, are taught to fight hostile images in their dreams, during the sleep state, by altering the end of the dream in a positive direction. In this way they avert the end of what otherwise would have been a nightmare. This method of treating unpleasant dreams was adopted by Faraday (1974) in England.

The foregoing discussion points to yet another important difference between the clinical role playing approach to the treatment of dreams and the traditional psychodynamic approach. The latter will treat or interpret *any* dream, while the former only *special* dreams. The Dream techique is indicated only in those instances where it appears that dream activities have failed to adequately serve the dreamer. Indications of such a failure are often unclear and may become a matter of interpretation. Nonetheless, there are three instances where expressions of such a failure are unmistakably clear. These are disturbing dreams, that is, dreams that seem important but puzzling to the dreamer, nightmares, and repetitive dreams.

The Progression of the Dream Technique

The enactment of dreams represents a special treatment situation. Unlike other day-to-day problem situations, dreams may become quite bizarre and surrealistic. This poses certain directorial problems which the therapist must cope with if he or she wishes to make some sense out of the role playing portrayals. Most of these problems have been discussed in several case reports (e.g.,Moreno, 1951; Nolte, Weistart, &

Wyatt, 1977; Yablonsky, 1976). The following will summarize the six parts of the Dream technique.

The session begins with a brief warm-up. Customarily this includes a short discussion in the form of an informal interview regarding the protagonist's attitude towards dreams and his or her dreaming habits. The protagonist is *not* encouraged to describe the details of the troubling dream at this point. These ought to be disclosed for the first time during the action stage. The Dream technique proper begins at the end of this discussion and progresses in six steps as follows:

1. Warming-up to the dream situation. The protagonist describes the place where he or she went to sleep the night that the dream occurred. The scene is then arranged and the protagonist lies down on the floor or on a mattress. The protagonist is now instructed to close his or her eyes and reenact the "going to sleep" part of the dream situation.

The therapist now kneels next to the protagonist, rests his or her fingers on the closed eyes, and begins to induce a sleep-like state with the following instructions:

> "Close your eyes. Your are about to fall asleep. Your eyes are getting heavier and heavier, heavier and heavier. Your eyelids are getting heavier and heavier. You begin to feel drowsy. Breathe deeply and pay a particular attention to your breathing, especially when you exhale. Gradually, your breathing becomes smoother and smoother. Now you may feel drowsy and close to falling asleep. I would like you now to begin to visualize the dream. But do not tell me anything yet, just try to visualize the dream as vividly as you can. As soon as you begin to see the dream, please get up and describe to me the place where you are and who else is there."

In warming-up the protagonist to the dream situation, the therapist may deliver these instructions in a soft monotone. These instructions should be long enough to allow the protagonist to experience the sleep state but *not* enough to make him or her sleep or hypnotized.

2. Beginning the action: The enactment of the original dream. The protagonist gets up and sets the dream scene. He or she may use auxiliaries to portray other human figures or objects that appear in the dream. Then the dream scenario is reenacted. The protagonist describes what is happening and together with the auxiliaries the scene is relived. It is important to remember that at this point the dream is portrayed *uninterrupted* by role playing techniques.

3. Deciphering the dream. Once the entire dream (or series of dreams) has been reenacted the therapist asks the protagonist to begin all over again. This time, however, further elaborations are introduced into the original dream scenario. The protagonist may now reverse roles with the auxiliaries, whether or not they represent real people or objects, and interact with them. The therapist may introduce the Double technique, for example, or any of the specific techniques and their typical combinations. By employing these role playing techniques, the therapist attempts to "fill the gaps" left in the original dream, to make sense out of its sporadic pieces, and to gain insight into the message that the dream conveys. This segment of the Dream technique may have to explore several parts of the dream; hence it may be longer than the original presentation.

4. A continuation of the sleep state. At this point the protagonist is asked to go back to sleep in the original place, described above (#1). The reason for this is that the dream occurred in the context of sleep and the role playing enactment has to retain that aspect. Again, the protagonist closes his or her eyes and remains "asleep."

5. Redreaming. The protagonist is now given the opportunity to dream the dream the way he or she would like it to be. In order to do so the following instructions are given: "I would like you now to get up and reenact the dream the way you would have liked it to be. You may change any part of the dream any way you wish. Get up and set the place of the dream. You may choose an auxiliary to portray other persons or objects; tell then what they should do or say, and then reenact the new dream." The dream is now reenacted in the form of redreaming.

6. Going back to sleep and waking up. As soon as the redreaming part is completed, the protagonist is instructed to go back to his or her bed and continue to sleep. The therapist may repeat the suggestions for inducing a sleep-like state described above (#1). But at the end of these instructions the therapist will ask the protagonist to wake up and open his or her eyes, and maybe greet him or her with a "Good morning."

This point of the session marks the end of the action stage and the end of the Dream technique. The rest of the session comprises the closing stage, that is, sharing, analysis, and discussion by the protagonist, the participating auxiliaries, and anyone else who was present during the role playing enactment.

Instruction. The specific instructions for implementing the Dream technique were described in each of the six parts of the foregoing procedure, and therefore need not be repeated.

Indications. The Dream technique is typically used when the protagonist complains of any of the following:

1. Having dreamt something that is very puzzling yet seems important to him or her.
2. Having a nightmare that may or may not result in sudden awakening.
3. Having a recurrent dream.

Contraindications. The clinical role playing approach to dream analysis maintains that only special dreams become the subject for treatment. These were mentioned under Indications. Similarly, dreams are not used as a means to understand behavior in general. Therefore, there is no need to treat dreams unless training in redreaming is necessary.

Psychodramatic Shock

Psychodramatic shock is a clinical role playing technique devised as a form of treatment of psychotic attacks (i.e., hallucinations and delusions) (Moreno, 1939 a,b). The technique is most effective when applied after the termination of the psychotic attacks, at the point where the protagonist has regained relative lucidity. The basic idea of this technique is as follows: The therapist asks the protagonist to throw himself back into the hallucinatory experience when it is most vivid in his mind and to reenact it, with the aid of auxiliaries. The scene(s) is (are) portrayed as a regular clinical role playing enactment using a variety of specific (basic) techniques as needed. Often, however, the portrayal may look, at first, bizarre, surrealistic, and confused—similar to the characteristics of the original psychotic episode. Only in subsequent scenes may a greater coherence become evident.

The term *shock* was ascribed to this technique because of the reaction of protagonists to the suggestion of reexperiencing the psychotic episode. Usually, they evince a violent resistance against being thrown back into the painful experience from which they have just emerged. Their natural inclination is to forget rather than confront it. Typically, at this point they will be full of fears that their new freedom may be shattered. The mere suggestion—and still more the prospect—of going through the actual process again frightens them. Nonetheless, it is the task of the therapist to encourage such a protagonist "to throw himself into the psychotic state, to lose himself entirely in it, however awful, ugly and unreal it may seem to him at the moment" (Moreno, 1939b, p. 2).

Obviously, because the Psychodramatic shock, like other shock techniques, is such a radical intervention, it must be administered sparingly and with extreme caution. When treating psychotic patients who could be potential candidates for such an intervention, the therapist is advised to have a professional colleague at hand in order to consult on the advisability of using the Psychodramatic shock.

The use of Psychodramatic shock for therapeutic purposes stems from a positive outlook, one that does not view psychotic attacks merely as a sign of malignant disease, but also as evidence of some strength. Such an approach was also espoused by Cameron (1963) who considered hallucinations and delusions as an attempt at self-cure, a form of coping. He described this aspect of psychotic attacks as follows:

> The hallucinating and the delusional patient is often trying to re-constitute his reality representations in such a way as to form a compromise—a compromise between *impulses* and *fantasies* which are flooding his psychodynamic system and the external realities which comdemn or contradict them. At the very least, hallucinations and delusions can keep a patient in contact with reality. (Cameron, 1963, pp. 237-238)

The principle of asking the patient to reproduce the aberrant behavior that characterized his or her problem and use it as a part of the therapeutic intervention was adopted by a variety of psychotherapists. For instance, Sechehaye (1956, 1961) used "symbolic regressions" with her patients and then helped them overcome basic conflicts through "symbolic realization." Another example is Milton H. Erickson's "strategic therapy" approach. One of the main principles of this approach calls for the acceptance of what the patient has to offer as the basis for subsequent therapeutic gains. In practice this may take the form of putting the patient back in the unhappy situation he or she complained about and only then to introduce a change (e.g., Haley, 1967, 1973).

There are also several behavior therapy techniques where the extinction of maladaptive behavior is sought through repetitions of the very same behavior (Rimm & Masters, 1974). Early in the 1930s, Dunlap (1932) introduced the technique of *negative practice*, that is, practicing behaviors not to perfect their performance but to eliminate them. Such a treatment was reported for a variety of problems such as enuresis, homosexuality, tics, stuttering, and speech blocking. Ayllon (1963) reported a case of treating a psychotic patient with the technique of *stimulus satiation*. This involved the repeated presentation of the stimulus that triggered the psychotic behavior until its attraction was reduced. Hull (1943) suggested the technique of *mass practice* for eliminating the practiced behavior.

In Psychodramatic shock the psychotic behavior is repeated through role playing enactment in order to bring about a cathartic effect and, perhaps more importantly, to help the protagonist gain control over such behavior. The protagonist is shown that he or she can get in and out of it at will and even change the content of the hallucination in the end.

This reminds us of the *Dream technique* described in the previous section. Indeed, to some extent the three parts that comprise the Psychodramatic shock resemble the six parts of the Dream technique. These three parts are as follows:

1. *Entry, the beginning of the hallucination or the delusion:* The protagonist is put back in the situation that preceded the psychotic attack or triggered it.
2. *The hallucination or the delusion proper:* The protagonist portrays the hallucination or the delusion with the aid of auxiliaries. This may involve a single scene or a series of scenes. Usually, the scenes are bizarre and lack coherence, but, they are portrayed as closely to the original ones as possible.
3. *The change:* The scene portrayed in the preceding, second part may be repeated, but now the protagonist may change something in it.

Instructions. There are no specific instructions for this technique. Instructions for each scene and each part are given as the situation demands. The therapist must only be aware of the initial resistance on the part of the protagonist to agree to go back and reenact the psychotic episode. Here proper encouragement and prompting are required.

Indications. The technique may be used with psychotic patients following the termination of their hallucinatory or delusional state. Ideally, it should begin immediately after the natural termination of the psychotic episode.

Contraindications.

1. Before the psychotic episode has burnt itself out.
2. When the circumstances (i.e., the psychological state of the protagonist or the balance between his or her strengths and weaknesses) raise a serious possibility that psychodramatic shock may
   cause more harm than help.

Role Playing Under Hypnosis (or in an Altered State of Consciousness)

The last of the general (basic) techniques to be described in this chapter
is *Role playing under hypnosis*. This is the same technique as *Hypnodrama*,
that is, a combination of hypnosis and psychodrama originally introduced by Moreno (1950). The following is an excerpt from Supple (1962)
which describes how the technique came into being:

> Hypnodrama is a synthesis of psychodrama and hypnosis. The idea
> of hypnodrama came to Dr. Moreno through an accident. In the
> summer of 1939 the late Dr. Bruno Solby brought a young woman
> for treatment. She suffered from paranoid delusions accompanied
> by nightmares; every night the devil came to visit her. She was
> unable to get into a psychodramatic re-enactment of the incident.
> After trying the self-directed technique and the method of mild
> prompting without results he became highly directive; this put the
> patient unexpectedly into a hypnotic trance. Dr. Moreno decided
> to try a psychodrama under these novel circumstances. With the
> aid of two male auxiliary egos the patient was able to portray two
> meetings with the devil, one as it had happened the night before,
> one as she expected it to happen the following night. Apparently,
> hynosis operated as a "starter" and spurred her spontaneity. (Sup-
> ple, 1962, p. 58)

The practice of combining hypnosis with other forms of psychotherapy
might have been a novelty in the late 1930s. Hypnosis has been combined
with psychodrama and clinical role playing (e.g., Moreno, 1950; Enneis,
1950; Naruse, 1959; Supple, 1962). It was also combined, for example,
with various behavior modification procedures (e.g., Kroger & Fezler,
1976). These, as well as numerous other reports, discuss the advantages
and the circumstances for using such combinations and under what
condition they would be superior to the use of psychotherapy without
hypnosis.

The technique of Role playing under hypnosis is conducted as follows:

The protagonist is warmed up and then enters the action space. He or she describes a specific scene related to the presenting complaint: a scene in the kitchen, in the living room, etc. Once the physical setting of the scene becomes real to the protagonist, the therapist starts suggestive techniques for the induction of hypnosis. When the protagonist is hypnotized, the action stage part of a regular clinical role playing session may be conducted. It may be a brief enactment comprised of two episodes or a full production including several scenes. The therapist uses auxiliaries as needed as well as any specific role playing techniques or their typical combinations. It should be pointed out that only the protagonist enacts under hypnosis. The auxiliaries are *not* hypnotized. Before the beginning of the closure stage the protagonist is awakened from the hypnosis. The sharing and the analysis are conducted as a regular closing stage.

Clinical role playing under hypnosis may be conducted along the model of the Dream technique. Thus, the hypnotic induction part parallels the "going to sleep" part. The first episode is parallel to the presentation of the dream; the exploration scene may be parallel to the exploration of the meaning of the dream; and the last scene may be used for role playing a resolution, a wishful thinking behavior. The awakening from the hypnotic state is similar to the awakening from the sleep that ends the dream technique.

Clinical role playing under hypnosis may be also used for diagnostic purposes. This is indicated whenever the therapist finds it necessary to uncover subconscious material that cannot be elicited otherwise. In this case the action stage usually comprises two or three scenes without a scene of retraining or resolution seeking. The technique may also be used as a regular clinical role playing treatment session, especially when the therapist is dealing with self-control problems such as overeating, drinking, smoking, or the management of anxiety.

Finally, a proper administration of both treatment procedures—Clinical role playing and hypnosis—requires expertise and experience. Each of these forms of treatment, separately, has its own characteristics. Therefore, the therapist must be familiar with the indications and contraindications for each before electing to apply Role playing and hypnosis together as a combined psychotherapeutic technique.

Instructions. The technique is introduced in general terms, taking into consideration the fact that the protagonist has already experienced both hypnosis and the clinical role playing procedure separately. The therapist explains that hypnosis will be introduced while the protagonist is inside the action space and after he or she has described and arranged the first scene. The protagonist is also told that the awakening from the hypnotic state will occur at the completion of the action stage.

Indications.

1. When the protagonist has already had experiences with hypnosis and with clinical role playing treatment separately.
2. When the protagonist finds it difficult to become adequately involved in scenes where Future-projection or Time-regression techniques are called for.
3. When the therapist feels that under the hypnotic trance he or she may obtain information that cannot be easily elicited otherwise.
4. When dealing with psychological or behavioral difficulties concerning deficits in self-control and the management of undue anxiety.

Contraindications.

1. When the therapist is lacking experience with hypnosis.
2. When hypnosis is contraindicated with a given protagonist and/or the particular disorder under treatment (e.g., Crasilneck & Hall, 1985, pp. 417-427).

Another variant of administering clinical role playing to protagonists who are in an altered state of consciousness is the combination of clinical role playing with *narcosynthesis*. Narcosynthesis (Grinker & Spiegel, 1945), also sometimes referred to as narcotherapy or narcoanalysis, is a form of therapeutic intervention in which a pharmacological agent, usually sodium amytal or sodium pentothal, is administered intravenously in order to facilitate emotional abreaction and communication. Thus, the use of clinical role playing either under hypnosis or in conjunction with narcosynthesis is similar and represents two instances of its application with clients who are in an altered state of consciousness. In the former case such a state is created through suggestion, and in the latter it is produced chemically.

The idea of using pharmacological agents to facilitate abreaction arose from earlier applications of barbiturates and other agents as a method of treating exited, agitated, or insomniac patients. The first report of this technique appeared about 60 years ago (Blackwenn, 1923). One of the early attempts to apply psychoanalytic insights to this treament was reported by Horsley (1936). During World War II narcosynthesis was prescribed for rapid resolution of such symptoms as stupor, mutism, confusion, and various conversion paralyses. Since then it has been prescribed mostly for treatment of acute post-traumatic stress disorders, particularly when expressed in seriously impairing social symptoms. Alteration of consciousness by intravenous injection of drugs is used also less frequently in order to facilitate diagnosis, to obtain personal histories, and to encourage free associations. These applications extend beyond the treatment of post-traumatic states.

The use of narcosynthesis is rooted in the notion that it facilitates emotional abreaction and hence cathartic experience as a means of bringing relief from debilitating symptoms. Abreaction has also been conceptualized as an interpersonal event. It usually releases affects of primitive fear, rage, and helplessness associated with shame, anxiety, sadness, guilt, and sometimes also triumph and revenge. According to Kolb (1984) the rationale for using this technique is that "beyond the psychodynamic and interpersonal explanations of the therapeutic value of narcosynthesis, this psychopharmaceutic intervention releases cerebral cortical functions concerned with the control of conscious inhibiting processes" (p. 742).

The relevance of role playing to narcosynthesis is that after the drug has been administered, the therapist simulates through verbal suggestions the traumatic event and asks the client to respond. If it is a post-traumatic event due to war, for example, the therapist may use instead of verbal suggestions other more realistic means, for example, playing 30 seconds of audiotape depicting battle sounds, gun shots, mortars, artillery shells, tanks, or planes and then asking the client to reenact the original episode. This may be followed by verbal clarifications or instructions for further enactments. Towards the termination of the session the therapist indicates sympathetically and firmly that the experience is over and that it has been a dream. As the client recovers consciousness, he or she is encouraged to rest in bed and sleep for a period. The treatment may be limited to one session or may be administered repeatedly in several sessions. The length of eash session may vary from half an hour to one or even two hours.

The application of clinical role playing with narcosynthesis depends, first of all, on the indications and contraindications for the use of narcosynthesis. It is said to be indicated as a treatment of acute symptoms of post-traumatic stress disorders. The contraindications concern the physiological and psychological risks that need to be taken into consideration before a decision to apply narcosynthesis is made. One risk of using barbiturates is respiratory delay or paralysis. It should not be undertaken by clients with severe cardiac, pulmonary, liver, or kidney diseases, and should be absolutely avoided in cases of porphyria. Psychologically, the risks center around the possible breakdown of the client's defenses and the occurrence of psychotic regression. Therefore, it should not be administered to clients diagnosed with prepsychotic personality. When dealing with post-traumatic stress disorders of war, the potential of a post-narcosynthetic depressive affective state should be seriously considered, particularly when there is likelihood of revealing the commitment of atrocities or sanctioned acts (Kolb, 1984).

To complete this chapter on the general (basic) techniques subgroup, a final comment is needed on the relation of the six techniques to each other. Each of the techniques that belong to the first three and to the second three stands on its own and cannot be combined, that is, used simultaneously with any of the remaining two within the *same triad*. This, however, is not the case with regard to techniques that belong to *different triads*. Thus, each of the three techniques associated with the reality dimension, the Dream technique, Psychodramatic shock, and Role playing Under Hypnosis (or in an Altered State of Consciousness), may be combined with one or two techniques associated with the time dimension.

How can, say, the Dream technique be combined with *two* techniques associated with the time dimension if each of the latter two stands on its own? The answer is that the two reality related techniques are introduced in a *consecutive fashion*, each general technique in a different scene. In fact this practice is quite common. One action stage may include a scene that uses Time-regression and another scene, typically before the end of that stage, that uses the Future-projection technique.

CHAPTER 8

The Situational Techniques: Principles and Paradigm

The apparent need for distinguishing between two broad categories of role playing techniques stems from the observation that techniques tend to vary with regard to their relationship to the content aspect of the events portrayed in the course of the treatment session. Some techniques, notably those classified as basic (both specific and general) appear to be more independent of the content aspect proper. On the other hand, other techniques (i.e., those classified under the situational category) appear dependent and inseparable from the content of the scenarios. Generally defined, situational techniques are acts that transform content—events as well as ideas—into actional modes of expression. They represent contents conveyed through concrete manifestations, verbal and nonverbal, of the issue(s) under exploration. The distinct features that characterize each one of them are determined by the particular scenarios they portray.

The problems encountered in our examination of the main determinants of the *basic* techniques surface again in the present chapter, but this time, the seriousness and the magnitude of the problems are on a larger scale. In the discussion of the specific and the general subgroups of the *basic* techniques category, the formulation of a coherent and logical structure concerned only a handful of interventions. The situation is noticeably different when we face the same task with regard to the situational techniques. There are hundreds of publicly known, published techniques of this kind and probably an equal number of unpublished ones. Furthermore, given that situational techniques are content-bound and that the content of human suffering is limitless, the qualitative disparity among techniques subsumed under this category of role playing intervention is considerably greater. Therefore, the task which we face now is far more complicated than that posed in the case of the basic techniques and the challenge is more exciting.

But before we embark on meeting this challenge it is important to clarify what constitutes a situational technique. The analysis presented in the next section will reveal that the answer to this question broadens the definition of the kind of interventions included in the situational techniques category.

ENACTMENTS VS. TECHNIQUES

The content of the protagonist's complaints may be expressed in terms of pains and fears, confusions and worries, burdening dilemmas and perceived ineptitude, or fantasies and misconceptions. Regardless of how the complaints are described, they are always dealt with in the form of simulated vignettes. This is the unique feature of clinical role playing therapy. Unfortunately, the language used to characterize the concretizing of contents into events is inconsistent. Sometimes they are described in the literature as role playing enactments, role playing portrayals, behaving out, acting out, or even acting-in (Blatner, 1973). Sometimes they are simply referred to as role playing techniques. The most frequent expressions used, however, are *enactments* and *techniques*. Is there a real difference between these two expressions or are they interchangeable, more or less synonymous concepts? It is quite possible that the inconsistency with regard to the labeling as shown in the literature is no more than a semantic inexactitude. But it is also possible, and in my opinion quite probable, that it reflects a fundamental confusion about what constitutes a role playing technique. As a point of interest it ought to be emphasized that this suspected lack of clarity does not seem to concern those techniques that were classified under the *basic* category. These have always been referred to as *techniques* and not as enactments. It is primarily in the proposed category of situational techniques that the confusion is most prominent.

The following examples illustrate the need for a clearer definition of the kind of activities that fall within the perimeters of the situational techniques category. Let us imagine a hypothetical case of a female protagonist whose presenting problem centers on her guilt over the way she fulfills her maternal duties. The translation of this problem into role playing portrayals may vary from one director to another. Here are four different versions. The first director in our hypothetical illustration asks the protagonist to recall a typical situation where she became aware of her guilt feelings. The protagonist mentions a recent discussion with her husband. At the request of the director the protagonist sets the scene and proceeds to act it out using an auxiliary, a group member, to represent her spouse. A second director may ask our protagonist if she would be willing to show the group the kind of roles she finds most difficult to cope with. The protagonist identifies the different aspects of her maternal duties and then singles out the one or two that she perceives as the most troublesome. The ensuing scene involves an encounter between the protagonist and each of the identified aspects as personified by auxiliaries. A third director may approach the same issue in an entirely different way. He puts the protagonist in an imaginary courtroom. There she has to face a judge, a jury, and a prosecutor all represented by auxiliaries (members of the therapy group) as she stands accused of neglecting some aspects of her maternal responsibilities.

Let us now turn to the fourth imaginary director. This one finds himself in an interesting situation. Before he gets a chance to set up a scene, the protagonist (who has had previous exposure to clinical role playing therapy) takes the initiative.

Protagonist: I suppose that you would like to see the whole thing role played, right?

Director: (smiling) Well, yes. By all means.

Protagonist: OK, let me show you and the group when I get those guilt feelings. Here's the kitchen *(she picks up a couple of chairs and arranges them in her kitchen)* and here I'm standing next to the sink and my daughter comes in. *(turning to the group)* Linda, would you like to come up and help me? You will be my daughter.

The protagonist proceeds to act out the situation with her daughter as portrayed by the auxiliary.

Now, which of the four examples ought to be considered a *technique* and which one, if any, is an *enactment*? If the question is put to a large group of role playing experts we may find that some cases are easier to answer than others. Labeling the intervention used by the first director could elicit some disagreement. We would not be surprised if some experts call it a technique and some an enactment. Labeling the interventions displayed by the second and the third directors will probably reveal the greatest consensus. Most experts will define the second intervention as a technique, specifically a variation of the Barrier Technique, and all of them will describe the third intervention as the Trial or the Judgment Technique.

What, then, is the basis for the problem in labeling the first example in our illustration? We can only conjecture that people find it easy to label an intervention as a *technique* when there is evidence that it was a preplanned, scripted episode initiated by the director. On the other hand, a spontaneous portrayal initiated by the protagonist is something else, which in the absence of a better term may be called an enactment. Using this line of reasoning one would be in a bind with regard to labeling the first example in the illustration because, although it was initiated by the director, it did not appear as a scenario scripted by him. Moreover, according to this criterion, the fourth example has to be branded an enactment. Obviously the considerations, "who initiated the scene" and "the extent that it was a preplanned scenario" ought to be rejected as viable determinants because they themselves are difficult to define. There are cases of joint initiations as well as various degrees of preplanning. I believe that the basis for differentiating techniques from enactments lies elsewhere.

The approach I adhere to is quite simple. It stems from the premise that role playing techniques are therapeutic *instruments* characterized by the transformation of content material described in the abstract into concrete, simulated vignettes. Such conversions are considered techniques irrespective of who introduced them to the scene or how they came to be. *Every portrayal displayed in the course of a clinical role playing session constitutes a technique or a set of techniques.* And there can be only two categories of techniques: basic (divided into specific and general ones) and situational. In my view there is no contest between the terms *techniques* and *enactments.* To be precise, an enactment is a generic expression indicating that an issue is being concretely displayed rather than merely talked about. A technique, on the other hand, concerns the *specific shape* and *form* that this mode of expression assumes.

GENERAL CONSIDERATIONS

In this section a few general considerations specifically relevant to the situational techniques group will be discussed. These include the differences among the impromptu, the adaptive and the rehearsed situational techniques, the objectives of situational techniques, and the relationship of the basic techniques to the situational ones.

Impromptu, Adaptive, and Rehearsed Techniques

The processes leading to the creation of situational techniques vary. This is perhaps one of the factors responsible for the impression that this category of techniques is extremely diversified and internally disorganized. The following analysis will attempt to dispel this impression by discussing the interrelated, intricate aspects of situational techniques in an orderly fashion. Let us begin with the creation of situational techniques. When we observe someone using such techniques, the first thought that may strike us is where does the inspiration come from? How do these techniques come into existence? In order to answer these questions it is necessary to distinguish among three separate creative sources: the impromptu, the adaptive, and the rehearsed processes.

The *impromptu* process is by far the most creative and, not surprisingly, is one of the least frequent forms of devising situational techniques. As its name suggests this process begins as a sudden inspiration. Often, the onset of the idea appears unpredictably but sometimes it is the result of a premeditated thought. Typically, an invention of this kind becomes a *bona fide* situational technique in the following way. The first step is to translate the idea into a concrete episode, usually in the context of a plot or a story. Once it has been planned as a simulated vignette, it is tried out with one or two protagonists and then changed or refined as necessary. The last step involves a few more trials and adding the final touches. The most salient aspect of this process is that it begins as an *ad lib original* invention.

The *adaptive* process is more common. This creative approach has produced a large number of situational techniques in the past. In fact many of the so-called psychodramatic techniques were devised through the adaptive process. This is a "variation on a theme" approach, where the inventor uses an already existing technique as his or her prime model and then proceeds to design a version of it that appears to be more relevant to the issue at hand. Situational techniques of the adaptive mode follow one of two models: (a) an already existing technique or (b) a basic clinical role playing principle. In the case of the first model a known technique is being altered. The changes may take the form of altering the key characters or redefining the place of the action, but typically the process and the structure of the original technique are retained. In the case of the second model the newly devised technique represents a specific example of a general rule.

The way the adaptive mode operates in practice may become clearer with the following illustrations. Suppose a therapist wishes to help a female protagonist who expresses a need to explore her feelings towards her family background. In the interest of expediency, the therapist decides to act swiftly and to use the Empty-chair technique (described in Chapter 6) as a model for a new technique. The Empty-chair, it might be recalled, is a specific (basic) technique. But it may become a situational one if adjusted to a particular content issue. The original technique requires the protagonist to face an empty chair and imagine that someone is sitting on it. Let us also assume, for the purpose of this illustration, that the protagonist told the therapist that she has in her possession a family Bible that contains a page featuring her family tree. Now, the therapist places a chair in front of the protagonist, but this time it represents the page with the family tree on it. The task of the protagonist is to confront and interact with this imaginary family tree. This technique would be considered as a variation of the Empty-chair theme, but may also be entitled the Family Tree Technique.

In another similar example the therapist designs a situational technique modeled after the Lost-in-the-Desert Technique. This technique puts members of a therapeutic group in an imaginary constellation where they are lost in a desert and have to find their own way out or wait for a rescue team to arrive. Until then, they have to organize their own small commune. Our therapist decides to change the original technique and produce a different version of it. This time he tells the group to imagine that the ship they took for a pleasure cruise sank. They are survivors who landed on a small uninhabited island. Again, they are instructed to form their own society while they wait to be rescued.

The use of a clinical role playing principle as a model for inventing new situational techniques of the adaptive mode is a fairly easy operation. For instance, there are numerous colloquial idioms and common expressions that describe emotional states in terms of physical analogues. Let us consider two such phrases in order to illustrate the point. One describes the state of having a social or moral burden as "a heavy responsibility on one's shoulders," and the other pictures the state of indecisiveness as "being torn between two alternatives." The principle that can serve as a constructive model for turning these phrases into situational techniques is the principle of *concretization*. Simply stated it calls for converting abstract metaphors into concrete events. Thus, the therapist who wishes to apply the principle to the first phrase may ask the protagonist to sit on the floor or on a chair. Then he will ask an auxiliary to represent the "heavy responsibility" and to physically lean on the protagonist by pressing down his hands on the protagonist's shoulders. A therapist interested in applying the principle to the second phrase will ask for two auxiliaries and instruct each one to grab one of the protagonist's hands. The auxiliaries will pull the hands in opposite directions, thus portraying the dilemma in action in addition to causing the protagonist to experience pain associated with his or her conflict. There are endless analogues and metaphors that can be turned into situational techniques in this way.

The *rehearsed* process is the most popular way of introducing a situational technique into the therapeutic session. This mode does not require the creation of an entirely new technique nor does it call for creative improvisation. It is a copying mode, a borrowing operation where an already existing technique is used again in its original form without any significant changes. The therapist who has learned and memorized a broad repertoire of situational techniques selects the one most appropriate for the situation at hand and reapplies it.

As far as the clinical practice is concerned, there is no substantive advantage of one process over the others. It is true that the first two modes in the above discussion require more creativity on the part of the therapist; hence, they tend to have a greater appeal. They pose an interesting challenge, which makes them more attractive to some director-therapists. This preference, however, is an issue that relates to the personality of the therapist. It has no bearing on the quality of the treatment per se. These comments notwithstanding, sometimes the adaptive mode may have an advantage over the rehearsed mode. Being a tailor-made adaptation, potentially it may fit better the special predicaments of a given protagonist and, at times, be more sensitive to the unique nuances of the particular problem.

Objectives of Situational Techniques

The overall purpose of all situational techniques is to address the therapeutic needs evident in the course of the treatment session. But needs may be looked upon from different points of view. In terms of the consumer of the treatment the needs may be those of the individual protagonist, and in a group setting (including marital and family therapy) they also pertain to those of a few selected members of a larger group, or needs shared by the entire therapy group. Needs may also be organized in terms of their content. But here one faces the problem of choosing among a variety of theories of motivation and systems of needs classification (e.g., Cofer & Appley, 1964; Maslow, 1970; McClelland, 1961). Psychologists have argued that people have from three to several hundred needs and even with the adoption of stringent definitions, the conclusion as stated in the literature is that "unfortunately, at the moment there is not enough research evidence to allow us to state conclusively which listing of needs leads to the greatest predictability" (Lawler, 1983, p. 16). Therapeutic needs also can be viewed from an entirely different perspective, that is, in terms of the functions that they serve in the treatment procedure. It is this perspective that elicits the least controvertible classification of the objectives of situational techniques. Granted that this approach is likely to yield only broad categories of objectives, nonetheless it is possible to point to four general objectives as follows: diagnostic, catalytic, experimental, and demonstrational. Most situational techniques will have one of these objectives but it is quite common for a given technique to have *more than one* objective.

Diagnostic objectives. Situational techniques designed for diagnostic purposes are primarily employed for the benefit of the therapist. Like any other diagnostic, psychological, or behavioral instrument, they must be constructed to have the capacity for eliciting the information needed in order to understand the protagonist's problems and conflicts. They must be able to provide the therapist with reliable data regarding the severity of the expressed difficulties, the variables that tend to maintain and sustain the existing problems, and the direct as well as the indirect consequences of the observed emotional, cognitive, and behavioral deficits. Like any other diagnostic tool, situational techniques may be used for such a purpose only after fulfilling the basic requirements concerning reliability and validity. In addition to the familiar issues of test-retest and interscorers (observers) reliability, testing by means of role playing involves a special form of validity. In the words of Shaw, Corsini, Blake, and Mouton (1980), "the validity of role playing as a test depends on the degree of reality measurement that takes place: whether the individual in real life or whether the artificial situation and the contrived problem elicit behavior that is typical of the individual" (p. 111).

The use of situational techniques for diagnostic purposes provide the therapist with two sources of information: one derived from the verbal content expressed in the scene and the other from the actional "language," the nonverbal component of the protagonist's performance. Techniques with diagnostic objectives tend to be used more in the beginning portion of the session. But they are not limited to that phase and may be applied at any time as needed.

Catalytic objectives. Situational techniques designed to promote catalytic objectives tend to be more sophisticated than those employed for diagnostic goals. Their prime purpose is to serve as triggers: to stimulate psychotherapeutic activities and to stir them toward particular outcomes to the extent that this can be done. Specifically, these techniques "set the stage" so that a desired psychological process will begin to operate and may culminate in appropriate realizations and insights. Goldman and Morrison (1984) made a distinction between what they called the *content* and the *process* of the protagonists' responses. In their nomenclature, content is the subject matter, the story of the client. Process, on the other hand, is "the manner in which the individual responds internally to the content and how he/she then acts in life" (p. 21). Using this distinction, the catalytic objectives refer to the stimulation of the factors and forces that determine the process.

The catalytic property of role playing techniques was discussed in Chapter 6 in connection with the basic techniques and therefore need not be repeated again. It will be sufficient to reiterate that such techniques possess an immense therapeutic value and that they constitute a large portion of all the remedial effort invested in the course of the treatment.

Experimental objectives. Situational techniques classified under this category are essentially training experiences. Their expressed objectives are to offer protagonists the opportunities to experiment; to try out, to rehearse, and to practice new learnings gleaned during the treatment. Franz Alexander (1965) pointed out that in corrective emotional experience, intellectual insight alone is not sufficient and that the essence of the curative mechanism is the accompanying reality testing. In clinical role playing therapy, reality testing is expressed best through techniques that accentuate the experimental objectives. Furthermore, these techniques are useful vehicles for the acquisition of new life skills, and for modifying or perfecting existing ones. The following excerpt from Shaw, Corsini, Blake, and Mouton (1980) summarizes this aspect of role playing.

> Role playing also gives people the opportunity to try out new behaviors in a "safe" setting. One can discover—surprisingly well—how comfortable new behaviors are and which of several alternative actions "fits" best. One can practice and repractice, try out minor variations repeatedly. Thus, weeks, months, and even years of real-life experience can be simulated in a few role-play sessions. Although the learning may not be quite as powerful as in a real setting, this lack is more than compensated for by the ease, safety, and creative learning potential of the role-play situation. (p. 25)

Indeed, the ability of situational techniques to act as a disinhibition agent—to minimize resistance to change—must be underscored. The comparison between in-vitro experiences (simulated practice opportunities conducted in the therapy room) and in-vivo experiences (practice in real life, in terms of their respective effectiveness) is often uncalled for. There is substantial evidence that the effectiveness of the latter often cannot be surpassed by other means. But as soon as one encounters a problem of fear of change and renitent protagonists, in-vitro learning through situational techniques becomes the most effective intervention modality.

Like the preceding catalytic objectives, the experimental ones, too, are characterized as remedial and corrective goals. Their prime purpose is to benefit the protagonists to overcome whatever handicap from which they may suffer. Again, situational techniques with such objectives represent a major portion of the entire repertoire of role playing techniques.

Demonstrational objectives. This category of objectives is somewhat different from the preceding ones because it has an additive property. It is uncommon to find situational techniques specifically designed for such objectives. Instead, each of the aforementioned categories may also assume demonstrational properties when used for didactic purposes. Role playing techniques employed for demonstrational purposes serve as a teaching vehicle; they substitute the lecturing approach with a more lively and engaging form of tutoring. In the clinical area, these objectives gain prominence when applied for the benefit of the observers as much as, and often more than, that of the protagonists themselves. The most typical clinical circumstances where these objectives tend to be emphasized are as follows:

(a) In clinical supervision for training clinical students.
(b) In clinical supervision when supervisees are encouraged to present their case reports in the form of role playing reenactments of the therapy sessions.
(c) When an issue shared by a group of clients emerged during the treatment session. The therapist-director may ask one or two members to portray the problem as spokesperson(s) for many group members. Once the problem and its ramifications have been demonstrated, the group will discuss various solutions and coping strategies.
(d) In situations when either the protagonist or the therapist need the advice of the observing members. The behavior in question may be portrayed by means of role playing enactments in a manner similar to the traditional presentation of case material in clinical case conferences. Following the presentation the observers' feedback is sought. It should be pointed out, however, that unlike (b) above, the presenter here is the protagonist.

The use of situational techniques for demonstrational purposes is not restricted to the clinical area. On the contrary, often role playing is employed in nontherapeutic contexts such as in the training of parents to deal with their children, in the training of teachers, in raising social issues, ethical dilemmas, etc. Although such applications do not utilize the fullest potential of situational techniques, nonetheless the practice is widespread and has many advantages.

The division of objectives into four broad categories raises the question of the practical advantages of this conceptual analysis. What are the application consequences of this exercise? The answer to this question is fairly obvious. Recognizing the different objectives of situational techniques we can now turn back to the structure of the therapy session and identify the stages where each objective's category is most indicated. The catalytic objectives seem to be appropriate in the warm-up stage where the therapist must strike a sensitive compromise between the need to structure the session and the need to let spontaneity evolve within the group. This situation was described by Weiner and Sacks (1969) as follows:

> Many. . . warm-up techniques operate by means of the director's establishing some definition to an otherwise unstructured situation. He sets certain "rules of the game" within which the group members can behave spontaneously. While a completely unstructured situation leaves maximal opportunity for free behavior, it also may raise the threat of overwhelming unconscious flow with a consequent blocking of the flow altogether. The painful and unproductive silences in certain non-directive groups are familiar. While some individuals and groups need a great deal of this structuring to reduce anxiety to the point where functioning begins, others require little or none. (p. 88)

Catalytic objectives also seem appropriate during the second segment of the action stage.

The diagnostic objectives are mostly indicated in the beginning of the session, in the first segment of the action stage where the problem is presented. The experimental objectives are clearly called for in the third segment of the action stage. It should be emphasized that none of the three objective categories—the diagnostic, the catalytic, and the experimental—are limited to one stage or a segment of a stage of the session. Each one of them may become relevant at many points during the treatment session.

It is also clear from the above discussion that the division of objectives into four broad categories cannot serve as a good basis for a general system of classifying situational techniques. Too many techniques have several objectives that tend to shift depending on the context in which they are used. The basis for classifying situational techniques under a more stable system must lie elsewhere.

The Relationship Between the Basic and the Situational Techniques

In general, all role playing techniques are closely related, although some more so than others. Our apparent emphasis on the differences among the various techniques' categories has conceptual and heuristic purposes, while in practice one is more impressed with the tendency of techniques to complement each other. Still, we maintain that more can be gleaned from looking at the specific patterns in which various techniques' categories are interrelated; a good example of this is the relation between the basic and the situational techniques. This relationship seems to be expressed in two patterns: an additive and a transformational pattern.

An *additive* property implies a state of complementarity. It suggests that basic techniques and situational techniques may be added to each other. And indeed, it is quite common to find therapists combining basic techniques, especially those of the specific category, with situational techniques. In fact, the therapeutic value of most situational techniques can be greatly increased when reinforced with techniques such as the Soliloquy, the Role-reversal, the Double and the Multiple Doubles, or the Empty-Chair. It is appropriate to conclude, therefore, that every basic technique, whether specific or general, may be used in conjuntion with situational techniques provided that the indications for its application fit the situation and that the contraindications do not apply.

Transformational relationships imply that one category of techniques may be redefined, restructured, and readjusted to assume the characteristics of another category. With regard to the basic and the situational techniques such a metamorphosis may occur in one direction only. Basic techniques may become situational ones, but not vice versa. It might be recalled from our earlier discussion in Chapter 6 that the basic techniques possess a universal psychological attribute, that is, their application in the role playing scenes is not contingent upon the specific content of a particular problem or conflict. This quality makes them malleable enough to assume content-bound characteristics and thus be transformed into situational techniques.

Let us illustrate the way in which basic techniques change their characteristics so that they actually become situational techniques. Here are a couple of examples. Picture a situation where, in the course of a therapy session, the therapist realizes that one of the protagonist's problems is that he tends to dominate every social relationship in which he is involved. With this tendency, the protagonist is ill-equipped and unable to form mutually satisfying relationships with other people. As long as this tendency persists, the protagonist faces a serious obstacle which arrests his social development. The therapist decides at this point to confront the protagonist with this tendency by using the Empty-chair technique. Only this time the empty chair is transformed to become the Obstacle (i.e., the tendency to dominate social interactions). The ensuing scene portrays the encounter between the protagonist and his barrier.

Or consider another example, this time with the Role-playing technique. Suppose a protagonist complains that she is mistreated by her friends. She feels that people take advantage of her, show disregard for her feelings and opinions, and act rudely towards her. The therapist immediately develops in his mind an image of "a chaos in the jungle." In pursuit of this image, the therapist asks the protagonist to assume the role of an animal of her choice, that is, to assume the identity of that creature. He then asks her to select a few auxiliaries to represent "people" or her friends and also assign roles of animals to them. The ensuing scene portrays the "star-animal" (the protagonist) interacting with the rest of the animals (the auxiliaries) in the jungle. Thus, the Role-playing technique became the core of a specially designed episode and in the process assumed situational technique attributes.

THE SITUATIONAL TECHNIQUES' PARADIGM

Except for a handful of basic techniques, all other interventions commonly referred to by practitioners and researchers as role playing techniques are classified under the situational techniques category. The concept of situational techniques is a new term and, to the best of my knowledge, has not been introduced before in the sense in which it is suggested here. Instead, references to techniques of the situational type in the literature have been characteristically inconsistent. A quick glance at the published material reveals many different labels and titles used for grouping such techniques under broader categories. Some of the more familiar ones are role playing (separate words) techniques, educational exercises, warm-up techniques, group experiences, simulation games, modeling techniques, structure exercises, behavior rehearsal techniques, and psychodramatic techniques, to mention only a few.

Given the popularity of these types of interventions, there is good evidence to suspect that a comprehensive and detailed list of all the known techniques and their variations will hold hundreds of entries. For example, the two books written by Morris and Cinnamon—a handbook of verbal group exercises (1974), and a handbook of nonverbal group exercises (1975)—each contained a couple of hundred techniques. Pfeiffer and Jones (1973-1979) have edited and compiled books and lists that describe several hundred such techniques. In addition there are other lists and techniques that appear in separate articles or are scattered in various books by many other authors (e.g., Blatner, 1973; Cohen & Smith, 1976; Corsini, 1966; Eiben & Milliren, 1976; Haskell, 1975; Maier, Solem, & Maier, 1975; Schutzenberger, 1970; Shaw, Corsini, Blake, & Mouton, 1980; Siroka, Siroka, & Schloss, 1971; Starr, 1977; Thayer, 1976; Weil, 1967; Weiner & Sacks, 1969; Yablonsky, 1976). This bibliographic list is far from being a complete one. It only cites some of the better known sources. Also, it should be borne in mind that it contains the published lists. It is estimated that as many techniques have been invented by practicing clinicians who have never reported them in the literature.

The need for creating a workable system that will organize all these techniques and sort them into manageable subgroups is obvious. It is extremely difficult, if not impossible, to master that enormous repertoire of techniques if they are left alone as an encyclopedic list. Thus it is necessary to decide what criteria should be selected as the basis for a meaningful classification system.

The realization of this need had already struck role playing experts several years ago. This resulted in various classification proposals, which ranged from very simplistic to more elaborate systems. For instance, techniques were divided into verbal and nonverbal categories (Morris & Cinnamon, 1974; 1975). Another dichotomous classification idea was suggested by Weiner and Sacks (1969) who categorized techniques according to the stages of the clinical role playing session (i.e., into warm-up and sum-up techniques). Techniques were also grouped according to their formally designated objectives as well as their formal settings. These include categories such as personal growth techniques, skill training techniques, experiential learning techniques, group exercises, or business games. A somewhat more elaborate system was proposed by Hollander and Hollander (1978), but their system was limited to warm-up techniques. One of the most sophisticated and complex categorization systems to be proposed recently was designed by Pfeiffer and Jones (1980). That system classifies situational techniques into a few dozen subcategories according to goals of activity. In addition, a cross-system is provided where each technique is rated according to the structural complexity of its design, the amount of feeling it generates and the impact on the audience, and the difficulty of its process as far as the learning effort is concerned.

These classification proposals are good illustrations of the attempts that have been made in the past to sort situational techniques into meaningful and practical organization systems. It appears that the overriding concern addressed by these proposals is a utilitarian one, that is, to provide the users an easy access to the techniques, to offer a workable retrieval mechanism. But a careful examination of the above examples also highlights some of the unresolved problems that still exist. Obviously the dichotomous systems do not eliminate the inconvenience of having excessively long lists of techniques under each category. A useful system must include several categories and subcategories. The classification of techniques according to their objectives, whether one uses the four we have suggested or other lists of objectives, is also problematic, as mentioned earlier. Many techniques have several objectives and the decision about which one is more prominent does not necessarily depend on their design but rather on *how* they are used and *under what* circumstances. Is it better, then, to classify techniques according to topical categories such as leadership, decision making, building trust, social skills, marital tensions, guilt, shame, and so forth? The pragmatic advantage of systems of this kind, especially as means for selecting and retrieving techniques, is considerable indeed. The problem, however, is that topics can be subdivided and reclassified endlessly, and whatever system is offered, one will have to keep adding more categories as well as revising the existing ones.

But there is an additional point to be made in connection with the discussion of the existing classification systems. Although the utilization consequences of any attempt to offer a classification system for the situational techniques must remain a prime consideration, it is equally important that a good classification system provide prospective inventors clues about how to design techniques more effectively.

Is there, then, a perfect system? The question is not easy to answer. In theory there is no reason why such a classification scheme cannot be devised. Of course, it would have to be an elaborate, multilevel codification system. In practice, however, the most difficult challenge is to produce an inclusive system which at the same time will be sensitive and delicate enough to detect all the important nuances that separate one situational technique from another. At present, I am not aware of the existence of such a system. I also do not pretend that the key for devising an ideal system is in my hands. But I would like to propose new foundations for classifying situational techniques with the hope that in the future these may lead to the formulation of a sound, general classification scheme.

The Paradigm

I begin with a prerequisite assumption for embarking on any classification endeavor, namely, that there is a logical order underlying what at first glance appear to be scattered, diversified, and unrelated events. An interesting corollary to this assumption is that situational techniques—both those that are invented intuitively and those that are created through careful preplanning—actually follow the same principles. This holds true even if the intuitive inventor is not cognizant of the underlying principles.

My next step is to define the general considerations that need to be taken into account in devising the new paradigm for the situational techniques. These governing considerations are as follows:

1. *Inclusiveness and simplicity.* It is imperative that the paradigm be broad enough to include every kind of situational technique but at the same time it should be as simple as possible. Thus, every effort must be made to avoid the formulation of a cumbersome and unduly complicated scheme.
2. *Insight and applicability.* The paradigm should help us understand the fundamental structure of situational techniques. It is also expected to provide clues concerning how to design a situational technique. These clues, assuming that they are indeed essential, ought to make the design of such techniques much easier.
3. *Process orientation.* The paradigm should be based on factors that refer to the processes that situational techniques tend to emphasize. The reason for focusing on processes rather than on objectives and content is that the former represent a far more stable attribute than the latter.

Bearing in mind these considerations, I have found a set of organized factors (i.e., basic principles) that unveil the internal structure of situational techniques. These factors can be illustrated graphically so that their relationships to each other are clear, as shown in Figure 8.1. A glance at Figure 8.1 reveals that the paradigm is organized in the form of two concentric circles and two axes. These, in fact, represent *three* dimensions (factors). One dimension is represented by the vertical axis, another one by the horizontal axis, and the third dimension is shown in the form of two concentric circles: the inner versus the outer. These three dimensions are the key elements of the paradigm.

Consider first the vertical axis that cuts across the two circles. This axis represents a dimension called *Modes of Eliciting the Issue.* As its title suggests, it concerns the ways in which a given issue is elicited (i.e., brought out into the open) through the technique. Before we continue, it should be pointed out that the term *issue* as used in this context refers to a behavioral or an emotional deficit, a psychotherapeutic process, or a remedial experience. Now, according to this dimension, psychological issues can be elicited in two ways or modes. One, which is described as

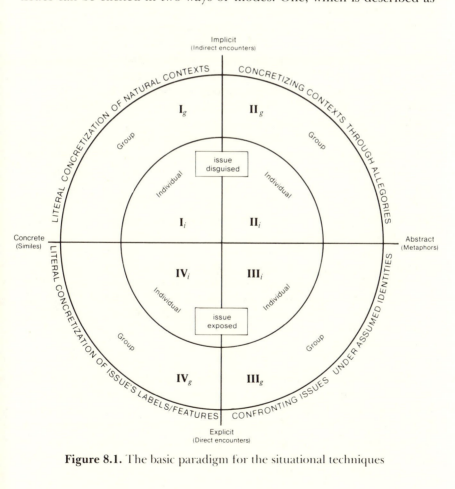

Figure 8.1. The basic paradigm for the situational techniques

an *Implicit* mode (see the top of the outer circle), tends to evoke the target issue(s) in a subtle way, in a covert, roundabout manner. Protagonists, here, have neither an advance knowledge nor a clear awareness of what is the exact issue they are working on or what psychological processes they are expected to activate. All they are asked to do is to become involved in the scene that is designed to produce the desired processes. The encounter with the issue is expected to occur *indirectly* and it appears to be the result of the protagonists' portrayals rather than the initiative of the therapist. Implicit elicitations may be accomplished best by keeping the target issues somewhat *disguised* (see the box in the upper half of the inner circle) and instead investing the major efforts of designing the techniques in the concretization of the contextual environment where the ensuing action will take place.

An intervention strategy of this kind is quite common in most forms of psychotherapy, if not all of them. Some may use it frequently, while others perhaps less so; and, in spite of its apparent manipulative quality, often there are good and sound clinical reasons to support its application. In a recent evaluation of self-development games and simulations, Farra (1980) discussed the ways that objectives are achieved. He made the point that "not only is it important to examine and evaluate the various objectives, but it is also helpful to know how obvious these objectives are to the players. The success of objectives is often related to the way they are achieved. Learning objectives are more effective when realized with subtlety" (p. 226). Yalom (1980), too, addressed the importance of the indirect strategy in his discussion of clinical strategy and techniques of making decisions in connection with "willing." Under the heading, "Therapeutic Approaches to Decision: Unconscious Levels," he wrote:

> How can the therapist approach the unconscious aspects of decision making—what Faber refers to as the "first realm of will?" The answer: "Indirectly." Much as they might wish to, therapists cannot create will or commitment. But they can influence the factors that influence willing. . . . *Thus, the therapist's task is not to create will, but to disencumber it.* (p. 332)

The implicit process is philosophically congruent with the often cited statement about the purpose of psychological treatment, namely, "to help people to help themselves."

The second mode of eliciting the issue is the exact opposite of the Implicit one and has appropriately been labeled the *Explicit* mode (see the bottom of the outer circle). This one tends to evoke the target issue(s) through *direct,* head-on confrontations. Protagonists are fully aware of what they are expected to do with the exposed problems, deficits, or conflicts that afflict them. As far as the design of the scene is concerned, the major effort centers on the concretization of the issue(s). In contrast with the design strategy employed in the case of the Implicit mode, a meticulous concretization of the environment where the confrontation might take place is less important with the Explicit mode. Often, whether or not the environment is concretized is quite immaterial.

The Implicit-Explicit polarity reflects the degree to which the therapist may control the protagonist's state of awareness with regard to each and every step of the psychotherapeutic process. True, "awareness of one's own feelings constitutes a therapist's most important instrument for identifying a patient's contribution to his or her life predicament" (Yalom, 1980, p. 235). Sometimes the best curative results occur when the protagonist's attention is completely focused on the therapeutic process. But, paradoxically, quite often the best outcomes are attained by *shifting* the protagonist's attention from the process.

An interesting illustration of these two approaches is described in Kipper (1980) who reported the treatment of two nyctophobic patients (people suffering from fear of darkness). Although the therapeutic modality used was not clinical role playing therapy but in-vivo desensitization, the treatment highlights the difference between the Implicit and the Explicit strategies. One of the patients was a young male in his early twenties, who developed a fear of darkness. He would not step outside his home after sunset. He would spend every afternoon figuring out how to get home before dark. The therapist decided to use an in-vivo desensitization procedure in order to help the patient. In essence this kind of treatment is based on actually exposing the patient to darkness in a controlled, gradual manner, one step at a time.

The way this was carried out was as follows: The patient was taught a muscular relaxation technique until he became proficient enough to be able to relax himself more or less instantaneously. In the ensuing sessions he would come to the treatment session before dusk; as soon as it became dark both the therapist and the patient stepped outside. The treatment began with the therapist instructing the patient to walk a few yards in the darkness, at first together with him and then alone. In each subsequent session the distance was gradually increased until finally the patient was able to walk alone half a mile. During this process the patient was asked to be aware of the fact that it was dark, and whenever he felt anxiety he would relax himself on the spot. The philosophy behind this approach fits the Explicit mode. But at this stage of treatment an interesting phenomenon was observed. In spite of the fact that the patient was able to walk a considerable distance alone, the fear did not disappear. At the end of each walk he would perspire heavily. So the therapist decided to change the strategy. He instructed the patient to shift his attention away from the darkness and asked him to become preoccupied with other thoughts as he walked in the dark. This did it. A few practice sessions later the patient was able not only to walk in the dark but also to overcome the feeling of fear. The attention-shifting strategy, the diversion of the awareness from the issue proper (i.e., the darkness) to other thoughts is an example of the idea that characterizes the Implicit mode.

Another example of the difference in therapeutic approaches congruent with the notions of the Implicit mode and the Explicit mode can be observed in Moreno's and Fritz Perls' treatments of stuttering. Moreno's technique will be described in greater detail in the next chapter. Briefly, his approach was quite similar to the attention-shifting strategy discussed above and seemed to be in line with the Implicit mode. His stuttering patient was instructed not to think about the words with which he chose to express himself. Instead, he was asked to role play emotionally laden situations—the ones that caused him to stutter—using a "personal language" comprised of nonsensical syllables. Perls, on the other hand, described a treatment of a stutterer using the opposite approach. His method required the patient to pay attention to the stuttering, that he or she confront it head on in a manner agreeable with the Explicit mode. The following excerpt describes Perls' approach.

> Two weeks ago I had a wonderful experience—not that it was a cure, but at least it was an opening up. This man was a stammerer, and I asked him to increase his stammer. As he stammered, I asked him what he feels in his throat, and he said "I feel like choking myself." So, I gave him my arm and said "Now, choke me." "God damn, I could kill you!" he said. He got really in touch with his anger and spoke loudly, without any difficulties. So, I showed him he had an existential choice, to be an angry man or to be a stutterer. (1969, p. 80)

The horizontal axis in Figure 8.1 represents the second dimension entitled: *Modes of structuring the issue.* This dimension refers to the actual structuring, the concrete implementation, of the issue. The structuring is predicated on the type of associations model (i.e., the images and ideations) the inventor of situational techniques has in his or her mind when the role playing episode is put into concrete form.

Before we continue to discuss this dimension it might be useful to sharpen the distinction between this and the previous dimensions because the two are interrelated and sometimes appear undifferentiated. Indeed, both dimensions address the design of role playing situational techniques. However, their common denominator essentially ends here. What is, then, the difference between the two dimensions? In the first, the modes of *eliciting the issue* addresses the aspect of strategy. It refers to the phase that *precedes* the actual implementation. In this phase the therapist is called upon to make a decision regarding the way he or she would like to see the curative process flow. Should it unfold by making the protagonist aware of the disturbing issue or should it emerge by diverting the protagonist's attention from the debilitating issue? The second dimension—modes of *structuring the issue*—deals with the implementation aspect. Once a decision is made regarding the flow, the next task is to decide what kind of concrete form the intervention should assume. There are two such forms: One is called *Similes* (see the left end of the horizontal axis) and the other is called *Metaphors* (see the right end of the horizontal axis).

Simile is defined in Webster's New World Dictionary, Second College Edition, as "a figure of speech by which one thing is likened to another, dissimilar thing." In other words, a thing, action, or relation is explicitly compared in one or more aspects to something of a different kind or quality. In the present context, *Similes* (in the plural) refer to the concretization of contexts or issues through *literal association*. These associations are based on conceptualizing qualities, relationships, actions, and things in terms of images that have natural relatedness to what they are supposed to represent. In other words, the quality that makes these images literal is that their presentation does not go beyond the actual facts, and that they appear in the role play situations similar to the way in which they would appear in one's own imagination if one is asked to visualize them as concrete, natural events.

Metaphors, on the other hand, refer to a different mode of concretization. This mode is exactly the opposite of the Similes. Unlike the Similes mode, contexts (or issues) are *not* represented here in the form of their natural occurrences or in ways commonly associated with them. Instead, the images and association that lead to the metaphoric modes are primarily alllegories. By allegories we mean plots and stories where people or events appear as symbolic representations to substitute those which characterize the original ones. The way the Metaphor mode is expressed in the structuring of the situational techniques is twofold:

(a) by concretizing stories—imaginary plots or fables—that highlight the issue under investigation as the result of logical inferences.

In other words, the relevance of the intervention to the issue is made by conceptualizing the relations in the *abstract*, on a symbolic level, and then translating the found analogue into a concrete form;

(b) by asking players to address the identified issue(s) under an *assumed identity*. The metaphoric conceptualization is not that of a context or of a hypothetical issue as in (a) above. Rather, the issue remains in its original form. The *role* of the player(s) becomes metaphorical (i.e., impersonal).

Let us try to illustrate this with another analogy. A city planner wants to have access to a water source. The first task is to decide where one drills the well. There are two possibilities: One is to find a place whose geophysical structure ensures the presence of natural pressures that will force the water up to the surface of the earth; the other possibility is to drill wherever a water source is to be found and to bring it up with a hydrolic pump. This is a matter of flow. In either case the final outcome is the same; the water will appear from beneath the earth. The next task is to decide how to drill the well. We are aware that the analogy of the Similes/Metaphors modes may seem awkward here; nonetheless, let us see how these will be used in this example. Using the Similes image one would think of the most natural way of drilling deep holes and rent ordinary drilling equipment. Using the Metaphors association, one would hire a fighter-bomber to fly over the designated spot and fire a successive series of high velocity air-to-ground missiles, or to bomb the place until this creates a deep enough hole to reach the water. The metaphoric association is that the purpose of missiles and bombs is to make holes in things.

How do these two modes reflect themselves in psychotherapy? In what way is a technique designed as *Similes* (literal concretization) different from that designed on the basis of *Metaphoric* structuring? The following are examples of the application of the Similes mode. Suppose a protagonist describes her predicament as "Everybody pushes me around." The therapist will concretize the phrase by asking several auxiliaries to come to the action space and push the protagonist. Or, suppose a protagonist expresses the need to be protected, to have unconditional support. The therapist will ask a few auxiliaries to form a supportive circle around the protagonist and to convey warmth and sympathy towards her. Similarly, a state of indecision may be concretized by having two auxiliaries push the protagonist back and forth. A need to withdraw is portrayed by allowing the protagonist to hide behind a wall of chairs. A conflict between a person's feelings and thoughts can be demonstrated by asking the protagonist to assume the role of his own heart while another auxiliary takes an adversary position, representing the protagonist's brain.

The Similes mode can also be utilized in techniques involving an entire group. Consider a situation in which a sharp disagreement emerges between females and males, all members of a therapy group. The therapist may draw an imaginary diagonal line that separates the room into two parts (some therapists actually draw a line with chalk). The therapist now sends all the male members to one corner of the room and the female members to the opposite corner. "This is the line of disagreement that separates the men and the women into two opposing camps," the therapist may say. "I would like to see if one camp can persuade members of the other to 'cross the line' and come over to its side. Let's see what it takes to have a mixed majority in one of the two corners."

Let us consider a different example. Suppose a therapist decides to provide members of a therapeutic group the opportunity to engage in self-introspection with regard to the subject of "the importance of their existence." In order to facilitate this aim he introduces the technique known as the Life Boat (e.g., Yablonsky, 1976). Briefly, the technique puts people in a boat floating in the middle of the ocean. They are survivors of a sunken ship. As time passes, food and water become scarce and all of them face the prospect of death unless they discard two or three people who will be thrown into the sea. People in the boat must now fight for their lives by convincing their comrades why they should be spared. This technique, according to our system, is an example of the *metaphoric* approach (mode). The element that is concretized here is the story of the boat. The "survival" issue is the by-product of that story. It does not represent literal concretization because the lifeboat analogy is not a *common* example where one naturally ponders his or her *raison d'être*. The most typical situations giving rise to such self-examination thoughts are important anniversaries or significant promotions, painful failures, demotions, and the like. Finding oneself in a lifeboat situation is a very *unusual* event. It was devised as a Metaphoric situation not because it is a common occurrence, but rather because it forces the issue well.

Again, it is our contention that situational techniques differ according to the ways they are designed, either as Similes concretization or concretization of Metaphors. Furthermore, we maintain that these aspects represent fundamental attributes of the structuring of the therapeutic issues in the context of clinical role playing interventions.

The third dimension of the paradigm shown in Figure 8.1 is represented by the two concentric circles. This dimension refers to the *Constituency of the techniques*. Situational techniques have been typically constructed to be used by either an *individual* protagonist or a number of participants simultaneously, i.e., by a *group*. I have retained that distinction in the paradigm because many techniques were originally devised that way. Thus, the inner circle pertains to techniques addressed for individual clients *even if the treatment is conducted in the presence of other persons* such as group members or members of one's own family. The outer circle refers to techniques designed as group interventions. Sometimes, however, the same situational technique may be applied either with individual clients or with a group. A technique that may have been invented originally for individual application can also be adopted with slight modifications for group treatment situations, and vice versa. In such a case the two applications of the technique will appear in the paradigm once in the appropriate portion of the inner circle and once in the corresponding portion of the outer circle.

To summarize, then, the first two dimensions, depicted in Figure 8.1 as the vertical and the horizontal axes, produce four quadrants. Each of these four represents a different kind of situational techniques' *prototype*. A *prototype* stands for a well-defined set of principles that characterize a certain class of situational techniques and ascribes to it a unique identity. Figure 8.1 shows that the four prototypes, moving from the upper left quadrant in a clockwise direction, are marked as Ii and g, IIi and g, IIIi and g, and IVi and g. The letters i and g represent the third dimension and denote techniques invented for *individual* or alternatively for *group* application. I propose that these four prototypes constitute the fundamental infrastructure of a classification scheme for clinical role playing techniques of the situational category. At the same time, I also recognize that the suggested division only represents a basic first step in the effort to uncover the overall patterns that characterize these techniques. There is considerable merit in the argument that further subcategorization of techniques into content areas and other clinically useful topics is also needed in order to turn the scheme into a complete and comprehensive classification system. Though respecting this need, nonetheless, I consider such subcategorizations to be of a secondary value. Given the complexity of the task involved, I was content with the decision to focus on the basic prototypes knowing that room was left for subsequent refinements.

CHAPTER 9

Prototypes of Situational Techniques

As we have seen, the basic paradigm shown in Figure 8.1 (p. 227) suggests that every situational technique can be sorted into one of four *prototypes* which represent the various combinations of the following: one of the two modes of eliciting the issue, the Implicit or the Explicit; one of the two modes of structuring the issue, the Similes or the Metaphors; and the two kinds of the techniques' constituency, the Individual and the Group clientele. The four prototypes, therefore, may be labeled as:

Prototype I : Implicit elicitation/Similes presentation for Individuals and Groups

Prototype II: Implicit elicitation/presentation by Metaphors for Individuals and Groups

Prototype III: Explicit elicitation/Similes presentation for Individuals and Groups

Prototype IV: Explicit elicitation/presentation by Metaphors for Individuals and Groups.

What are the *specific* characteristics of each of these four prototypes? What kinds of interventions serve as classic examples of these prototypes? The answers to the questions may require an extended discussion, which is the subject of the present chapter. Let us, then, examine the principles underlying each prototype in detail and see *a few* typical examples.

PROTOTYPE I: IMPLICIT/SIMILES COMBINATION

This prototype is represented in the paradigm in the form of the upper left quadrant (Figure 8.1) marked Ii and Ig as illustrated in the small, highlighted replica shown in Figure 9.1.

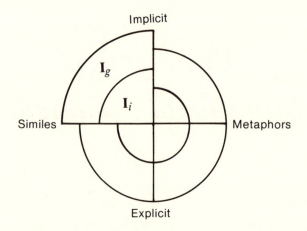

Figure 9.1. Prototype I

Underlying Principles

The prototype is based on the following principles. First, regarding the therapeutic issues, the target remedial experiences under treatment remain disguised and are not spelled out in advance. Second, the design of the role playing interventions focuses on structuring the environments—the circumstantial contexts where the ensuing action takes place. The environments, however, must be portrayed as *literal concretizations* of typical and natural backgrounds associated with the emergence of the treated issues.

Special Characteristics

The characteristics associated with techniques of this kind are:

1. The protagonists involved in these techniques always portray themselves in their *original identities.*
2. Nonverbal techniques are typically categorized under this prototype. These may include techniques conducted in a complete silence as well as those which, in addition, allow for brief vocal utterances in the form of either meaningful words or nonsensical and nonword sounds.
3. The simulated surroundings (i.e., the environmental backgrounds where the ensuing actions may take place) represent common and natural contexts associated with the identified problem issues.

4. This prototype also includes techniques designed to convey messages of interpretations, also known as action interpretations (Moreno & Moreno, 1969). Serving in this capacity, the interpretative messages are translated into concrete events or situations which by themselves carry subtle hints regarding the insight(s) that ought to be gleaned. It is hoped that through such manipulations protagonists may understand and accept the intended messages via the process of self-realization.

The following discussion will describe in detail examples of situational techniques most typical of this prototype. As a general rule the primary constituency of each technique will be indicated in brackets next to the title. The word "Individual" signifies that the technique was designed to be applied with an individual protagonist, and the word "Group" denotes that its primary application is with a number of individuals simultaneously.

Kicking an Obstacle (Individual)

The objective of this situational technique is to facilitate the expression of locked anger or frustration when dealing with protagonists who are unable to express these feelings willingly.

The way the technique is designed is as follows: The therapist-director asks the protagonist to walk in a circle around the action space. The idea of walking in a circle is to enable the protagonist to walk *forward* continuously rather than pacing back and forth, which usually causes annoyance. As the protagonist begins the stroll, obstacles are placed in his or her way. The obstacles may be in the form of chairs laid upside down or, as is often advisable, objects made from softer material such as plastic wastepaper baskets, balls, small and empty cardboard boxes, and so forth. The protagonist is instructed to kick the obstacle away and at the same time utter a sound or a scream. The process is repeated several times until the protagonist is able to express the anger quite explicitly. This technique should last for a few minutes only. If the protagonist is not responsive enough, it is advisable to terminate it after five minutes or so and either suggest a different technique or wait for a more appropriate opportunity.

An intriguing adaptation of the combination of nonverbal techniques coupled with the use of nonsensical utterances was reported by J.L. Moreno (1964a). He described an example of the psychodramatic approach to stuttering with a client, Joe, age 20, who was gifted in mathematics and physics. Joe had a long history of stuttering and stammering.

Moreno, the director in this case, formulated the problem as an incongruous development of the mental processes and the psychosemantic interactions. In order to facilitate a greater harmony between these two developmental areas, the expressions of emotional states in blocked utterances had to be removed through a new training device. This took the form of portrayals of situations using a "Joe language," that is, a mode of communication made up of nonsensical syllables. For example, an auxiliary was called up to represent Joe's girl friend. The two enacted situations that made Joe experience various emotions, e.g., sympathy, anxiety, or anger. These were situations that caused Joe to stutter. Only this time, instead of talking English, Joe (and the auxiliary) were instructed to speak in nonsensical syllables:

> The patient is told to resist the emergence of verbal utterances and to produce sounds and words which are nonsensical. The vowels and consonants are to be brought together into any possible combination as they come to him spontaneously. This exercise is useful in the training of stutterers and stammerers. "None of the stutterers and the stammerers whom I have treated stuttered during this test." (Moreno, 1964a, p. 217)

Examples of this mode are:

> (Sympathy—25 seconds) "Oh ma cour ta ti, lou tu ca, la ma, ma dar, tu tu, who cro ma, to jou, ho, ha, oh, ah, ohh."
> (Anxiety—20 seconds) "Ho cru ho ho ho no no no, you, no car, car ca ter tutu, tu tu cum tu oh no na no, oh, ah, ahaaa, no no no mi pa ne croi, oh long, oh long, oh long, good bi, gu ib, ohhh."
> (Anger—25 seconds) "Ta pugh pugh pugh pers frual, fer, me sta pu a tu a tu pugh tu a, poir ti, tu ah, cou, couc, ta la mi, cou ptugh ah."

The Letter (Individual)

This technique, invented by Sacks (1974), consists of the protagonist "writing" a letter aloud. The technique may be administered in individual sessions or in front of a group. The therapist-director, after spending a few moments for warming up, asks the protagonist (or potential protagonists in a group setting) to name someone with whom he or she might have something to discuss. A useful instruction is also to "name someone with whom you have not always been entirely honest." The writer is asked to lean forward in a writing position with his or her eyes cast down. The letter begins with a formal salutation such as "Dear. . . " and closes with the signature of the writer. It is important that the writer understands that this is an entirely hypothetical letter so that one need not be confined to what one would actually write in real life. It ought to be clear to the writer that he or she may express whatever comes to his or her mind freely, irrespective of the cautions that might be exercised in real life. The letter is written by using an imaginary pen and paper and is expressed aloud.

The technique is said to facilitate the exploration of one's feelings towards other people. It "helps to minimize resistance based on vagueness and abstractions. Many patients who otherwise get lost in philosophical generalities drained of affect become focused on highly concrete material as soon as they begin their letter to a specific person" (Sacks, 1974, p. 186). Sacks points out that in his experience the technique tends to liberate intense abreactive emotions, and that the characteristic emotions arising in this technique are rejection, grief, and longing. Often, after finishing the letter, the protagonist feels stronger, ready to reassert himself or herself in a situation that requires a direct confrontation with the issues or the person addressed in the letter.

When the technique is used in a group therapy situation, several members of the group take turns and write their own letters. Here, as a variation, a Double may be introduced to add a "P.S." after each letter. Following the Double's intervention, the writer may respond with a "P.P.S." This small addition is not restricted to group application of the technique and can be employed in individual administration as well.

Again, there are numerous variations of this technique. The core design remains the same, but instead of writing a letter a different task is introduced. One of the better known versions is the technique called "A Telephone Call" to be described next.

A Telephone Call (Individual)

The purpose of this technique is to facilitate open expression of feelings towards another person. The technique is quite simple. A protagonist is asked to place an imaginary telephone call to a person with whom he or she has an unfinished business that needs to be resolved. The conversation can be a one-way monologue, but it is helpful to have an auxiliary on the receiving end of the line. The way this technique is done is as follows: The therapist-director instructs the protagonist to describe the place where the telephone is located. Then the protagonist is asked to dial, using the imaginary telephone, the number of the person for whom this call is intended, to hold the imaginary receiver in his or her hand, and start the conversation with the words, "Hi, this is—speaking. I am calling you to. . . ." The protagonist is encouraged to say anything that comes to his or her mind and to use the opportunity for maximizing spontaneous and free expression, even if this would be quite different from what he or she would dare to say in real life. If an auxiliary is used to represent the person on the other end of the line, the director may say to the protagonist, "This person (pointing to the auxiliary) is not the real person you have the conflict with. You can tell him or her anything you like. He or she will not take it personally." In the event that an auxiliary is introduced, his or her role in the conversation is limited to encourage the protagonist to talk openly. There is no need to represent accurately the real-life partner to the conversation. The technique ordinarily lasts for 10 minutes or so. If the protagonist becomes unresponsive, it is advisable to have him or her reverse roles with the auxiliary for a moment and to be the receiver of the call. Often this small manipulation encourages further dialogue.

This technique, like the preceding one, aims at helping protagonists to extricate themselves from an emotional and attitudinal disarray and to set them on a track that will clarify and organize their discourse with reality. It seems particularly beneficial for persons who display a mental state described by Csikszentmihalyi (1982) as psychic *entropy*. Psychic entropy is a state of the self that occurs when attention is withdrawn from the outside world to reconcile conflicting information in consciousness. A conflict is the result of "a mismatch between information being processed and goals or intentions developed by the self. The ensuing subjective experiences are anxiety, self-pity, jealousy, boredom, and so forth. They are all characterized by self-consciousness, that is, the *involuntary* turning inward of attention to restore order in the self" (Csikszentmihalyi, 1982, p. 170). The way the present technique attempts to alter this state of psychic entropy is by introducing a measure of distancing. Distancing is achieved by making the interaction hypothetical and a non-face-to-face encounter, i.e., a telephone confrontation. The underlying rationale is that distancing helps to restore objectivity and suppresses the magnitude of emotional interference.

Finally, this technique ought not be confused with a situation where protagonists are asked to replicate telephone calls that *have actually occurred* in the past. The situational technique of a Telephone Call refers to calls that were never made. A demonstration of telephone calls that occurred in the past is simply a combination of the Self-presentation and the Role-playing (basic) specific techniques.

The Womb: Rebirth (Individual)

Suppose a protagonist says, "I wish I could start it (life) all over again" and the underlying issue is a deep feeling of uncertainty with regard to how welcomed he or she was upon arriving in this world. The act of rebirth can be concretized in a simulated fashion, and the technique is called the Womb or the Rebirth. The design of this technique is as follows: The therapist-director simulates a womb by asking the assistance of a few auxiliaries. They are instructed to kneel down facing each other in pairs and to put their hands on the shoulder of their partners. In this way they create a small human tunnel, now representing the womb. The lights in the room may be dimmed, and the protagonist is instructed to crawl into the womb and lie there in an embryonic position. The protagonist may stay in the womb for a few minutes either quietly or soliloquizing about his or her feelings inside "mother's womb," about the future, or about anything that seems to be important. When the moment of birth arrives the auxiliaries who form the womb begin to push and shove the "baby in the uterus" to signal that labor has started. The director, or an additional auxiliary, may assume the role of the obstetrician and pull out the protagonist, now the "new born baby."

Once the protagonist is out of the "uterus" he or she may be given a loving mother (or father), also represented by an auxiliary. The development of the scenario from this point is left open.

The notion of regressing the patient to an earlier stage or stages of development for curative purposes has been discussed by other therapists, especially in the treatment of the psychoses. (e.g., Burton, 1961).

In hypnotherapy, the technique of age regression is used with a variety of patients and it is not necessarily limited to psychotics (e.g., LeCron, 1965; Zeig, 1982). Meares (1961) identified several types of regression. One of them, which seems to be close to that used in the Womb: Rebirth technique, is revivification.

> We distinguish revivification as a type of regression in which the patient returns to a former age and really relives his past experiences. If he regresses to some period of childhood, he may relive an incident so that he actually re-experiences the event as a child. He sees the event with the eyes of a child, not as an adult; he experiences the emotions evoked by the event in a way that a child experiences emotions. In a state of revivication the patient speaks and behaves as a child. Revivication is thus a very much more complete type of regression than is simple age regression. The

reliving of the event and the experience of the emotion as it was felt at the time of the event have greater therapeutic effect than age regression. (p. 388)

The Womb: Rebirth technique is essentially based on a similar rationale; however, it is not conducted under an hypnotic trance, but rather as a role playing experience.

There are numerous variations of this technique that also recreate significant moments in the protagonist's past. It should be borne in mind that this kind of technique concerns the recreation of somewhat imaginary events—moments the protagonist is unable to recall (or completely recall) or is not expected to remember. Once protagonists are "thrown" into these situations they are left to their own devices, to experience them as they please.

A slightly modified adaptation of the principles underlying this kind of situational technique can be observed with another, yet related, group of techniques. These are employed primarily for diagnostic purposes, that is, as a means for identifying therapeutic issues that may require professional attention. The reason why this kind of technique is subsumed under prototype I is quite obvious; it is impossible to spell out unidentified issues in advance. Perhaps one of the better known examples of such interventions is the Psychodramatic Body Building (Robbins & Robbins, 1970) or other versions of the Ego Building technique (Feinberg, 1959). In the Body Building technique the protagonist is asked to build a "replica" of his or her body using auxiliaries to portray various body parts. Then the protagonist reverses roles with the auxiliaries, one at a time, in an effort to further explore his or her attitudes and feeling towards these parts. This simple procedure helps to bring out intrapersonal conflicts that may manifest themselves, symbolically, through a friction in various parts of one's own body.

Growing Big or Small (Individual)

Perhaps the most intriguing and sophisticated role playing interventions are those employed as messages of interpretation. One of the difficulties that therapists must anticipate in the course of the psychotherapeutic process is resistance on the part of their clients to gain insight with respect to their problems. Often insight may be disparaged as superficial because it is not accompanied by appropriate feelings or because it does not lead to action. This is what Schlesinger (1982) described as resistance against the action component of response:

One of the general goals of all psychotherapy is to promote a patient's own activity in therapy. A major style of resisting is to avoid becoming active. A major task for interpretation and follow-up interpretation is to promote activity in this sense. By 'action' I mean first of all, a conscious effort by the patient to become active in relation to the interpretation, to grapple with the new idea, to test its truth and make it his own or modify it or reject it. (p. 36)

In clinical role playing therapy it is advisable to impart the interpretive message through enactment rather than verbally. Needless to say, this calls for an artistic and creative undertaking. It requires the translation of interpretative ideas into concrete forms by structuring situations leading—hopefully—to an inevitable insight on the part of the protagonist regarding the intended message. Insight, therefore, is gained through a process of self-discovery, through firsthand experiences and through active interactions with the elements in the simulated situation. There are many ways, both told and untold, to convey interpretations via role playing interventions, and the Growing Big or Growing Small techniques serve only as representative examples. Suppose a protagonist evinces an authoritarian approach in his or her dealings with other people and tends to dominate every social interaction. Let us also assume that this protagonist is either unaware of this behavior or fails, even refuses, to acknowledge it. Using the Growing Big technique, the therapist-director will ask the protagonist to stand on a chair and conduct his or her affairs from this position. Experience has shown that most protagonists become uncomfortable standing high above everyone else and after a while may respond by saying, "Am I really behaving as if I am above everyone?" or "I really don't like bossing people around, though maybe it looks as if I do."

The Growing Small technique is the reverse of the Growing Big and is intended for people who display an attitude (and behavior) marked by inferiority and self-depreciation. Here, the director may instruct them to sit low on the floor or to squeeze themselves under a low table into a sitting position and continue with the scene from that position. Again, protagonists usually respond to this intervention by saying something like, "I feel terrible not being able to stand up to people" or "Is this the way I present myself? Do I always belittle myself this way?"

Nonverbal Exercises (Group)

Most typical group techniques subsumed under prototype I are those commonly known as Nonverbal Group Exercises. As suggested by the title, the salient characteristic of these group interventions is that members interact with each other in complete silence. Discussions and verbal sharing of experiences take place only at the termination of the exercise proper. The basic idea is that such exercises provide opportunities for experientially based learning devoid of verbal mediations and that they promote self-awareness, sensitivity, group cohesion, and mutual trust. The interested reader may find lists of these techniques elsewhere (e.g., Schutz, 1967; Weiner & Sacks, 1969). Here, we will describe a couple of examples to illustrate the main characteristics of such techniques.

The "Take That" exercise. This particular example is taken from Morris and Cinnamon (1975). The authors list five subsidiary goals for this technique: to give and receive feedback, to become aware of nonverbal cues, to learn to constructively handle anger, to open hidden agendas, and to explore the dynamics involved in dominance and submission. The technique may be applied with groups of 12 members or less and usually lasts for 15 to 20 minutes. The instructions are as follows: The director asks members to silently form dyads with other members toward whom they have neutral or negative feelings. Then the director instructs the pairs to remain standing, with the taller member's hands on the shoulders of the smaller member. When the director says, "Begin," the taller person must try to force his or her partner down by pushing on his or her shoulder. After a few minutes the director will stop the action and instruct the taller member to help the partner up, reverse roles, and repeat the process. After the completion of the exercise, members are encouraged to discuss feelings that they had toward their partners, to state whether or not they felt angry and how they coped with it, and to describe what they were aware of during the exercise.

Blindfolded encounters. This technique, or variations of it, is said to be particularly effective during the very early stages of the group formation. Its primary objectives are to break the distance and the lack of acquaintance among group members, to increase one's sensitivity to nonverbal cues and to provide initial feedback in a nonthreatening manner. The technique is administered in the following way: Group members are asked to form two equal-size circles, one within the other. Then they are told that the rest of the exercise will be conducted with their eyes closed. The people in the inner circle are instructed to move slowly in a clockwise direction and those in the outer circle in a counterclockwise direction. When the director says, "Stop," everyone comes to a standstill. At this point each member in the outer circle is asked to feel the face of his or her inner circle partner with the hands. After three minutes or so, the director instructs the members in the inner circle to do the same with their outer circle counterparts. Then members are instructed to open their eyes and describe their impressions of the partners using only motions and gestures. In the end members are encouraged to supplement their nonverbal communication with questions and clarifying statements.

It should be pointed out that many nonverbal techniques are conducted in a manner that *does spell out* clearly, *at the onset of the exercise,* the issue at hand. A large number of the exercises described in Morris and Cinnamon (1975), for example, seem to follow such an instructional strategy. For instance, in a technique called Lift and Rock, a member of the group lies down on the floor. He or she is then lifted up, still in a straight horizontal position, by the group members and gently tossed up and down. The process is repeated with each member, one at a time. This is an example of an exercise that aims at promoting risk taking and trust. Morris and Cinnamon (1975) describe the facilitator's instructions as follows: "The facilitator makes the following statement, 'The exploration of our feelings of trust is an extremely important dynamic to consider. This exercise is designed to allow us to experience trust in terms of dependency on the group' " (p.248); then the facilitator continues with the rest of the instruction. Preambling a nonverbal exercise with such an introduction makes the issue quite *Explicit,* hence the technique can no longer belong to Prototype I—the *Implicit* elicitation/Similes presentation category. Thus, not all group nonverbal exercises are automatically classified under Prototype I. The phrasing of the initial instructions often constitutes the deciding factor for casting the technique under one prototype or another.

A Temporary "Demise" and the "Revival" of the Group (Group)

There are also *verbal* group techniques that belong to Prototype I. A good example of such a technique is the Temporary "Demise" and the "Revival" of the Group. Imagine a situation where the group has temporarily ceased to function properly because of resistance, because of the presence of a debilitating tension or anxiety that caused members to withdraw, or for any other reason. The therapist-director may decide at this point to portray the situation using literal concretization approach. Thus he or she may ask for a volunteer to come forward to represent the group: "You are now 'the group' and you are temporarily dysfunctional, in fact you are in a coma-like state," the director may say. "I would like you to lie down on the floor and remain motionless. You can, however, talk and respond to questions put to you by group members. But do not answer people who talk to you from their seats, only those who come close to you. Talk sparingly, and remember, you are in a coma so you need not answer every question." Now the director turns to the group members and says, "Here is the group, lying down incapacitated. Find out if it is still potentially healthy and if it wants to be revived. You can do anything you like: Bury it or revive it. You may start now." The rest of the scene is left open to be developed by the group members.

PROTOTYPE II: IMPLICIT/METAPHORIC COMBINATION

This prototype is represented in the paradigm in the form of the upper right quadrant (Figure 8.1) marked II*i* and II*g* as illustrated in the small, highlighted replica shown in Figure 9.2.

Underlying Principles

The principles that describe this prototype are as follows. First, regarding the therapeutic issues, the remedial experiences under treatment remain disguised and are not spelled out in advance. Second, the design of the role playing interventions focuses on planning the contexts—the simulated backgrounds where the ensuing action takes place. These backgrounds are imaginary metaphors. Their relationship to the problem is allegorical, i.e., while they do elicit the psychological processes appropriate to the issues under treatment, they are constellations that rarely or never occur in real life the way they are portrayed in the session.

Special Characteristics

The characteristics associated with techniques that follow these principles are:

1. The protagonists involved in these techniques always portray themselves in their *original identities*. Only the situational context is designed as a fantasy, an unusual event, or an allegory.
2. The context, or the simulated environment, represents a plot that relates to the underlying issue through *symbolic associations* rather than through natural backgrounds associated with the identified problem(s) in real life.

3. With very few exceptions, these techniques require the assistance of several auxiliaries. Therefore, they are most applicable in group situations, that is, the treatment of an individual protagonist within a group context or the treatment of several group members simultaneously.

The way these principles and special characteristics are manifested in the techniques themselves can be seen in the following examples.

The Magic Shop (Individual)

The underlying objectives of the Magic Shop technique are to facilitate protagonists in identifying their developmental needs, to help them rearrange their priorities, and to provide them with the opportunity to test the strength of their intrinsic motivation with regard to their own improvement. The Magic Shop (e.g., Moreno, 1964a, pp. X-XI) is conducted in the following manner. The therapist-director may introduce the technique by saying,

"I would like to invite you today to visit a special shop. It is called the Magic Shop because you may purchase there anything you like, provided it is nonmaterial. The shop deals with intangible qualities such as traits and skills. You may try and buy there a quality you already have but you may need more of it. You may also try and

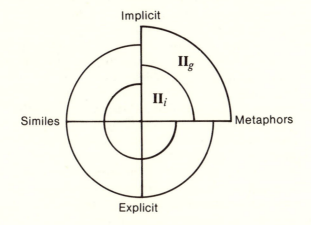

Figure 9.2. Prototype II

get an intangible quality you never had. The shop is run by a shopkeeper who will be most happy to oblige you provided he has the 'goods' you wish to buy from his stock. However, it is possible that he might not have it. This little establishment operates by using the barter principle. Once you have ascertained that the shopkeeper has what you want, you must give him something in turn. The trade, too, is done with intangible qualities, i.e., traits and skills you currently possess, that you are willing to exchange in favor of your new purchase. In principle, the exchange is with 'goods' of equal *value,* not necessarily of the same *kind.* The shopkeeper is trained to make this judgment. Everyone may visit the shop and no one is under obligation to complete the transaction. If you do not like the deal you may leave the shop emptyhanded. That is perfectly all right."

At this point the director may pause for questions and clarifications, and then proceed:

"Here is the Magic Shop (pointing to the action space). It is surrounded by invisible walls. You, the people sitting outside the shop, can see and hear anything that happens inside. But those who are inside the shop can neither hear nor see the outside. There are two chairs in the shop. No scales and no measures can be used. There is also an imaginary door on this side. You are invited to enter the shop, one person at a time, and try to trade. Any questions?"

Now, the director ends the instructions by saying, "I will be the shopkeeper. I am going to enter the shop and stay there for 30 (or 45) minutes. See you inside."

Often, it takes a few moments for the first volunteer to enter the shop. Sometimes members of the group wait to see if the shopkeeper really intends to stay inside the store, oblivious of anything that occurs on the outside. It is advisable to keep each transaction relatively short, about eight to 12 minutes per individual client. Otherwise, the director may risk losing the attention of the observing members. For this reason, it is also recommended to have no more than four or five clients, and then to close the shop.

Different shopkeepers run their businesses differently. There is no one style that is best. My own preference is to portray a shopkeeper who is a 500-year-old gentlemen and who has been inside the store all that time. In this way the shopkeeper can afford to portray someone who is relatively ignorant of things protagonists take for granted.

Let me illustrate this technique with an excerpt from an actual Magic

Shop session. Following the initial instruction, the shopkeeper sat in his chair and waited for the first customer. The first one to enter the shop was Carl, a 45-year-old businessman.

Carl: (knocks on the imaginary door) May I come in? *(He does not wait for an answer and steps inside the shop. Then he sits down in front of the shop-keeper.)*

Shopkeeper: What can I do for you, sir?

Carl: I heard that you have this marvelous store, so I decided to see it.

Shopkeeper: That is nice of you, sir. Did you have anything particular in mind or did you plan to make this a social visit?

Carl: Oh, no. I definitely want to buy something. You don't sell cars, do you?

Shopkeeper: (maintains a straight face) No, I don't sell anything of that sort. Is that what you heard my shop carries?

Carl: No, no. I was just kidding. I know what this store is all about.

Shopkeeper: That is very good. You see, I have sat in this shop for over 500 years, and I don't get out. So I don't know what goes on in the outside world. It is very easy to pull my leg, that is, if you want to do it.

Carl: No, no, no. Forgive me for not being serious. Seriously, I would like to buy some energy. Do you have energy to sell?

Shopkeeper: What do you mean by energy? There are different energies for different things. Can you describe it to me? You see, I must find out *exactly* what it is you want. I have to be very careful not to give people things they don't ask for.

Carl: I understand and appreciate this. You see, I'm 45 years old, not as old as you, but I'm no youngster anymore. I find that I'm tired by the time I come home from work, and there are only so many things I can do.

Shopkeeper: When do you usually come home and what is it exactly that you do?

Carl: I'm the executive director of this big company that produces electronic devices, and usually I get home around 8 P.M.

Shopkeeper: You must be working very hard. Is it important for you to work so much?

Carl: I like to work. Well, I suppose you may say that I'm a workaholic. Do I need it? Well, not for the money. I just like to work.

Shopkeeper: And you wish to buy more energy, is that right?

Carl: Yes, I want to be able to continue as I used to be.

Shopkeeper: To work maybe 22 hours a day?

Carl: (a little uncomfortable) No, this is an exaggeration, I. . .

Shopkeeper: Why? If you like to work, why not 22 hours a day?

Carl: Well, that's not the point. I just feel I need more energy.

Shopkeeper: Ah! Maybe you need it to be able to spend more time doing things with your family?

Carl: Well, that's another story.

Shopkeeper: If you say that that's another story, I'm not going to argue with you. Maybe you want to have more energy so that you'll feel young again, so that you won't feel you're middle aged. Is that it? You don't mind me ruminating like this, do you?

Carl: To tell you the truth, I didn't think about it that way. Hmmm, that is an interesting notion.

Shopkeeper: So, you want to buy energy. Is this like buying more vitality?

Carl: I suppose so. Yes, vitality is a good word for it. Do you have it in stock?

Shopkeeper: And you want to spend it on your work, not with your family, correct?

Carl: When I came in I thought only of my work, but I should also be more actively involved with my wife and children. But that, as I told you is another story.

Shopkeeper: I really seem to be getting old, because I don't know how you can have the vitality to spend 22 hours a day at work and another six hours with your family. In my time they used to have only 24 hours in a day. Do they have more nowadays? OK, if that is what you want, so be it. What are you going to offer me in turn? I do have vitality and energy to sell, but you have to give me something of equivalent value in return. You know that?

Carl: Yes, well, I thought that you might be interested in humor. I can give you some of that. It is a good commodity. Many people may want it.

Shopkeeper: It is not important what I'm interested in. I do not buy things for myself. But what did you mean by "some" humor?

Carl: Well, some, not all of it.

Shopkeeper: I have to know what I'm getting for my store. So "some" means what? Half a bag? Two pounds?

Carl: I'm not going to give you all of it.

Shopkeeper: Why not?

Carl: I need to keep some. In my work environment that is one of the things that keeps me sane. Well, if you don't want some humor, how about I give you fatigue?

Shopkeeper: Nope, you can't give me that, because once you get your vitality and energy, your fatigue will dissipate automatically.

Carl: How about some musical talent. Oh! We have the same problem again. What is "some"? I'll tell you what, you can have all my musical talent. Mind you, it's a big sacrifice on my part.

Shopkeeper: Is it? If you work so hard, when do you have time or energy to enjoy your musical talent?

Carl: That's true, I don't use it much. Not lately, anyhow.

Shopkeeper: If that's the case, I don't think that your musical talent is equivalent to what you want to buy. Give me something more substantial.

Carl: Substantial? *(thinks for a while)* I really don't know what to offer you. Why don't you make me an offer, tell me what *you* want?

Shopkeeper: How can I? I don't know you, sir. How do I know what you have that you are willing to give up?

Carl: Listen, I really want that energy. I'll pay for it.

Shopkeeper: You will? Even if it is a considerable price?

Carl: Only if it is reasonable.

Shopkeeper: I'll tell you, I don't usually do that kind of thing, but for you I'll make an exception. Give me a portion of your ambition. Your ambition "to be better" than your colleagues, those who are on your level in the organization.

Carl: (looks surprised) Do you think that there is a connection between my ambition and what I want to buy? I never thought of it that way. How about a *little* portion of my ambition. . .

Shopkeeper: That is my proposal, take it or leave it.

Carl: (sits quietly for two minutes) Gosh, it's difficult but I'll take it.

Shopkeeper: (shakes hands with Carl) The shop is open all the time. If this exchange does not work for you, you can come again and make a new deal. You don't even have to come to me. Just visit the Magic Shop you have in your own heart.

It is true that ordinarily Magic shopkeepers ought to refrain from making counterproposals. These should be saved for the few occasions when protagonists are sincerely unable to produce reasonable offers, or, as in the above example, when the protagonist is the first customer and the director wants to end the first interaction on a positive note to encourage other protagonists to come forward and use the shop.

The Judgment Techniques (Individual)

The idea of using trial scenes with protagonists who feel guilty for having certain thoughts and feelings, or for having behaved in the past

in an unsavory manner towards significant persons in their life, has led
to the creation of a few interesting techniques. Probably the earliest
model for such techniques was offered by J.L. Moreno (1937) almost 50
years ago. In that version an imaginary courtroom was set up where the
protagonist stood accused of whatever he or she felt guilty about. The
objective of this intervention was to provide the protagonist an opportunity to repent or expiate his or her "sins." The Courtroom technique
was designed as follows. The action space became a courtroom with
tables and chairs. One auxiliary was assigned the role of a judge, one
auxiliary became the prosecutor, and another was nominated as the
defense attorney. The protagonist was the accused, and the remaining
group members served as the jury. The protagonist stated his or her
(perceived) "crime" and the trial took place. At the end a verdict was
passed and a "psychological" punishment suggested. There are different
ways of ordering the final sentence. It can be suggested to the judge by
the director. The judge may decide it alone. Each member of the jury
may take the role of the judge and suggest the punishment, thus leaving
it to the protagonist to select the most appropriate one.

A different version of a somewhat similar idea was suggested by Sacks
(1965) who invented the Judgment Technique. In this version, however,
the accused is *not* the protagonist himself or herself, but rather someone
towards whom the protagonist has *latent hostility*. Thus, the objective of
the Judgment technique is to deal with this feeling on the part of the
protagonist and to hopefully dissipate it. In this technique, an auxiliary
is selected to take the role of God. "God" then explains to the protagonist
that unfortunately the latter has died, but that happily he or she is now
living in heaven and will continue to be there for eternity. But now,
another applicant is at the door of heaven and God has not yet decided
the fate of that applicant: to be admitted to heaven to be with the protagonist or to be sent to hell. God also says that he is aware of the fact
that the new applicant has done wrong to the protagonist; he wants the
protagonist first to clarify this with the applicant and then advise God
what to do. The applicant is portrayed by an auxiliary, who first takes
the stance of denying all wrongdoing; only if the protagonist confronts
him or her effectively will the auxiliary finally admit the "sins" of self-
ishness, cruelty, neglect, and so forth. Another auxiliary is assigned the
role of a soul-hungry Satan who tries to convince the protagonist that
the applicant should not be forgiven. The protagonist has only 10 minutes or so before God will make the final decision.

The author of the technique emphasized the need to be cautious in
introducing the Role-reversal technique here, especially reversing role
with God. Some religious protagonists may be diffident about the idea

and should be permitted not to do it. Also, reversing role with God should be used advisedly with psychotic protagonists.

Another technique that may be classified under the Judgment Techniques' group is that known as *The Death Scene.* It was created by Siroka and Schloss (1968) who described its underlying rationale as follows:

> Unless man takes his own life, he has no control over his own death. Every choice he makes becomes meaningful, becomes heroic, becomes a responsible commitment when the individual makes that choice with the knowledge of its potential irrevocability. Therefore, each choice represents a confrontation with death and an affirmation of his own existence, an affirmation of life. (p. 202)

The Death Scene technique is introduced to potential protagonists as a role playing opportunity for a confrontation with death. Its main purpose is to alleviate debilitating feelings and biased perceptions that prevent them from making new choices and commitments. The past is looked upon as "the death of the old life" and the future as "the birth of new life." The general structure of this technique will be described next, but it should be emphasized that modifications might be made to suit specific needs of each individual protagonist.

The protagonist, standing alone in the action space, is told by the therapist-director that he or she died. Then the protagonist is asked to reflect on this state and express loudly how it feels to be dead. If this monologue conveys rage and hostility, a Mephistopheles, represented by an auxiliary, is introduced. Mephisto tells the protagonist that he has the power to give revenge. If the protagonist agrees to bargain, he is given the opportunity to express his revenge. On the other hand, if the protagonist expresses in the monologue self-doubt and inability to relate to others, St. Peter, represented by another auxiliary, comes along in the form of a kindly, elderly gentleman. St. Peter slowly and innocuously questions the protagonist for further elucidations on his or her inability to take responsibilities and to relate to others. He also asks for further corroborations for which the protagonist may bring a witness, someone who knows him or her well (an auxiliary). At this point the director may ask the protagonist and the friend to reverse roles.

Now a judge, appointed by the director, enters and instructs the protagonist to select a few auxiliaries to serve as jurors. The jury represents both the externalization of the protagonist's own conscience as well as that of the collective group. The jurors weigh the evidence and share their personal feelings with him or her before reaching a verdict. But the jury does not judge the protagonist. Before the trial is over, the judge gives his role to the protagonist who now, standing alone in the action space, must pass judgment and propose recommendations for the future. The scene ends here, and the protagonist is told to "come back to life."

Deserted Island (Group)

The prime objectives of this group technique are to enhance the process of mutual acquaintance among group members and to initiate the establishment of more cohesive subgrouping. This technique is usually indicated in the initial stages of the group formation. In line with the principles that govern the Implicit/Metaphoric combination of Prototype II, the group is not advised of these goals. Instead, the therapist-director informs the group that their ship unfortunately sank. But they survived the disaster and managed to get into two or three small boats of four people each (the number of the boats and people in each depend on the size of the group). The boats drifted away in the ocean for two weeks until they reached different, small deserted islands. Now that each group has safely landed on an island, it must be prepared to settle in, conceivably forever. Each subgroup is sent to a different corner of the room to build their new home(s). After a few minutes the director may further instruct the groups to "write a collective letter to their families and then put it in a sealed bottle to be thrown into the sea," or to "celebrate their first year anniversary on the island," or "to give birthday presents," and so forth. But most of the exercise is conducted without interferences on the part of the therapist-director. The exercise may last for half an hour or so. It ends when the director says, "You are very lucky. A ship passing by is about to rescue you and take you back home. Please prepare to leave your respective islands. You have a few minutes to do so."

The Deserted Island technique has generated numerous variations with the same underlying goals. In these variations only the story has been changed (e.g., reaching an oasis in the desert, becoming trapped in a jungle, or being stuck on the moon). The original Deserted Island technique may also be designed with a slight change of plot. The therapist may send two subgroups to each island representing the natives and the newcomers (the survivors of the sunken ship).

The Life Boat Technique (Group)

This technique was already described in the previous chapter. The theme is familiar. A sunken ship and a boat full of survivors floats aimlessly in the middle of the ocean. The purpose of the Life Boat Technique (Yablonsky, 1976) is to provide the members of the group an opportunity to reflect on their *raison d'être*, to examine the meaning of their lives (Thorson, 1978). The therapist-director asks six or seven people to sit in the middle of the room in an imaginary boat. Then they are told,

> "You have been in this boat for seven long days. You are very tired, sunburned, and hungry. You supply of food and water is getting low and unless you get rid of at least two people you will die. During the last week you have not seen any ship on the horizon. I would like you to select the two people who will be thrown into the sea. But first, let each one of you persuade the group why his or her life should be spared. Then you will decide."

Some groups tend to duck the painful process by deciding to be together in life and death. The director must decide whether to allow them to reach such a decision or to make it clear in advance that this is not a viable option for them.

As with the former technique, here, too, are several variations of the Life Boat theme. The common denominator of all of them is that they depict people in extreme life-threatening situations who are faced with the task of deciding who shall and who shall not survive. Some of the known versions are jumping from a crippled airplane having a limited number of parachutes, leaving people behind in the desert with only two or three camels to ride on, hiding in an atomic shelter where food and water become scarce, and the like.

Forming a Band (Group)

This brief situational technique is an example of a class of group interventions known as warm-up techniques. Its main purpose is to facilitate an atmosphere of openness and candor. Often, however, additional objectives may be attained. These include fostering an atmosphere of cooperation, emphasizing the importance of the collective effort, or enhancing internal cohesion. In the Forming a Band technique (Weiner & Sacks, 1969), members of the group are asked to come forward and form a band. They select a conductor and then play invisible musical instruments. Each player may hum the tune of his or her particular musical instrument. They may be allowed to rehearse before their official performance.

Other techniques such as Bridge Building or Picture Making may use actual material, rather than imaginary instruments. This may include pieces of paper, colored pencils, matches, bricks, and playing cards. Each member of the group holds to some parts of the material so that the entire project can be accomplished only by cooperation on the part of each group member.

The Problem Solving Fantasy (Weiner & Sacks, 1969), for instance, is a group technique that tends to promote an atmosphere of cooperation in a different way. The entire group is instructed to break into small subgroups of three or four members each. Then they are instructed to plan—that is, to dream and design but not to role play—their own utopia. Basically, the request is to conceptualize a new society by deciding on their preferred form of government, community structure, norms for maintaining the social order, their preferred hierarchy of values, the location of the new society, the climate, and so forth. The planning period need not exceed 20 minutes, and at its end each of the participating subgroups presents its model. The groups are also instructed to convince the rest of the members to adopt their particular ideal world.

Problem-Solving Fantasies with Solutions (Group)

The preceding three group techniques—the Deserted Island, the Life Boat, the Forming a Band—and their variations put the participating group members in problem situations with dilemmas that actually have *no ideal,* that is, *preferred solutions.* There is no "true" or "best" answer(s) to these problems and whatever the members may decide is accepted. In these kinds of techniques the focus is only on the process(es) leading to the solution and not on its outcome.

There is, however, a large body of situational techniques that includes problem-solving situations *with* solutions. Here, unlike the preceding techniques, the problems posed *do have* "true" or "best" solutions. These solutions are based either on factual data or on the consensus of experts in the problem areas.

On their face value, these techniques appear to belong in the Explicit part of the paradigm, not in the Implicit part. This is because the problem, or the issue, is spelled out clearly to the group in an attempt to arrive at the solution. But there is an element of "deception" here. The ostensibly formal issue often is *not the real* purpose for using the techniques. Instead, the therapist-director expects that by working through a given problem another hidden process will take place. And it is the hidden process that is the true focus of the therapeutic intervention. For this reason these kinds of techniques are classified under the Implicit mode of eliciting the issue.

For instance, one such technique is the Lost in the Desert situations. It involves seven to 10 participants who are told that their airplane crashed in the middle of the desert, but miraculously they survived without harm. However, the pilot and the navigator died in the crash. They are also told that they must move on from the crash site because it is unsafe. At this point they are given a sheet of paper with a list of 15 items that are available to them. Of these they may take only 10 that are essential for their future survival. The task of the group is to decide which items to select (sometimes they may be also asked to rank the chosen items in terms of their importance). The final decision must be unanimous. The group solution is then compared with an existing so-lution made by experts in survival techniques. If the initial purpose for introducing this technique was to foster group cohesion and collabora-tion, and *not* to demonstrate the decision-making process, the technique must end here without any further discussion. In that case it will be considered an Implicit/Metaphoric type. However, if the initial objective for introducing this technique was indeed to analyze the decision-making process in a group, or to demonstrate that collaborative solutions are better than individual ones, then further discussion regarding the group performance is quite in order. But in that case the technique will be classified as an example of Prototype III: the Explicit/Metaphoric com-bination, which we will describe next.

PROTOTYPE III: EXPLICIT/METAPHORIC COMBINATION

This prototype is represented in the paradigm in the form of the lower right quadrant (Figure 8.1) marked III*i* and III*g* as illustrated in the small, highlighted replica in Figure 9.3.

Underlying Principles

This prototype is based on the following principles. First, regarding the therapeutic issues, the remedial processes under treatment, including the objectives of the techniques, are clearly stated to the protagonists at the onset of the role playing episodes. In this way the central issues may be dealt with explicitly and directly. Second, these encounters occur in the contexts of imaginary circumstances, which may vary in their alle-gorical quality from extremely unusual to bearing resemblance to typical real-life situations. However, the most important point is that the met-

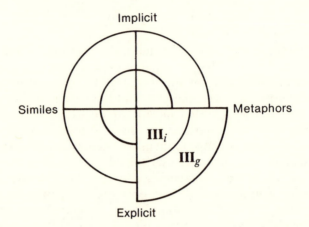

Figure 9.3. Prototype III

aphoric quality is achieved by having the protagonists assume roles, or adopt attitudes, that are *not their own;* they portray assumed identities.

Special Characteristics

The characteristics associated with techniques subsumed under this prototype are:

1. Protagonists involved in these techniques *rarely* portray themselves in their original identities. In the absence of an explicit request to *become* someone else, they are, at least, instructed to *think* as if they were different kinds of people.
2. The situational contexts (the simulated role playing environments) may represent realities related to the main issues through symbolic associations as well as common and natural realities.
3. Because protagonists, in these techniques, play roles that are *not* their own, it is often recommended that they be adequately warmed up in advance. The therapist-director needs to ascertain that they are genuinely ready to portray their assigned roles to the best of their ability.

The following will describe a few examples of situational techniques most typical of this prototype.

Personification of Animals or Objects (Individual)

There are endless brief situational vignettes where the protagonists are asked to assume a role or an identity of something else. Usually, the reason for a request of this sort is to facilitate free expression of the issue under treatment. Since people are not in the habit of being something else, especially not animals or objects, obviously it is incumbent upon the therapist to explain what the issue is and why he or she wants them to change identities. Here are a few examples. A therapist may say to the protagonist, "Mary, it seems to me that you handle the situation with your boyfriend with extreme inflexibility. Let me show you what it felt like to me. I want you to be a talking giraffe; move slowly, do not bend, and be very cautious. Your boyfriend will be a dancer. Let's see how the two of you get along." Suppose a protagonist says that his wife complains that he is "infuriatingly dependable." The therapist may assign him a role of a (speaking) rock, perhaps the Rock of Gibraltar. The personification approach may be used for remedial and retraining purposes as well. An inflexible protagonist may be asked to be a very flexible creature—an otter, for example—and so on.

Often, operating under an assumed (borrowed) identity permits shy, reticent, and withdrawn persons to disclose themselves. Under the protective shield (mimetic-pretend behavior) they may feel safer. Consider the following example.

A group of eight people were in a session. The director asked each one to become an animal that might typify his or her personality. All members complied with the request save one, who insistently claimed, "I am nothing." So the director told him to be nothing and instructed the rest of the animals (members) to treat him as such. After being shoved, pushed, and jumped over by the group members, he suddenly imitated a lion's roar and screamed, "I am a lion, and I've had enough of you stupid animals. I'll show you who is in charge here. You will see exactly what I am. Anyone who dares touch me again will be taught an unforgettable lesson." He continued to be a lion to the end of the exercise.

The Chessboard Technique (Individual)

This simple situational technique was reported by Weiner and Sacks (1969), who considered it a warm-up intervention but perhaps more as a diagnostic means for assessing the protagonist's support system. The idea is that coping in various social situations may be likened to a game of chess. Therefore, the support one expects from one's family members, friends, and associates may be pictorially demonstrated using the chess-board analogy. The therapist-director may present the techniques as follows: "Often, people need to rely on others, especially family members and friends, to get along in certain life situations. Think of a situation in your past when you needed such help. Let us look at your position in that situation as follows: The action space will become a chessboard and you will become the King figure. The King needs to be helped and defended by the other figures. Think of the persons whom you expect to support you and assign them the roles of the Bishops, the Queen, the Knights, the Castle, and the Pawns. Make these assignments according to the way you perceive their help. You may assign the roles as an ideal situation or as a current, perhaps disappointing, situation. Please tell us which of these two alternatives it is."

The roles of the figures is played by auxiliaries who may move either on their own or as instructed by the King into defending or other po-tentially dangerous positions. The symbolic meaning of the roles as-signed to various significant persons in the protagonist's life, the positions they assume (or refuse to assume), and the interactions between them and the protagonist provide a diagnostic impression of the pro-tagonist familial and social support system. It can suggest areas of con-flicts and difficulties that need to be explored in different scenes with the aid of different role playing techniques.

The Keyes—Sutton Case (Individual)

This situational role playing technique is typically employed in non-clinical settings; nonetheless, it deserves our attention because it serves as a classic illustration of many other techniques that may have potential therapeutic application. Two group members are handed two separate sheets of instructions that describe a fictitious situation. Each member is given a new identity; one becomes a Frank Keyes and the other a Phil Sutton. Mr. Keyes is the advertising manager of a large company, and Mr. Sutton is a staff member of the advertising department and reports directly to Mr. Keyes. The two handouts describe a situation where Mr. Sutton, who is a very talented and aspiring marketing specialist, abused the encouragement and support given to him by his superior, Mr. Keyes, to develop a relationship with the president of the company. It came to the point that Phil Sutton presented a project to the president without the knowledge of Frank Keyes. When asked about the project by the vice-president, Frank had no idea what it was, and despite his embarrassment managed to bluff his way through. Each sheet of paper describes the situation somewhat differently, one from Sutton's point of view and one from Keyes' perspective. The role playing episode portrays a meeting called by Frank Keyes to discuss the incident with his subordinate Phil Sutton.

Using this methodology, inventors have produced an abundance of cases and situations where a critical incident is portrayed as an imaginary situation and the key players are given new identities, usually described in detail via a handout. Most of these cases involve two people. Although they are dyadic role plays, we classify them as techniques aimed at an individual protagonist because often the problem depicted by the enacted situation has a greater relevance to one of the two participants. But some cases are more complex (e.g., Towers, 1969) and involve larger groups of up to a dozen key players. In these instances the technique can no longer be considered for individual application. Now it has become a group application technique.

It is true that these kinds of techniques tend to be more common in training communication, leadership, and managerial skills. When applied in the context of psychotherapy, the roles and the descriptions of the situations are *rarely* produced in the form of prepared scripts available as typed handouts. Instead they are designed, on the spot, as impromptu vignettes triggered by clues from the protagonists, the auxiliaries, or anyone present in the session.

The Russian Doll (Individual)

This technique uses a small wooden toy known as the Russian Doll, the "Babushka" or the "Matrioshka" Doll (Robbins, 1973). It is a simple container in the shape of a bottle painted as an old Russian lady. It can be opened into two halves; inside there is a smaller replica of the bigger doll. The second replica can be opened, and again inside there is a smaller replica of the bigger doll, and so on. Altogether there are seven or eight replicas of the Russian lady, each smaller in size than the one before. The way these are utilized as a role playing technique is as follows. The therapist-director tells the protagonist that the exercise is designed to encourage self-exploration:

> "We would like to know who you are, and what is behind the external appearance that you put on. People have many layers. Some are external and publicly known to everyone. At the other extreme there are layers that are personal, intimate, and very pre-

cious. I would like you to be that doll. First, describe yourself as you appear to the world. Then, open the doll and you will find a hidden version of you, a layer that is just below your outer layer. Describe this too. Then open the next one and you will find an even more hidden layer. Please proceed to describe each layer until you get to the one that is very intimate, the one that you do not wish to divulge or expose to us."

Once the protagonist agrees to come forward and present himself or herself, the director may say, "Please hold the doll in your hand and begin by saying 'This is me, (state your name) as I appear to the world. . . .' "

There are several techniques that use an "intermediary object." This intermediary object, according to Rojas-Bermudez (1969), allows us to protect the self against the discomfort that we feel when another person enters our personal territory: "The 'intermediary object' is able to cross the barrier of the self without releasing alarm reactions; this neutral quality enables it to be used as a therapeutic tool" (p. 152).

It is true that in the Russian Doll technique, and for that matter in other variations where an intermediary object is employed, the protagonist does not operate under a *bona fide* assumed identity. To be exact, the protagonist *hides* in a semiconspicuous manner behind an external mask, while keeping his or her own identity more or less intact. There is no doubt that the allegorical quality of techniques using such methods is being greatly compromised. Nonetheless, the provision of symbolic protection to the self in the form of such objects is a sufficient reason to justify the classification of these techniques under the Explicit/Metaphoric prototype.

The Candle Technique (Group)

One of the most sensitive issues in every form of group psychotherapy is that of providing a protagonist with an honest feedback about himself or herself in a relatively nonthreatening manner. While ideally it is expected that feedback provided by group members will be based on more or less objective observations, there is always the potential danger that they may use the opportunity for launching personal attacks on the feedback recipient. Furthermore, providing feedback to only one person may sometimes be misinterpreted as a license for making him or her the scapegoat of the group.

The Candle Technique (Kipper, 1975) represents an attempt to structure a role playing situation where evaluative feedback can be offered in a relatively nonthreatening atmosphere, where the personal integrity of the target person is more or less safeguarded, and where none of the group members is singled out. The therapist-director introduces the technique as an exercise in providing feedback and says, "I would like each of you to think of what you would like to be if you had the chance to be someone or something else. You may choose to become a different person, an object, an animal or perhaps a plant." After a few moments each member describes his or her new identity. The director then says that he has now become a candle (hence the title of the technique), which gives light:

> "If you put me next to something, you may see it better and clearer. I cannot talk. The only sound I can utter is 'pss pss.' I would like one of you to move me and place me behind each member at a time. Leave me there for awhile, and as I stand there the rest of you may tell that person or object what you see in him or her in the new identity. Tell both the desirable and the undesirable features that you see. But as soon as I say 'pss pss,' move me to another person."

Experience has shown that members tend to receive the feedback and consider it seriously. The protective shield (i.e., the temporary new identity) minimizes undesirable emotional reactions and accentuates objective-rational attitudes.

Work Values Exercise: Blue-Collar Blues (Group)

The Work Values Exercise: Blue-Collar Blues is a classic example of many similar techniques that may be employed in both therapeutic and nontherapeutic settings. The objectives of these interventions are usually to demonstrate the advantage of group decision processes, to analyze the interpersonal communication modes prevalent in the group, and, to some extent, to unify the group around a common task. Typically, the exercise is conducted in a group of about 10 participants in a "fishbowl" manner, that is, six or seven members are doing the required task while the remaining ones observe them and provide feedback about various aspects: leadership, atmosphere, patterns of collaboration, and communication styles. An important ingredient in all such techniques is that *there is a true* or *best solution* to the problem posed to the group. This solution is based either on factual data or on a readily available solution arrived at by experts in the problem area. The Work Values: Blue-Collar Exercise is conducted as follows. Each member of the group is given a sheet of paper with instructions.

"A research study was published in 1974 regarding the values of American youth in the 1970s. The research was based on extensive questionnaires filled out by American youth from all walks of life. The part of the survey that we are concerned with in this exercise is a survey of *blue-collar workers* in their *early twenties* who are *high school graduates*, who have no college degree, and who *hold jobs that require moderate skill and intelligence*. Among other questions, this group was asked to specify the things that they want most from a job. They have named 15 items which are listed here in a random order. These are:

——Seeing the results of their work
——Chance to make a lot of money later on
——Not too demanding job
——Chance to use their minds
——Interesting work
——Not expected to do things not paid for
——Job in growing field/industry
——Good pay
——Having a job that does not involve hard physical work
——Chance to develop skills/abilities
——Recognition for a job well done
——Socially useful work
——Participation in decisions regarding job
——Good pension plan
——Not being caught up in a big impersonal organization

Your task is to rank these items the way you think these youngsters did. Put yourself in their frame of mind and use the numbers 1 to 15 for the ranking, where 1 represents the most important item and 15 the least important one."

Once each member of the group had completed his or her individual ranking, the director will ask six or seven people to volunteer and become a problem-solving team. The team will be instructed to arrive at a consensus with regard to the way the items on the list ought to be ranked. The team will not be allowed to adopt a statistical approach, that is, to calculate the averages of the individual rankings and make these the final list. Customarily, the team will be given about 45 minutes to finish the job.

Once the team has completed its task, the director will distribute the Work Values: Blue-Collar Blues Survey Results sheet shown in Table 9.1.

TABLE 9.1

Work Values: Blue-Collar Blues Survey Results

Items	Individual Difference	Individual Rank	Survey Rank	Team Rank	Team Difference
Seeing results	___	___	3	___	___
Chance to Make Money	___	___	8	___	___
Not Demanding	___	___	13	___	___
Chance to Use Mind	___	___	4	___	___
Interesting Work	___	___	1	___	___
No Work Without Pay	___	___	14	___	___
Job in Growing Field	___	___	10	___	___
Good Pay	___	___	2	___	___
No Hard Physical Work	___	___	15	___	___
Chance to Develop	___	___	5	___	___
Recognition	___	___	7	___	___
Socially Useful Work	___	___	11	___	___
Participant in Decisions	___	___	6	___	___
Good Pension	___	___	9	___	___
Not Big, Impersonal	___	___	12	___	___
Total Individual Difference	[ ]			Total Team Difference	[ ]

Now each member of the entire group will enter his or her individual ranking in the column "Individual Rank" (second from left). Members of the problem-solving team will enter, in addition, the ranking of the team in the column "Team Rank" (second from the right). These rankings are compared with the actual findings of the survey, which are printed in the middle column. The two boxes at the bottom of Table 9.1, Total Individual Difference and Total Team Difference, represent the sum of the deviations from the survey ranking, irrespective of the direction (negative or positive).

At this point, the group may discuss the performance of the team in terms of the accuracy of their problem-solving task, their communication style, decision-making strategy, and so forth. Sometimes the director allows the observing members to interrupt the team's deliberations at predetermined points and to provide feedback about the performance of individual members as well as the team as a whole.

PROTOTYPE IV: EXPLICIT/SIMILES COMBINATION

This prototype is represented in the paradigm in the form of the lower left quadrant (Figure 8.1) marked IVi and IVg as illustrated in the small highlighted replica in Figure 9.4.

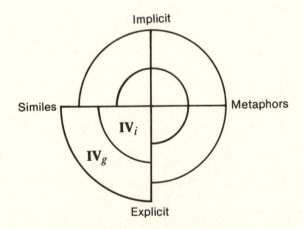

Figure 9.4. Prototype IV

Underlying Principles

This prototype is based on the following two principles. First, regarding the therapeutic issues that are under treatment or are the subjects of the enactments, these are clearly stated to the protagonists at the onset of the role playing episodes. In this way they can be dealt with directly. Second, in designing the interventions the main creative effort is focused on the concretization of the issues proper, that is, translating the words, phrases, or features that describe the issues into simulated, tangible manifestations.

1. Protagonists involved in these techniques always portray themselves in their *original identities*.
2. The portrayals of the context—the simulated backgrounds where subsequent actions may occur—take a special form here. In the present prototype the contextual backgrounds are the *issues themselves* put into concrete forms.
3. Many of the techniques subsumed under this prototype can be used in individual therapy. The presence of live auxiliaries may be substituted by the introduction of objects such as chairs, tables, boxes, or pillows.

The following will describe examples of situational techniques most typical of this prototype.

The Outside–Inside Technique (Individual)

The Outside-Inside technique (Kipper, 1977) is a variation of the Russian Doll technique described under Prototype III: the Explicit/Metaphoric combination. The design of this technique is as follows. The therapist-director arranges six or seven chairs in a row and places them in such a way that each chair faces the back of the one in front of it. Now the director explains that the purpose of the exercise is to facilitate self-presentation. The chairs represent "different layers of one's personality." The chair on the extreme left end of the row stands for the outward layer, that which is visible to the world and is publicly known. The chair situated on the other end of the row, the extreme right end, represents the innermost layer, the core of one's personality. The rest of the chairs stand for various levels of the personality between these two extremes. The director may say,

"What I would like you to do, is to come forward, one person at a time, take the extreme left chair, sit on it, and describe yourself the way you appear to people externally. Then, move to the next chair and describe yourself as you are in the layer underneath the very external one. You may continue to describe each layer of your personality by moving from one chair to another. Remember, you are under no obligation to go through *all* the layers. You may stop at any point (chair) that you feel is too uncomfortable, that is, that requires you to disclose intimate material you are not ready to reveal at this time."

The director may also designate one member of the group to serve as an interviewer to elicit further information on various points that may call for clarification.

There is a fine difference between the Russian Doll technique described earlier and the present Outside-Inside one. That difference is responsible for classifying the former technique in Prototype III: Explicit/Metaphoric combination and the latter here in Prototype IV: Explicit/Similes one. The Russian Doll uses an allegorical symbol to mediate between the threat caused by the potential violation of one's own privacy and the emergence of defense mechanisms. The incorporation of such symbolic protections to the "self" in the design of a situational technique would, almost by definition, classify it under the Metaphoric category. On the other hand, the Outside-Inside technique dispenses with mediating means to soften the threat that self-disclosure may incur to the self. In essence it is a harsher technique which leaves the self more exposed. The only protection protagonists have is their control over the process, the approval—by the director and by the group members—of their legitimate right to stop the process at any point at which they feel uncomfortable. The issue itself—the various levels of the personality—is concretely displayed in the form of the row of chairs.

Confronting Role-Repertoire (Individual)

Confrontations between protagonists and the roles they fulfill in various areas of their lives have been the subject of several versions of situational techniques. The specific objectives of such confrontations may, of course, vary from one case to another. Generally, however, they focus on one or more of the following aims: to facilitate a greater understanding of these roles and the responsibilities associated with them, to clarify the protagonist's attitudes towards the roles, and to sort out disorganized and unprioritized role-repertoires.

An example of this kind of technique is the one known as Confronting Your Own Role-Repertoire. The protagonist is asked to identify by name the most important roles in his or her life. Each role is represented by an empty chair. The chairs must be arranged by the protagonist so that the ones representing the most important roles are to be placed close to him or her, and those representing the less important roles are to be placed farther away. The director asks the protagonist to select auxiliaries to represent the various roles and to sit on the chairs. Now the participating auxiliaries are instructed to state their respective positions aloud (and simultaneously, if they wish) and to convince each other why they should be given prominence. In the beginning the protagonist may watch the ensuing chaos silently. But as the discussion unfolds, he or she may be asked to reverse roles with one or several auxiliaries and to attempt to sort out the situation. The progress of the scene largely depends on the action(s) the protagonist chooses to pursue. Occasionally some protagonists become overwhelmed by the chaos and elect to withdraw, to give up, or to break into tears. In such circumstances the director has to intervene and help them with ideas so that they may assume control over the "unruly" auxiliaries and the seemingly unsolvable situation.

There are several variations of this technique that do not necessarily deal with role-repertoires. Instead, protagonists may be offered an encounter with fears and wishes they have, or traits they possess that cause them discomfort. These confrontations usually involve one or two auxiliaries only. The protagonist is asked to identify by name the fear, the wish, or the troubling trait and to select an auxiliary to represent it. The two players are instructed to discuss with each other the problem(s) they have as the auxiliary must defend its right to exist. Often the ensuing encounter may require several role reversals where the protagonist assumes the role of the troubling issue, while the auxiliary temporarily becomes the protagonist.

The Barrier technique. One of the better known versions of such encounters is the Barrier technique (e.g., Robbins, 1968; Weiner, Allen, Moss, & Costa, 1966). Again, the protagonist identifies a trait, a skill (or the lack of it), an attitude, or a fear that constitutes an impediment—a barrier in his or her aspiration to achieve a desirable goal(s). This "barrier" may be portrayed by a pile of chairs or a row of chairs, also known as the Wall or the Fence technique (Weiner & Sacks, 1969), and personified by an auxiliary. It is not unusual to have a protagonist who reports several barriers. The director may choose to have him or her encounter them one at a time, or to have them all in one scene. In the latter case several chairs or piles of chairs may be arranged, each representing one stumbling block. The ensuing confrontation will resemble the Confronting Your Own Role-Repertoire technique described above. Typically, a successful end of such scenes is concretized by making the (physical) barrier small enough, or by creating a space between two chairs, so that the protagonist can jump over or walk through effortlessly.

Ackernecht (1967) described another version of the same approach in his method of role playing of embarrassing situations. This approach is slightly more involved because a scene of an embarrassing situation is portrayed by auxiliaries at the protagonist's request. The protagonist, on the other hand, observes the scene and then confronts it by reversing role with one auxiliary.

The Swing (Individual)

There is another subgroup of techniques subsumed under Prototype IV: Explicit/Similes combination, where the confrontation with the issue is attained by means of a different form of concretization. The protagonist's predicament is exposed in a literal manner. A classic example of these is the Swing (Weiner & Sacks, 1969). Suppose a protagonist is besieged by a problem that leaves him or her in an uncomfortable state of indecision. The therapist-director may confront the protagonist with the indecisiveness in the following way. Two auxiliaries will be asked to come forward to the action space and hold hands as if they were a swing. The protagonist is asked to sit on the auxiliaries' hands and then he or she will be swung back and forth while contemplating the troubling problem. The auxiliaries will have to swing the protagonist in such a way that he or she is quite uncomfortable. This may continue for a few moments with the hope that the protagonist will be compelled to reach a decision in order to stop the swinging.

The same issue of indecisiveness may be handled in a different manner also, that is, the Torn Between Alternatives technique. Again, our protagonist is in a dilemma, unable to decide one way or the other. The director asks two auxiliaries to come forward and has one grab the right hand and the other the left hand of the protagonist. "Each one of you," the director tells the auxiliaries, "represents one of the two alternatives. Please tell the protagonist, simultaneously, why you should be chosen, and at the same time, pull his or her hand in your direction." (Thus they pull in opposing directions.) The protagonist is told to talk with the auxiliaries as he or she is "torn between the two alternatives." Most protagonists make a choice in a few moments, if only to stop the pulling. *A note of caution:* Before introducing this technique it should be ascertained that the protagonist's health permits this kind of physical pressure. *This practice should be the general rule before subjecting any protagonist to a physically demanding clinical role playing technique.*

The consequences of the protagonist's choice, if he or she made one, may be either discussed or enacted in a separate scene. If it turned out to be unsatisfactory, the other alternative may be explored. Needless to say, techniques based on concretizations of this sort are too many to enumerate because ideas for such confrontations are only as limited as the boundaries of their inventors' creative imagination.

The Photo-Album Technique (Individual)

This technique (Kipper, 1977) is actually a spin-off of the Empty-chair technique (described in Chapter 6). Its purpose is to provide protagonists with the opportunity to reexamine their self-evaluation and self-development. The design of the technique is quite simple. The therapist-director asks the protagonist to look at an empty chair and put on it, in his or her imagination, a picture showing him or her in the past. Specifically, the protagonist is told to "select a picture of yourself from those you have in your photo album." Once the picture had been described, the protagonist chooses an auxiliary to represent himself or herself in that picture. "What I want you to do now," the director may say, "is to look at you as you appear in the picture and talk with yourself *about* yourself, about the way you grew up, and about what has become of you." The director may also ask the protagonist to reverse roles with the picture, thus allowing him or her to interview the "grown-up version" and ask questions.

In the Photo-Album technique only one protagonist, and perhaps one auxiliary, can be active at any given moment. There are, however, other versions of confrontation techniques in which the entire group participates in an auxiliary capacity. Although these techniques involve group activities, the fact that only one person serves as the protagonist is a sufficient reason to classify them in the "individual" category (see p. 234). Among the more popular ones are the Behind-Your-Back technique (Corsini, 1953) or variations of the Hot Seat technique (e.g., Goodman & Timko, 1976). In the former technique the protagonist stands with his or her back to the group as group members discuss openly his or her good and bad qualities. The protagonist may respond to the statements made about him or her only at the end of the discussion (sometimes no responses are permitted at all). In the latter, the Hot Seat technique, members of the group are allowed to verbally attack the protagonist who sits on a chair designated as the "hot seat." They may continue their attack as long as the protagonist defends and rationalizes the deeds for which he or she is criticized; but as soon as the protagonist evinces reactions of remorse, helplessness, and regret, the group members respond with compassion and care. In general, it should be pointed out that the simulation component built into these techniques is minimal. In any case, as far as their classification in our paradigm is concerned, they also belong in Prototype IV: the Explicit/Similes type.

The Crib Scene Technique (Group)

The Crib Scene technique (Allen, 1966) is an example of situational techniques designed as a group exercise. In other words, it is a technique applied to several individual protagonists simultaneously. Its main purpose is to offer protagonists the opportunity to experience again the feeling of babyhood, of being taken care of by a loving mother. The therapist-director may introduce the technique as follows:

> "Today we can be babies, young infants in the crib. Get down out of your chairs and lie on the floor. And although you are not really babies you can pretend for a few moments that you are. It is possible to feel like a baby if you think about it. Just lie on the floor like a baby."

The director now assumes the role of a nurturing mother, walks around from one protagonist to another, patting each on the head and covering each with imaginary blankets "so baby goes to sleep, warm and quiet." The director may continue:

> "Baby feels drowsier and drowsier, and goes to sleep. So baby sleeps and sleeps, closes his eyes and goes to sleep. Gets heavy and goes to sleep. And the mother comes and loves the baby, takes care of the baby, covers the baby, and keeps him warm. Mother feeds the baby and gives him milk. She pats the baby and watches over the baby while the baby sleeps and sleeps."

These instructions are repeated over and over again in a soft and somewhat monotonous voice to induce the desirable atmosphere and to allow the protagonists to experience the "baby-like state."

This state of "voluntary regression" may last for no more than 20 minutes. To end the Crib Scene, the director says:

> "So the baby begins to wake up, begins to move a little and to stretch a little. The baby sits up. Now he feels alert, feels happy, good and content, and gets back to the chair. Now that you sit back in your chairs you are adults again, behaving, feeling, and thinking like adults."

It should be mentioned that therapists subscribing to behavioral approaches may find the regressive type of techniques (e.g., the Crib Scene and the Womb: Rebirth [see pp. 241-242]) incompatible with their views of the psychotherapeutic process. But even for those who find such techniques acceptable, a word of caution needs to be added. Regressive techniques must be used sparingly and cautiously, especially if they are intended to be applied to psychotic patients or highly suggestible persons.

The Concretization of Silence (Group)

Suppose, in a group therapy situation, members of the group become silent. No one speaks, and a heavy mood of inaction descends on the group. The therapist-director decides to concretize that situation in the following manner. "It seems to me," he or she might comment, "that everyone is caught in the atmosphere of silence. I would like to know what this silence means. Let us put a chair in the middle of the group. The chair will represent the 'silence in the group.' I would like one of you, anyone who feels like it, to come forward and sit in the chair and be that silence." As soon as a volunteer has emerged, the director turns to him or her and says, "You are the silence that has descended upon this group. You personify that silence, and in that capacity you can talk, explain yourself, ask group members questions, or respond to their questions." Turning now to the rest of the members, the director says, "Here is your silence. Could you please start by telling it why you have brought it to the session today? Do you want it to continue in its presence here, or would you like it to change, and how?"

This highly sophisticated manipulation achieves two immediate goals. First, it breaks the silence as members begin to converse with it and among themselves. Second, it retains the issue of the silence of the group, clarifies its role and meaning, and implicitly conveys the message that

silence is not necessarily a negative phenomenon. The way the technique
might work is illustrated as follows. After the introduction of the exercise
by the the director, the member who personifies the silence begins to
ruminate.

The Silence: I like to be here. I'm glad to have the opportunity to be with
you guys. I'm not entirely sure why you've brought me here, but
be that as it may, I'm content. *(Members of the group remain silent but
a few begin to smile.)* John, why did you bring me here?

John: Gee, I really don't know. Suddenly, everyone became silent, so I
decided to follow the herd. If no one talks, why should I be the
first one?

Dean: (to John) What's wrong with being the first one?

John: Don't you start with me, Dean. I'm not going to let you make me
talk first.

Dean: It seems to me that you have already started. You were the first
to talk. *(laughter in the group).*

The Silence: The way I see it, you guys seem to me quite uptight.

Mary: Why do you say so?

The Silence: Because, that's how. . .

Pat: Let's not play games, Mary. Don't you think we look pretty uptight?
I know I am. I just feel that if I start talking everyone will converge
on me and ask me questions and criticize me. Who needs it? Why
should I stick my neck out. I'll take my own time.

The Silence: Wonderful, Pat. You stick with me and I'll protect you. As
long as you stay with me you'll not have to say a word for weeks.

Pat: I don't need you that much, don't get too excited.

The Silence: That's too bad. But I think that Dave will be my buddy, right
Dave?

Dave: (nods yes)

The Silence: You see, I told you. I've one friend here. Come Dave, come
and sit with me.

Dave: I don't want to. I'm quite comfortable here on my chair.

John: Why Dave, you don't look very comfortable to me.

Dave: You're wrong. I am. And don't project your feelings on others.
If you're uncomfortable, speak for yourself.

Jane: Boy, oh boy! You sound very hostile, Dave.

Dave: No, I'm not. I'm telling you I am quite content watching the group.

Dean: Watching the group! What is it to you? A show? A zoo?

Dave: I didn't say that. I'm telling you I want to be quiet.

The Silence: So do I, Dave. You be my friend.

Pat: I don't know about you guys, but I think that I feel uncomfortable because—and don't get me wrong—I don't trust you enough yet. I'm not accusing anyone, but I don't know you enough to be open with you, so I take my time.

Mary: I agree with you. I feel the same way, only that I wouldn't mind talking about myself if not for this guy *(points at the Silence)* who makes things worse.

The Silence: Thank you, Mary, you made my day.

Mary: What are you so proud about! Are you going to sit there in the middle and make us feel uneasy?

The Silence: You bet.

Mary: Well, I'm not going to let you. Pat, help me. Let's do something.

Pat: We can kick that guy *(points to the Silence)* out of his chair.

Dave: What's that going to accomplish? You guys say that we need to establish more trust in the group. Playing football with a chair is not going to help.

John: Be constructive, Dave. Do you have an idea of what we should do?

Dave: No, and frankly I don't want to think about it. I told you, I am happy as I am.

Pat: I know, let's get the Silence out of the way. Anyway, we already did because we aren't silent anymore. And instead, let's put someone in the chair who'll represent something else. Perhaps somebody will represent our discomfort.

John: "Discomfort" does not sound to me very constructive.

Mary: But it's true, isn't it? We—except Dave—said that we were uncomfortable. So, why avoid the issue?

Dean: OK. Why don't we put Trust in the chair, our need to trust each other?

John: I like that.

The Silence: I'm not moving out of this chair. I'll stay right here as long as I can.

John: Come on guys, let's get this clown out of his chair.

Three members get up and push the member who represents the silence out of the middle of the group.

The decision of the group to replace the Silence with another role—someone who will represent Trust—points to the many variations of this technique. Depending on what transpires in the group, the salient psychological or sociometric characteristics that prevail at a given moment can be concretized in the same fashion. One may place a chair in the middle of the group with a group member who personifies Trust, Discomfort, Resistance, Domination, Hostility, and so forth.

Action Sociometry (Group)

In his book *Who Shall Survive*, first published in 1934, J.L. Moreno laid the foundations of sociometry, which is the study of the structure and the organization of groups through the analysis of the interpersonal relationship patterns of their members. In order to uncover these patterns a paper and pencil instrument known as the Sociometric Test was designed. Briefly, group members are asked to describe their relationships to other members of the group by writing the names of those members towards whom they feel attraction as well as those towards whom they feel rejection. These choices are then portrayed graphically with sets or arrows: blue ones for positive choices (attractions) and red ones for negative choices (rejections). This pictorial representation of the structure of members' choices is called the Sociogram. The Sociometric Test is, of course, more complicated, bearing in mind that other factors need to be taken into consideration (e.g., the criteria by which members are chosen or rejected, the order of the choices—first, second, third, etc., and the reasons given for the choices).

The Action Sociometry technique, however is a simplified role playing version of the Sociometric Test. The therapist-director may ask the group member to mill around the room and make choices with regard to a variety of topics. For instance, he or she may ask the group member to "look around and put your hand on the shoulder of the person whom you would like to be your brother (your sister, your mother, your boss, etc.)" or "look around the room and put your hand on the shoulder of the person you feel most uneasy with." In this way it will become immediately apparent who is the star (the most popular person or people in the group), who remains an isolate (unchosen), and who are the people who tend to cluster together. Members of the group are now asked to sit with the people of their choice and explain the reason for their choices. This technique is also known as the Sociometric Tag (Weiner & Sacks, 1969).

The purpose of this technique is threefold. It allows group members to express their perceptions and feelings towards each other. It allows members of the group to see the structure of the interpersonal relationships in their group. It also provides participants with the sometimes uncomfortable, if not embarrassing, opportunity to deal with each other openly by facing directly the interpersonal dynamics in the group.

Action Problem Solving (Group)

This technique is a variation of the preceding two group techniques. Typically, it is introduced as a follow-up of the Action Sociometry described above. Suppose, in a group therapy situation, members are concerned with the problem of what to do with a consistently uncooperative member. The group is sharply divided on that issue. Some participants hold that unless the member in question begins to cooperate there is no room in the group for such a person. Others may argue that it is the responsibility of each and every member to help that person change his or her uncooperative attitude. A third opinion is voiced by members who maintain that the group ought to be tolerant, do nothing, and wait for a change whenever it may occur. The therapist-director then sends the holders of these three opinions to separate corners of the room. He or she may say, "Here, you are sharply divided. Each subgroup must try very hard to convince the other two to accept its position. You must persuade the other members to come to your corner. This exercise will end once the majority of you will cluster in one corner." The member in question stands at the side of the action space with the director, or preferably with a Double, so that he or she does not feel completely alienated. The group must also understand that its solution will be regarded merely as a recommendation to the therapist who, in turn, has the right to negotiate with the group.

CLINICAL CONSIDERATIONS

Now that the situational techniques' paradigm and its four prototypes have been presented, we are not only struck by the orderly structure underlying the many kinds of role playing interventions, but have also well positioned ourselves to proceed to examine some of the broader implications that this discovery holds for the clinical practitioner. We may begin by discussing the question: What clinical insights can be gleaned from having identified four different prototypes? Phrasing the question differently we may ask: To what extent has the division of situational techniques into four prototypes contributed to the attainment of a better fit in the matching of role playing interventions with the clinical characteristics of the therapy situation?

From a clinical standpoint, the Implicit and the Explicit modes are concerned with the protagonist's readiness to take risks (some may refer to it as his or her ego strength and the likelihood of evincing resistance), as well as with the level of consciousness in which the expected changes need to occur. The Implicit mode uses a diversionary approach. Diversion connotes a second-best option barring the feasibility of direct access. In terms of clinical skills we associate diversionary approaches with wisdom and creativity more than with manipulations and intrigues. The Implicit mode, therefore, suits low risk-takers and tends to minimize provocations to the existing defense mechanism system of the individual.

Furthermore, sometimes new experiences are integrated best on a subconscious level. There seem to be reciprocal relationships between the conscious and the subconscious levels, where modifications in one cause changes in the other. Curiously enough, the changes are often evolutional rather than parallel. In other words, changes on one level result in *different kinds* of changes in the other, as if the second-order changes represent elaborations (the consequences) of the first-order ones. The Implicit mode tends to be instrumental in producing such a chain of effects. The Explicit mode, on the other hand, is well suited for high risk-takers who are likely to profit from direct encounters without resorting to avoidance and other distracting tactics. Such challenges to one's own existing attitudes, lack of appropriate skills, and emotional constraints are perceived as enrichments of one's coping ability rather than painful violations of it. The Explicit mode also addresses changes that can be dealt with on a conscious level where a state of complete awareness of the treated issues constitutes an asset rather than a liability.

The clinical significance of the Similes and the Metaphors modes of structuring the issue is a different matter altogether. Similes and Metaphors modes represent various degrees of *distancing*, where Similes emphasize a sense of immediacy, of being a part of the issue, while Metaphors foster observational, reflective, and philosophical states of involvement. Because of this difference, the two modes tend to facilitate slightly different psychological processes in order to attain the desirable therapeutic objectives. It should be made clear that we are dealing here with degrees of emphasis and not with exclusivity, that is, I do not wish to give the impression that one mode activates psychological processes that are never activated by the other mode. Such a clear-cut delineation is not possible. Nonetheless, the Similes mode is likely to support emotional release and to encourage catharsis (and under certain conditions also to improve performance skills). The Metaphors mode utilizes cognitive and introspective processes for the same purpose.

The four prototypes are sets of combinations, each comprised of two modes: one from the Implicit-Explicit dimension and one from the Similes-Metaphors dimension. These permit us to address a greater variety of clinical constellations and introduce a measure of further refinement in the utilization of the techniques as shown in Figure 9.5.

This figure presents the main features of the original situational technique's paradigm. Again we have the two concentric circles representing the Individual-Group application dimension, the vertical axis that stands for the Implicit-Explicit modes of eliciting the issue, and the horizontal one showing the Similes-Metaphors modes of structuring the issue. The two axes form the four prototypes marked I through IV. The new addition, however, is portrayed by the two diagonal arrows that illustrate the clinical characteristics of each prototype.

The arrow tilted to the left of the diagram cuts across Prototypes I and III and is called "Avoidance and inhibition." It suggests that techniques classified under these two prototypes are particularly indicated

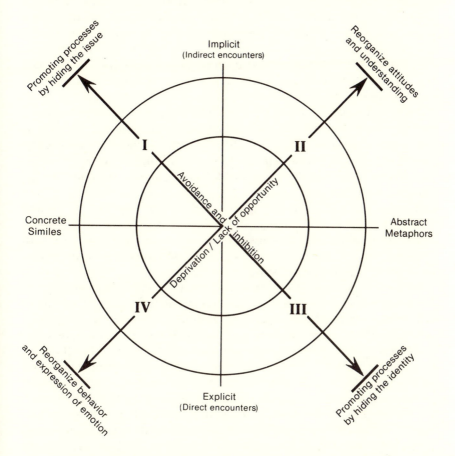

Figure 9.5. Clinical applications of the four techniques' prototypes

for protagonists who might *not* be ready to face the issues associated with their presenting problems. Protagonists suspected by the therapist to be unduly threatened by direct confrontations (resisting or otherwise inhibited protagonists) are likely to benefit most from techniques belonging to these two prototypes. Each of these prototypes includes techniques that protect protagonists in different ways. Techniques subsumed under Prototype I are concerned primarily with resistance. They retain the protagonists' involvements through emphasizing emotional experiences but at the same time disguise the target issue(s). The greatest part of the therapeutic effects achieved with such techniques is believed to occur on the subawareness level. Techniques subsumed under Prototype III, on the other hand, protect the protagonists through anonymity or partial anonymity. They tend to produce a disinhibition effect, a desensitization process, by turning *direct* confrontations into *impersonal* encounters. This kind of distancing fosters cognitive activities and deemphasizes emotional reactions. Distancing, of course, permits protagonists to stay with the issue(s), thus allowing the therapeutic effects to occur on the level of awareness.

The arrow tilted to the right of the diagram cuts across Prototypes II and IV and is labeled "Deprivation/lack of opportunities." It suggests that techniques classified under these two prototypes are particularly indicated for protagonists whose problems and difficulties might be attributed (at least partially) to lack of appropriate opportunities to reintegrate their past experiences or to learn new, satisfactory coping behavior. Although such deficiencies and deprivations may be related to resistance or fear of change, the main therapeutic thrust here is focused on the relearning process. There is only a nominal concern with the impact of the threat on the protagonists' defense mechanism systems or with the likelihood of meeting resistance.

Each of these two prototypes contains techniques that provide the remedial effects differently. Techniques subsumed under Prototype II offer opportunities for reorganizing attitudes, self-concepts, and value systems through introspection and cognitive reconstructions of emotional reactions. The consequences of such reappraisals and evaluations could be strengthened commitments to the already existing values and perceptions. They could also produce modifications of the old attitudes or even acquisitions of new ones. But the disguised aspect of these techniques suggests an additional therapeutic quality. It points to the fact that the intended therapeutic effects are not limited to changes observed in the overt content of the plots portrayed through these techniques. Other covert, consequential outcomes are also expected to occur, first perhaps on a subliminal level and then on the overt one. These second-order effects are as much part and parcel of the main therapeutic effort as the explicit, overt ones.

Techniques subsumed under Prototype IV offer protagonists opportunities to reorganize, and hopefully enrich, their emotional lives. They provide chances to express hitherto suppressed feelings, to facilitate a clearer communication of feelings, and to better synchronize feelings with actions and thoughts. These techniques also provide opportunities for developing new learning skills, for abandoning damaging ones, and for perfecting those in need of improvement. The discussion of the clinical application of techniques subsumed under Prototype III earlier mentioned that these may also be used for skill training. In Prototype III I was addressing inhibited and somewhat guarded protagonists. Prototype IV techniques are used for the same purpose but when protagonists are thought to be strong enough to face head-on confrontations.

At this point a cautionary note must be entered: The foregoing attempt to ascribe separate clinical indications to each of the four prototypes is more suggestive than definitive. The reason for this qualifying statement is that it is conceivable to encounter techniques that may not conform exactly to my analysis, though I believe that these represent exceptions to the rule. In view of the fact that each prototype includes many variations of different techniques, clinical implications arising out of delicate nuances that separate one variation from another may occasionally require a fresh examination. Some techniques were originally designed to have multiple therapeutic objectives which, taken together, would suit more than a single prototype. Since all these goals cannot be equally attained at one time, the classification of such techniques depends on which of the goals is emphasized in a given administration. This point is quite important and deserves to be reiterated again. Often the classification of a particular technique is a function of the *way it is executed* and not necessarily a function of its basic design. For example, a technique originally built along the Implicit/Similes guidelines (Prototype I) may easily be changed to become an Explicit/Similes one (Prototype IV) if the therapist chooses to clarify the issue in advance rather than let it evolve indirectly.

Uncovering the principal dimensions that form the situational techniques' paradigm also allows us to shed further light on another practical matter of clinical significance, namely the formulation of guidelines for inventing simulation interventions. Indeed, how does one devise a role playing technique? Curiously enough, the literature seems to offer only a partial answer to this question. Thayer (1977) for example, discussed some of the key variables that need to be reviewed before embarking on the actual development of simulation vignettes. These include a careful consideration of the particular treatment issue, the importance of taking into consideration the phase of the counseling or the therapeutic process, the need to assess the intensity of the emotional state of the prospective player, and appraising the ability of the protagonist to comprehend a problem.

Other discussions (e.g., Towers, 1969) analyzed the differences between role playing in therapy and dramaturgical acting. In these discussions the uniqueness of role playing was demonstrated by specifying the skills and characteristics of both the actor (client) and the director (therapist) as factors affecting the simulation procedures, and by alluding to the problem of casting the players in simulation scenes. There have also been attempts to provide general outlines for role playing exercises (e.g., Morris & Cinnamon, 1974, 1975) that highlight some of the important issues involved in designing such techniques. These include defining the goal(s) and the duration of each technique, specifying the kind of materials that is required, having clear instructions for administration, and identifying possible variations of the techniques.

Considering all this useful and valuable information, one is still left with the distinct impression that a good inventor of role playing techniques must be endowed with special talents—creativity, imagination, and resourcefulness—or that by reading and practice somehow these talents may flourish.

There is certainly a great advantage to having such talents, and learning through modeling coupled with practice is equally important. Yet the skill and artistry required for developing new techniques do not deserve the aura of mystery that was created around them. Having discovered the dimensions that comprise the techniques' paradigm, we are in an improved position to advise prospective inventors about the considerations that need to be taken into account in the design process.

At the point when the therapist has the idea for the role playing intervention, a new set of considerations needs to be entertained. Let me present these in the form of questions that therapists must raise and answer. Should the therapeutic issue, or the troubling issue, be made explicit to the protagonist in advance? Would the protagonist benefit more by having the issue disguised? Suppose that the answer to the first question is affirmative. What is the therapist's assessment of the protagonist's strengths? Is he or she ready to face the issue with or without protecting measures? Is the Similes mode appropriate here or should one introduce the impersonal Metaphors mode? Suppose that the answer to the second question is affirmative, should the therapist try to activate cognitive processes to initiate the therapeutic processes by using the Metaphors modes or is the Similes mode of structuring more beneficial? I propose that the answers to these questions must be given *before* the therapist proceeds to formulate the instructions to determine the administrative aspects of the intervention and to assess the impact of the intervention on the observing audience.

The preceding four chapters represent a significant portion of my concentrated effort to unravel the internal organization of the interventions used by clinical role playing. In the course of the analysis I have attempted to highlight those aspects that pointed to the systematic quality of this treatment modality. Slowly, it became increasingly apparent that the notion of "techniques" is a central component of this mode of treatment. Although the advantages of this proposition speak for themselves, one can ill afford to be oblivious of the (unintended) potential misleading conclusions that such a concept may cause.

One potential danger is that the formulation of the therapist's interventions in terms of techniques might be misinterpreted as a deliberate attempt to compromise the *essence* of psychotherapy by glorifying the *form*. The insistence that all role playing interventions ought to be viewed as techniques, basic and situational, can easily be misunderstood as shifting the main focus of the psychotherapeutic endeavor away from its true meaning and purpose. I am quite aware of this danger, including the fact that the very choice of the word "techniques" might be misleading. I am also aware of the danger that, if subjected to a superficial analysis, clinical role playing is likely to be regarded as a reductionistic approach where psychotherapy is seen as a compendium of gimmicks, as a form of treatment where structure supercedes substance.

These potential dangers have been discussed already in another context by Yalom (1975). Yalom raised the issue of the role of what he called the "structure exercises" in group psychotherapy, especially in reference to T-groups and gestalt therapy. His criticism there has relevance to the present discussion, too. The following excerpt describes the main contention quite poignantly.

Structured exercises were first described in group work in the T-groups of the 1950's and became even more common and variegated with the evolution of the encounter group. . . . In recent years the gestalt therapy field has provided an additional source of structured procedures. The use of these procedures has grown to the extent that many group-leader training programs are technique-oriented and novitiates lead groups clutching only a grab bag of gimmicks into which they reach whenever the proceedings flag. . . . This development is most unfortunate and a gross miscarriage of the intent of the approaches which originally spawned these techniques. (Yalom, 1975, p. 446)

After discussing the ramifications of this unfortunate development and its causes, Yalom makes it patently clear that the objection is not against the basic notion of using techniques ("structured exercises," as he terms them). In principle, these serve a useful therapeutic function. Here is an excerpt from the conclusion of his discussion.

In voicing these objections to the excessive use of structured exercises, I have overstated the case. Surely there is a middle ground between, on the one hand, allowing the group to flounder and mire profitlessly in some unproductive sequence and, on the other hand, to assume a frenetically active, structured leadership role. The Lieberman, Yalom, and Miles encounter group study reached that very conclusion. It was demonstrated that the degree to which leaders assume an 'executive,' managerial function was related to outcome in a curvilinear fashion—i.e., too much and too little were negatively correlated with good outcome. (Yalom, 1975, p. 452)

Has clinical role playing therapy with its heavy emphasis on techniques fallen victim to such an unfortunate development, and does it force the therapist into a role characterized by excessive executive and managerial behavior? Obviously, my own answer to both parts of the question is that it has not. But it is also not too difficult to see that proponents of a few psychodynamic approaches may think otherwise. A therapeutic approach that is based on applying the behavior simulation model in psychological treatments must contain a considerable measure of structure. The kind of control that is exercised—the "managerial" aspect of the therapist's responsibility—is delicately focused and tightly confined to the *catalytic function*, that is, to the skill of setting those circumstances that might have the greatest probability of activating the desirable curative processes. The balance of that control is delicate indeed and can easily be violated. Stepping out of line would be in evidence when the therapist assumes control over the content of the explored issues and by tampering with the process itself.

But perhaps the most fundamental difference between the concept of techniques as used in clinical role playing therapy and in other forms of therapy is that, in the former, techniques are one piece in a chain of concepts, whereas in the latter they represent a self-contained entity. In clinical role playing the therapist's interventions are expressed in terms of the triad: scenario—scenes—techniques. The scenario consists of several scenes involving a score of techniques, and the *move from one scene to another* within the general scope of the scenario gives this form of therapy its strength. Separating one component of the triad from the others (i.e., singling out the techniques part) would, in all likelihood, reduce the overall therapeutic effectiveness of the intervention. Structure experiences, on the other hand, are designed as *one-scene* scenarios. It is not surprising, therefore, that it has been repeatedly argued that these have limited therapeutic value; hence they need to be employed advisedly. Because of this limitation, structured experiences and one-scene techniques have customarily been designed for specific objectives.

Clinical role playing techniques may be used in two ways: 1) as a part of the scenario—scene—techniques triad, which is their primary function anyway; and 2) as one-scene scenarios similar to structure experiences. However, this latter practice is mostly limited to the treatment of simple problems and a reduced use of behavior simulation. The fact that I have devoted four chapters to the basic and the situational techniques categories by no means implies that clinical role playing is regarded as a form of therapy based on a group of techniques. The topic of "techniques" was discussed separately in order to make the presentation orderly and coherent. The same rationale governed the decision to discuss each technique separately. Although it is true that some of the described techniques may be used one at a time as the sole simulation vignette during a treatment session, the majority of them serve a different and a broader function. The essence of clinical role playing therapy is the comprehensive utilization of behavior simulation procedures in a given session, not a sporadic, occasional use of one technique or another. It is the latter application of role playing that in my view, represents a reductionistic approach. The extended analysis of techniques is due partly to the complexity of this topic, and partly to the special meaning ascribed to the concept of techniques in this book.

The definition of "techniques" within the context of clinical role playing has been broadened and extended beyond the common meaning that it connotes in behavioral science. This point was already discussed at the beginning of the preceding chapter and need not be repeated again. At this juncture it is sufficient to be reminded of the fact that the concept of techniques pertains to *every form of roles in action*. Therefore, it also includes behaviors labeled the Dialogue technique, the Self-presentation techniques, the Aside technique, the Telephone Call technique, to mention only a few—behaviors that ordinarily would not be classified as techniques. This atypical and liberal use of the term techniques is partly responsible for the central position it has occupied in our discussion.

CHAPTER 10

Application in
Group Psychotherapy

Originally, clinical role playing (as represented by the method of psychodrama) was designed to be used in a group psychotherapy setting. The presence of several clients who assemble together gave rise to the idea of involving auxiliaries as an essential component of the treatment procedure. It also made the implementation of this idea possible. But the group format of clinical role playing therapy has an interesting characteristic. Although there are occasions and corresponding role playing techniques that involve the entire group or most of its members simultaneously, typically clinical role playing addresses one protagonist at a time. This form of therapy, therefore, may be more precisely defined as the treatment of an individual protagonist in the context of group setting. One person, the protagonist, is treated directly whereas the others (i.e., the auxiliaries and the observing members) are helped indirectly. The auxiliaries may be helped in the sense that their role performance may resemble the idea of Fixed-Role Therapy (Kelly, 1955), and the observing members may be indirectly helped through processes such as identifications with the players (protagonists and/or auxiliaries) or vicarious modeling. Since the group setting was the cradle of clinical role playing as a therapeutic modality, it is fitting that the first illustration of a complete session will be that of a group therapy.

The special characteristic of clinical role playing as applied in the context of group therapy, however, does not alter the need to adhere to the general issues: processes and rules, which govern giving any other form of group therapy. A detailed discussion of these is beyond the scope of the present chapter and the interested reader is advised to consult other sources (e.g., Yalom, 1975).

Given the decision to dispense with such a discussion it, still, might be helpful to point to the importance of some of the general rules that govern the conduct of group therapy. Recognizing the tendency of clinical role playing directors to focus on the individual protagonist, it is a good idea to be reminded of the following rules.

1. Therapists must be aware of the personal needs of every individual member of the group. This becomes a particularly important issue in the context of clinical role playing where customarily one member, the protagonist, attracts most of the attention.
2. Therapists must be aware and attend to the group processes that evolve among the members. Again, focusing on a single protagonist cannot be at the expense of ignoring such processes.
3. The application of clinical role playing procedures does not override other important needs of members of the group. Therefore, therapists must be ready to defer simulation interventions in favor of verbal discussions whenever needed.
4. Therapists must be familiar with the literature concerning the principles for selecting clients to a given group. These principles deal with the criteria for creating a homogeneous vs. hetrogeneous group as far as factors such as age, sex, educational and socioeconomic backgrounds, or diagnostic categories are concerned.

A CASE ILLUSTRATION

The following illustration is based on a session conducted with a group comprised of nine adult clients. The majority of the members were college graduates and the others had at least one year of college education. Six members were females and three were males. Of these, five were married, two divorced, and two single. The coping difficulties that prompted them to seek therapy varied, but none was severe enough to require hospitalization. The group met once a week for a period of about an hour and a half.

When the group was set up it was agreed that it would last for 30 weeks. It was also agreed that by the 25th session the agreement would be reviewed with an option to either terminate the group according to the original plan or to extend the initial agreement for an additional period. The session to be described below was the 10th meeting. At that point, members were already familiar with the main procedures of clinical role playing and its basic technical terms. Every member had a chance to be protagonist either for a full session or for a brief encounter. Also, all the members had chances to serve as auxiliaries several times. The first three sessions were completely devoted to the purpose of warming up the group. These included a few brief discussions and role playing of some situational techniques such as the Magic Shop, the Letter technique, and Action Sociometry. During that period members became familiar with most of the specific basic techniques. By the time the 10th session was about to begin, members were reasonably comfortable and willing to participate as protagonists.

Session 10: The Warm-Up Stage

The session started with a discussion of the previous meeting. (This was construed as the continuation of the "analysis" portion of the Closure stage of the ninth meeting, as well as an introduction to the Warm-up stage of the 10th meeting.) The director asked the member who served as the protagonist in the previous week for comments. This included his evaluation of the session, now that he had had a few days to reflect upon it and to report if and how it affected him during the past week. Members of the group were also asked to offer their insights and feedback. The protagonist's perception was discussed for about seven minutes and then the director turned to the group and asked, "Who would like to be protagonist today?" Following a minute of silence, Carol started.

Carol: I have a problem that bothers me. Actually I thought about it last week, but Jim seemed to have a more important issue to deal with, so I kept quiet. I'm still not sure whether it's worthwhile talking about, and I certainly don't want to take up the group's time. If someone has a more pressing need, I can wait.

Jim: I didn't know you had something on your mind last week. I do appreciate your willingness to give me a chance. That was really nice of you. . .

John: (somewhat cynically) Carol is a nice person.

Jim: I didn't mean to say that the way you say it, John,. . .

Betty: What is the matter with you John? It *was* very considerate of her and I don't see any reason to make fun of it. If you have a great need to mock everything, maybe you should be a protagonist, because maybe you do have a problem.

John: Hey! Get off my back, will you please. OK, I'm sorry, Carol.

Carol: I think John is right. I'm a "nice" person. I'm too nice to people, and that's what I wanted to talk about. Sometimes I feel that people take advantage of me.

Stacy: I can sympathize with that. But in my case, it's always men who do it to me. . . . Oh! and my mother, too.

(The director noticed that Linda opened her purse and took out tissue papers to wipe her nose. Her face became red, too.)

Director: Linda, what are you thinking of?

John: She probably has a cold.

(The director ignores John's remark and motions with his hand to Linda signaling a permission to continue.)

Linda: I don't know. All that discussion, the bickering, and everything that has been going on here makes me sad. I don't know why, but it reminds me of my husband. But don't get me wrong, he doesn't make fun of me. I wonder why I'm thinking of him. Maybe I should be a protagonist, what do you think?

Jim: What about Carol? What is it? She started to say something, then everyone jumps in with all kinds of comments, and we still don't know what bothers her. And now suddenly we focus on Linda. What's going on here? I want to hear from Carol.

Virginia: Gee whiz! What's gotten into you? What are you mad about?

Jim: Carol gave me a chance last week, so I owe her one. And I'm not going to let all of you take advantage of the fact that she is nice and unassertive and. . .

Carol: Thanks, Jim, but I felt I did say what troubles me. We didn't hear Linda's problem and she's upset. So maybe her problem is more important than mine, and if she. . .

Jim: Please, Carol, don't do that again.

Betty: Don't push her Jim. I know that you mean well. But pushing, even out of consideration and gratitude, won't do.

Jim: Well, I just wanted to help, and *(turning to Linda)* I didn't mean to hurt you. I'm not angry at you. *(turning to the director)* You must have some technique that can sort all this out. Maybe something that gets both Carol and Linda on board.

Ellen: They can do that thing when you walk around and talk with a double.

Bill: You mean the soliloquy, don't you?

Ellen: Yes, that's right. I couldn't remember the name of it.

Linda: I don't feel like doing this. Let Carol be the protagonist. I didn't say I wanted to be one anyway. *(wipes her eyes)* No, truly, I can wait.

John: I don't understand what's going on. Everyone who wants to be a protagonist and has an important problem suddenly decides that it is not so important and it can wait. If we could wait, why did we come to therapy anyway? We could have waited another five, 10 years. . .

Bill: By that time we wouldn't be able to afford it, the way you guys run the economy.

John: I don't run the economy. . .

Bill: That's what everyone is saying. No one is willing to take responsibility for anything, anymore.

Stacy: (giggles) Oh, knock it off, Bill! We are all responsible here.

Linda: If there is something that can get me and Carol involved, then I am willing to talk, but I want her to start first.

Director: We could do something that might help us. *(gets up and picks a chair and moves it to the center)* Let me put this empty chair in the middle of the action space. I would like both Carol and Linda to look at this chair for a moment. Keep looking at the chair and try to put, in your imagination, someone whom you wish to talk to about the things you mentioned here. The person you wish to put in the chair may be someone who is alive or dead, someone who lives close by or far away. Try to visualize that person sitting in this chair as vividly as you can.

(The director waited for a minute or so. Then he turned to both Carol and Linda and asked them: Whom did you put in the chair?)

Carol: Well, at first it was hard, because as soon as I tried to visualize one person, another one suddenly appeared. It was like a parade of persons.

Director: Did you manage to get one to sit for a while?

Carol: Well, yes. First I tried hard to put my brother in the chair, but that didn't work; he refused to stay. So I got to sit my boss there.

Director: How about you, Linda?

Linda: Oh, I had no trouble at all putting my husband in the chair. He sat there, and I have the feeling that he would have stayed there forever.

Director: OK. *(picks up the empty chair and places it in front of Carol)* Carol, I would like you to put your boss, again, in the chair. Is your boss a male or a female?

Carol: A female. Her name is Lilly.

Director: OK. Try to imagine Lilly in the chair, and then would you tell her why you have brought her here, or anything else you wish to tell her. Try to do it by talking to the empty chair. If you find it difficult, we can ask someone to represent Lilly and actually sit in the empty chair.

Carol: Oh, no, that's all right. I have no problem addressing the empty chair. *(pauses for a moment)* Hi, Lilly, you probably wonder why I brought you here today. Well, there is something I wanted to talk with you about, but frankly, I couldn't bring myself to do that until now. *(a pause)* Well, you probably wonder why. Look, I'm scared of you. I'm afraid that you will criticize me, and I don't know why.

You know, even if you don't say anything about my work, I have the feeling that you may not like it. Gosh, it is so difficult to please you. I know that you don't understand this. You always say that I have a problem with my self-image and that this is *my* problem, not yours. And I certainly agree with you that I have a problem. But you know what? Sometimes I feel that you manipulate me. You say this because you know I will believe it. And in fact, you are not exactly the darling angel you like everyone to think you are.

Director: Reverse roles. Move to Lilly's chair, and be Lilly.

(Lilly): Look, I really don't know what you want from me. Why don't you explain yourself clearly?

Director: Reverse roles. Carol, move to your own chair and be yourself again.

Carol: What do I want from you? I don't know what I want from you. I want to tell you that I'm afraid of you. Well, I just told you this. I thought that if I manage to tell you this it will make me feel better. But having said it I really don't feel any better. So, what do I want from you? I know. I want you to be different. I want you to behave so that I won't be intimidated by you. *(raises her voice)* Be different, you hear! That's what I want from you!

Director: Reverse roles.

(Lilly): That's silly, Carol. I don't have a need to change, and you can be assured that I am not going to do this just because you want me to change. It's your problem. You should change!

Director: Reverse roles.

Carol: Right! *I* should change. The only problem is that I don't know how.

Director: Thank you, Carol. Let's move the empty chair to Linda. Linda, can you visualize your husband in the chair again?

Linda: Sure.

Director: Good. Will you tell him why you brought him to this session, and anything else you want to tell him now?

Linda: Look Bob. . . *(pauses for a moment)* I didn't plan to bring you here. It just happened that suddenly you came into my mind. Jim tried to protect Carol, and then John made his usual sarcastic remarks, and I don't know what triggered me to become sad. But I was. And suddenly I thought of you. Look, I'm disorganized now, and I don't know if I make sense at all. Probably not. You always say that when I'm emotional you have trouble following my thoughts. What I want to say is. . . I feel trapped. No, that's not accurate. I feel helpless. Yes, that's more like it. Sometimes I feel very dependent around you—dependent and helpless. And this feeling drives me nuts. I don't understand it and I can't control it.

Director: Reverse roles. Move to the empty chair and be Bob.

(Bob): I know you feel that way, and I wish I could help you. But I don't know how. Anyway, how did you get me involved in all this? I'm not sarcastic to you, am I?

Director: Reverse roles.

Linda: No, Bob, you're not. But there is something about the way you behave that makes me feel inadequate. And I'm not even sure that it is you. Maybe you just remind me of someone else? Oh, Bob, I don't know. It doesn't make sense. I'm not trying to tell you that you should be different. I do love you as you are. Maybe *I* should be different.

Director: Reverse roles.

(Bob): Look honey, this is not the first time you've told me this. If it troubles you so much why don't you talk about it with your therapist?

(Linda reverses roles spontaneously and moves to her chair.)

Linda: (smiling) I am talking to him right now. *(general laughter)*

Director: Thank you, Linda. *(turning to the entire group)* Well, we heard both Carol and Linda. We can't have them both protagonists at the same time. So what do you think we should do now? Any suggestions? *(the group members shared their impressions with each other, and Carol said that she sees similarities between her problem and Linda's so she might learn about her own problem by observing her session. The group made her commit herself to become the protagonist next week, and in the meantime they all will read about assertiveness. The director suggested a popular, short book on the subject, written by an expert in assertiveness training.)*

The Action Stage

A. First Segment (Presenting the Problem)

(This segment contains one key scene and one connecting scene.)

Director: OK, Linda, we have heard you talking to the empty chair, to Bob in the empty chair. You said that there is something about him that sometimes makes you feel inadequate. Can you say more about it? Is it something that he does or doesn't do?

Linda: The truth is that honestly I don't know what it is. Well, I wouldn't say that I like everything he does. Like every normal couple we have arguments, disagreements, and once in a great while, a serious fight. But I really don't know. That's what drives me nuts. I know I'm not crazy, but sometimes it feels as if I am. *(turning to the group)* I don't know if you guys ever felt that way, but let me tell you, it's weird and scary.

Director: Can you remember a typical situation, say in the last six months, when you felt that way? I mean, a situation involving you and Bob?

Linda: Sure. There are many of them.

Director: Do they usually involve disagreements or one of your occasional fights?

Linda: Not necessarily. In fact, usually I feel it when we do not have real disagreements. But you are right. I usually feel this way when I need something from Bob. That's right. It doesn't have to be an argument. This feeling comes up when I need something from him.

Director: Fine. Can you think of a typical situation and tell me a little about it—a general description without the details?

Linda: It was about, oh, three months ago, during the winter. Bob came home from work, and I was waiting to talk with him about something that happened to me earlier in the day. But you probably want me to tell it as if it happens now, in the present, correct?

Director: That's right. We will move the clock back. It is winter now and the time is, what? Five-thirty, six o'clock in the evening? *(Linda nods.)* Tell us where you are and arrange the place you are in.

Key scene 1. The scene is set in Linda and Bob's living room. In the middle there is a couch and a love seat which she represents by four empty chairs. The room also has two additional chairs, a large bookcase, a brown upright piano, and a TV set which were described by Linda but were not concretely represented in the scene. The time was set as six o'clock in the evening. Linda chose Jim to be the auxiliary to play the role of Bob, her husband. The scene begins as Linda sits and watches the evening news.

(Bob): *(Knocks on the door)*

Linda: *(to the director)* No, that's not right. He doesn't knock on the door, he uses his keys.

(Bob): *(starts again)* Hi, honey, I'm home.

Director: *(to Linda)* Is that how it begins?

Linda: Perfect! *(to Jim, gets up and hugs him)* Hi, Bob, how was your day?

(Bob): Oh, it was terrible, we had such a hassle in the office.

Linda: (to the director) No, no! Bob rarely says that he had a bad day in the office. He might say he is tired, that he has a headache, but not that he had a terrible day.

(Bob): It was OK, how was yours? Where is Ronny? Anything new?

Linda: Ronny is fine. He's in the back, in his room. . .

(Bob): (yells) Hi, Ronny!

Linda: (to the director) Right! He always yells from the living room. *(to Bob)* May I talk with you alone, before dinner? *(to the director)* He really doesn't insist on having dinner right away. He likes to read the mail first, to chat with our little boy, or just relax for 10 minutes or so.

> *(Note that Linda repeatedly "falls out of her role" with explanatory comments to the director. Ordinarily, this kind of behavior signifies resistance. But at the very beginning of the plot it is difficult to determine whether it represents a serious form of resistance—an attempt to avoid the issue that needs to be addressed promptly and separately—or simply a lack of involvement due to insufficient warming up. The director decides to wait a little longer, and if needed, to ask the auxiliary to try and get the protagonist more involved. This decision is based on the supposition that the slow start indicates a minor hesitation to face the issue, which is likely to disappear with increased involvement. Since it is the simpler hypothesis of the two and also easier to check and deal with, it ought to be considered first. If the next few minutes show no improvement in Linda's involvement, as marked by a cessation of the "falling out of the role" behavior, the second hypothesis, i.e., of resistance, will have to be considered.)*

(Bob): Where's the mail?

Linda: (surprised, turns to the director) Perfect! That's typical of him.

Director: Linda, please talk to your husband, not to me. I'm not in your living room. If you need to correct him, tell him so directly. Bob, keep talking to her so that she will not "neglect" you and talk to people who are not in your home right now.

> *(The director could have said, "Don't talk to me, you are falling out of your role." This would be quite acceptable. But, in my opinion, it is always preferable to keep the instructions congruent with the context of the simulation. The statement "Don't talk to me, you are falling out of your role" has a disapproving connotation, and may enhance resistance. The statement "I'm not in the living room" is perfectly logical. It represents a description of the "objective" simulation reality. Not only does it make sense, it also signifies to the protagonist that the reality of the simulation environment is the overriding context of the session and it should be adhered to.)*

(Bob): Where's the mail?

Linda: The mail can wait. Can we talk alone for a minute?

(Bob): What happened?

Linda: It's OK. I just have to talk to you about something I discussed with Sherri [a friend] today.

(Bob): Hmmm. . . What's she up to nowadays?

Linda: She is involved in many different things, most of them you wouldn't be interested in. You know, she is into decorating and Jack is planning an expansion of his business, but there are complications with his father. Incidently, did you know that Jack's father was once a diplomat? Imagine him a diplomat! With all the troubles that he creates for Jack, I would have thought that he was a bull fighter rather than a diplomat. If there is anyone in that family who seems like a diplomat it is Jack's mother. What a lady! She knows how to get around diplomatically. There you have a woman I admire. I wish I could be like her. Don't you think she's a great lady?

(Bob): Is that what you wanted to talk to me about? I mean, are you planning a personality change? I don't know. I like you as you are.

Linda: Oh, Bobby, I'm not planning a personality change. I was just saying to myself, "Here you have a true, marvellous lady." Don't you agree with me?

(Bob): I agree, she is really a swell lady. But what difference does it make? Ask Jack, she's his mother. Anyway, I'm completely lost. What did you want to tell me about Sherri?

Director: (to Linda) Is that how Bob reacts?

Linda: He (Jim) is terrific in the role.

(Bob): (repeats the last sentence) Anyway, I'm completely lost. What has this got to do with your discussion with Sherri?

Linda: Oh, right! How did I get to Jack's mother?

(Bob): Beats me! I was about to read the mail and you started talking about Sherri, and three minutes later I found myself discussing Jack's mother. *(General laughter. Linda smiles, too, but blushes, as if she was caught misbehaving.)* So what about your discussion with Sherri?

Linda: Never mind, it's not that important. Let's have dinner. *(She gets up from her chair [the couch] visibly perturbed and walks toward the dining room.)*

(Bob): Come on, Linda, you said it was important. What did I do to upset you? Look, I'm listening to you. It's only that sometimes you seem to wander away from the main thought and I get confused. I'm interested in what you have to say. So, would you please come back and tell me about your telephone conversation with Sherri.

Linda: What did you say?

(Bob): I said that I'm really interested in hearing about your conversation with Sherri, and the part you wanted to talk with me about.

Linda: No, before that.

(Bob): Before what?

Linda: Before that. You said that I was confused or something like that.

(Bob): Oh, I'm sorry, honey. I didn't want to upset you. Look, I didn't mean to criticize you; I'm used to your way of chatting. I just tried to be funny, that's all. I should have remembered that you are sensitive about being made fun of.

Linda: No, there was something you said that was important.

(Bob): The important thing to me is that I don't want to offend you with my sense of humor.

Linda: Oh, Bobby, you know that I like kidding you, too, and I like your sense of humor. I don't even mind when, sometimes, you humor my seriousness. That's OK, too. It's only that you are so organized in your thoughts and I'm not.

(Bob): *(raises his hands in a gesture of helplessness)* So what? What difference does it make anyway, and who cares that much?

Linda: I do, and maybe that's the trouble with me. You did say something before, and as soon as I heard it I had those feelings of being trapped and helpless. But for the life of me, I can't put my finger on it. What the hell was it? Oh well, let's go and eat dinner.

Director: OK. Thank you, Jim. *(Jim, the auxiliary, returns to his seat with the rest of the group members.)*

Connecting scene 1. The first scene did not provide a clear clue as to how to proceed next. Although there are several options, the director is still looking for a good clue. A connecting scene, using the Soliloquy technique, is usually indicated in such situations. Therefore, the director asked Linda to walk around the action space and say loudly what she is thinking and feeling right now. The director told her that this walk represents the walk from the living room to the dining area. "In real life," he explained, "the walk from the living room to the dining table may last a few seconds. But in simulation we can freeze time and stretch it as long as it is necessary. So, go ahead; walk around and soliloquize loudly."

Linda: *(begins to walk)* I really don't feel good right now. I don't know if I want to cry or not. He said something that hit my adrenalin like a gunshot. Suddenly I had those feelings. I only wish I could remember what the exact words were. Maybe the words are not important, and I'm reacting to something else, but what? *(It is obvious that Linda is locked in a "mental set." She repeats the same ideas, the same questions, and the same words, unable to extricate herself from this line of thinking. She needs help from an external source, i.e., an auxiliary. The auxiliary will have to free her from the cognitive "set" and move her to explore other possibilities. The best technique for this purpose is the Double.)*

Director: Linda, would you like to have a Double to help you?

Linda: Yes, I think I can use the help of a Double.

Director: OK. Why don't you look around and pick your Double from the group members.

It is recommended that whenever possible protagonists be given the opportunity to select their own auxiliaries. Protagonists tend to choose people they feel are best for the role(s) and with whom they have appropriate relationships. Selecting auxiliaries on the basis of the sociometric structure of the group proves to be extremely advantageous. The only justifications for departing from this practice are: (a) when the director has reasons to believe that it would be therapeutically beneficial for a particular member to practice a particular role; and (b) when a given member of the group has demonstrated a special talent in portraying certain role(s). The use of such a member may expedite the process and add to its quality.

Linda: (looks around) Stacy, would you like to be my Double?

Stacy: Sure. *(She gets up, enters the action space and stands beside Linda.)*

Director: OK, Stacy, you now assume the role of Linda. As Linda, you speak in the first person regardless of whether you refer to yourself or to the real Linda, who will be next to you. The two of you represent different voices inside one person. You talk to each other as if it was an internal debate, only this time everyone can hear it. Your task is to help Linda express her thoughts and feelings more clearly and openly. Avoid using questions as much as you can and try to use statements. Also, remember that the Double must not talk more than the protagonist. Now, Linda, when your Double says things you agree with, please tell her so. If, however, you disagree with your Double, correct her. We have done the Double many times before and you know the drill, right?

Double: I feel trapped and helpless.

Linda: Right.

Double: I feel a lump in my throat. What is he doing to me?

Linda: What am I doing to myself? I'm not sure he is doing anything to me. . .

Double: I feel angry.

Linda: No, I don't feel angry. . . well, actually, it's true. I do feel angry. I think I don't deserve to be a victim of these feelings.

Double: It's difficult for me to admit that I feel anger, especially towards Bob.

Linda: Hmmm!. . Well, I don't know. Usually I don't have difficulties in expressing anger.

Double: But it is more difficult with Bob because I love him. And it's difficult to be angry with someone I love.

Linda: That's true. It's definitely more difficult to be angry with someone you love because it makes you feel guilty once you finish venting your frustration. So maybe I'm more careful in getting angry with Bob because guilt is hard, too. That's true.

Double: I like to be a nice person.

Linda: Yes, I suppose so. There's nothing wrong with being nice. I would like to believe that people think of me as good person. I'm a good mother. I think little Ronny is happy with his mother.

Double: It's hard being nice and being angry at the same time.

Linda: No, not really. I can be a "bitch" for a few moments.

Double: But not with Bob.

Linda: Oh, yes. With Bob, too. Mind you, I don't like it particularly. But when he deserves my "bitching" at him, he gets it.

Double: Yeah, I can be a "bitch" when I want.

Linda: Bob is different! He's cool and controlled. Well, I suppose he gets all his anger out when he plays tennis, or when he watches a basketball game. Boy, does he get expressive watching those games. Sometimes I think that maybe this is a better way. Keep cool at home and at work, and then get it all out where no one can get hurt.

Double: I'm different, though. . .

Linda: That's for sure. We're different kind of people.

Double: I envy Bob.

Linda: Sometimes, but I don't think that this is my problem.

It is obvious that the Double is not getting anywhere with Linda, although some interesting points have emerged during the doubling. It seems that the Double's attempt to find clues suggesting the existence of a problem between Linda and Bob is not very productive. Linda does not indicate that she and her husband do not get along. The Double should start again empathizing with the feeling of being trapped and helpless and explore a different avenue. The director decided to stir the Double to a new line of doubling.

Director: Double, what about the feelings of helplessness?
Double: (catches the signal immediately) I still feel upset.
Linda: That's true. You know what? I think that I get these feelings only when I'm with adults.
Double: Adults give me these feelings. It's not only Bob. Other adults make me feel that way too.
Linda: That's right. Well, most of the time, of course, it is in the presence of Bobby that I feel that way. But I get it in the presence of others, too.
Double: Right, it isn't only Bobby. But it's usually men who make me feel that way.
Linda: I haven't thought about that. You may be right. But I'm not sure about that. I think that sometimes I feel the same with my female friends. Not with the good and close ones, with them I never feel that way.
Double: Anyway, I know that I feel like that around Bob. . .
Linda: Sometimes.
Double: Right, sometimes, and in any event, it's only with adults.
Linda: Right. I don't feel like that when I'm around children. Not that I've so many children around me. The ones I see are usually Ronny, and maybe a friend or two. But that's interesting.
Double: Yeah, I don't feel that way when I'm in control.
Linda: (stops walking and looks a little surprised) Hmmmm! Do you think that it has to do with control? I haven't looked at it that way. It's an interesting idea.
Double: I like to control.
Linda: (still seems preoccupied with her previous thoughts) You know what? I remember now that I did have these feelings, quite intensely, once when I was with Ronny. I remember it now because at the time I really got scared for a moment.
Director: OK, let's stop it there. Thank you, Stacy. *(She returns to her seat.)* Linda, it might be quite useful to see that scene. Would you like to do that?
Linda: Sure, why not?

Two of the several clues that emerged in the last part of the soliloquy seemed to have captured Linda's attention. These were the issue of *control* and the *incident with Ronny.* Which one should the director choose? There is a great temptation to select the former clue because it happened to be conveniently defined psychologically and because, at last, we have a clear direction on how to proceed with the next scenes. It should also be pointed out that once "control" was mentioned by the Double, it startled Linda for a moment. Indeed, many therapists are attracted to clues defined by the players in clear psychological labels. On the other hand, the second clue (i.e., the incident with Ronny) seems important, too, because the protagonist singled it out and because she said that it was an unusual experience for her. True, at this point of the session we do not have a clear idea where this clue may lead us. Following this clue may leave us uncertain a little longer. But since it was labeled by the protagonist as an important experience, it might be advised to follow her lead. There is a risk in pursuing this strategy. It is possible that the protagonist is leading the director, consciously or unconsciously, astray, away from the real problem. But as long as directors are aware of that possibility and keep reminding themselves of its existence, it might be interesting to pursue the second clue.

The Action Stage

B. Second Segment (Explorations and Interpretations)

(This segment includes two key scenes and one connecting scene.)

Director: Would you like to set the place where the situation occurred? Use chairs to denote the important objects in the situation. Also, tell us what time it is and who the people involved are.

Key scene 2. The scene is set in a public playground. The area is sealed by a fence, and it includes trees, benches, a sandbox, and several kinds of swings and slides. It is winter, either January or February. It is cold outside and there are still a few patches of snow on the ground. There are several children in the playground with their mothers. Ronny, who is three and a half years old, is playing with two other children in the sand box. Linda sits on a bench nearby, talking with another mother whom she became acquainted with during her visits to the playground.

Director: OK. We need someone to be Ronny and someone to be the other lady at the playground. How shall we call her?
Linda: By her real name, I suppose. Wilma.

Director: Now, you pick a Ronny and a Wilma. And let's have two volunteers to represent the two kids.

Linda: Jim can be Ronny, and Ellen, would you like to be Wilma?

Ellen: Yes.

Director: Can we have two volunteers to be Ronny's playmates? *(Carol and
Virginia volunteer. They sit on the floor together with Jim, who portrays
the role of Ronny, and play in the "sandbox." Linda and Wilma sit on a
bench, talking to each other.)*

Linda: So, how have you been, Wilma? I haven't seen you since last week.

Wilma: Oh, fine, thank you. And what about you?

Linda: I'm just fine, thank you. How's Tracy? How did you resolve the
problem she had with the piano teacher?

*Wilma: (She looks at the director helplessly, signaling that she has no idea how
to respond to that question. This is the time to use the Role-reversal technique.
Linda knows the story. She can become Wilma and model it for Ellen.)*

Director: Reverse roles. Linda, please move to Wilma's chair, and be her.
Ellen, please move to Linda's chair, and be her. Now, Ellen, what's
your name?

(Linda): Ellen. No, I mean Linda.

Director: Right. So, Linda, please repeat the last sentence that was said
by the real Linda when she sat in this chair.

(Linda): (laughs) I don't remember.

Director: You said something about Tracy and the piano teacher.

(Linda): That's right, now I remember. Yes, what happened with Tracy
and the problem with the piano teacher?

(Wilma): Oh, that? Well, now, listen to this. I went to the teacher and
told her the problem, and what do you think she said to me?

(Linda): What?

(Wilma): She said that she thought Tracy was just lazy, and that's why
she put all this pressure on her. Well, I was really angry. I told her
that she should have checked it with me before she yelled at Tracy,
and that I was surprised that with her teaching experience she
hadn't thought about it.

Director: Reverse roles again. Linda, please move back to your original
chair and be yourself. Ellen, you can move to the other chair and
be Wilma. Now, repeat Wilma's last sentence.

(Wilma): I was angry at her and told her she should've checked it with
me before yelling at Tracy.

Linda: But how did you convince Tracy to agree to go back to the piano
lessons?

(Wilma): Oh, I told her that everything was OK.

Linda: (to the director) No, that's not it. She didn't say this.

Director: (wondering whether it is important to continue with these role reversals for a conversation that seems to lead nowhere) OK, reverse roles, change chairs and identities.

(Wilma): I told her that I spoke with the teacher and apparently it was a case of misunderstanding. But I also told her what had happened, and maybe in the future she will be more open with her. I believe that children should be encouraged to stand on their own and be able to solve some problems by themselves. I mean, I don't mind doing the groundwork for her—after all, teachers can be over-powering—but Tracy is 11. She should be able to clear the mess herself. Don't you think so?

(Linda): Oh, I don't know. Maybe you were too harsh with her.

Linda: (falls out of her role as Wilma) That's exactly what I told her! I thought she was a little too demanding not only as mother but also as a person. She is a tough female. *(resumes her role as Wilma.)*

(Wilma): Oh, Linda. You've no idea how much easier it is when you let the kids clean up their own mess with some background help from us. *(pauses for a minute)* Look at that, Linda. Look at Ronny. He throws sand all over the place. Ronny, *(she yells)* come here!

Director: OK. Reverse roles back, everyone to her original role. Wilma (Ellen) would you repeat the last sentence.

(Wilma): (yells) Ronny, come here!

Linda: (to the director) I need a Double.

Director: Fine, choose anyone you want.

Linda: Stacy was a good Double. Would you like to do that again, Stacy?

Stacy: Sure. *(picks up a chair and sits beside Linda)*

(Wilma): (repeats the sentence again, yelling) Ronny, come here!

Linda: (to the Double) Wilma is all right. She's OK. She's a very responsible person and fun to be with. But I don't like this yelling at Ronny. It doesn't sound right.

Double: I don't like her yelling at *my* child.

Linda: Right.

Double: She should yell at her child if she wants to yell.

Linda: Right.

Double: I'm Ronny's mother.

Linda: Right.

Double: I don't like that.

Linda: No, I don't. *(It is obvious that, contrary to the practice of the technique, the Double is talking more than the protagonist. Ordinarily this calls for intervention on the part of the director who has to coach the Double not to dominate the conversation and instead draw the protagonist out. This is simply done by instructing the Double in front of the protagonist and sometimes by whispering the instruction in the Double's ear without interrupting the interaction. But in the present scene it appears that in voicing Linda's internal feelings and thoughts the Double managed to get her progressively agitated. So the director decided to let the Double continue to be the more verbal of the two and watch for Linda's reaction.)*

Double: She may be a fun person to be with, but I'm the mother. If she doesn't like what Ronny is doing she should tell me and ask me to do something about it.

Linda: Yeah, that's true. But what makes me really uneasy is the tone of her voice.

Double: The yelling is unpleasant.

Linda: Right.

Double: It's frightening.

Linda: It gives me the creeps.

Double: So, what am I going to do about it?

Linda: Nothing. I'll put Ronny on my lap and talk to him softly. He'll calm down that way.

Double: I would have liked to tell Wilma to mind her own business, but I am not going to do so.

Linda: That's right.

Double: I'm a coward.

Linda: If that's what you want to call it, then I'm a coward. But I don't see it that way.

Double: I'm very good at rationalizing things. Here I feel my privacy is invaded, and I'm not going to do anything about it.

Linda: (visibly upset) You're damned right that's what I'm going to do. I'm going to protect my baby. *(At this point, the director can cut the action. There are two possible clues for moving on to the next scene. One is Linda's reluctance to tell Wilma to mind her own business and leave Ronny alone. The second clue is Linda's need to protect her child. Linda behaves, however, in a manner that suggests that something is about to happen. She seems to be progressively uneasy yet still evinces a great measure of self-control. Furthermore, to the objective observer the scene has not been sufficiently upsetting until now to deserve her earlier description of it as a "scary incident." Therefore, it should be allowed to continue for a short while.)*

Linda: Ronny, come here for a moment!

(Ronny): I don't want to.

Linda: Come here! I want to tell you something.

(Ronny): I'm busy, Mom.

Director: Reverse roles. Ronny, change roles with your mother. *(Jim and Linda reverse roles. He goes to the bench, and Linda goes to the sandbox.)* Now, Ronny *(portrayed by Linda),* please repeat the last words you said to your mother before the role reversal.

(Ronny): (portrayed by Linda) I don't want to!

(Linda): (portrayed by Jim) Come here, I need to tell you something.

(Ronny): I don't want to!

(Linda): Ronny, I told you to come to me right now!

(Ronny): OK. *(Reluctantly leaves the sandbox and approaches Linda and Wilma)* What?!

Director: (to Ronny/Linda) What's the matter Ronny? Are you upset about something?

(Ronny): Of course, I'm upset. I was in the middle of something important when she interrupted me. That's not fair.

Director: I can understand that. But maybe she has to tell you something important.

(Ronny): Everything is important to her.

Director: Well, why don't you tell her what's on your mind. I know that you are a little boy and you can't express yourself like an adult. But here you can try.

(Ronny): I'm a good boy, right Mommy? *(to the director)* Let's reverse roles again. I want to be Linda and Jim can be Ronny. *(They reverse roles.)*

(Ronny): (repeats sheepishly.) I'm a good boy, right Mommy?

Linda: (tries to seat him on her lap, but Jim is too big; Laughter) Yes, you're a good boy.

(Ronny): Can I go back to play now?

Linda: (to the director) Now he suddenly runs away from me.

(Ronny): (runs away)

Linda: (shouts) Ronny, don't run away! Ronny!

Double: He runs away from me.

Linda: Right. I don't like it when he runs away from me like that. I can't stand it!

Director: Thank you, all the helpers. *(The helpers return to their seats among the rest of the group members. Linda remains in the action space.)*

Connecting scene 2. The director and Linda are in the middle of the action space.

Director: You said "I can't stand it." What did you mean?

Linda: I don't know. It's a strange thing. I simply can't stand him running

away from me. When he behaves that way I have the same feelings
of helplessness I had when I spoke with Bob.

Director: What does "running away" remind you of?

Linda: (thinks for a while) I don't know.

Director: OK. I want you to run around the action space and as you do
this please say whatever comes to your mind. I'll ask the group to
encourage you and repeat the words, "Run, run, Linda, run."

Linda: What? Do you want me to run here?

Director: Yes.

Linda: Do I have to do it?

Director: No, you don't have to. But I'd like you to do it. It may help.

Linda: OK. *(She begins to run, first slowly and then faster.)*

Group: Run, Linda, run. *(rhythmically)* Run. . . run. . . run. . .

*Linda: (She runs faster six or seven rounds and then she suddenly stops, grabs
her head in her hand, and sobs, pronouncing the words slowly.)* Oh, hell!
Now I do remember.

Director: (waits a moment and lets her cry) What's the matter? What are you
crying about?

Linda: (still sobbing) I don't want to run away. It reminds me of something
frightful that happened a long time ago.

Director: When was that?

Linda: A long time ago. I was seven or eight years old.

Director: Let's see that scene. We'll wind the clock back to the time that
you were eight years old. Where are you? And who are the people
involved in the situation?

Key scene 3. Linda is eight years old. She is alone in front of her parents'
house. She has just come back from school and no one is at home. It is
cold outside and there is snow on the ground. She has been waiting for
a while. The time is about four o'clock in the afternoon.

Linda: (sits on the fence of the house talking to herself) Where is everybody?
I don't want to be alone. I'm waiting a long time. I don't know what
to do. I have all kinds of thoughts in my head and I don't know
what to do. I'm afraid to be alone, I'm afraid to be alone, I'm afraid
to be alone. . . *(cries again)* What can I do? I've got to do something.
I'll go around the block and see if I can find anybody I know. *(She
walks around the action space aimlessly, first slowly, then she runs and
cries.)*

Director: (Asks Stacy, quietly, to join Linda as a Double.) I'm going to give
you a Double, Linda, OK?

Linda: (cries quietly) Mommy! Daddy! Where are you?

Double: (overwhelmed by the situation, begins to cry as well) I don't want to be alone, I'm afraid.

Linda: I'm a little girl. I don't know what to do.

Double: I'm frightened.

Linda: I'm frightened.

Double: What shall I do? Maybe I should stay in front of the house. They'll come along soon. They know it's the time for me to come home from school.

Linda: They aren't here. What shall I do? I can't think and I can't decide.

Director: What happens next?

Linda: My mother finally comes.

Director: Who can portray your mother?

Linda: Maybe Carol? *(The director motions to Carol to come in.)*

(Mother): Linda! *(Linda runs and hugs her, still crying.)* What's the matter, darling, why are you crying?

Linda: Mommy, mommy, where have you been?

(Mother): I went shopping. What is the matter?

Linda: I was afraid you'd never come back.

(Mother): Of course, I'll come back. I would never leave you. Never.

Linda: But you did. *(The director signals to the Double to leave the action space.)*

(Mother): I was delayed in traffic for a little while. Oh, I'm so sorry you had to wait outside alone. I really am. You were really frightened, weren't you? Oh, my darling, I'm so sorry.

Director: (to Linda) Is this OK? Is that how mother responds?

Linda: Yes. It's pretty close. She also said that I should have used my head and gone to Mrs. Dora, the neighbor, and waited there. She would have taken care of the situation.

(Mother): Oh, Linda, poor thing. I'm so sorry, but you should have used your head and gone to Mrs. Dora and waited there.

Linda: I didn't know what to think. I didn't know what to do.

Director: Reverse roles. Linda, change with your mother. *(The director wants to get Linda out of her role so she becomes less emotional. A change of role usually accomplishes that purpose.)*

(Mother, portrayed by Linda): (stops crying) Look, next time don't wait outside. Go to Mrs. Dora and wait for us there.

(Linda, portrayed by Carol): OK.

(Mother): I hope that this will never happen again. But if by chance it does, please use your head and wait for me or Daddy at Mrs. Dora's. Would you do this?

Director: Reverse roles again.
(Mother): *(repeats last words)* Would you do this?
Linda: *(nods her head affirmatively)*
(Mother): Everything is fine now. Let's go inside.
Director: OK, thank you.

C. *Third Segment (Alternative Behavior)*

(This segment contains two key scenes.)

Key scene 4. The idea for this scene is suggested by the director. It takes place in the action place and in the present.

Linda: *(to the director)* You know, I'd totally forgotten this incident until today. Maybe my uneasiness with regard to not thinking straight has to do with this experience.
Director: Maybe. Look, let's move the clock forward to the present. Now you're an adult again. What I would like to do is to have a meeting between Linda, the adult, and Linda, the eight-year-old girl, right here in this room. Perhaps the two of you should meet and you can explain to little Linda the whole situation from an adult's perspective. Would you like to do this?
Linda: That sounds like a good idea.
Director: Who can represent little Linda?
Linda: *(looks around)* How about Carol? *(Carol comes inside the action space. Linda puts two chairs, one facing the other, and sits on one of them. Carol sits on the other chair.)*
Big Linda: Let me ask you a question, Linda. Do you think that the feeling of helplessness and entrapment I feel when I talk with Bob, when my thoughts wander away, are related to this incident? *(looks at the director)* That's what he said.
Director: Who? What?
Linda: Bob. He said something about my "thoughts wandering away." And that's what upset me. *(turns to little Linda)* Well, do you?
Little Linda: I don't know.
Director: Reverse roles. *(The reason for the role reversal is twofold: first, to get more information since Carol, in the role of little Linda, couldn't answer the question; second, now that Linda sees the experience from an adult's point of view, the Role-reversal will create a further distance from the present and hopefully will help her to see things in a new light. To start with, it might be a good idea to show Linda the absurdity of all this.)*

(Little Linda, portrayed by the real Linda): It looks like it. I think I carry with me the feelings I had in this experience and connect them with any hint of implied criticism for not using my head, for not thinking straight.

(Big Linda, now portrayed by Carol): But you're a little girl. You're entitled to think that way.

(Little Linda): I know. As a matter of fact, I do feel upset for not being able to use straight thinking.

(Big Linda): Would you believe me if I told you I still feel that way now, too?

(Little Linda): Really, after all these years?

(Big Linda): Yes.

(Little Linda): But that's silly.

Director: Reverse roles, again. Linda, move over here and be big Linda. And Carol, you will represent little Linda.

(Little Linda): (repeats) But that's silly.

(Big Linda): I know, it does sound silly, doesn't it?

(Little Linda): You mean you can't grow out of it? Gee, it looks as if I'm going to suffer from it for the rest of my life.

(Big Linda): Perhaps not. Now I'm determined to do something about it.

(Little Linda): Well, don't count on me. I'm a little girl. I'm not sure I can help you there.

(Big Linda): Don't worry. I'm not going to ask you to bail me out. It's not your responsibility, it's mine.

(Little Linda): What can you do then? Please tell me.

(Big Linda): Maybe now that I know where these feelings come from I won't have them anymore.

(Little Linda): OK, if you say so.

Director: (to little Linda) Are you completely convinced?

(Little Linda): (gets the hint) As a matter of fact, I'm not completely convinced. This might not be sufficient.

(Big Linda): Hmmmm. . . what do you suggest?

(Little Linda): Maybe you could go home and write 50 times, "Linda is not a little girl anymore. She can think freely any way she wants." That's what the teacher makes us do in school.

(Big Linda): (smiles) Yes, I'm not surprised. It makes sense that you would suggest this for me.

(Little Linda): Well, I'm only eight years old. I told you that I'm a little girl.

(Big Linda): That's fine. You're a smart girl, Linda.

(Little Linda): Am I going to remain smart when I grow up and be like you?

(Big Linda): Yes, that I can promise you. You'll remain smart.

(Little Linda): Oh, that's wonderful. May I go now? I want to play.

(Big Linda): Yes, you may go. *(Carol returns to her seat among the group members. Linda remains in the action space.)*

Director: Was she helpful to you?

Linda: Not really, but she's a little girl. What do you expect of her?

Director: Well, I don't know. According to you, your reactions to any hint of criticism about the way you think are also based on the responses of an eight-year-old girl.

Linda: That's true. But I'm not going to write that sentence 50 times. That's ridiculous. I think that now that I know where all that comes from, I'll be fine.

Director: Little Linda said she wasn't completely convinced. She wanted you to do more.

Linda: What do you suggest?

Director: Maybe you can talk about it with someone. Is there any person who might be able to help you in the future?

Linda: Bob is the best person I can think of.

Director: So, let's bring Bob here and do it.

Key scene 5. The scene is set in Bob and Linda's living room. It is a Future Projection situation— a discussion which never took place, but may occur in the future. Linda arranges the room: the couch, the chairs, etc. She asks Jim to represent Bob again. The time is late evening after Ronny has gone to bed.

Linda: Bobby, I had a very interesting experience I want to share with you.

(Bob): Oh, what was that?

Linda: I found out that my sensitivity to any implied criticism about the way my thoughts tend to wander is related to something that happened to me when I was a little girl.

(Bob): Aha! It turned out to be psychological after all. What's the story?

Linda: Well, when I was eight years old, I came home from school one day and no one was home. I got scared, of course. When my mother finally came home and found me crying, she told me that I should have used my head and stayed with the neighbors instead of waiting for her in the street. But I was so frightened that I couldn't think straight.

(Bob): And since then every time I tell you that I can't follow your way of thinking it brings out those feelings, is that what it is?

Linda: Yes, but it isn't only you. That's what I'm trying to tell you. There's nothing personal against you, you see. It's true for anyone who makes such innuendos.

(Bob): I'm sure glad it has nothing to do with *my* behavior. I always wondered what I was doing to upset you. I didn't think it had anything to do with my humor, because you seem to like it. Now it makes sense to me. OK, from now on I promise that I'll try to be more careful with my reactions to you when you free associate. You don't do it all the time, you know.

Linda: Well, that's what I want to talk with you about. I appreciate your willingness to be more careful, but I need some help.

(Bob): Oh, what kind of help?

Linda: I need to get rid of that sensitivity.

(Bob): And you think that if I change my behavior it wouldn't help you to overcome it. That makes sense. So you need to change, not I, right?

Linda: I think so.

(Bob): It sounds logical. How can I help you, then?

Linda: I think that having found this out by myself is going to help a lot. But little Linda thought it wouldn't be enough.

(Bob): I beg your pardon? Little Linda? Who's she?

Linda: Oh, I did this role playing and I met with myself as a little girl. Someone was myself as an eight-year-old girl. *(smiles)* She suggested that I write 50 times the sentence, "Linda is not a little girl anymore" or something like that.

(Bob): (smiles) Little girl's idea of correcting behavior, eh?

Linda: Well, yes. But seriously, how can I remind myself that these feelings aren't relevant anymore?

(Bob): (looks at the director) We need an expert's help here. *(Linda nods her head in agreement.)*

Director: You may decide to agree on a code word so that whenever Linda feels that she'll use it, you will say something to her.

Linda: That's an idea!

(Bob): Let's decide on something funny. That'll take the seriousness out of the whole thing.

Linda: C'mon, Bobby, this *is* serious!

(Bob): I know, I know. What I mean is that we can make it look funny. *(to the director)* Isn't there something in psychology that says if you think that something is funny, you eventually believe it is?

Director: Yes, there is. Often the way you feel depends on what you are telling yourself.

(Bob): (to Linda) You see, there you are!

Linda: OK, so what if, whenever I get these feelings, I say "Bingo"?

(Bob): And I'll respond: B-8.

Linda: No, you should say "DON'T be 8." *(They laugh.)*

(Bob): That's funny, but will you remember to say it?

Linda: Oh, probably not. But what the heck. Let's try it. If it doesn't work we'll think of something else.

Director: Thank you all. *(Jim returns to his seat. The director and Linda sit on two chairs in the middle of the action space. They are ready now to proceed with the last portion of the session, the Closure stage.)*

The Closure Stage

A. Sharing

Director: (to Linda) Would you like to hear sharing from the group members?

Linda: Sure.

Director: (to the group) Linda shared with us some of her personal experiences. Perhaps you are now ready to share with her some of yours. If there is anything in your life that is somewhat similar to the situations, reactions, and feelings demonstrated by Linda, would you be willing to tell us about them? Also, if Linda's portrayal triggered something within you, please tell us about it. This is the time for mutual sharing, not for critical feedback. Who wants to start?

Betty: I wasn't involved as an auxiliary, but boy, was I involved in the scenes! You know, when you were there as a little girl, frightened and helpless, I couldn't help crying, too. What an experience, wow! I identified with you so much. I really did. *(Some other group members join Betty in agreement.)*

Stacy: I suppose that as a Double I had the best opportunity to empathize with you, Linda. You say that I was crying, too. And I wasn't acting. Actually, I was crying partly for you and partly for me. It reminded me of all those times that I felt misunderstood by *my* own parents. As you know, I'm still struggling with some of these feelings. I saw that your mother tried to be understanding; I suppose mine does, or did, too. But parents can say, maybe unintentionally, harmful things to their children. And these things stay with us for years.

Maybe they can't avoid it. After all, they can't watch every word they say. It's unnatural. You're lucky that you were able to trace it to something specific. Maybe this will help you understand why you're behaving the way you do. But sometimes we aren't so lucky. Then what?

John: Then we go to a therapist.

Stacy: Very funny, John. Do you have anything to share?

Jim: C'mon, John.

John: Strangely enough, I did identify with Bob. Not that I wasn't touched by your experience, Linda. I was. But I don't remember a similar experience in my life. As a man, I found it easier to identify with Bob. It reminded me of my ex-wife who used to complain that I didn't understand her. And we forever had arguments because I didn't have a clue as to what she was talking about or what I was doing wrong. I'm not saying that my situation is exactly similar to the one that exists between you and Bob. The two of you seem to have a good marriage. Mine was rocky. But I could see Bob's side of being helpless, too, of not knowing what to do. I can tell you it's a lousy situation to be in. You're frustrated, angry, and helpless. So what do you do? You spread your anger all around, particularly on your family.

Bill: Or you go and act it out elsewhere.

Virginia: What do you mean?

Bill: You feel that you're better off being away from home. Then you hang out in singles' bars drinking and chasing other women.

Virginia: I was intrigued by Carol's portrayal of little Linda. She really stuck to her role beautifully. And when Linda, that is, big Linda, asked her for advice she told her to write a sentence 50 times; a great line from an eight-year-old girl. I thought that this was terrific. Good for you, Carol!

Linda: Right, I thought so too, Carol. I think that that line showed me the absurdity of the whole situation. I thought to myself, "Hey, what do you want from this little girl? Let her play peacefully. That's kids' stuff."

Carol: (blushing) Well, I decided to remain the little girl I was supposed to be.

Linda: And I'm glad you did, Carol. Obviously you can be decisive when you want.

Carol: It is easier to do when you're someone else. My problem is to be decisive when I'm myself.

Director: Carol, in the beginning of the session you said that you had the feeling that Linda's problem might have some bearings on yours. What did you find out?

Carol: Well, the feelings of helplessness are the same. As you can guess, I often have the same feelings. But my reaction is to give up and do nothing. Linda was upset about these feelings. I become paralyzed, depressed, and shameful. But I think that Linda's session and Jim's, too, give me more courage to become a protagonist next time. I'll try to keep that courage for the next session. Anyway, I promised that I would be the next protagonist. So, let's not talk about me now. I'll have my turn next week, I hope.

Bill: I must admit, Linda, that I envy both you and Bob. I wished I could be as open to my ex-wife as Bob. Maybe it takes a good marriage to do it. Or perhaps having a good sense of humor does it. But from what I've gathered, Bob can diffuse a lot of tension with this approach. I become so serious and tense when I find myself in conflict situations that sometimes I feel that my reaction makes things even worse. Well, I don't know how open Bob is. Maybe you portrayed him that way?

Linda: I wouldn't describe him as a very open person, maybe because he tends to be an introvert. When you compare his controlled reactions to my enthusiasm, he is anything but "very open." But you're right that he is an understanding person. Of course, his sense of humor is often a great asset.

Bill: Be that as it may, I sat here feeling a little envious.

Linda: Thank you, Bill, it's nice of you to say so.

Bill: I really mean it, Linda.

Linda: I can see that.

Virginia: I liked the fact that the problem wasn't left at the point that you had your good cry. I know that it helps a lot, and some of us here also wiped our eyes. Don't get me wrong, I think that this kind of crying warms your heart and makes you feel better. But I thought that it was very important to have the final session with Bob—to discuss the problem and find a practical solution for it.

John: What? Do you think that the "Bingo" business is a practical solution?

Virginia: Why not? If it helps her to change the reaction from an irrelevant childish one to a more rational, adult reaction, what does it matter if it is "Bingo" or anything else? I liked it. Why do we always have to look for deadly serious solutions?

John: I don't know. I hope it works well for Linda.

Virginia: Look, if this one doesn't, at least both of them know what the issue is and they can find something else that will work. I know from my experience that sometimes I can change my attitude by doing really little things. I remember that once I thought that I had to educate everyone around me by telling them what they should or shouldn't do. And I mean *everyone!* Then, one day I met a guy who I liked. Naturally, I started telling him what to do and what not to do. One evening he came to my apartment with a little bag, went to the bathroom and put on a skirt. It was so funny. He didn't say anything but I got the message: If I wanted to make him be like me, he'd become something funny and ridiculous.

John: Maybe you're right. I'm skeptical.

Virginia: But John, that's you. You're a skeptical person. I've the feeling that behind your skepticism there's a warm pussycat.

John: No kidding! I thought I hid it very well.

Virginia: You have to try harder. (*general laughter*)

Director: Any other sharing?

Stacy: I just wanted to thank you, Linda, for being the protagonist today.

The Closure Stage

B. Analysis

This last portion of the session is devoted to summarizing the learning that occurred during the treatment hour. But in Linda's case it seemed unnecessary. First, part of it had already been discussed during the sharing. Second, if there were any need for additional interpretation, it could wait until the next session when Linda would be asked to review her therapeutic experience of this session. So at this point the director thanked Linda and the rest of the group, and the meeting was adjourned.

CHAPTER 11

Applications in Family and Individual Therapy

Customarily, group psychotherapy is thought of as a form of treatment involving a number of clients who serve as a miniature therapeutic community. Two of the many characteristics of this therapeutic setting are: 1) the number of its participants, which ranges from seven to 10 (e.g., Yalom, 1975, pp. 284-285); and 2) the fact that the group is assembled by the therapist and becomes an integral unit only *after* it has been established. But there are other forms of psychotherapy where these two characteristics are absent. These involve a smaller number of clients who already constitute an integral unit prior to their involvement in therapy. The best known examples of these are family therapy, the treatment of dyads (most notably marital therapy) and, of course, individual treatment. The present chapter will describe the principles for the application of clinical role playing in family therapy and in individual treatment, along with case illustrations.

The use of clinical role playing in marital therapy actually falls between these two forms of therapy and has some characteristics of both. It can be conducted in a group format, that is, with the participation of eight to 10 clients comprising several married couples. In that respect it is similar to the application of the *multiple families setting,* which will be described under the family therapy section. Or it can be conducted in dyads, that is, with one married couple. In that case the principles for its application are a combination of those discussed under the treatment of *a single family unit* and that of *an individual client.* For the sake of avoiding tedious repetition it was decided that marital therapy would be left out.

FAMILY THERAPY WITH CLINICAL ROLE PLAYING

Clinical role playing has been an integral part of family therapy for many years. The ways in which it has been utilized in this form of therapy has varied both in terms of importance and purpose. In some instances it constituted a central intervention modality, as evidenced in the psychodramatic approach (e.g., Starr, 1977). In other instances it was introduced to the treatment of families in conjunction with other therapeutic approaches (Guldner, 1983; Hollander, 1983), often in a peripheral, secondary capacity. Some approaches utilized clinical role playing for both diagnostic and remedial purposes. But some applied it primarily for diagnostic purposes, that is, to make the clients aware of their family problem(s), whereas others introduced it mainly to facilitate the acquisition of better, alternative behaviors.

When clinical role playing is applied as the main form of intervention, it is important to distinguish between two kinds of family therapy settings: (a) the treatment of multiple families, and (b) the treatment of a single family unit.

Multiple Families Setting

This kind of family therapy (e.g., Guldner, 1982) is similar to the group therapy setting. It, too, involves between seven to 10 clients or whatever number that allows for three or four family units—parents and their children (nine years and older)—who participate as one group. Guldner, for instance, included even more participants in his group, up to five or six family units. Although it is true that, in general, the procedures used for the treatment of this group are the same as those recommended for group therapy, often some changes are required given the special characteristics of the multiple families group. These characteristics are as follows:

- The multiple families group consists of several cohesive subgroups. These subgroups (i. e., the different family units) have been formed prior to the formation of the therapeutic group and should remain that way throughout the treatment. In other words, in regular therapy groups the sociometric structure of any given group is formed as the treatment progresses. With multiple families treatment, the situation is quite different. There, the sociometric structure of the group has been formed in advance and its integrity must remain intact. In fact, any attempt to dissolve this structure and replace it with another one will be contraindicative and destructive.

• In each subgroup of clients who participate in the treatment are the original members (or players) involved in the protagonist's problem(s). In a regular therapy group *all* the protagonists' auxiliaries represent people in absentia. In a multiple families group the auxiliaries may be either the persons originally involved in the portrayed situations or substitutes for these original players.

A typical clinical role playing session with multiple families groups begins with the emergence of a protagonist. Since the protagonist's problem involves other members of his or her family, the first segment of the Action stage, presenting the problem, is portrayed with the participation of all the original members who are available in the session. The second segment of the Action stage (i.e., explorations and interpretations) is conducted the same way one conducts a regular group therapy session. Generally, therefore, the selected auxiliaries here will be members of *other* family units who will represent the original members. The original members of the protagonist's family will be called again to serve as auxiliaries in the third segment of the Action stage where alternative behaviors are explored. The greatest departure from the procedure employed in a regular group therapy is evident in the Closure stage. There, each family unit discusses *separately* the relevance of the protagonist's portrayal to their own family constellation; only then do all reconvene to share with the entire group the learning gleaned from the session.

A Single Family Unit

This therapeutic setting is the conventional form of family therapy. It involves members of one family unit, which typically consists of three to five persons (parents and their children). Given the unique nature of this group (i. e., the small number of the participating clients and their already established common history), its internal dynamic is considerably different from that evident in a regular therapy group. Some of the special characteristics of the single family group are as follows:

• All the members have extremely intense emotional ties to each other. The difficulties of one member strongly influence the behavior and feelings of other members. This makes it harder to introduce a change in the behavior of one person without affecting that of the others.

- The strong emotional ties among the family members also make it difficult to introduce new objective perceptions. It is important, therefore, to ask members to assume not only their own original roles but also those of the other members who are present in the session. In addition, in this form of psychotherapy the therapist-director often actively participates in the production. He or she may assume the role of a Double and is often required to provide more active guidance to the auxiliaries.

- Because of the emotional interdependency among the family members, the difficulties of the declared protagonist are often reinforced and maintained (sometimes even created) either by the personal attitudes and behavior of each of the other members or by the family structure and culture. A change in the protagonist's perception and behavior may require a similar change in one or more other family members. Given the existence of such a constellation, it is not unusual to alter the protagonist in some of the enacted scenes. The prime protagonist is always the individual who volunteered first to present the complaint. Although that individual will always remain the protagonist in the first and third segments of the Action stage, other members of the family may temporarily become protagonists during the second—exploration and interpretation—segment. This practice is typically reserved for family therapy. It is not recommended in the use of clinical role playing in either group psychotherapy or in individual treatment. The preferred guideline there is that the protagonist remains the same person throughout the session.

The progression of the treatment session with a single family follows the same general guidelines and stages of every clinical role playing session. It begins with the Warm-up stage and proceeds to the Action stage, which contains three segments. The Closure stage often provides opportunities to explore alternatives for better coping behaviors with regard not only to the protagonist's personal difficulties, but also to the behavior of other family members.

Of the two family therapy settings mentioned above I have chosen to illustrate a case of treating a single family unit.

A CASE ILLUSTRATION

The family included four members: the parents and their two teenage children. The father, Richard, age 45, worked as a manager in a large company. The mother, Gloria, age 43, was employed as a part-time music teacher. Richard and Gloria had been married for 18 years. The family sought psychological treatment because their youngest child, Sara, was displaying behavioral difficulties both at home and in school. Sara, age 14, was described by her parents as "an unmanageable and undisciplined person." At home she constantly fought with her parents, especially with her mother who complained that she was "tired of Sara's defiant, aggressive, and erratic behavior." In school she tended to be uncooperative and quarrelsome, and would often miss classes, that is, disappear for an hour or two. Her scholastic achievements were low in spite of the fact that she was considered an intelligent person. The school counselor who worked with Sara for a while thought that her problems were related to the family constellation and advised the mother to seek family therapy. Sara's brother, Adam, age 16, was a brilliant student—sharp and witty. The parents were very proud of Adam and his achievements and considered him to be "a wonderful son, and a fun person to be with." Adam loved his sister but did not know how to relate to her volatile behavior. He labeled Sara's frequent fights with her parents as "the battles of Sara-jevo" referring to the famous assassination of Archduke Francis Ferdinand in Sarajevo, Yugoslavia, 1914 (the incident that precipitated World War I).

The session to be described below begins with the Action stage. The session itself started with a brief warm-up in which all the participants discussed the previous session and its effect on the behavior of each member of the family. Then Gloria described a couple of unpleasant incidents involving Sara and her that had occurred during the past week. The director suggested that it might be useful to focus on these issues; then, turning to Gloria and Sara he asked: "Who would like to be the protagonist today?"

Gloria: I don't mind being the protagonist since I brought up the subject. But I don't know which of the two incidents you want me to describe.
Director: Perhaps you can tell us, briefly, about them?
Sara: (interrupts) Why don't you bring up the issue of my request to go away for the weekend?
Gloria: OK. I don't mind doing that one.

The Action Stage

A. *First Segment (Presenting the Problem)*

(This segment included one key scene and one connecting scene.)

Key scene 1. The scene is held in the living room. There is a couch, two armchairs, a piano, and one wall unit. The time is Thursday evening, Dick sits on the couch (*made of a couple of chairs*) and reads a newspaper while Gloria watches TV. Adam is not there. Dick and Gloria assume their positions. A minute later, Sara enters the room and sits next to her mother.

Sara: Mom, can I go for the weekend to Pickville?
Gloria: What do you mean "for the weekend"?
Sara: For the weekend, you know. Saturday and Sunday.
Gloria: You mean staying overnight in Pickville?
Sara: Yes.
Gloria: Absolutely not!
Sara: (to the director) That's exactly how she always responds (*mimics her mother's voice*) "Absolutely not!" Always "Absolutely not." Everytime I ask her something for myself she always refuses me.
Gloria: I don't understand. What on earth are you going to do in Pickville? How are you going to get there? Are you planning to go there alone?
Sara: (to the director) You see! That's typical of her. First she says "no" and then she asks questions.
    (Sara has twice talked to the director instead of addressing her mother. It is obvious that she still finds it difficult to get into the role playing. This behavior raises the possibility that Sara resists the request to become involved in the role playing or that she tries to manipulate her mother by using the director. The director plans to ignore Sara's attempts to use him against the mother, and to let the scene continue for a while without interference, in the hope that Sara will become involved. A direct intervention will be necessary only if the noncooperative behavior persists too long.)
Gloria: Well?
Sara: Now you're asking? Julie invited me, Suzie, Mike, and Rob to visit her grandparents' farm in Pickville and spend the night there. Did you think that I'm stupid enough to go to Pickville alone? *(raises her voice)* Why don't you ask all these questions first instead of saying "no"? Why can everybody else spend the night with their friends whenever they want, and I'm treated like a retarded child?
Gloria: I'm not treating you as a retarded child, and you'd better stop that nonsense.
Sara: What nonsense? *(begins to yell)* You see? Now you tell me that I talk nonsense.
Gloria: There's no need to shout. If you want to discuss something with me, that's fine. But I'll not do it through shouting or fighting.

Dick: (raises his head from behind the imaginary newspaper) What's that noise all about?

Gloria: Sara wants to go to Pickville for the *whole* weekend.

Dick: Is that a reason to shout? Why can't I have some peace and quiet here?

Sara: (angrily) What's so great about "peace and quiet"? Everytime I try to say something I get this speech about "peace and quiet." What is it? Are we supposed to live in an aquarium?

Dick: Look, I don't know why you get upset every three minutes. If you've something to ask your mother, think of ways of doing it without letting all our neighbors into the details of the conversation.

Sara: Is that what you're concerned about? The neighbors? What about me? Why is it always me against the neighbors?

Dick: I'm not concerned about the neighbors, Sara. That wasn't my point. I just wish you would learn to talk to us without shouting. There's no reason for that style. We're not deaf.

Gloria: (to Dick) What about the weekend? What do you think?

Dick: What weekend?

Gloria: The weekend Sara wants to spend in Pickville?

Dick: What about it?

Sara: This is ridiculous! What's the matter with everybody? No one hears anything. *(upset)* That's the reason I have to shout. Maybe if I yell, someone will hear me.

Dick: Look, if you plan on being rude, you'd better leave the room.

Sara: (angrily) Fine!!! *(She leaves the room swearing.)*

Gloria: (to the director) You see, that's how it is. I'm really tired of it.

Connecting scene 1. Gloria remains alone in the action space. The director asks her to soliloquize. He instructs her to walk around the action space and say loudly what she is feeling and thinking at this moment (i.e., following the end of the first scene).

Gloria: I'm tired of these conversations with her. Why is it that most of our discussions end with bitterness, accusations, and fights? Sometimes I really want to cry, or to yell "Enough of that!" What did I do wrong? OK, I admit that sometimes I say "no" before I ask questions. But I tried to correct it. I asked her questions about the trip. I also asked Dick for his opinion. And before I was given a chance to think it over we had another fight. Now she's left the room angry. It's becoming too much for me.

Director: May I be your Double, Gloria?

Gloria: Sure.

(Typically, the director is not supposed to assume an auxiliary role and leave the session unattended. But in this kind of family therapy such brief involvements in the enactment are necessary. The decision to become an auxiliary was based on the director's reasoning that a brief Soliloquy is needed in order to move to the next key scene as soon as possible. For this, a meaningful clue had to be identified. Trusting his own ability to find such a clue through the introduction of the Double technique, the director offered himself as a Double.)

Gloria: As I said, I'm tired of being the target of her anger.

Double: I'm tired of it.

Gloria: Right.

Double: Sometimes I want to yell "Enough!" or even cry.

Gloria: The truth is that sometimes I do cry. But I do it at night so that no one sees it.

Double: I cry because I'm hurting.

Gloria: And also because I feel guilty.

Double: I feel guilty because I'm supposed to be a good mother.

Gloria: (tears appear in her eyes) I want to be a good loving mother, and I behave like . . . . Oh, I don't know . . . sometimes I hate the way I behave.

Double: I feel that I'm a failure.

Gloria: That's it. I think you've got it. I feel that I've failed as a mother. This is a more accurate description of my feeling—a failure.

Double: And I find this feeling unbearable.

Gloria: It's hurting, it's really hurting. I wanted so much to be a good mother. I remember myself when she was born, all the dreams and the hopes for the future. It's so different now.

(At this point the director stopped the Soliloquy and decided to use the last sentence as a clue for the next scene.)

B. Second Segment (Explorations and Interpretations)

(This segment includes three key scenes.)

Key scene 2. The scene is set 14 years earlier. Sara is an infant. She has just come home from the hospital with her mother. Gloria has arranged a crib out of three chairs and Sara is in the crib. Dick and Gloria are standing by the crib, admiring their new baby.

Gloria: Look at her, Dick. She's so cute. Look at these little fingers. She's such an adorable baby!

Dick: I think she looks a little like me.

Gloria: Yes, there's a resemblance to you. But I think that her eyes and mouth are like mine.

Dick: (smiling) You mean she's going to grow up talking like you?

Gloria: Dick, what's wrong with the way I talk?

Dick: Oh, nothing. I only hope she won't talk on the phone as long as you do.

Gloria: That's not fair, Dick.

Dick: (smiling) Forget it, I was just kidding.

Gloria: Oh, Dick, I'm so happy. Isn't it wonderful to have a tiny little person like this in the house. She's so cute and adorable. I could kiss her the whole day. I hope I'll be a good mother to her. Oh, Dick, I want to be the best mother there is.

Director: Sara and Gloria, I would like you to reverse roles. Gloria, please get into the crib. Sara, you be Gloria. You're now the new mother. Dick, you remain youself. Sara, please repeat the last sentence said by Gloria before you reversed role with her.

(Gloria, portrayed by Sara): She's so cute *(starts laughing and turns to the director)*. It's funny to see my mother cuddled like a little baby.

Director: (to Sara, now portrayed by Gloria) Sara, I know that you're a little baby and can't talk, because you really don't know how. But here you may talk to your mother and father. This is a special situation. OK? Perhaps you want to ask her what kind of a mother she wants to be?

(Baby Sara): (in a childish voice) Mommy, I don't know you yet. Can you tell me what kind of a mother you are?

(Gloria): (finds it difficult to answer the question and hesitates for a moment) I'll be a good mother.

(Baby Sara): And what does that mean?

(Gloria): I don't know. *(to the director)* What do you want me to tell her? I've no idea what she (referring to Gloria) will say.

> *(Evidently, Sara finds it difficult to empathize with her mother, a difficulty manifested in falling out of the ascribed role, which typically signifies resistance. But resistance to what? Given that Sara did not experience such difficulties in portraying her own self, there is a good reason to assume that the resistance is not with regard to her participation in role playing in general, but rather to the portrayal of the particular role of her mother. Apparently, being in the role of her mother exacerbates the conflict between her anger and love towards Gloria. Instead of trying to solve the conflict she prefers to avoid it by falling out of the role. The director decided to test this assumption by putting a little more pressure on Sara to stay in the role of Gloria. If, however, Sara will persist in resisting the role, the director will have to reverse roles again and perhaps try the Mirror technique.)*

Director: Look, you're a new mother and you've a new adorable baby. I'm sure that you've hopes and ideas about the future. I'm sure you plan to be a loving mother. So tell her about these.

(Gloria): Well, I'll try to be a good mother.

(Baby Sara): I hope you'll be a wonderful mother. I would like to have a wonderful mother. Little babies need a loving mother. Even when I grow up I'll need a loving and understanding mother.

(Gloria): (to the director) Now, what am I supposed to say?

Director: Reverse roles, again. Gloria, you will resume your own role, and Sara, you can be yourself. In fact, Sara, I would like you to leave the action space and watch the development of the scene. Adam, perhaps you can be baby Sara for a few moments. Get in the crib and let's see how the scene continues. You can begin by asking your mother what kind of a mother she hopes to be. Sara, the two of us will watch the scene. Anytime you want to say something or intervene in the scene, you may do so without asking my permission. OK? *(Sara nods her head in agreement.)*

(Baby Sara, now portrayed by Adam): So, what kind of a mother will you be?

Gloria: Oh, darling, I'll be the best there is. I will try to be a good mother to you and I hope that when you grow up we'll be good friends.

Dick: We'll go out and play together. We'll have fun together. And I hope we won't have fights and big disagreements.

(Baby Sara): Oh, I don't know about that. Children always fight with their parents. I will, too, you know.

Gloria: That's all right. But I want you to know that I'll never hurt you on purpose. Anything I do for you will be out of love. I think we will have wonderful relationships.

(Baby Sara): I hope so, Mom. I would hate to grow up fighting with you and Dad.

Sara: (interrupts from her seat) Tough luck, baby.

(Baby Sara, portrayed by Adam): (to the real Sara) What do you mean?

Sara: You're going to be surprised, baby.

(Baby Sara): Why don't you come up and be me? I can use some help.

Sara: You're on you own, baby.

(Baby Sara): Come here to the crib.

Sara: I don't want to. I feel safer here where I am.

Director: (tries to see if Sara is ready now to assume the role of her mother without resistance) Perhaps you want to be a Double to your mother?

Sara: Do I have to do it?

Director: Only if you can and want to.

(Baby Sara): You can also join me and I'll be your Double.

Sara: He *(referring to Adam)* wants me to be the baby, and you want me
    to be my mother. I can see that in a few moments I'll be all by
    myself in the action space doing all the roles. No thank you.
Director: You can be there all by yourself being yourself. Maybe you want
    to present your side of the issue?
Sara: But it'll have to be as myself now, not as a baby.
(Baby Sara): Hey! I've an idea. You come and be Mom, and I'll be the
    baby and we'll do it between the two of us. How about that?
Sara: I don't feel like being Mom. It's silly.
Director: That's all right. You can be yourself if you want. Let's continue.
    Thank you Gloria, Dick, and Adam.

Key scene 3. Sara becomes the protagonist for the next scene. She may
remain the protagonist for a while, but towards the end of the session
Gloria will have to resume the role of the protagonist. The director asks
Sara to put out two chairs, one facing the other. The two chairs represent
two aspects of her own self. The plan is that she will not remain alone
in the action space. She will be provided with an auxiliary. But the
auxiliary will be a part of her.

Director: You said that you felt uncomfortable in the role of your mother.
    Can you tell me more about it?
Sara: I didn't say I was uncomfortable. I said it was silly.
Director: OK. What was silly about it?
Sara: I don't know. The whole situation was ridiculous. There I was
    standing next to the crib with Dad. And mother was lying on the
    chairs like a baby. Why would a grown-up person do that? I thought
    the whole situation was silly.
    *(Sara is still resisting any attempt to make her see her mother's side, and
    to empathize with her. The description of the scene indicated a complete lack
    of involvement. The next step is to get her involved in the enactment. But
    how? The clue came from Sara herself. She said she was willing to role
    play, but as herself. If it is possible to have her disclose some of her own
    fears and concerns, she might be ready to empathize with those of her mother.
    The director decided to try and move the scene in this direction.)*
Director: And how did you feel when you stood there by the crib, in the
    role of your mother? I understand that the situation seemed silly
    to you. That's what you thought about it. What did you think about
    portraying the role?
Sara: I thought that I didn't want to do it.
Director: Why?

Sara: Because I didn't like it.

Director: Why?

Sara: (laughing) You want me to say that I felt uncomfortable. OK, you win. I guess I was uncomfortable. So what?

Director: I just wanted to know what we can do with these two chairs. I suppose one chair can represent the feeling of discomfort and . . .

Sara: . . . and what will I do?

Director: You will sit on the other chair and be yourself. Talk with the feeling and find out whatever you can about it. Shall we leave the chair empty that represents the feeling of discomfort or would you rather have someone sit on it?

Sara: I think it will be better to talk to a real person rather than to a chair. I suppose you want me to select someone?

Director: (nods)

Sara: How about Adam? He's smart. *(Adam enters the action space and sits on the chair opposite Sara.)*

Director: (to Adam) You now represent Sara's feeling of discomfort. Think about yourself as the expression of "discomfort." For the rest of the scene I'm going to call you "Discomfort," OK? *(Adam agrees.)*

Discomfort: I feel uneasy.

Sara: I know.

Discomfort: If you know, then why do you use me so often?

Sara: I don't know. It just happens.

Discomfort: I can't imagine that you enjoy me. Perhaps you shouldn't use me so often. Can't you control me?

Sara: I don't know how. Maybe you can tell me how to do it. You're smart.

Discomfort: Oh, I'm not sure about it. *(smiles)* I bet you that I'm more a pain in the neck.

Sara: (smiles) That's right. And it's true for you as "Discomfort" as well as for you as "Adam."

Discomfort: You know what I think? I think that you like me?

Sara: Nonsense! Why should I like you? I don't like being uncomfortable.

Discomfort: But you don't do anything to overcome me. If you really hated me you would do something to get rid of me. I know you. If you want something, you turn the world upside down to get it.

Sara: What do you mean?

Director: Reverse roles. Sara, change places with Adam. Now you will be the feeling of discomfort and Adam will be Sara. Adam will you repeat the last sentence said by Sara?

(Sara, portrayed by Adam): What do you mean?

(Discomfort, now portrayed by Sara): When you want something, you make
    . . . I don't remember what he said?

Director: He said that when you want something you . . .

(Discomfort, portrayed by Sara): Oh, yes. I remember. When you want some-
    thing, you make sure that you get it one way or another.

Director: (to Adam as Sara) Ask her what she is uncomfortable about.

(Sara): OK. What are you uncomfortable about?

(Discomfort): I don't know.

(Sara): Look, don't play games with me. I'm smart, too, you know. If I
    make you uncomfortable, that's OK. It's my job. But don't play
    games with me.

(Discomfort): (gets angry) I'm not playing games with you. I just don't
    know.

(Sara): Oh, yes, you know. You're just afraid to tell me. That's what it's
    all about. You're just afraid.

(Discomfort): I'm not playing games, and I'm not afraid.

(Sara): I want the truth. If you're not interested in telling the truth, I'll
    leave.

(Discomfort): (shouts) You can leave if you want. *(waits a moment)* You want
    the truth? I'll tell you the truth. You can leave! Just leave me alone.

(Sara): How can you be happy being alone? You always say, "Leave me
    alone."

(Discomfort): I'm not playing games.

(Sara): What about being alone?

(Discomfort): You want to know about that? OK. I'll tell you about that.
    (gets very upset) I'm used to being alone. *(She falls out of the role and
    talks as Sara to Adam.)* It's easy for you to talk. You're my smart
    brother, right? The bright one, right? You're the pride of the
    family. You're the terrific kid and I'm the black sheep in the family,
    the troublemaker. So, why are you surprised that I feel alone?
    Don't you understand? I'm alone against Mom, alone against Dad,
    alone against Mom and Dad together, and alone against you. And
    if you want to know, I'm also alone against you and Dad. Why is
    it that the two of you always have fun together and I'm the bad
    one? I'll tell you why. It's because I don't count. That's right, I
    don't count anymore. So, now you know and I hope you're satisfied.
    (She begins to cry quietly.)

(Sara, portrayed by Adam): (to Sara) I'm sorry Sara. *(to the Director)* Now
    what have I done? I shouldn't have asked.

Director: You're doing fine.

Adam: But I made her cry. What shall I do now?

    (Both Adam and Sara fell out of their roles. Now they are relating to each

other in their original roles, that is, as a brother and a sister. Sara became emotionally involved as she revealed her feelings of loneliness in the family. Adam, who insisted that she tell the truth, has been taken aback and is overwhelmed with guilt. It is time to reverse roles again and end the scene here. But it is also important that the dialogue between Sara and Adam be continued and their conflict resolved. The director decided to move smoothly to a new scene without much interruption. Therefore, the next step will be designed as if this and the new scene are almost one.)

Director: Reverse roles again. Sara, you be yourself and Adam, you sit on the other chair. As a matter of fact, Adam, I would like you to be yourself, too. Please move your chair closer to Sara if you feel like doing this. Continue the conversation in your original roles as a brother and sister. *(Adam moves his chair closer to Sara.)*
(The little gesture of changing the physical arrangement of the action space is meant to signify that a new scene is about to start. It is a small, yet important, manifestation that a new situation has been created, and that the players interact now in different roles.)

Key scene 4. Sara and Adam sit together. Sara is still tearful, and Adam tries to comfort her.

Adam: Are you OK, Sara?
Sara: Don't worry, I'll be all right.
Adam: I'm very sorry, Sara. I didn't mean to make you cry. I just thought that you tried to be . . . ah . . . ,what I mean is that I'm sorry I pushed so hard. I'd no idea that it would make you so upset.
Sara: Don't worry about me.
Adam: Maybe I shouldn't have done it?
Sara: Oh, I don't know. Perhaps it's time that they *(points to Gloria and Dick, who sit outside the action stage)* and you know what you're doing to me. *(Gloria and Dick, who are obviously deeply moved by the scene, get up from their chairs and move towards Sara. The director motions to them to sit back down.)*
Adam: Well, I didn't realize this.
Sara: Well, you're a clever kid. You tell me: Why does it take someone to cry and make a scene before anyone pays attention to you? Tell me the truth Adam, would you notice that if I didn't make such a big noise about it?
Adam: Probably not.
Sara: You see. This is your answer. And you said that I was playing games!
Adam: What can I tell you? I guess you're right. But still, I don't know.

I, for example, get attention without making big noises. So, why is it that I can get by without causing a "Sara-jevo" and you can't? I don't understand that.

Sara: (*points to the director*) Why don't you ask him? He may be able to explain it to you. All I know is that I don't get attention unless I make a big noise.

Adam: Is this also the reason for all the noise you're making at home?

Sara: Maybe. I don't know because I don't think about it before I start something. For me it's an automatic reaction.

Adam: Do you like it that way?

Sara: As I said, I don't know anymore.

Adam: You must know whether you like it or not. And you must be aware how people react to you when you do it.

Sara: When I set myself to win, I don't care whether the others win or lose.

Adam: But in the family, it's *us* who lose.

Sara: (*sits quietly, staring at the floor*).

Adam: Did you hear me?

Sara: (*whispers*) I heard you.

Adam: Well?

Sara: (*continues to sit quietly, staring at the floor*).

Adam: Well?

Sara: Do you feel like a loser?

Adam: I didn't until today. But now I do. I feel defeated and I resent it.

Director: Adam, describe to me the idea of "feeling defeated."

Adam: (*somewhat upset*) "Defeated" is a plain English word.

Director: What are you angry about?

Adam: (*angrily*) I'm not angry.

Sara: Yes, you are. At least you sound as if you are.

Adam: So what if I am? It's not a great joy to realize that you have lost, that you can't do anything.

Sara: Now you know how I feel.

Adam: You gave me the knockout punch. Is that what you really want? Is that what makes you happy?

Sara: No, I didn't say that it makes me happy.

Director: (*to Adam*) Why don't you lie flat on your back as if this is a boxing ring and you were just beaten down to the floor? Let's see that. (*Adam lies on the floor on his back with his arms spread.*)

Sara: Adam, don't be ridiculous.

Adam: (*ignores her remark*) I'm done. I lost. It's all over with—finished, kaput, finis.

Sara: What are you talking about?

Adam: You win. I lose.

Director: Reverse roles. *(Adam becomes Sara. Sara assumes the role of the defeated Adam and lies on the floor.)* Let's hear the last words said by Adam before the role reversal.

(Adam, portrayed by Sara): You win. I lose.

(Sara, portrayed by Adam): What are you talking about?

(Adam): I just want to show you how I feel.

(Sara): But I don't want you to feel that way.

(Adam): What can I do? I feel that way because you're trying to win the attention at my expense.

(Sara): At your expense?

(Adam): That's right! The atmosphere you create affects me, too.

(Sara): What is it to you? You're not part of this.

(Adam): Yes, I am.

(Sara): How so?

Director: Reverse roles. Adam, please lie on the floor. Sara, you become yourself and please repeat the question.

Sara: How so?

Adam: Because I also try to avoid you when you make trouble. So I cause you to be alone, too.

Sara: But you don't do it deliberately, do you?

Adam: (pauses for a moment) If I lose my sister, it hurts the same whether I do it deliberately or not. It's just the same.

Sara: (kneels next to Adam) You'll not lose me, Adam. Please, get up. I don't want to lose you. Help me to win in a different way.

Director: Let's stop her and call mother again. Thank you, Sara and Adam.

C. Third Segment (Alternative Behavior)

Director: (to Gloria) Here you are again in the action space. You started as the protagonist, and it's only right that you get the opportunity to end the session as the protagonist. What would you like to do with regard to the problem you raised at the beginning of the session?

Gloria: I really have no definite idea. But I want to say that the scenes done by Sara and Adam were very important to me. I was really moved. I never realized that Sara felt so isolated in the family. It was awful . . . I mean very difficult to watch, I can tell you that. I feel really guilty, especially when I think of our relationships nowadays compared with the dreams I had about our future re-

lationships when she was a baby. Sara ended the last scene asking
Adam for help. I must do the same. I need help as well. So do
whatever you think is going to help me.

Dick: (talks from his seat) I agree with Gloria. It hurt me, too, to watch
Sara's difficult position. But I don't think that Gloria should be the
only protagonist now. Well, I don't know about the rules of role
playing. You [*the director*] always try to have only one protagonist
up there. This time you really need to bend the rules because I'm
in this mess as much as Gloria. So we both need help, and I would
like to be a co-protagonist, or whatever you call it. But only if that's
OK with you, Gloria. I don't want to steal your time.

Gloria: Oh, I can use any help I can get, Dick. Of course it's fine with
me.

Dick: (already in the middle of the action space) And I really think that, as
you *(the director)* said to us sometime ago, the whole family is the
protagonist now. Maybe we all can come up to the center. *(to the
director)* Can you handle that? I mean, can you do something with
all of us together?

Director: You've got to ask Gloria if she wants everybody in the action
space, because she's the protagonist. And, of course, you also have
to ask Adam and Sara if they want to participate now.

Gloria: I have no objections.

Adam: It's OK with me. *(to Sara)* Let's join them, what do you say?

Sara: All right.

Director: I'll tell you what I'm going to do. We'll have everyone up here,
but in pairs. We'll start with Gloria and Dick, and then we'll have
Adam and Sara.

*(The Director did not want to act against the unifying spirit expressed by
Dick, and therefore decided against asking each member of the family to
take turns and role play alone for a short while. He also thought that, at
this moment, getting the whole family in one scene might lead to a premature—perhaps superficial—closure. Since Sara asked Adam's help, and
Dick volunteered to be Gloria's "co-protagonist," these two pairs seemed to
emerge as potentially reinforcing sociometric dyads. It appeared safer to
design a scene that might further strengthen this development.)*

Key scene 5. Gloria and Dick sit in the center of the action space
facing each other, and Sara and Adam sit in the corner. The time
is *now* and the space is the treatment room.

Director: OK, Gloria and Dick, I would like you two to reverse roles with
the children. Gloria, you'll be Sara, and Dick, you'll be Adam. Your

task is to discuss and agree on a list of things that you want your parents to do in order to improve the difficulties we've seen portrayed here today.

Dick: (to the director) I should have known that you might pull something like this on us. It's difficult, you know.

Director: I know. But try and give it your best shot.

(Adam, portrayed by Dick): OK, Sara, we've got a job to do. Let's have a list for the old folks.

(Sara, portrayed by Gloria): First thing I want is to stop being considered the black sheep of the family.

(Adam): I agree. That's important. But how can they do it? It's already in their mind. How can they change their attitude?

(Sara): I know, but they should try.

(Adam): We need to have a more concrete recommendation for them.

(Sara): How about if they stop saying "no" before they hear me out. And maybe they could avoid saying "no" to me at all for a while.

(Adam): That's pushing it to the extreme. But they must reduce the number of refusals at least by half. How about that?

(Sara): That's a good start. I also think that mother must stop bothering me.

(Adam): What does that mean?

(Sara): Asking me questions and telling me what to do or not to do.

(Adam): Be reasonable Sara. You don't want her to stop talking to you, do you? She can't calculate every word she speaks to you. It's unnatural.

(Sara): But she does bother me a lot, and Dad, too. She demands too much and he wants peace and quiet every time I have something to say.

(Adam): Correction. He wants it every time you *shout* something.

(Sara): You must admit that he treats you and me differently.

(Adam): In what way does he do it?

(Sara): As I said, he's more willing to listen to you than me. He agrees more often with you than with me. And in general, he seems to be more patient with you.

(Adam): OK, we'll put on the list a joint petition for more equality. We can ask both of them to work on being impartial in the way they treat you and me. We'll ask that they hear you and me with the same degree of openness, and that they exercise the same degree of patience, or impatience, towards you and me. How about that? I doubt that this will eliminate all the problems you have with them but at least it won't make you feel discriminated against compared to me. Is that acceptable to you?

(Sara): It's definitely an improvement.

(Adam): I hate to bring this up now, but what about your anger towards them, especially towards mother?

(Sara): What do you mean?

(Adam): Well, you sound so angry when you talk to mother. And, besides, I'm afraid that it might be difficult for you to get rid of the grudge you hold against her. Actually, I'm concerned that after all these years that it might be deeply engrained in your personality and that no amount of goodwill can change it. What do you think?

(Sara): I don't understand. What are you driving at?

(Adam): Well, I guess I'm saying that maybe the problem of your relationship with Mom is more complicated than it appears on the surface. And that in spite of her effort—assuming that she'll make one—nothing will be changed. What I'm afraid of is that after all this we may find ourselves back where we started. And that goes with regard to Dad, too.

(Sara): Are you trying to tell me that we shouldn't work on the list because it's doomed to fail? That's a very depressing thought.

(Adam): But if they try hard and it wouldn't work out satisfactorily because there's no chance for improvement to begin with, the frustration will be even greater. Then we'll be even more depressed.

(Sara): What can I tell you? I really don't know. I think we ought to give it a try. I would like to think that the problem is solvable and that if we try hard, we'll make it. That's all I can say.

Director: OK, thank you "kids." Let's have the "parents" now and see what they can come up with. Sara and Adam, please sit on these two chairs in the center and remember that you have reversed roles with your parents. Sara, you represent Gloria, and Adam is playing Dick.

(Dick, portrayed by Adam): I guess we should agree on things we want the children, I mean us . . . ,that is, them, . . . Oh, *(to the director)* I'm confused.

Director: You're the father now, and your name is Dick. You sit here with your wife, Gloria (points to Sara). I'm asking the two of you to agree on what it is that you want your children to do in order to solve the issue portrayed in today's session. Is it still confusing?

(Dick): No, that's clear. OK, Gloria *(referring to Sara, who sits opposite him).* What do we want the kids to do differently?

(Gloria, portrayed by Sara): They should be nicer to us.

(Dick): Nicer?

(Gloria): I mean, they need to talk nicer to us, to stop quarreling and be more positive. If I ask Sara to help me in household chores, to

clean the mess she creates, etc., she has to quit arguing with me every time and quit those temper tantrums.

(Dick): But it's normal for teenagers to behave that way.

(Gloria): I don't now about that.

(Dick): What is that supposed to mean?

(Gloria): If it were normal, why are we here in therapy?

(Dick): Maybe she exaggerates a bit. I'll give you that.

Director: Ask her for specifics. What does she want Sara to do?

(Dick): Well . . .

(Gloria): It might be helpful to have a list of things she has to do. And these she should do without arguing. I think that Adam should have a list of things, too.

(Dick): I agree. A similar list for both of them.

(Gloria): Maybe it can be one separate list for Adam and one separate list for Sara. We also may want a joint list of chores that Sara will be responsible for one day and Adam the next day. Maybe they can take turns.

(Dick): That's a good idea. But what about all these "Sara-jevo" incidents? We can't continue with them because they upset the whole family.

(Gloria): If we approach this more positively, I don't think we'll have them as often.

(Dick): I still don't know how this will happen.

(Gloria): Sara needs to have her wishes fulfilled sometimes.

(Dick): I agree. We need to provide her with ideas about how she can do that without making such a big fuss.

(Gloria): I know, but I haven't got a clue what to tell her.

(Dick): Me neither.

(Gloria): We're stuck!

(Dick): Maybe she can imitate Adam?

(Gloria): No, she can't do that. She doesn't like Adam's style. She's more expressive than him. Besides, why can't she have her own way? Remember, we're not making Adam the best example anymore.

(Dick): I forgot. You're absolutely right. Well, there must be something she can do differently! I can't believe that her way to win is the only one. There must be an alternative.

(Gloria): Like what?

(Dick): We have to ask her. I know what I would do. But we agreed that it has to be her way, that is, something that she can feel comfortable with. We do agree that in principle there should be more cooperation. And that whenever there are differences, they should not be dealt with by shouting and leaving the room in a noisy protest. Right?

(Gloria): That's it!

(Dick): What have I done now?

(Gloria): I've got it! You're great. We'll ask Sara to change her way of arguing. From now on she can't leave the room in a protest in the middle of a discussion. She must stay and try to bring it to a resolution.

(Dick): Even if she doesn't win every time.

(Gloria): I guess so.

(Dick): And without shouting.

(Gloria): Well, with less shouting. She can't change that all of a sudden.

(Dick): Fair enough.

(Gloria): So, that's it. Anything else we should do?

(Dick): Just a minute. One more thing.

(Gloria): What?

(Dick): We're recommending something new, and we hope that it will improve the situation. But it's a new system and it's possible that, at least in the beginning, it may not work well. What if everyone continues the old habits? How can we make sure that we're reminded of the new system?

(Gloria): We'll try harder.

(Dick): Let's see if we can build a "reminder" into the new system.

(Gloria): OK. Do you have an idea?

(Dick): Well, if one of us continues to behave in the old way, the other person can say something . . . maybe, "The 'new deal,' please." These words can remind us to change.

(Gloria): OK.

Director: Thank you, all. It's a good time to end here. The two of you can be yourselves again. Let's talk a little bit about the session before we adjourn.

The Closure Stage

Gloria: I think that today's session was a very good one. I have a feeling that we've made an important step forward. I feel good about it.

Sara: I feel better, too. I only hope that something good will come of it.

Dick: I must say, right now I'm quite hopeful. I have a positive feeling about the session. We worked hard, especially Sara, and I'm optimistic about the future. I really am. I think we all have to thank Sara for it.

Gloria: (smiling) What about the protagonist? What about her? *(referring to herself, of course)*

Dick: (smiling) The protagonist was terrific! But Sara set us on the correct track.

Gloria: I guess you're right, Dick. I'm only kidding.

Dick: I know.

Adam: (to the director) I raised the question whether or not Sara can change her behavior. Because I don't know if it has or hasn't become an inseparable part of her personality. What do you think?

Dick: In the role play, Sara said that you must give it a try. Why do you bring this question up again?

Adam: I know she said it. I only wonder if there is anything in psychology that can assure me that there is a chance for success.

Sara: Adam, leave this issue alone. We'll wait and see. I think that this is the best we can do. So let's do it.

Director: If everyone is committed to improve the situation, it will get better. My question, Adam, is how do *you* feel about it? Because it seems to me that the "new deal" changes your position. Do you feel that you've been unduly deprived of your privileges?

Adam: Well, maybe a little.

Sara: It's about time that you join the collective effort as well. You can't sit on the sidelines and be an uninvolved "peacemaker" all the time. It's not going to be easy for me, either, you know.

Adam: I know.

Sara: But you're still unhappy about it, right?

Adam: Not much.

Director: Maybe you'd like to be the protagonist next time?

Adam: We'll see. I'm not sure.

Director: It's better to talk about it, Adam. Because if this is a "bad deal" for you, we need to explore other alternatives. There's no sense in doing something that leaves one member of the family bitter about it. We're not in a rush to make a final decision now.

Adam: I'm not bitter about it. Only for me, it was nice so far. Now because of Sara's problem, I've got to change, too. That's all.

Sara: Now you blame me for all this.

Adam: No, it's not a question of blame.

Dick: I suppose you're sorry that you can't hide anymore.

Adam: Yeah! Well, maybe it wouldn't be so difficult, after all. Let's give it a try.

Sara: Are you sure about it?

Adam: I guess so.

Gloria: We'll help you, Adam. In fact, we'll help each other.

Dick: We should have taped the session. I'm not sure I remember what was on all the lists.

Sara: I think I remember.

Adam: Oh, I remember, too.

Director: Would it make sense to ask you to put the things you said on your lists in writing, and perhaps add more if you can come up with additional ideas?

Dick: I like that idea. We can do that and bring the lists next week to review them again.

Director: We'll do even more than that. Next session we can role play some difficult scenes from the past using the new deal, and see if it seems to work better. We can experiment with it and refine it, if needed. Then, Adam, you can also judge for yourself how you can relate to it. We'll need your OK before we decide.

Adam: That makes sense. And what if I don't like it?

Sara: (smiling) You know him *(referring to the director).* He'll ask you to be the protagonist.

Adam: (smiling) Yeah. That'll be the day. Maybe I'm better off going along with our plan than to be a protagonist. It sure seems easier.

Gloria: I'm not trying to pick on you, Adam. What I don't understand is, if you had reservations and uneasy feelings about the whole thing, why didn't you say so during the role plays?

Adam: You guys don't understand me. I'm not saying that I don't like the new deal. What I'm saying is that until now I was out of it, and now I have become involved. I'm a little apprehensive, that's all.

Dick: I can understand this. I find myself in the same position. I tended to leave the fights to Mom and Sara and stay out of them. I guess we found today that this is not possible. We're all involved—even if that realization is, selfishly, uncomfortable. Maybe I'm sorry a little bit to have to abandon my secure hiding spot.

Adam: That's exactly what I feel.

Dick: Well, you and I, Adam, must come out of our hiding places. It doesn't work anymore. And I agree that it would have been more comfortable if we could have stayed where we were.

Adam: Yes.

Director: Any more comments? If not, let's adjourn. I'll see you all next week.

PSYCHODRAMA À DEUX: THE APPLICATION OF CLINICAL ROLE PLAYING IN INDIVIDUAL TREATMENT

The idea that clinical role playing can serve as an effective mode of intervention in individual therapy is not as popular as that which advocates its application in group psychotherapy. Even the expression, "Psychodrama *à Deux*," which denotes such use of clinical role playing in individual treatment (e.g., May, 1981), is probably hardly known outside the circle of ardent psychodramatists. *À deux* means "for two" or "intimate." It has been introduced to the role playing nomenclature because it adequately captures the two fundamental aspects of the individual therapy setting: (a) the presence of two people, a therapist and a client, and (b) the atmosphere of complete privacy. In the interest of maintaining a semantic clarity, it ought to be emphasized that the decision to adhere to the term *psychodrama* à deux, or, to replace it with *clinical role playing* à deux, is largely a matter of personal and theoretical preferences. As far as the practice of psychotherapy is concerned, the adoption of one term or another is inconsequential.

Traditionally, the use of behavior simulation and its clinical role playing techniques has not been associated with the practice of individual therapy. Why? There are several reasons that may account for this.

First it should be recalled that the early systematic introduction of role playing to psychotherapy began with the advent of psychodrama. Two historical developments proved to be of a considerable significance in the shaping of the present popular view of the applicability of role playing. One was the association of role playing with psychodrama, and the other, the association of psychodrama with J. L. Moreno. But Moreno was primarily interested in group processes and group psychotherapy. The fact that psychodrama was designed as a form of group psychotherapy is probably responsible for the conventional notion that associates role playing with group therapy.

Second, an effective use of clinical role playing requires the participation of auxiliaries who portray a wide variety of roles in the protagonist's life. The group setting provides the therapeutic process with an easy access to persons who can assume such roles. No wonder, therefore, that the group setting was considered the ideal medium for the application of role playing both in terms of convenience and cost effectiveness. There is, undoubtedly, a great deal of truth in the conventional belief which holds, that whereas in verbal therapy conducting group treatment appears to be far more complicated than individual treatment, in clinical role playing the degree of difficulty is reversed.

Third, one of the points repeatedly emphasized by most therapeutic approaches concerns the uninvolved posture therapists must assume in conducting their psychotherapeutic interventions. It is imperative that therapists are as objective as possible and that they appropriately distance themselves both from the emotional anguish expressed by their clients and their own personal reaction to it. This requirement has been expressed in a variety of concepts such as guardedness against countertransference and counterconditioning, helping clients to help themselves, adopting as much of a value-free attitude as possible, and so forth. If clinical role playing is to be used in individual therapy, the therapist will have to participate as an auxiliary and assume various roles in the life of the protagonist. This form of involvement is sometimes seen as at odds with an impartial attitude on the part of the therapist. Although performing auxiliary roles does not necessarily result in subjective involvements with the client, the line that separates these two can be quite delicate. A healthy separation requires a substantial degree of self-control and self-awareness on the part of the therapist. The tendency to shy away from applying clinical role playing techniques in individual therapy may represent an attempt to avoid both the temptation and the likelihood of crossing that line.

Finally, the model that provided the classic setting for conducting individual therapy was established years before the advent of clinical role playing. That model, originally set by psychoanalysis, was based on the notion that verbal language is the vehicle for treating psychological aberrations. When role playing was introduced into psychotherapy in the early 1930s, it was harder to change the tradition and redesign the already existing model. Instead it was considerably easier to incorporate actional concepts in a new therapeutic modality such as group psychotherapy. The decision resulting from this "political" strategy marked the beginning of the association between role playing and the treatment of groups.

One of the hallmarks of the general development in the area of psychotherapy during the last two decades is a gradual, yet steady shift from the tendency to adhere to old (perhaps somewhat dogmatic), conventional practices towards a greater degree of openness to change. Traditional notions and practices are valued as long as they continue to be functionally valuable. Otherwise, expediency may supersede the need for upholding the tradition. That shift also applies to the issue of using clinical role playing in individual therapy. There are good reasons for retaining the old association between role playing and group therapy. But this need not imply the exclusion of role playing from the practice of individual treatment. On the contrary, there are valid arguments in favor of incorporating clinical role playing in individual settings.

- One of the limitations of the group therapy situation is the absence of opportunities for complete privacy. The presence of a number of group members sometimes inhibits clients who prefer to reveal certain personal difficulties in private (J. L. Moreno, 1973). If clinical role playing is deemed as effective therapeutic intervention, such clients should be given the option to benefit from it in the more intimate setting of individual therapy.

- Some clients are disinclined to participate in group therapy. They feel uncomfortable being in groups for numerous reasons (e.g., a preference for exclusivity, their temperament, a lack of social skills, or the need to maintain a public image). In fact, there are instances where group psychotherapy is not the treatment of choice for the difficulties expressed by clients. Instead, the preferred mode of treatment is the individual setting.

- Individual treatment is the most common form of psychotherapy. Its prevalence is far greater than that of group therapy. Expertly done, there is really no compelling reason to argue for the exclusion of clinical role playing from the kind of treatment therapists do most.

In view of the above discussion, therapists are advised to *use the Empty-chair technique and its variations as often as possible.* If they have to actively assume auxiliary roles, these should be kept *short and brief,* not exceeding a few minutes. *Jumping in and out of auxiliary roles* is a safeguard against intense emotional investment in, and an undue identification with, any particular portrayal.

As a result of these recommendations the length of the clinical role playing interventions employed in each individual therapy session is *much shorter* than the length of such interventions during a group therapy session. The curtailed duration affects the complexity as well; the interventions tend to become simpler and involve fewer scenes, which intersperse with more verbal discussions.

Another ramification of the absence of group members is the need to pay extra attention to the issue of protagonists' involvement in the role plays. In a group setting, group pressure and massive reinforcement from several members can help protagonists overcome resistance to become involved. Active auxiliaries can swiftly immerse protagonists into action and encourage them to loosen their inhibitions and excessive controls. In individual treatment the therapist has to cultivate his or her protagonist's readiness and involvement alone. The therapist must be prepared to allocate the necessary time and effort for this undertaking.

There are two kinds of clinical role playing interventions in individual therapy. One is the portrayal of a single episode, and the other is the portrayal of a sequential role playing. Each of these has its own special characteristics and, therefore, is indicated for different purposes and under different therapeutic conditions.

Role Playing of a Single Episode

This kind of clinical role playing is confined to the portrayal of one key scene. Obviously, an intervention of this sort represents the simplest form of role playing, a fact that perhaps also explains the reason for its relative popularity. As one weighs the therapeutic advantages and disadvantages of portraying a single key scene, it becomes apparent that its merit may be twofold: (a) for diagnostic purposes, that is, a method of obtaining a clearer scope of the presenting complaint(s), and (b) for the training of specific skills.

(a) The enactment of a single key scene for diagnostic purposes. The protagonist is asked to role play one episode. Typically, the scene will depict a situation that demonstrates either the protagonist's psychological and behavioral difficulties or his or her current proficiency in using various coping skill(s). It may concretize what has been previously discussed in the session, a new improvised situation, or an already existing situational technique. For optimal therapeutic expediency the portrayed scene has to include one or more specific basic techniques (e. g., Role-reversal, the Soliloquy, the Empty-chair, or the Double). The introduction of role playing of a single key scene during a traditional, verbal therapy is by no means limited to one enactment per session. In principle, given sufficient time, one session may contain two (or more) single episodes. However, these are not inherently connected. Each constitutes a separate episode and is enacted at different times during the session.

(b) The repeated portrayal of a single episode. The objective of this kind of clinical role playing is to provide protagonists with the opportunity to experiment with, and practice, new skills. Here too, only one key scene is enacted. But rather than limiting it to a single portrayal, protagonists may, if dissatisfied with the outcome(s), repeat the same (or similar) scene several times. Thus the one scene can be practiced in several ways. This use of clinical role playing is common in the training of social, heterosexual, communication, leadership, or assertive skills, for example. It is also common as an added intervention in desensitization treatment. The repeated portrayal may continue until it reaches a desired proficiency. Again, applying clinical role playing appropriately

requires the simulation to be reinforced with at least one or more of the basic techniques.

Sequential Role Playing

This kind of clinical role playing in individual therapy is actually a miniature version of the expanded form of this therapeutic modality. It contains all the three segments of the Action stage, namely, the presentation of the problem, the explorations and interpretations, and the practice of alternative(s) or the consequences of the portrayed behavior. Unlike the enactment of a single episode, the sequential role playing is comprised of *three* key scenes, one for each of the three segments. Unlike the expanded procedure used in group or family therapy, it is a shorter version of clinical role playing. The brevity is mostly expressed in the second segment where typically only one scene is allocated for procedures of explorations and interpretations. This limitation is imposed due to the absence of individuals who can serve as auxiliaries. For this reason the application of the sequential role playing in individual therapy is restricted to simple and well-defined issues where extensive explorations are not needed. The three key scenes form a continuous progression, that is, one evolves from the other. Sometimes they can also be supplemented with one connecting scene in the form of a Soliloquy (with or without a Double).

The example chosen in order to illustrate the use of clinical role playing in individual therapy includes a case of the repeated portrayal of a single episode.

A CASE ILLUSTRATION: A REPEATED PORTRAYAL OF A SINGLE EPISODE

The client, Susan, came for therapy complaining of a feeling of unhappiness and frequent, brief periods of mild depression. At the age of 31 she felt she was shy and insecure. Her social circle included two close female friends, and although she had been dating occasionally, her relationships with males were kept short. This was done intentionally in order to avoid intense involvements. At work, although a dedicated and hard worker, she could not escape feeling unappreciated by her colleagues and superior. During the initial stages of treatment a few areas of difficulty were identified. One of them was a fear of criticism coupled with a lack of assertiveness. This problem area had been addressed in previous sessions, and the clinical role playing to be described below was considered a continuation of this treatment effort. Specifically, it focused on providing Susan with an opportunity to practice some assertive skills to help her cope in situations involving the "threat" of criticism.

Key scene. The scene was taken from the work environment. The place was the office of Susan's supervisor, and the time was set as the previous Monday at about 11 a.m. Susan arranged three chairs and a small table to represent Jean's (the supervisor's) office. The director explained to Susan that the scene would be enacted in the present, as if it were occurring now for the first time. He also told her that he would assume the role of the auxiliaries, as needed.

The scene depicted a discussion between Jean and Susan concerning a report she had written the previous day. Susan described some of Jean's characteristics and the necessary details pertaining to the report.

Director: Sue, before we begin, let me tell you about the Aside technique. Sometimes the things people say overtly do not reflect their internal feelings and thoughts. This usually occurs when they have reason to rightly or wrongly believe that there is a great risk in revealing their true opinions, and that candor might harm them. The Aside technique is designed to reveal such unspoken feelings and thoughts and make them public, at least here in this room. The technique is very simple. In the course of role playing, whenever you find yourself in such a situation, please cover the side of your mouth with your hand as if you're telling a secret, and say these feelings or thoughts. The fact that the disclosure is expressed as an Aside means that the auxiliary must ignore it. Feel free to do the Aside as many times as you want. You need not wait for my instructions. OK? Now, let's begin. *(Jean, portrayed by the director, sits in her office as Susan enters.)*

Sue: Hi, Jean. Did you want to see me?

(Jean): Oh, hi, Sue. Yes. Come in. *(motions to her to sit down)* I want to discuss with you the report you sent me yesterday.

Sue: OK.

(Jean): I read it carefully, and on the whole I think you've done a good job . . .

Sue: (interrupts) Thank you, Jean. I must tell you that I put a lot of work into it, and I'm sure you'll appreciate that. *(Sue practices some of the points raised during the previous sessions. She remembers that in order to reinforce her self-confidence, she needs to focus her attention on the positive*

*aspects of her performance. She even tries to go one step further and make
Jean do so as well.)*

(Jean): I do appreciate it. But what I want to talk with you about is not
the effort you made in composing this report. As I said, it's fine.
The reason I called you in is that I want to ask you about your
conclusions and suggestions that appear in the last section of the
report. I can see what you're trying to say, but I'm not sure I agree
with you. In fact, I don't understand how you could have come to
such conclusions.

Sue: I can explain them. (Aside: Here we go again. Why can't she discuss
a report without finding something wrong with it? When will I see
the day she tells me: "Sue, you've done a great job, period"? But
I'm going to take a deep breath and stay cool.)

(Jean): Wait a minute. Don't you want to know my reservations?

Sue: OK. Go ahead. (Aside: The truth is that I prefer not to hear her
her criticism. I'll discuss her reservations as long as I keep remembering that we discuss options, not personalities. The reservations
do not reflect on me, personally. Anyway, what the hell does she
know about me? And she's not my prime candidate for the title of
Ms. TRUTH.)

(Jean): Your opinion is that the art department will reject your conclusions, and therefore our first problem is to address the attitudinal
difficulty and not the issue of production. Right?

Sue: Correct. They'll give us a hard time. And if we're going to try to
convince them in the way we always do, we'll lose a lot of valuable
time. Therefore, I recommend that we approach it in an entirely
different way.

(Jean): I don't understand how you can say this.

Sue: (Aside: Here we go again! Maybe I don't make sense?) All right,
you can change the end of the report if you want.

Director: (stepping out of Jean's role) I'm going to leave Jean's place empty,
and become your Double. *(He pulls up a chair and sits beside Sue.)*

Double: I'm going to let her change my work if she disagrees with me.
After all, she's my boss.

Sue: Correct. She's the boss.

Double: She's in charge and I'm not in charge of anyone. I need to please
her.

Sue: Well, I prefer to "disapper" before it's too late.

Double: Too late? I'd say before I get hurt.

Sue: But I also don't mind if she makes changes in the report.

Double: It's her right to mess up my work.

Sue: No, I can't agree with that.

Double: I'm not kidding myself. You may disagree with me. But my behavior expresses the belief that her rights are more important than mine.

Sue: Why do you put it as an issue of "rights"?

Double: Because I feel frustrated that my opinion is not appreciated. Don't you feel that way?

Sue: I don't know.

Double: And I thought that by now I do know what I feel.

Sue: So, what if I'm frustrated and angry? Anger doesn't solve anything. It has never solved anything for me. It only gets me into more trouble.

Double: Right.

Sue: I can tell you many stories about that, if you really want to know.

Double: I do. Do I want to talk about this now?

Sue: I suppose it's possible that my inability to handle anger causes my avoidance of such situations. *(The director makes a "mental note" to bring up the issue of Sue's past experience with anger later, following the end of the role playing.)*

Double: Correct. I'll tell you what's in my mind. If I let her change the report her way, I wouldn't have to face the criticism anymore. This way I can end this "agony" in a minute.

Sue: Is that what I'm doing? I suppose you're right. But oddly enough I don't feel very uncomfortable right now. Does this mean that I don't have the fear of criticism?

Double: I don't feel the urge to end the confrontation.

Sue: Well, I'm not exactly happy to be here, but I feel strong enough to continue.

Double: I feel uncomfortable, and you can't fool me.

Sue: OK. So I do feel uncomfortable and angry. What's next?

(Interestingly, Susan's awareness of her anxiety produces new, encouraging responses. She does not manifest the panic symptoms she used to display in the past in similar situations, and she's trying to think rationally. Nonetheless, she still evinces a preference to avoid confrontations with the source that criticizes her judgment. Where should the director lead the scene from here? One possibility is to explore the history of her reaction to anger and frustration and assist her to develop new perspectives. But this will require at least one full clinical role playing session. Another possibility is to familiarize her with effective communication skills to cope with Jean. Given

that the session was initially planned to have only one clinical role playing scene, the director chose the second option.)

Double: Fight back, that's what I feel like doing.

Sue: You know what? You're absolutely right. I'll fight back.

Double: I'm ready, are you?

Sue: You bet. *(turns to the empty chair, representing Jean)* Look here, Jean, I wrote the report as clearly as I could. You don't have to accept my conclusions if you don't want.

Director: Reverse roles. I'd like you, Sue, to move to Jean's chair and become Jean. Please respond to Sue, that is, to the empty chair where Sue sat a minute ago.

(Jean, portrayed by Sue): What are you angry about? I only wanted to understand the reasons for your conclusions. That's not like you, you know.

Director: Reverse roles again.

Sue: I know. But I think that I did a good job, and I explained my reasoning in the report. Take it or leave it. *(She gets up and leaves the office.)*

(The Director sat with Sue to discuss her performance in the scene.)

Director: How do you feel right now, Sue?

Sue: Angry, but happy that I defended my position.

Director: Do you like what you did?

Sue: Yes and no. As I said I feel strong, but inside I'm burning with anger. I'm furious.

Director: What about?

Sue: (smiles) That I actually didn't win. I thought that it was childish to run away from her office. That's terrible. Anyway, I'll never do it in real life. She'd fire me.

Director: Would you like to do the scene again? You can try to behave differently if you want. Perhaps you can try to behave in a manner that is also acceptable in real life.

Sue: Yes, I'd like that.

Director: Let me give you a couple of tips. One, try to maintain eye contact with Jean. Second, ask her questions. You cast yourself in the role of defender all the time. You see, it was interesting that when you spoke with Jean, you let her ask the questions and you answered her like an "accused" person who must defend herself. But when you spoke with your Double, you asked a lot of questions. Obviously, you felt secure and comfortable with your Double. Am I right?

Sue: Yes, I wasn't aware of that. But I felt good and in control talking to the Double.

Director: Could you do the same with Jean?

Sue: I'll try. So, let's do it again.

Key Scene: First Repeat

Sue: Hi, Jean. Did you want to see me?

(Jean): Oh, hi, Sue. Come in. The reason I called you is that I need to discuss with you the report you wrote.

Sue: You know that I put in a lot of hard work to get it done. I hope you like it.

(Jean): Yes, I can see that. I read it carefully and I can appreciate the work you've done . . .

Sue: (interrupts her quickly) Do you have any questions? Have I done something wrong?

Director: Let me be your Double, Sue. *(moves from Jean's chair to the chair of the Double, next to Sue)*

Double: Here I go again.

Sue: What now?

Double: I expressed my worries before she told me that I'd actually done something wrong.

Sue: You're right. I must remember not to criticize myself. I'm to be positive, right?

Double: I like to think positively about myself. It's a nice feeling.

Sue: (to Jean, again portrayed by the Director.) Let's start again. Do you have any questions about the report?

(Jean): As a matter of fact I do. I don't understand one of you conclusions, the one that . . .

Sue: (interrupts) Which one?

(Jean): I was about to say that I don't understand your recommendation that we have an attitude problem with the art department. You said that you expect them to reject your analysis, and if we try to convince them as we usually do, we'll lose a lot of valuable time.

Sue: Well, this is my opinion. I thought you would understand it.

(Jean): I don't. How could you have said this?

Sue: (hesitates for a minute) Well . . .

(Jean): Well, what?

Sue: (falls out of her role and laughs) I want to stop it. It's funny. It's ridiculous. I don't believe it!

Director: What's the matter?

Sue: Jean looks so funny. Suddenly I felt I'd the power to say what I want. I don't believe it.
Director: Did I say something funny?
Sue: No, you did your part well.
Director: Do you mean that this is how it happened in real life?
Sue: Yes. *(laughs)*
Director: I still want to see you going through the entire episode, Sue.
Sue: Those tips you gave me really work. I felt quite comfortable.
Director: How about doing it again, from the beginning to the end?

Key Scene: Second Repeat

Sue: Hi, Jean. Did you want to see me?
(Jean): Oh, hi, Sue. Come in.
Sue: What's up, Jean?
(Jean): The reason I called you is that I need to discuss your report.
Sue: You know, Jean, I worked very hard on it.
(Jean): I know, and I do appreciate the effort you put into it. My problem is with your conclusions and suggestions. For instance, you suggest that the problem of convincing the art department regarding the merit of your analysis will be greater than the production issue. And you also recommended that we deal with the attitudinal problem in a different manner. I don't understand it. How could you say such a thing?
Sue: Well, I did the analysis and that's what I came up with.
(Jean): But it doesn't make sense.
Sue: Why not?
(Jean): Do you really mean that the problem of the attitude of the art department is more important than the production issue? How do you expect me to agree to such an idea?
Sue: Frankly, I did not expect this type of a reaction from you. I was hoping you would see it my way. But you still haven't told me your reason for not accepting my view.
(Jean): Don't you know the reason? You know that I don't have the authority to change the procedures here.
Sue: Even if it makes sense to do so?
(Jean): That's correct. I want you to think of a way we can act on the results of your analysis using the existing channels of communication. I can't see us experimenting with new procedures.
Sue: I don't know what to tell you, Jean. There's always room for innovations.

Director: (leaves Jean's chair) I'd like to be your Double, Sue. But I want to be a special Double, the one that represents your fear of criticism. OK?

Fear: Hi, there. Do you recognize me?

Sue: Of course I do. You're my fear of criticism.

Fear: Right. Would you mind telling me what the hell you are doing? I'm scared of your boldness.

Sue: You know what? I like it. It's a new discovery for me. And the fact that I can do it makes me feel good about myself.

Fear: I'm scared. You're risking so much!

Sue: What am I risking? I talk nicely to her. I don't offend her.

Fear: But it's so dangerous. She may become angry at me for not accepting her opinion and for challenging her. And in a minute she's going to criticize me. It's better to give up. I should bend my head, and get the hell out of here before I get hurt. I'm small and weak. *(sits on the floor curled up, head in hands)*

Sue: Look at you! Aren't you ashamed of yourself sitting down like this?

Fear: It's safer here.

Sue: It's not. If you don't mind me saying it, you look pretty miserable.

Fear: But no one can hurt me! I disappear before there's a chance to get hurt. So I'm on the safe side, and you're exposing yourself to danger. You'll be sorry.

Sue: Yes, I might get hurt. But there's no insurance against it—not for me and not for you. Don't tell me that you feel great down there. So what's the big deal? I certainly don't wish to look like you.

Fear: I don't understand what happened to you. You're not yourself. I'm frightened at the change I see in you. In being bold you'll become careless and you'll regret it.

Sue: I'll try to be careful.

Fear: You know that I'm going to stay here. I'll never leave you. Come down and be with me. *(tries to pull her down to the floor to be with him)*

Sue: (struggles with him) Leave me alone!

Fear: You belong here with me, Sue. *(keeps pulling her down)*

Sue: (angrily) Leave me alone, you hear!

Fear: (stops pulling her) All right. But I'm not going anywhere. I'll stay with you whether you like it or not.

Sue: Fine. Just make sure that you keep on remaining small and insignificant.

Fear: I'm going to stay here.

Sue: You know what? Maybe it's a good idea. You can remain here and remind me that I shouldn't go overboard with my newly discovered power. You can keep an eye on me. At the same time I can look at you and remind myself how I was. So stay here.

Fear: OK *(The Director gets up and resumes the role of Jean.)*

Sue: (to Jean) What shall we do next?

(Jean): Look, Sue. I don't want to dump your report. It's good. Why don't I write you a memo about my reservation and you can think about it.

Sue: And then what?

(Jean): I'll get you my memo today. Why don't you get something in writing and then let's get together again at the end of the week, maybe on Friday.

Sue: But you do like my report, don't you?

(Jean): Yes, except that particular conclusion. See if you can get me something by the end of the week. OK?

Sue: I'll do my best. Is there anything else you want to discuss with me?

(Jean): No, that's all.

Sue: OK. I'll see you on Friday then. *(She leaves Jean's office.)*

The remainder of the session continued as a traditional verbal therapy. The ensuing discussion focused on Susan's reaction to her newly discovered assertive behavior. Clearly, it was necessary to reflect on it beyond the immediate aura of excitement concerning the strength she found in herself. Like any other euphoric experience, the present one too evoked an immense sense of self-gratification. But such experiences tend to be short-lived. The next task, therefore, was to integrate it both into Susan's self-concept and into her routine behavior. To accomplish this, the therapist decided to proceed with practices of assertive behavior in the next meeting. The outcome of this session supported the presently chosen strategy, that is, a continuation of the repeated portrayals of the single episodes format.

Another issue that needed therapeutic explorations concerned Susan's allusions of her long-lasting belief that anger constitutes a debilitating feeling that cannot be used as a constructive force. This belief raised the possibility of a difficulty with regard to her attitude towards the expression of aggression. This issue remained to be explored in future sessions.

CHAPTER 12

Clinical Role Playing: Present and Future

We have come a long way from the beginning of the discussion of clinical role playing. Slowly, step by step, the process of understanding this therapeutic modality proceeded from an examination of its historical antecedents through the formulation of its basic concepts and principles to detailed descriptions of its specific forms of intervention.

Now it is time to pause for a moment and take a look once more at the method as a whole. What is the prospect of clinical role playing? Has it demonstrated a sufficient strength to warrant an increase in popularity? What directions should it pursue? What is still missing that needs to be done, and which of the pursuits that already have began need to be further developed? Obviously, the answers to these questions are predicated on the formation of an overall perception of the effectiveness of clinical role playing as a treatment procedure given both its strengths and weaknesses. Conventional wisdom suggests that in order to determine where we can go from here it is incumbent upon us to know where are we now.

Although allusions to the present status of clinical role playing have already been made in various parts of the book, still there are two important issues that deserve special attention. These are the therapeutic relevance of clinical role playing and its appropriate position among the many varieties of existing therapeutic approaches.

THERAPEUTIC RELEVANCE

A colleague of mine, with whom I worked several years ago, was once asked, "What kind of people are most suitable to be treated with role playing and psychodrama?" Without hesitation she replied, "Anyone who has or has had parents." Indeed, it is fair to say that the suitability of clinical role playing, whether it derives from Moreno's psychodrama theory or from the behavior simulation model, is not limited to a particular client population. In principle, every person can be a good potential candidate for such treatment. Having said this, we must acknowledge that in practice there are unsystematic individual preferences: Some individuals find the method of clinical role playing appealing and others do not.

The answer to the question of what kinds of problems are best suited to be treated with clinical role playing or psychodrama is a different matter. Here one would be wise to exercise a greater modesty and caution because the answer is not so simple. Contemporary thoughts on the effectiveness of psychotherapy suggest that efficacy is related to the availability of a wide range of treatments, and of these, some appear to be more effective with a particular kind of problem than are others. Based on both clinical experiences and research, a view has emerged that no single mode of treatment, clinical role playing included, can justifiably claim superior results for every clinical problem. Nonetheless, there is nothing improper in subscribing to one basic therapeutic approach, as long as its limitations are not ignored or easily discarded.

Given this view, the issue of the differential effectiveness of clinical role playing becomes even more interesting. In order to address it properly one first has to decide what criteria should be used for determining the therapeutic merits of clinical role playing.

The most convincing criteria, of course, would be research outcomes. In that respect we are somewhat limited due to the fact that at the moment there is only scant comparative research on the general effectiveness of role playing and psychodrama relative to other modes of therapy, as well as its effectiveness with selective groups of problems relative to other therapies. Therefore, conclusive statements about the differential efficacy of clinical role playing with specific problems are premature.

These introductory comments notwithstanding, there is a body of research that provides a general support for the efficacy of clinical role playing. Furthermore, there are also preliminary encouraging findings concerning its effectiveness with specific problems. A detailed review of these findings may be found elsewhere (e.g., Kipper, 1978). At this juncture we will limit ourselves to illustrating these points with a few examples.

For instance, clinical role playing and especially its Double technique were found to be effective in developing empathy both among normal teenage subjects (e.g., Kipper & Ben-Ely, 1979) and among retarded persons (Pilkey, Goldman, & Kleinman, 1961). Role playing was also found to increase feelings of dominance, self-confidence, and self-esteem (e.g., Ostrand & Creaser, 1978) and to enhance interpersonal consistency (i.e., the development of a strengthened identification with self and others), among sociopathic women (Naas, 1966).

Or, consider the following examples. The literature on desensitization procedures as applied in behavior therapy indicates that these are the treatments of choice for fears and phobias. Yet, comparisons of desensitization with clinical role playing revealed interesting results. In one study (Kipper & Giladi, 1978) it was found that structured psychodrama was as effective in reducing test anxiety among college students as systematic desensitization. In a second study, Decenteceo (1978) reported that role playing was more effective than both classic desensitization and no treatment groups in reducing fear of snakes. These results, by themselves, perhaps do not justify altering the conclusion regarding the effectiveness of desensitization procedures. Obviously, additional comparative studies with more severe phobias are needed before a different conclusion may be drawn. Nonetheless, the available findings suggest a potential usefulness of clinical role playing in treating these kinds of problems.

One of the topics thoroughly studied in child psychology has been the development of altruistic behavior. The applicability of role playing to this topic has also been explored. An example of one such study was reported by Staub (1971). In this particular investigation the efficacy of teaching children helping and sharing behaviors via role playing techniques was compared with that of an instructional method. The data showed that the former intervention produced superior results: better learning of "helping behavior" for girls and of "sharing behavior" for boys.

Another possible criterion for demonstrating the differential efficacy of clinical role playing with specific problems would be data based on case studies and clinical reports. Overall, this literature depicts an enthusiastic endorsement of this method of therapy. For example, role playing and psychodrama interventions were reported to be useful in the treatments of clinical problems such as drug addiction among adolescents, and alcoholism (e.g., Blume, Robins, & Brandston, 1968; Blume, 1971; Weiner, 1965; 1967). Some studies reported successful teaching of communication and interpersonal skills among the mentally retarded (e.g., Pankratz & Buchan, 1966; Taylor, 1969), aphasic patients (Schlanger & Schlanger, 1968), and deaf people (Clayton & Robinson,

1971). There were also descriptions suggesting that clinical role playing and psychodrama might be quite useful in treating hospitalized and psychotic patients. Numerous reports to that effect have been published during the last 20 years (e.g., Chase & Farnham, 1966; Polansky & Harkins, 1969; Rabiner & Drucker, 1967; Williams & Gasdick, 1970). Even this brief survey of a few selective examples indicates that clinical role playing is a psychotherapeutic approach relevant to a broad spectrum of clinical problems.

IS CLINICAL ROLE PLAYING AN ADJUNCT OR A MAIN THERAPY?

The above discussion leads us to another, perhaps corollary, issue concerning the overall position of clinical role playing in the entire therapeutic endeavor. Usually the issue is raised in the form of the question: Should clinical role playing be regarded as a main psychotherapeutic modality or is it limited to serve ancillary functions? There is no doubt that the clash between the two opposing views has produced undesirable consequences. Those who maintain that it is only an adjunctive method have been too quick to unjustly minimize its therapeutic merits. Conversely, those who applied it as a main form of therapy became over-enthusiastic in their unqualified endorsement of clinical role playing as a comprehensive therapeutic modality. My own position is that, as stated, the question is not constructive; the two options are restrictive and there is an equally viable third alternative. The latter suggests that the application of clinical role playing either as a primary mode of therapy or as one component of other kinds of therapeutic interventions may vary according to the circumstances. But since traditionally the question has been raised as a choice between two views, let me discuss it the way it is phrased above.

How does one decide in favor of one view or another? An objective examination reveals that such a decision may depend on the following three factors: (a) the therapist's primary approach and training, (b) the way therapists choose to apply clinical role playing, and, of course (c) the empirical data. The first two are matters of attitudes; the third is a matter of facts.

Therapists who subscribe to and have received their basic training in psychotherapeutic approaches other than clinical role playing naturally will use these as their main treatment interventions. If they wish to expand the repertoire of their techniques, they may occasionally borrow from other approaches—in our case, from clinical role playing. Their position as to which is a main approach and which is merely an adjunct has already been made, even before they decide to use role playing techniques. In short, their position reflects personal preferences and is an indication of their bias in favor of a particular theoretical view rather than an impartial evaluation of the therapeutic merit of role playing. Therapists who subscribe to and have received their basic training in clinical role playing will have the same bias, this time in favor of role playing. Their view has also been crystallized in advance. Sometimes, however, one may encounter therapists who do not operate under a preset notion about when clinical role playing should be regarded as a main therapeutic thrust and when as an auxiliary intervention. They keep an open mind and prefer to decide each time differently, depending on the merit of the individual case. Their application of various treatment modalities is based on a problem-solving orientation, and their decision becomes a matter of practical choice, not of a principle. For them, clinical role playing can be both a main as well as an adjunctive method.

Personal preferences aside, is there empirical evidence that can shed light on this issue? The short answer is: not really. The evidence is far from being equivocal, and there is sufficient data to uphold each of the two positions. In scrutinizing the evidence, however, an additional difficulty seems to emerge. Sometimes the data (in support of either view) are in themselves problematic. Often, designs of experiments and case studies which could clarify the issue already reflect the investigators' views. From the very beginning these cast role playing in either an adjunct or a main capacity. Some research designs provide only indirect inferential conclusions because they have avoided investigating the issue directly. A direct investigation would require studies where role playing is used alone compared with role playing used together with other therapeutic modalities. And these are scarce.

Let me illustrate this problem with three examples. The first concerns the use of clinical role playing as the primary modality. Consider the two reports of psychodrama treatments combined with videotape playback (Goldfield, 1968; Gonen, 1971). The very design of these two already reflects the author's views. There is no doubt that psychodrama was conceived as the main therapeutic modality because, by definition, videotape playback is not a major therapeutic approach but rather a helpful technique. The second example concerns the use of role playing as an adjunct method and comes from a study by Lipsky, Kassinove, and Miller (1980). These authors set to evaluate the efficacy of rational-emotive therapy combined with imagery, supportive therapy with relaxation, and no treatment. Obviously, the researchers' interest focused on verifying the efficacy of rational-emotive therapy, presumably because they considered this approach as their main therapeutic thrust. From the outset, role-reversal was introduced as an adjunct intervention. Therefore, the best findings one could hope for as far as role playing is concerned would support the efficacy of role reversal only in that capacity.

Now let us examine an entirely different third example. Blitch and Haynes (1972) reported a case of treating a homosexual female. The treatment, which lasted 14 sessions, included the following procedures: (a) relaxation training in situations involving physical touch, (b) role playing to acquire heterosexual skills, and (c) cognitive restructuring of fantasies accompanying masturbation. Was role playing considered here to be an adjunct method or the main treatment modality? One could try to determine this by looking at the time spent with each of the other two interventions. But there is no need to do that. Judging from the nature of the interventions, behavior therapy was the primary approach, not role playing. At the same time it would be inappropriate to say that role playing was introduced in an ancillary capacity. The case study shows that it was applied as one out of three procedures, that is, as part and parcel of the overall main approach. The therapist considered role playing not an adjunct technique but a central component of the treatment package, that is, a behavioral technique.

There is a difference between considering clinical role playing as an adjunctive therapy and considering it as a component of the primary modality. The former sees it as an inferior modality having a small contribution to the overall curative endeavor, whereas the latter sees it as a central intervention having a restricted scope. The former sees it in a *supplementary* capacity, whereas the latter as a main intervention for a *limited purpose*. Behavior therapy is indeed an interesting example of a system that incorporated role playing as a genuine component of its main thrust. This view has been demonstrated in many case reports and controlled clinical outcome research. Accordingly, subjects are exposed to treatment in which role playing is combined with one or more of the following procedures: modeling, direct coaching, cognitive restructuring, and home assignments, to mention a few (e.g., Bornstein, Winegardner, Rychtarik, Paul, Naifeh, Sweeney, & Justman, 1979; Hersen, Bellack, & Himmelhoch, 1980), and the list is very long indeed.

The incorporation of one approach into another can go in either direction. Just as role playing can be incorporated into behavior therapy as a main treatment of choice for specific issues and purposes, proponents of clinical role playing can incorporate behavior therapy or other techniques into their approach, forming a merger of treatment procedures. A comprehensive clinical role playing approach to psychotherapy holds that interventions originally developed outside the behavior stimulation approach may be adopted in two ways as follows:

(a) *Redefining the intervention in terms of behavior simulation frame of reference.* For example, the techniques of modeling and coaching typically associated with behavior therapy are congruent with the behavior simulation concept of mimetic-replication (and sometimes also with mimetic-pretend) behavior. When introduced in role playing episodes, they become *bona fide* clinical role playing techniques. The same would apply in instances where techniques used in other nonbehavioristic therapeutic approaches are sought to be integrated into clinical role playing.

(b) *Borrowing techniques for specific occasions.* In this way clinical role playing borrows techniques based on different principles and procedures. Although these cannot be translated into behavior simulation nomenclature, nonetheless, they do *not* seem to be in conflict with the application of role playing. It is an act of pairing techniques for the sake of expediency. Examples of these would be the adoption of the principles of operant conditioning, shaping of behavior through reinforcements, or self-control. Some forms of cognitive restructuring and other verbal interactions would also fall under this category.

It is perhaps clear now why I have claimed at the outset that discussing the position of clinical role playing vis-à-vis the question of whether it constitutes a major therapeutic modality or merely an adjunct method is not helpful. The fact that the evidence suggests that it can be either of these two possibilities and that experience shows that there is a third possibility lead us to the conclusion that the question asked was inappropriate. The view put forward in this volume maintains that in principle all major therapeutic techniques ought to be considered as main interventions. Often, two or more need to be merged in order to maximize therapeutic effectiveness and the relative contribution of each component of the integrated package may vary from one case to another. The traditional question, therefore, has to be replaced by a different one, namely, under what circumstances should one decide to incorporate other therapeutic techniques into role playing and when should role playing techniques be used more or less alone? Unfortunately, at the present state of knowledge, a clear answer to this question must await further research. We will be advised to bear in mind that until such empirical evidence is produced, current answers are influenced by the respondents' theoretical preferences. Proponents of clinical role playing may decide differently from proponents of other therapeutic approaches.

CONSIDERATIONS FOR THE FUTURE

As we look at the principles, paradigms, procedures, and techniques of the method of clinical role playing, three general observations emerge. One is the straightforwardness of the logic associated with its assumptions. All that is required is accepting the premises that the subject of psychotherapy is behavior, overt as well as covert, as expressed in real life, that such behavior can be simulated more or less accurately, and that the concretization of human experiences is therapeutically valuable. Second, in contrast to the simplicity of the underlying assumptions, the practical, implemental aspects of the method are quite complex. An expert utilization of clinical role playing involves, in addition to having the appropriate clinical knowledge, a mastery of the many facets of the method. It also demands considerable creativity, ingenuity, and resourcefulness on the part of the therapist. The third observation is that the method is well organized and follows a number of models. Previous descriptions of role playing could have easily led to the conclusion that it consists of a few procedures accompanied by a few interesting techniques which otherwise have little in common and are unrelated to each other. Hopefully, our analysis has dispelled this misleading impression.

The process of formulating the present view was long, indeed. It began with a historical survey of role playing and its emergence as a recognized form of therapy. The second and third chapters described an attempt to fill the void created by the absence of a general model for the use of clinical role playing. This effort resulted in the formulation of a general model for behavior simulation and its application in clinical practice. The ensuing two chapters described the design of the treatment session. These were followed by four chapters that provided a classification system for the various techniques along with paradigms showing the rationale for the proposed categorization. And the next two chapters contained illustrations of the application of clinical role playing in different forms of therapy.

We began the book by looking back at the historical path of role playing in the hope of demonstrating the contribution of the past to the shaping of the present. It is fitting that the concluding comments will examine the road that lies ahead.

TOWARDS A WIDER ACCEPTANCE OF CLINICAL ROLE PLAYING

The popularity of role playing as a form of therapy has increased in the last two decades. This trend, however, still largely rests on impressions derived from positive, often sporadic, clinical experiences rather than on accepting the basic conceptual foundations. Part of the difficulty is that the hindering effects of the past have not been completely eradicated. Still, the receptivity of role playing as a *bona fide* form of therapy is somewhat marred by its association with Moreno's theory. This does not mean to imply a criticism of the theory. Quite the contrary, it had a significant contribution to the development of behavioral science. But, as I have already indicated, there were political and other reasons for the discomfort expressed with regard to this association. One is that in spite of his genius, Moreno acquired the reputation of a controversial figure. Second, his theory lacked the scope and breadth of a general theory of personality. Furthermore, from the early days of psychodrama its followers adopted an exclusive stance. They made an unfortunate "political" decision to become tightly entrenched in their own system. No wonder that the acceptance of role playing was hindered by such isolation from the rest of the professional community.

As a matter of fact, traditional skepticism towards role playing as identified with Moreno's particular formulation of psychodrama had many roots. In a recent monograph, Blatner (1985) enumerated several reasons for such resistance. His list is long and contains 20 points. Here are a few examples. Unlike sociometry, another innovation by Moreno, psychodrama failed to capture the imagination of academicians. For some reason it lacked the inspiration that characterized humanistic psychology and did not arouse the same excitement and scientific challenges posed by modern behaviorism. As a result, it was these two—humanistic psychology and behaviorism—that became the "radical approaches" accepted by academic psychology.

By repeatedly contrasting himself with the dominant school of psychoanalysis, Moreno defied the intellectual trend of the early period of psychotherapy only to acquire the reputation of a maverick. Also, his direct approach to psychotherapy and the emphasis on activity in the form of concrete enactments were incongruent with the then prevailing principle of psychological treatment.

Some modes of therapy, which branded themselves as spin-offs of psychodrama, acquired a questionable respectability. Undeservedly, psychodrama was blamed for this, thus losing some of its due credibility. Furthermore,

"Religion and philosophy were also themes that had become separated from science in the early part of this century, and this separation was guarded with as much emotion as the separation of
church and state. Moreno's inclusion of such themes in his writings
and personal presentations went against the norm. . . .
[These]. . . were seen as potentially affecting negatively on the
emerging field of psychiatry, which was trying to attain the mantle
of scientific and medical respectability. (Blatner, 1985, pp. 49-50)

These comments notwithstanding, it should be emphasized that the
association of role playing with psychodrama is not the only reason for
its past low popularity. Another of the reasons, for instance, is that its
adoption by behavior therapy posed a problem for those who subscribed
to psychodynamic approaches. And this, too, added to the traditional
skepticism towards role playing.

Nowadays, however, many of these reasons either do not apply or
have diminished in significance. I believe that future efforts must focus
on offering new perspectives, new formulations, and new evidence in
support of models such as behavior simulation. This holds the best hope
for continuing the trend of increased acceptance of clinical role playing
as a valuable therapeutic modality.

RESEARCH

The plea for a vigorous research undertaking concerning the behavior
simulation model and the effectiveness of clinical role playing was made
several times throughout the book and need not be repeated again.
Instead, we would like to raise some general research issues that pose
a challenge for the future.

It might be helpful to begin the discussion with a point about the
distinction between role playing research in relation to social psychology
and that in relation to clinical psychology and psychotherapy.

Although these are the two areas where traditional role playing research took place, their focus of interest has been somewhat different.
For social psychologists, a key issue is determining the extent that role
playing adequately simulated the "true" reality as measured by real-life
behavior. Uncertainty in this regard would cast doubts about the pre-
dictive validity of role playing and the advisability of its inclusion in social
psychology studies. So far research outcomes have not been equivocal
on this issue. Although a correspondence between in-vivo and simulated
experiences is of interest to those who apply role playing in therapy,

their main preoccupation lies elsewhere. Clinicians are particularly interested in the therapeutic effects of simulations. In other words, they
need to identify the kinds of psychological processes that are activated
by various role playing interventions. For them, such knowledge is important in order to arrive at a better match between the interventions
proper and their intended therapeutic effects. Clinicians are also interested in the long-term impact of clinical role playing on subsequent
behavior outside the treatment room.

The importance of investigations designed to ascertain the similarity
between in-vivo behavior and its corresponding simulated portrayals is
undisputable. Certainly, research effort in this direction is highly desirable. Positive outcomes will assuredly lend further credence to the rationale advocating the use of clinical role playing in psychotherapy. In
particular, it will add to the affirmation of one of its basic assumptions,
namely, that real-life behavior can be accurately simulated in laboratory
conditions. Yet establishing or failing such *unqualified* support does not
carry the same weight for practicing therapists as it does for social psychologists. It is true that a congruence of this sort may increase the
possibility of transfer of learning—of generalization—from the treatment sessions to real-life. But the decision to use or refrain from using
any given therapeutic intervention does not rest solely on this issue.

The position held throughout the book is that clinical role playing
interventions (techniques) serve as therapeutic tools. In principle, therefore, their effectiveness depends on a good fit between the specific purposes for which they have been designed and the actual outcomes.
Although this is by no means a unique approach, it has not generated
sufficient research.

It seems that researchers have been more attracted to the global perspectives, that is, to the study of clinical role playing procedures that
contains a host of techniques lumped together. Our point is not to dis-
courage this type of research. On the contrary, the tradition of the past
needs to be carried into the future. Knowing the *overall* therapeutic
quality of clinical role playing is important given that this is the way it
is conducted in daily practice. This kind of research also holds the key
for providing answers to several questions previously raised in this book.
For instance, are there particular kinds of personalities who respond
favorably to this form of therapy? And conversely, are there any who
do not tend to benefit from it? What kinds of clinical problems are dealt
with best by means of role playing? Likewise, one should encourage a
continued research aimed at ascertaining the overall effectiveness of

clinical role playing therapy compared with other forms of treatment. The question to be answered here, however, is not how does clinical role playing pair with other therapies, but what is its comparative usefulness with regard to specific clinical problems?

Future research needs to focus on the specific merit of individual techiques, or several techniques subsumed under one kind of category or under one technique's prototype. Psychotherapeutic help is essentially an educational endeavor (although some may prefer to use the medical analogy, and consider it a curative undertaking). It is based on the activation of psychological processes that can eliminate maladjusted behavior and replace it with a functional behavior. Given that a wide range of such processes have been identified in psychology, should we not know what is the relationship between the use of a technique, or a subgroup of techniques, and the elicitation of specific psychological processes?

Pursuing this line of research may shed further light on a famous controversy that has been long evident in psychotherapy in general, and in clinical role playing in particular. I refer, of course, to the debate surrounding the centrality of catharsis as a curative factor. My contention is that characterizing the therapeutic process in terms of either catharsis or training (or even both) may prove to be a restrictive view. Catharsis is one process. Contrasting it with training, which involves a variety of learning processes, is an unbalanced comparison. More important, it is doubtful that catharsis and training adequately capture *all* the psychological processes that affect human behavior. In its beginning, behavior therapy limited itself to treatments based on different kinds of conditioning. Today, other psychological processes are subsumed under that form of treatment. It should be remembered that some of these (e.g., self-control, self-talk, and other cognitive processes) were totally rejected by the founders of modern behaviorism. As more and more processes become amenable to objective assessments, therapists of different persuasions begin to address themselves to such issues. Progress, therefore, appears to be associated with identifying a greater number of specific psychological processes that can be utilized in the course of therapy.

Finally, future research should also investigate the advantages of incorporating new, advanced technology into traditional practices of clinical role playing. This involves the use of television and other instruments capable of monitoring important physiological measures. Research in medical psychology and biofeedback have already demonstrated the therapeutic possibilities offered by such procedures. The tendency of traditional therapists to shy away from the use of modern technology may eventually prove to be a sign of anachronism rather than that of a sound clinical judgment.

* * *

Earlier in the book (see Chapter 9, Prototype II), I described the technique of the Magic Shop. This delightful imaginary shop allows us to entertain the possibility of acquiring what is in our own fantasy. It is a place where hidden wishes can be played out as if they have come true. Suppose we were given the opportunity to visit the Magic Shop and have our ideal vision of clinical role playing, what would that be?

So let us pretend that the shop is set in an imaginary action space, with two chairs in the middle: one for an imaginary shopkeeper and one for us. As we enter, the shopkeeper greets us with the question: What can I do for you today? At first, overwhelmed by this opportunity, we hesitate for a moment. Then we manage to muster our courage and say:

We have a vision of what therapy through clinical role playing should look like in the future. It is a form of psychotherapy based on a general model that emcompasses all other forms of simulations. It has a well organized structure and sets of many techniques that can be used in several ways. In principle, however, there are two prototypical formats. The elaborate one consists of about half a dozen interrelated scenes. It ascribes a great importance to the process of moving from one scene to another as a way of understanding the complexity of the protagonist's difficulties, creating the necessary conditions to abandon dysfunctional modes of thinking and behaving, and facilitating the formation of new perceptions and attitudes, or the practicing of new modes of coping. The second format is more focused and represents a shortened version of the former. Here, the main therapeutic effort centers on practicing alternatives to old, identifiable behavioral patterns, while other aspects of the treatment are rendered through different procedures.

In our vision, the method of clinical role playing is based on solid scientific evidence that substantiates its effectiveness. It also provides criteria for a differential utilization of techniques, that is, a set of directions for choosing the appropriate interventions in order to help protagonists activate the processes needed for the attainment of therapeutic targets.

In our vision, clinical role playing employs a variety of learning as well as other therapeutic principles in a systematic manner. It incorporates advanced technology. The treatment session is enriched by computerized data based on videotapes and other important physiological indices. This information is gathered without the awareness of the protagonist and is available instantaneously.

Well, dear shopkeeper, can we have our vision come true? Even if we cannot have it all exactly the way we want, a close approximation will suffice.

References

Ackernecht, L. K. (1967). Roleplaying of embarrassing situations. *Group Psychotherapy, 20*, 39-42.

Alexander, F. (1965). Unexplored areas in psychoanalytic theory and treatment. In G. Daniels (ed.), *New perspectives in psychoanalysis: Sandor Rado lectures 1957-1963*. New York: Grune & Stratton.

Allen, D. T. (1966). Psychodrama in the crib and in the family. *Group Psychotherapy, 19*, 22-28.

Alperson, J. R. (1976). Gone with the wind: Role-reversal desensitization for a wind phobic client. *Behavior Therapy, 7*, 405-407.

American Psychological Association (1977). *Ethical standards for psychologists* (Rev. ed.). Washington D. C.: Author.

Ayllon, T. (1963). Intensive treatment of psychotic behavior by stimulus satiation and food reinforcement. *Behavior Research and Therapy, 1*, 53-62.

Bandura, A. (1977). *Social learning theory.* Englewood Cliffs, N. J.: Prentice-Hall.

Barker, R. G. (1968). *Ecological psychology: Concepts and methods for studying the environment of human behavior.* Stanford, CA: Stanford University Press.

Beck, A. T., Emery, G., & Greenberg, R. L. (1985). *Anxiety disorders and phobias: A cognitive perspective.* New York: Basic Books.

Bellack, A. S., Hersen, M., & Lamparski, D. (1979). Role play tests for assessing social skills: Are they valid? Are they useful? *Journal of Consulting and Clinical Psychology, 47*, 335-342.

Bellack, A. S., Hersen, M., & Turner, S. M. (1978). Role playing for assessing social skills: Are they valid? *Behavior Therapy, 9*, 448-461.

Berger, M. M. (ed.). (1978). *Videotape techniques in psychiatric training and treatment* (Rev. ed.). New York: Brunner/Mazel.

Berne, E. (1961). *Transactional analysis in psychotherapy.* New York: Grove Press.

Bettelheim, B. (1967). *Empty fortress.* New York: Free Press.

Biddle, B. J. (1979). *Role theory: Expectations, identities, and behaviors.* New York: Academic Press.

Biddle, B. J., & Thomas, E. J. (1966). *Role theory: Concepts and research.* New York: Wiley & Sons.

367

Blackwenn, W. J. (1923). Narcosis as therapy in neuropsychiatric conditions. *Journal of the American Medical Association, 95,* 1168-1171.

Blatner, H. A. (1973). *Acting-In: Practical applications of psychodramatic methods.* New York: Springer.

Blatner, H. A. (1985). *Foundations of psychodrama: History, theory, practice and resources.* A monograph published by the author, San Marcos, Texas: San Marcos Treatment Center.

Blitch, J. W., & Haynes, R. B. (1972). Multiple techniques in a case of female homosexuality. *Journal of Behavior Therapy and Experimental Psychiatry, 3,* 319-322.

Blume, S. B. (1971). Group role reversal as a teaching technique in an alcoholism rehabilitation unit. *Group Psychotherapy and Psychodrama, 24,* 135-137.

Blume, S. B., Robins, J., & Brandston, A. (1968). Psychodrama techniques in the treatment of alcoholism. *Group Psychotherapy, 21,* 241-246.

Bohart, A. C. (1977). Role playing and interpersonal conflict reduction. *Journal of Counseling Psychology, 24,* 15-24.

Borgida, E., & Nisbett, R. E. (1977). The differential impact of abstract vs. concrete information on decision. *Journal of Applied Social Psychology, 7,* 258-271.

Bornstein, P. H., Winegardner, J., Rychtarik, R. G., Paul, W. P., Naifeh, S. J., Sweeney, T. M., & Justman, A. (1979). Interpersonal skills training: Evaluation of a program with adult male offenders. *Criminal Justice and Behavior, 6,* 119-132.

Bratter, T. (1967). Dynamics of role reversal. *Group Psychotherapy, 20,* 88-94.

Brind, A. B., & Brind, N. (1967). Role reversal. *Group Psychotherapy, 20,* 173-177.

Bronfenbrenner, U., & Newcomb, T. M. (1948). Improvization: An application of psychodrama in personality diagnosis. *Sociatry, 1,* 367-382.

Buchanan, D. R. (1984). Psychodrama. In American Psychiatric Association Commission on Psychiatric Therapies, T. B. Karasu (Chairman), *The psychiatric therapies.* Washington, D. C.: American Psychiatric Association.

Buck, R. (1984). *The communication of emotion.* New York: Guilford Press.

Burton, A. (ed.). (1961). *Psychotherapy of the psychoses.* New York: Basic Books.

Cameron, N. (1963). *Personality development and psychopathology: A dynamic approach.* Boston: Houghton Mifflin.

Carkhuff, R. R. (1969a). *Helping human relations: Vol. I: Selection and training.* New York: Holt, Rinehart & Winston.

Carkhuff, R. R. (1969b). *Helping human relations: Vol. II: Practice and research.* New York: Holt, Rinehart & Winston.

Carpenter, J. R. (1968). Role reversal in the classroom. *Group Psychotherapy, 21,* 155-167.

Chase, P., & Farnham, B. (1966). Psychodrama in a mental hospital. *Mental Hygiene, 50,* 262.

Clayton, L., & Robinson, L. D. (1971). Psychodrama with deaf people. *American Annals of the Deaf, 116,* 415-419.

Cofer, C. N., & Appley, M. H. (1964). *Motivation: Theory and research.* New York: Wiley & Sons.

Cohen, J. (1951). The technique of role reversal: A preliminary note. *Occupational Psychology, 25,* 64-66.

Cohen, A. M., & Smith, R. D. (1976). *The critical incident in growth groups: A manual for group leaders.* San Diego, CA: University Associates.

Colman, A. (1982). *Game theory and experimental games: The study of strategic interaction.* Oxford, England: Pergamon.

Corsini, R. J. (1953). The Behind-Your-Back technique in group psychotherapy and psychodrama. *Group Psychotherapy, 6,* 102-109.

Corsini, R. J. (1966). *Roleplaying in psychotherapy: A manual.* Chicago: Aldine.

Crasilneck, H. B., & Hall, J. A. (1985). *Clinical hypnosis: Principles and applications.* New York: Grune & Stratton.

Csikszentmihalyi, M. (1982). Learning, "flow," and happiness. In R. Gross (ed.), *Invitation to lifelong learning.* Chicago: Follett.

Curran, J. P. (1979). Pandora's box reopened? The assessment of social skills. *Journal of Behavioral Assessment, 1,* 55-71.

Decenteceo, E. T. (1978). *Systematic desensitization and roleplaying in the treatment of fear of snakes.* Unpublished Doctoral Dissertation, State University of New York at Stony Brook.

Dunlap, K. (1932). *Habits, their making and unmaking.* New York: Liveright.

Durkin, H. E. (ed.). (1981). *Living groups: Group psychotherapy and general system theory.* New York: Brunner/Mazel.

Eiben, R., & Milliren, A. (eds.). (1976). *Educational change: A humanistic approach.* San Diego, CA: University Associates.

Elms, A. C. (ed.). (1969). *Role playing, reward, and attitude change.* New York: Van Nostrand Reinhold.

Emmelkamp, P. M. G. (1982). Anxiety and fear. In A. S. Bellack, M. Hersen, & A. E. Kazdin (eds.), *International handbook of behavior modification and therapy.* New York: Plenum.

Enneis, J. M. (1950). The hypnodramatic technique. *Group Psychotherapy, 3,* 11-54.

Faraday, A. (1974). *The dream game.* New York: Perennial Library, Harper & Row.

Farra, H. (1980). Self-development games and simulation: An evaluation. In R. E. Horn & A. Cleaves (eds.), *The guide to simulations/games for education and training* (4th ed.). Beverly Hills, CA: Sage.

Feinberg, H. (1959). The Ego Building technique. *Group Psychotherapy, 12,* 230-235.

Fink, A. K. (1968). When is a director not a director? When he is a protagonist. *Group Psychotherapy, 21,* 38-39.

Fleming, M. (1974). *Hostility in recovering alcoholic women compared to non-alcoholic women and the effect of psychodrama in reducing hostility.* Unpublished Dissertation, United States International University.

Forrester, J. W. (1973). *World dynamics.* Cambridge, MA: Wright-Allen Press.

Freedman, J. L. (1969). Role playing: Psychology by consensus. *Journal of Personality and Social Psychology, 13,* 107-114.

Garfield, P. L. (1974). *Creative dreaming.* London: Futura Publications.

Gazda, G. M., & Powell, M. (1981). Multiple impact training: A model for teaching/training in life-skills. In G. M. Gazda (ed.), *Innovations to group psychotherapy* (2nd ed.). Springfield, IL: Charles C Thomas.

Geller, D. M. (1978). Involvement in role-playing simulations: A demonstration with studies on obedience. *Journal of Personality and Social Psychology, 36,* 219-235.

Glasser, W. (1965). *Reality therapy.* New York: Harper Colophon Books.

Goldberg, C. (1970). *Encounter: Group sensitivity training experience.* New York: Science House.

Goldfield, M. (1968). Use of TV videotape to enhance the value of psychodrama. *American Journal of Psychiatry, 125,* 690-692.

Goldfried, M. R., & Davison, G. C. (1976). *Clinical behavior therapy.* New York: Holt, Rinehart & Winston.

Goldman, E. E., & Morrison, D. C. (1984). *Psychodrama: Experience and process.* Dubuque, IA: Kendall/Hunt.

Goldstein, J. A. (1967). The effect of doubling on involvement in group psychotherapy as measured by number and duration of patient utterance. *Psychotherapy: Theory, Research and Practice, 7,* 57-60.

Goldstein, J. A. (1971). Investigation of doubling as a technique for involving withdrawn patients in group psychotherapy. *Journal of Consulting and Clinical Psychology, 37,* 155-162.

Goldstein, A. P., & Goedhart, A. (1973). The use of structural learning for empathy in paraprofessional psychotherapist training. *Journal of Community Psychology, 1,* 168-173.

Gonen, J. (1971). The use of psychodrama combined with videotape playback on an inpatient floor. *Psychiatry, 34,* 198-213.

Goodman, G. A., & Timko, M. G. (1976). Hot seats and aggressive behavior. *Academic Theory, 11,* 447-448.

Gorecki, R. R., Dickson, A. L., Anderson, H. N., & Jones, G. E. (1981). Relationship between contrived in vivo and role-play assertive behavior. *Journal of Clinical Psychology, 31,* 104-107.

Greenberg, M. (1967). Role playing: An alternative to deception. *Journal of Personality and Social Psychology, 7,* 152-157.

Grinker, R. R., & Spiegel, J. (1945). *Men under stress.* Philadelphia: Blakiston.

Guldner, C. A. (1982). Multiple family psychodramatic therapy. *Journal of Group Psychotherapy, Psychodrama and Sociometry, 35,* 47-56.

Guldner, C. A. (1983). Structuring and staging: A comparison of Minuchin's Structural Family Therapy and Moreno's Psychodramatic Therapy. *Journal of Group Psychotherapy, Psychodrama and Sociometry, 35,* 141-154.

Gutride, M. E., Goldstein, A. P., & Hunter, G. F. (1973). The use of modeling and role playing to increase social interaction among asocial psychiatric patients. *Journal of Consulting and Clinical Psychology, 40,* 408-413.

Haas, R. B., & Moreno, J. L. (1961). Psychodrama as a projective technique. In H. H. Anderson & G. L. Anderson (eds.), *An introduction to projective techniques.* Englewood Cliffs, N.J.: Prentice-Hall.

Haley, J. (ed.). (1967). *Advanced techniques of hypnosis and therapy: Selected papers of Milton H. Erickson, M. D.* New York: Grune & Stratton.

Haley, J. (1973). *Uncommon therapy.* New York: Norton.

Hamilton, V. L. (1978). Obedience and responsibility: A jury simulation. *Journal of Personality and Social Psychology, 36,* 126-146.

Haskell, M. R. (1957). Psychodramatic role training in preparation of release on parole. *Group Psychotherapy, 10,* 51-59.

Haskell, M. (1975). *Socioanalysis.* Long Beach, CA: Role Training Associates.

Hersen, M., & Bellack, A. S. (1978). Staff training and consultation. In M. Hersen & A. S. Bellack (eds.), *Behavior therapy in psychiatric setting.* Baltimore, MD: Williams & Wilkins.

Hersen, M., Bellack, A. S., & Himmelhoch, J. M. (1980). Treatment of unipolar depression with social skills training. *Behavior Therapy, 4,* 547-556.

Higgins, R. L., Alonso, R. R., & Pendleton, M. G. (1979). The validity of role-play assessment of assertiveness. *Behavior Therapy, 10,* 655-662.

Higgins, R. L., Frisch, M. B, & Smith, D. (1983). A comparison of role-played and natural responses to identical circumstances. *Behavior Therapy, 14,* 158-169.

Hollander, C. E. (1967). The mirror technique as a psychodramatic encounter. *Group Psychotherapy, 20,* 25-31.

Hollander, C. E. (1978). *A process for psychodrama training: The Hollander Psychodrama Curve.* Denver: Colorado Psychodrama Center.

Hollander, C. E. (1983). Comparative family systems of Moreno and Bowen. *Journal of Group Psychotherapy, Psychodrama and Sociometry, 36,* 1-12.

Hollander, C. E., & Hollander, S. L. (1978). *The warm-up box.* Denver: Colorado Psychodrama Center.

Horn, R. E., & Cleaves, A. (eds.). (1980). *The guide to simulations/games for education and training* (4th ed.). Beverly Hills, CA: Sage.

Horsley, J. S. (1936). Narco-analysis. *Lancet, 1,* 55.

Hull, C. L. (1943). *Principles of behavior.* New York: Appleton.

Janis, I. L., & Mann, L. (1965). Effectiveness of emotional role-playing in modifying smoking habits and attitudes. *Journal of Experimental Research in Personality, 1,* 84-90.

Janov, A. (1970). *The primal scream.* New York: Dell.

Johnson, D. W. (1967). The use of role reversal in intergroup competition. *Journal of Personality and Social Psychology, 7,* 135-141.

Johnson, D. W. (1971a). Effectiveness of role reversal: Actor or listener. *Psychological Reports, 28,* 275-282.

Johnson, D. W. (1971b). Role reversal: A summary and review of the research. *International Journal of Group Tensions, 1,* 318-334.

Johnson, D. W., & Dustin, R. (1970). The initiation of cooperation through role reversal. *Journal of Social Psychology, 82,* 193-203.

Kanfer, F. H., & Phillips, J. S. (1969). A survey of current behavior therapies and a proposal for classification. In C. M. Franks (ed.), *Behavior therapy: Appraisal and status.* New York: McGraw-Hill.

Kazdin, A. E. (1977). *The token economy.* New York: Plenum.

Kazdin, A. E. (1979). Situational specificity: The two-edged sword of behavioral assessment. *Behavioral Assessment, 1,* 57-75.

Kelly, G. A. (1955). *The psychology of personal constructs.* New York: Norton.

Kelly, J. A., & Drabman, R. S. (1977). Generalizing response suppression on self-injurious behavior through an overcorrection punishment procedure: A case study. *Behavior Therapy, 8,* 468-472.

Kelly, J. G., Blake, R. R., & Stomberg, C. E. (1957). The effect of role training on role reversal. *Group Psychotherapy, 10,* 95-104.

Kenderdine, J. M., & Keyes, B. (eds.). (1974). *Simulations, games and experiential learning techniques: On the road to a new frontier.* Proceedings of the first national ABSEL conference. Norman, Oklahoma: Center for Economics and Management Research, The University of Oklahoma.

Kipper, D. A. (1967). Spontaneity and the warming-up process in a new light. *Group Psychotherapy, 20,* 62-73.

Kipper, D. A. (1975). The Candle technique in psychodrama. *Group Psychotherapy and Psychodrama, 28,* 50-54.

Kipper, D. A. (1977). Towards a psychodramatic intake: Two techniques of self-introduction. *Group Psychotherapy, Psychodrama and Sociometry, 30,* 146-154.

Kipper, D. A. (1978). Trends in the research on the effectiveness of psychodrama: Retrospect and prospect. *Group Psychotherapy, Psychodrama and Sociometry, 31,* 5-18.

Kipper, D. A. (1980). In vivo desensitization of nyctophobia: Two case reports. *Psychotherapy: Theory, Research and Practice, 17,* 24-29.

Kipper, D. A. (1981). Behavior simulation interventions in group psychotherapy. In G. M. Gazda (ed.), *Innovations to group psychotherapy* (2nd ed.). Springfield, IL: Charles C Thomas.

Kipper, D. A. (1982). Behavior simulation: A model for the study of the simulation aspect of psychodrama. *Journal of Group Psychotherapy, Psychodrama and Sociometry, 35,* 1-17.

Kipper, D. A., & Ben-Ely, Z. (1979). The effectiveness of the psychodramatic double method, the reflection method, and lecturing on the training of empathy. *Journal of Clinical Psychology, 35,* 370-376.

Kipper, D. A., & Har-Even, D. (1980). *Changing attitudes towards newcomers' privileges: Effects of mimetic-replication and mimetic-pretend simulation situations.* Paper presented at the 17th Scientific Convention of the Israel Psychological Association, Ramat-Gan, Israel.

Kipper, D. A., & Har-Even, D. (1984). Role playing techniques: The differential effect of behavior simulation interventions on the readiness to inflict pain. *Journal of Clinical Psychology, 40,* 936-941.

Kipper, D. A., Har-Even, D., Rotenberg, M., & Dagan, M. (1982). Involvement in role playing as a function of the simulation procedure and level of imagination. *Journal of Group Psychotherapy, Psychodrama and Sociometry, 35,* 99-110.

Kipper, D. A., & Giladi, D. (1978). The effectiveness of structured psychodrama and systematic desensitization on reducing test anxiety. *Journal of Counseling Psychology, 25,* 499-505.

Kolb, L. C. (1984). Narcosynthesis. In T. B. Karasu (Chairman), *The psychiatric therapies.* Washington, D. C.: American Psychiatric Association.

Kreitler, H., & Eblinger, S. (1968). Validation of psychodramatic behavior against behavior in life. *British Journal of Medical Psychology, 41,* 185-192.

Kroger, W. S., & Fezler, W. D. (1976). *Hypnosis and behavior modification: Imagery conditioning.* Philadelphia: J. B. Lippincott.

Lawler, E. E. (1983). Drives, needs, and outcomes. In B. M. Staw (ed.), *Psychological foundations of organizational behavior* (2nd ed.). Glenview, IL: Scott, Foreman & Company.

Lazarus, A. A. (1966). Behavior rehearsal vs. non-directive therapy vs. advice in affecting behavior change. *Behavior Research and Therapy, 4,* 209-212.

Lazarus, A. A., & Fay, A. (1984). Behavior therapy. In T. B. Karasu (Chairman), *The psychiatric therapies.* Washington, D. C.: American Psychiatric Association.

LeCron, L. M. (ed.). (1965). *Experimental hypnosis.* New York: Citadel.

Lehman, R. S. (1977). *Computer simulation and modeling: An introduction.* Hillside, N.J.: Lawrence Erlbaum.

Linton, R. (1936). *The study of man.* New York: Appleton-Century.

Lippitt, R. (1958). The auxiliary chair technique. *Group Psychotherapy, 11,* 8-23.

Lipsky, M. J., Kassinove, H., & Miller, N. J. (1980). Effects of rational-emotive therapy, rational role reversal, and rational-emotive imagery on the emotional adjustment of community health center patients. *Journal of Consulting and Clinical Psychology, 48,* 366-374.

Maier, N. R. F., Solem, A. R., & Maier, A. A. (1975). *The role-play technique: A handbook for management and leadership practice.* San Diego, CA: University Associates.

Marks, I. M. (1978). Behavioral psychotherapy of adult neurosis. In S. L. Garfield & A. E. Bergin (eds.), *Handbook of psychotherapy and behavior change.* New York: Wiley & Sons.

Maslow, A. H. (1970). *Motivation and personality* (2nd ed.). New York: Harper & Row.

Mathew, A. M., Gelder, M. G., & Johnston, D. W. (1981). *Agorophobia: Nature and treatment.* New York: Guilford Press.

May, J. V. (1981). *Psychodrama à deux.* Grand Rapids, MI: Pine Rest Christian Hospital (a monograph).

McClelland, D. C. (1961). *The achieving society.* Princeton: Van Nostrand Reinhold.

Mead, G. H. (1934). *Mind, self and society.* Chicago: University of Chicago Press.

Meares, A. (ed.). (1961). *A system of medical hypnosis.* Philadelphia: W. B. Saunders.

Moreno, J. L. (1914). *Einladung zu einer begegnung.* Vienna: Anzengruber Verlag.

Moreno, J. L. (1934). *Who shall survive?* Washington, D. C.: Nervous and Mental Disease Publications (Rev. ed. Beacon, N. Y.: Beacon House, 1953).

Moreno, J. L. (1937). Psychodrama and the psychopathology of interpersonal relations. *Sociometry, 1,* 45-46.

Moreno, J. L. (1939a). Psychodramatic shock therapy. *Psychodrama and Group Psychotherapy Monographs* (Whole No. 5). Beacon, New York: Beacon House.

Moreno, J. L. (1939b). Psychodramatic shock therapy: A sociometric approach to the problem of mental disorder. *Sociometry, 2,* 1-30.

Moreno, J. L. (1950). Hypnodrama and psychodrama. *Group Psychotherapy, 3,* 1-10.

Moreno, J. L. (1951). Fragments from the psychodrama of dream. *Group Psychotherapy, 3,* 344-365.

Moreno, J. L. (1959). Theory of spontaneity-creativity. In J. L. Moreno (ed.), *Sociometry and the science of man.* Beacon, N. Y.: Beacon House.

Moreno, J. L. (ed.). (1960). *The sociometry reader.* Glencoe, IL: The Free Press.

Moreno, J. L. (1964a). *Psychodrama Vol. I.* (3rd. ed.). Beacon, New York: Beacon House.

Moreno, J. L. (1964b). The third psychiatric revolution and the scope of psychodrama. *Group Psychotherapy, 17,* 149-171.

Moreno, J. L. (1965). Therapeutic vehicles and the concept of surplus reality. *Group Psychotherapy, 18,* 211-216.

Moreno, J. L. (1966). Psychiatry of the twentieth century: Function of the universalia: Time, space, reality, and cosmos. *Group Psychotherapy, 19,* 146-158.

Moreno, J. L. (1973). Note on indications and contradictions for acting out in psychodrama. *Group Psychotherapy and Psychodrama, 26,* 23-24.

Moreno, J. L., & Kipper, D. A. (1968). Group psychodrama and community-centered counseling. In G. M. Gazda (ed.), *Basic approaches to group psychotherapy and group counseling* (1st ed.). Springfield, IL: Charles C Thomas.

Moreno, J. L., & Moreno, Z. T. (1969). *Psychodrama Vol. 3. Beacon, N. Y.: Beacon House.*

Moreno, Z. T. (1959). A survey of psychodramatic techniques. *Group Psychotherapy, 12,* 5-14.

Moreno, Z. T. (1965). Psychodramatic rules, techniques and adjunctive methods. *Group Psychotherapy, 18,* 73-86.

Moreno, Z. T. (1975). The significance of doubling and role reversal for cosmic man. *Group Psychotherapy and Psychodrama, 28,* 55-59.

Morris, K. T., & Cinnamon, K. M. (1974). *A handbook of verbal group exercises.* Springfield, IL: Charles C Thomas.

Morris, K. T., & Cinnamon, K. M. (1975). *A handbook of non-verbal exercises.* Springfield IL: Charles C Thomas.

Muney, B. F., & Deutch, M. (1968). The effect of role reversal during discussion of opposing view points. *Journal of Conflict Resolution, 12,* 345-346.

Naas, J. (1966). The use of actional procedures in group psychotherapy with sociopathic women. *International Journal of Group Psychotherapy, 16,* 190-197.

Narsue, G. (1959). Recent developments of psychodrama and hypnodrama in Japan. *Group Psychotherapy, 12,* 258-262.

Newton, F. B. (1974). The effect of systematic communication skill training on residence hall paraprofessionals. *Counselor Education and Supervision, 14,* 4-8.

Nichols, M. P., & Efran J. S. (1985). Catharsis in psychotherapy: A new perspective. *Psychotherapy: Theory, Research and Practice, 22,* 46-58.

Nisbett, R. E., Borgida, E., Crandall, R., & Reed, H. (1976). Popular induction: Information is not always informative. In J. Caroll & J. Payne (eds.), *Cognition and social behavior.* Hillsdale, N. J.: Erlbaum.

Nolte, J., Smallwood, C., & Weistart, J. (1975). Role reversal with God. *Group Psychotherapy and Psychodrama, 28,* 70-76.

Nolte, J., Weistart, J., & Wyatt, J. (1977). Psychodramatic production of dreams; "The end of the road." *Group Psychotherapy, Psychodrama and Sociometry, 30,* 37-48.

Noone, R. (1972). *In search of dreaming people.* New York: Morrow.

Ost, L. G., Gotestam, G., & Melin, L. (1976). A controlled study of two behavioral methods in the treatment of stuttering. *Behavior Therapy, 7,* 587-592.

Ostrand, J., & Creaser, J. (1978). Development of counselor candidate dominance in three learning conditions. *Journal of Psychology, 99,* 199-202.

Pankratz, L. D. (1971). Extended doubling and mirroring "in situ" in the mental hospital. *Group Psychotherapy and Psychodrama, 24,* 150-151.

Pankratz, L. D., & Buchan, G. (1966). Techniques of warm-ups in psychodrama with the retarded. *Mental Retardation, 4,* 12-16.

Park, R. E., & Burgess, E. W. (1921). *Introduction to the science of sociology.* Chicago: University of Chicago Press.

Perls, F. (1969). *Gestalt therapy verbatim.* New York: Bantam Books.

Pfeiffer, J. W., & Jones, J. E. (eds.). (1973-1979). *A handbook of structured experiences for human relations training* (Vol. I-VII). San Diego, CA: University Associates.

Pfeiffer, J. W., & Jones, J. E. (1980). *Structure experiences kit.* San Diego, CA: University Associates.

Pilkey, L., Goldman, M., & Kleinman, B. (1961). Psychodrama and emphatic ability in the mentally retarded. *American Journal of Mental Deficiency, 65,* 595-605.

Polansky, N. A., & Harkins, E. B. (1969). Psychodrama as an element in hospital treatment. *Psychiatry, 32,* 74-87.

Rabiner, C. J., & Drucker, M. (1967). Use of psychodrama with hospitalized schizophrenic patients. *Diseases of the Nervous System, 28,* 24.

Rimm, D. C., & Masters, J. C. (1974). *Behavior therapy: Techniques and empirical findings.* New York: Academic Press.

Robbins, M. (1973). Psychodramatic children's warm-ups for adults. *Group Psychotherapy and Psychodrama, 26,* 67-71,

Robbins, R. B. (1968). The re-acting barrier in psychodrama setting. *Group Psychotherapy, 21,* 140-143.

Robbins, R. B., & Robbins, G. J. (1970). Psychodramatic Body Building. *Group Psychotherapy and Psychodrama, 23,* 122-126.

Rogers, C. R. (1975). An unappreciated way of being. *Counseling Psychologist, 5,* 2-10.

Rojas-Bermudez, J. G. (1969). The intermediary object. *Group Psychotherapy, 22,* 149-154.

Sacks, J. M. (1965). The judgment technique in psychodrama. *Group Psychotherapy, 18,* 69-72.

Sacks, J. M. (1974). The Letter. *Group Psychotherapy and Psychodrama, 27,* 184-190.

Sarbin, T., & Allen, V. (1968). Role theory. In G. Lindzey & E. Aronson (eds.), *The handbook of social psychology* (Vol. 1). Reading, MA: Addison-Wesley.

Scheff, T. J. (1967). Toward a sociological model of consensus. *American Sociological Review, 32,* 32-46.

Schlanger, P. H., & Schlanger, B. B. (1968). Adapting role-playing activities with aphasic patients. *Journal of Speech and Hearing Disorders, 33,* 128-131.

Schlesinger, H. J. (1982). Resistance as process. In P. L. Wachtel (ed.), *Resistance, psychodynamic and behavioral approach.* New York: Plenum.

Schonke, M. (1978). Psychodrama in school and college. *Journal of Group Psychotherapy and Psychodrama, 28,* 168-179.

Schutz, W. C. (1967). *Joy: Expanding human awareness.* New York: Grove Press.

Schutzenberger, A. A. (1970). *Précis de psychodrama* (Rev. ed.). Paris: Editions Universitaires.

Sechehaye, M. A. (1956). *A new psychotherapy in schizophrenia: Relief of frustration by symbolic realization.* New York: Grune.

Sechehaye, M. A. (1961). The curative function of symbols in a case of traumatic neurosis with psychotic reaction. In A. Burton (ed.), *Psychopathology of the psychoses.* New York: Basic Books.

Shaw, M. E., Corsini, R. J., Blake, R. R., & Mouton, J. S. (1980). *Role playing: A practical manual for group facilitators.* San Diego, CA: University Associates.

Simmel, G. (1920). Zur philosophei des schauaspielers. (On the philosophy of actors.) *Logos, 1,* 339-362.

Siroka, R. W., & Schloss, G. (1968). The death scene in psychodrama. *Group Psychotherapy, 21,* 202-205.

Siroka, R. W., Siroka, E., & Schloss, G. (eds.). (1971). *Sensitivity training and group encounter: An introduction.* New York: Grossett and Dunlap.

Speroff, B. J. (1955). Empathy and role reversal as factors in industrial harmony. *Journal of Social Psychology, 41,* 163-165.

Starr, A. (1977). *Psychodrama: Rehearsal for living.* Chicago: Nelson-Hall.

Staub, E. (1971). The use of role playing and induction in children's learning of helping and sharing behavior. *Child Development, 42,* 805-816.

Stave, A. M. (1977). The effect of cockpit environment on long-term pilot performance. *Human Factors, 19,* 503-514.

Sturm, I. E. (1965). The behavioristic aspects of psychodrama. *Group Psychotherapy, 18,* 50-64.

Sturm, I. E. (1970). A behavioral outline of psychodrama. *Psychotherapy: Theory, Research and Practice, 7,* 245-247.

Sturm, I. E. (1971). Implication of role playing methodology for clinical procedure. *Behavior Therapy, 2,* 88-96.

Supple, L. K. (1962). Hypnodrama: A synthesis of hypnosis and psychodrama, a progress report. *Group Psychotherapy, 15,* 58-62.

Sylvester, J. D. (1970). Mental rigidity and the method of role reversal. *Studia Psychologica, 12,* 151-156.

Taylor, J. F. (1969). Role-playing with borderline and mildly retarded children in an institutional setting. *Exceptional Children, 36,* 206-208.

Thayer, L. (ed.). (1976). *50 strategies for experiential learning.* San Diego, CA: University Associates.

Thayer, L. (1977). Variables for developing simulated counseling vignettes. *Counselor Education and Supervision, 17,* 65-68.

Thorson, J. A. (1978). Lifeboat: Social values and decision making. *Death Education, 1,* 459-464.

Toeman, Z. (1948). The double situation in psychodrama. *Sociatry, 1,* 436-446.

Towers, J. M. (1969). *Role-playing for supervisors.* London: Pergamon.

Vinacke, W. (1954). Deceiving experimental subjects. *American Psychologist, 9,* 155.

Wachtel, P. L. (ed.). (1982). *Resistance: Psychodynamic and behavioral approaches.* New York: Plenum.

Wagenaar, W. A. (1975). Supertankers: Simulators for the study of steering. *American Psychologist, 30,* 440-444.

Warner, G. D. (1970). The didactic auxiliary chair. *Group Psychotherapy and Psychodrama, 23,* 31-34.

Weil, P. (1967). *Psicodrama.* Rio de Janeiro: Edicons Cepa.

Weiner, H. B. (1965). Treating the alcoholics with psychodrama. *Group Psychotherapy, 18,* 28-29.

Weiner, H. B. (1967). Psychodrama treatment for the alcoholic. In R. Fox (ed.), *Alcoholism: Behavioral research, therapeutic approaches.* New York: Springer.

Weiner, H. B., Allen, J., Moss, C. C., & Costa, J. (1966). *Psychodramatic treatment for the alcoholic, a manual.* New York: Spring Grove State Hospital.

Weiner, H. B., & Sacks, J. M. (1969). Warm-up and sum-up. *Group Psychotherapy, 22,* 85-102.

Wessberg, H. W., Mariotto, M. J., Conger, A. J., Farrell, A. D, & Conger, J. C. (1979). Ecological validity of role plays for assessing heterosocial anxiety and skill of male college students. *Journal of Consulting and Clinical Psychology, 47,* 525-535.

Williams, R. L., & Gasdick, J. M. (1970). Practical applications of psychodrama: An action therapy for chronic patients. *Hospital and Community Psychiatry, 21,* 187-189.

Wolpe, J. (1958). *Psychotherapy by reciprocal inhibition.* Stanford, CA: Stanford University Press.

Wolpe, J. (1969). *The practice of behavior therapy.* New York: Pergamon.

Wolpe, J., & Lazarus, A. A. (1966). *Behavior therapy techniques: A guide to the treatment of neuroses.* London: Pergamon.

Yablonsky, L. (1954). The future-projection technique. *Group Psychotherapy, 7,* 303-305.

Yablonsky, L. (1955). Preparing parolees for essential social roles. *Group Psychotherapy, 8,* 38-40.

Yablonsky, L. (1974). Future projection technique. In I. A. Greenberg (ed.), *Psychodrama theory and practice.* New York: Behavioral Publications.

Yablonsky, L. (1976). *Psychodrama: Resolving emotional problems through role-playing.* New York: Basic Books.

Yalom, I. D. (1975). *The theory and practice of group psychotherapy.* (2nd ed.). New York: Basic Books.

Yalom, I. D. (1980). *Existential psychotherapy.* New York: Basic Books.

Zeig, J. K. (1982). *Ericksonian approaches to hypnosis and psychotherapy.* New York: Brunner/Mazel.

Zilboorg, G., & Henry, G. W. (1941). *A history of medical psychology.* New York: Norton.

Zimbardo, P. G. (1965). The effect of effort and improvization on self-persuasion produced by role-playing. *Journal of Experimental Social Psychology, 1,* 103-120.

Author Index

Subject Index

significance of, 44-45
spontaneous and mimetic behavior, 32
Barrier technique (technique), 213, 269-270
Basic techniques
    definition and principles, 138
    subgroups, 138, 187-188
    vs. situational techniques, 139, 222-223
Behavior rehearsal
    history, 19-20
    procedure and stages, 22
    resemblance to theater, 21-22
Behavior simulation
    concept of, 29-30
    clinical role playing, 65-66
    factor B and paradigm, 30, 34
    factor E and diagram, 30, 50
    in psychotherapy, 62
    in specific (basic) techniques, 180-182
Behavior simulation patterns
    description and paradigm, 34, 35
    familiarity with the model, 41-44
    mixed/combined patterns, 36, 37, 40-41
    "pure" patterns, 36, 38, 39
Behavior therapy, 20, 48, 58, 138, 273
Behind-your-back (technique), 271-272
Blindfold encounters (technique), 244-245
Body building (technique), 242
Bridge building (technique), 256

Candle technique (technique), 263-264
Catharsis
    action catharsis, 15, 75
    catharsis of integration, 15-16
    curative factor, 15, 95, 363
Chessboard (technique), 259-260
Clinical role playing
    and behavior simulation, 65-66
    and in-vivo therapy, 58
    and role playing, 28
    criticism of, 360-361
    main and adjunct therapy, 355-359
    therapeutic principles
        authenticity, 67-70
        concrete portrayals, 66-67
        expanding learning experiences, 72-74
        interrelatedness of episodes, 74-75
        selective magnification, 70-72
Clinical role playing session
    action stage, 81-101
    closing stage, 101-110
    definition, 77-79
    structure, 79-81

warm-up stage, 81-92
Closing stage
    action vs. discussion, 107, 110
    characteristics, 80, 101
    premature closure, 110
    relation to action stage, 106-108
    temporary closure, 106, 107
    therapeutic aspects, 101-103
Clues
    and connecting scenes, 97
    and relation to scenes, 94-95
    based on incongruous behavior, 113-114
    in first segment, 95
    nonverbal, 112
    self and externally initiated, 116-117
    the selection of, 115-116
    verbal, 112
Cognitive processes, 48, 70, 80, 109
Comfort, 102-103
Conceptual neutrality, 24, 30
Concrete-abstract dimension. *See also* Metaphors; Similes
    clinical significance, 278
    description, 231-233
Concrete behavior
    and in-vivo behavior, 57-58
    in psychotherapy, 63-64
Concretization
    and enactments, 212
    definition in situational techniques, 271
    in techniques, 271
    literal associations, 231
    of silence, 273-276
    of physical analogues, 216
    principle of, 66-67
Conflict, 216, 270
Confrontation
    direct, 228-229, 230, 268-269, 270, 280
    indirect, 229, 280
Confronting self-repertoire (technique), 268-269
Constituency of techniques, 233-234
Co-therapist(s), 130, 131, 133, 134, 136
Couple's therapy. *See* Marital therapy
Creative act
    and spontaneity, 13
    and status nascendi, 15
    and the emergence of clues, 15
    characteristics, 13
Creativity, 15
Crib scence (technique), 272-273
Cultural conserves, 13, 14

Death scene (technique), 253-254